A GUIDE FOR LEADERS IN HIGHER EDUCATION

A GUIDE FOR LEADERS IN HIGHER EDUCATION

Core Concepts, Competencies, and Tools

Brent D. Ruben, Richard De Lisi,

and Ralph A. Gigliotti

Foreword by Doug Lederman

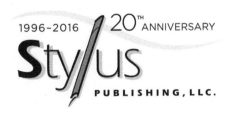

1996–2016 20TH ANNIVERSARY

Sty/us

PUBLISHING, LLC.

STERLING, VIRGINIA

Published by Stylus Publishing, LLC
22883 Quicksilver Drive
Sterling, Virginia 20166-2102

Library of Congress Cataloging-in-Publication Data
Names: Ruben, Brent D. | De Lisi, Richard
Title: A guide for leaders in higher education: core concepts,
competencies, and tools / Brent D. Ruben,
Richard De Lisi, and Ralph A. Gigliotti;
foreword by Doug Lederman.
Description: Sterling, Virginia : Stylus Publishing, 2017. |
Includes bibliographical references and index.
Identifiers: LCCN 2016016335 (print) |
LCCN 2016019551 (ebook) |
ISBN 9781620363911 (cloth : alk. paper) |
ISBN 9781620363928 (pbk. : alk.   paper) |
ISBN 9781620363935 (library networkable e-edition) |
ISBN 9781620363942 (consumer e-edition)
Subjects: LCSH: Education, Higher--Administration. |
Educational leadership.
Classification: LCC LB2341 .R727 2017 (print) |
LCC LB2341 (ebook) |
DDC 378.1/01--dc23
LC record available at https://lccn.loc.gov/2016016335

13-digit ISBN: 978-1-62036-391-1 (cloth)
13-digit ISBN: 978-1-62036-392-8 (paperback)
13-digit ISBN: 978-1-62036-393-5 (library networkable e-edition)
13-digit ISBN: 978-1-62036-394-2 (consumer e-edition)

Printed in the United States of America

All first editions printed on acid-free paper
that meets the American National Standards Institute
Z39-48 Standard.

Bulk Purchases

Quantity discounts are available for use in workshops and for
staff development.
Call 1-800-232-0223

First Edition, 2017

For their love and support, this book is dedicated to Jann, Colleen, and in memory of Ann McGillicuddy-De Lisi.

CONTENTS

PART THREE: APPLIED TOOLS FOR LEADERSHIP AND ORGANIZATIONAL EFFECTIVENESS

PART FOUR: LEADERSHIP DEVELOPMENT MODELS

FOREWORD

Thomas Friedman is not the pundit who has engaged in the most hyperbolic comments about the fragile future of American higher education in recent years; that honor would probably go to someone like Nathan Harden (author of a 2012 article in the *American Interest* titled "The End of the University as We Know It") or to Kevin Carey, who wrote the 2015 book *The End of College*. But Friedman, whose *New York Times* column bought in wholesale to the massive open online course (MOOC) phenomenon and offered such recent headlines as "Revolution Hits the Universities," might well be the highest-profile prognosticator to predict serious peril ahead for colleges and universities, given the multiple pressures of financial constraints, technology-driven competition, and changing demographics and student needs.

Most of these commentators exaggerate the pending doom awaiting higher education. But they are not wrong to anticipate enormous change ahead for an industry that, in some segments, still looks fundamentally as it did 100 or more years ago. That reality is important for the conversation that this book's authors undertake because, as they write, "the dramatic changes in the landscape of higher education" (p. 5) have significantly altered "the nature of the requirements for college and university leadership. . . . To an increasing degree, such issues pose challenges for leaders at all levels and types of institutions, and require a knowledge and skill set that technical or disciplinary preparation alone do not adequately provide" (p. 6).

The unsettled state of higher education raises the stakes for college and university leaders, because it's a heck of a lot easier to navigate on a calm, sunny day than in a tempest. How turbulent and threatening the situation is in higher education can be debated. What follows is my attempt to assess the *strengths* and *weaknesses* of the higher education industry, and the *opportunities* and *threats* it faces. This SWOT analysis, as it is called in corporate parlance, is an exercise that looks at internal and external factors to understand an entity's positioning and prospects.

Brent Ruben, one of the authors of this volume, asked me to prepare a SWOT analysis for one of a series of talks I gave at Rutgers in April 2015. In nearly 30 years covering higher education, I had never undertaken such an analysis—I'm a lowly journalist, after all, not a management consultant—and I was surprised by the request. But the exercise proved fruitful and extremely interesting (to me, at least), and I present it here with the hope that it provides context for understanding the present state of higher education and, in turn, the leadership issues that this volume explores.

Let's begin with two caveats. First, in some ways, one overall analysis of an industry as broad and sweeping as higher education is illogical. The strengths, weaknesses, opportunities, and threats of public two-year institutions such as Northern Virginia or Cuyahoga Community Colleges differ significantly from, say, those of private research institutions such as Stanford or New York Universities. But ideally this framework can serve as a jumping-off point that others might adapt to look at specific sectors or groups of institutions.

Second, it became clear to me as I developed this analysis that attributes that look like strengths from one perspective can, when viewed from another perspective, appear to be weaknesses, and opportunities can, when turned to the flip side, emerge as threats. So this is a fluid document.

On to the analysis.

Strengths

Even as many Americans increasingly question the performance and value of the nation's colleges and universities, the U.S. higher education ecosystem remains the envy of much of the rest of the world. Here are its strengths.

Differentiation

American higher education is an incredibly diverse constellation (for reasons explained later, I avoid using the term *system* to describe it) of institutions, ranging from purely vocational schools offering certificates and associate degrees to major universities with extensive graduate programs and billion-dollar research portfolios—and everything in between. While the industry is often seen as slow-changing if not stagnant—more on that later, too—the reality is that, defined broadly, the *postsecondary enterprise* has adapted to meet the needs of a wide variety of consumers, from someone seeking to become a refrigerator mechanic to those who wish to study nothing but great books for four years. Entire sectors (community colleges, for-profit institutions) have been added, and new modes of delivery (think online) established.

History of Excellence

American postsecondary institutions are relative newcomers, at least compared to Europe's oldest universities. But some American colleges have been around for hundreds of years and have developed enormously strong brands.

The oldest private colleges like Harvard and Yale were bolstered in the nineteenth century by the emergence of major publicly supported flagship and land-grant universities and a long tradition of producing knowledge as well as educating the nation's citizens.

Democratization

Higher education in the United States was quicker than much of the rest of the world to embrace a democratic approach, buying into the idea that educating a larger proportion of the population would help individuals and the broader economy and society alike. The idea that a postsecondary education is key to pursuing the "American Dream" has been of enormous benefit to colleges and universities. While socioeconomic status in the United States causes larger-than-desirable gaps in accessibility to college, and other countries have more recently widened their own pipelines to higher education, the American postsecondary ecosystem's head start helped it win public support within its own borders and establish its reputation and reach globally as a bridge to social mobility.

Relative Independence

Compared to their counterparts elsewhere, colleges and universities in the United States are subject to relatively little government control (though their officials often complain to the contrary). The U.S. government asserts limited authority over colleges and universities; states vary in how much oversight and governance they inflict on the institutions they help to finance. In general, the United States has created an ecosystem that encourages competition and innovation, which are widely viewed as contributing to the sector's historical excellence.

Tradition of Liberal Education

The liberal arts disciplines are under attack at this moment as job-seeking students flock to other majors and coding academies are exploding amid fascination with digital technology. But the American tradition of undergirding even professional disciplines with a core of liberal education, which is gaining ground globally, has been a historic advantage for American higher education—and almost certainly remains an advantage, momentary consternation aside.

Colleges as Community Anchors

The plethora of colleges and universities in the United States means that many American metropolitan areas, cities, towns, and even hamlets have their own institution, and in most cases the college or university is a leading employer, driver of economic activity, and culture and arts provider, among other roles. Those links—not to mention the political support that institutions receive from their local legislators—give most colleges a base that has enabled them to flourish and protect them when times get tough.

Market Share

The sense that U.S. higher education has been the best in the world has contributed to its status as a destination for many of the world's best students and scholars.

Weaknesses

While it remains the envy of much of the rest of the world, U.S. higher education is increasingly perceived within American borders as underperforming. Following are some of the reasons why.

Labor-Intensiveness

Higher education is a "high-touch" industry; as much as three fourths of the operating expenditures of most colleges and universities are in employee costs, a primary factor in driving institutions' costs (and, in turn, their prices) to rise faster than the rate of inflation for more than two decades. Much of the perceived cost problem in higher education is blamed on the professoriate, but most of the recent growth in employee numbers has come on the administrative side of the house, driven, college leaders say, by growing student demand and increased government regulation.

Rising Prices

The assertion that the price of higher education has risen out of reach of most Americans is questionable, stoked by the mainstream media's focus on a too-narrow band of private and elite public colleges and universities and eye-popping student debt figures that blew past the cumulative $1 trillion mark this decade. The average annual price of a public college in the United States is under $20,000, including in-state tuition and room and board, and nearly half of Americans start out at a community college, where the price is about half that. But college prices undoubtedly continue to rise unsustainably, and we are at a point where perception and reality have become one.

Complacency and Resistance to Change

This weakness is the flip side of American higher education's tradition of excellence and the historical perception of its high quality. Institutions (made up, as they are, of human beings) tend, like people, to change only when they must. Given that what most colleges have done for tens (or hundreds) of years has "worked," in terms of sustained demand from paying students, most colleges have felt little pressure to change. That situation has begun to shift in the last decade or so, as more colleges and universities question the viability of their business models. While some colleges have cut back in ways that have affected their faculty and staff, many faculty members have been protected from that kind of pain and remain unpersuaded that the status quo is broken.

Lack of Measurement and Evidence of Performance

The pressures that virtually every industry has faced—of a demand for evidence and proof of quality, efficacy, and performance—came late to higher education, but they are here. Institutions have been slow to respond to them for a variety of reasons: they are decentralized, they haven't historically been held accountable in this way (and bristle at it), and much of what they do is difficult to measure, particularly in terms of student learning. The industry has simply been slow to develop and adopt tools for gauging what and how much students learn. Another factor is that the colleges and universities typically viewed as the leaders—elite and wealthy private and public colleges—have had the least incentive to develop a system that might measure educational quality, because they are the winners in the current setup in which the public equates quality with prestige. The difficulty in judging quality—combined with what inevitably is enormous variation in quality, because every industry has such variation—means that the existence of weak institutions hurts all institutions and the public's overall perception of quality of the higher education ecosystem.

Decentralization

I previously described higher education's differentiation and relative independence from government as strengths that have allowed for healthy competition and innovation. There is no "system" of higher education in the United States, in my view; it might more appropriately be called an "ecosystem." While most states have structures that organize (if not unify) some or all of their public colleges and universities, little to no formal organizing structure exists at the national level, as is true of many countries that have ministries to govern or oversee their institutions. That lack of organization and coherence not only allows for independence but also makes systemic change difficult, if not impossible, to bring about. Little can be mandated, and even good ideas and best practices can be difficult to implement or spread across institutions. This arrangement favors competition over cooperation, restricting collaboration at a time when many colleges could benefit from joining forces more.

The lack of systemic structure also means that real or perceived institutional interests generally trump public interests. Existing reward structures, such as institutional rankings may encourage colleges and universities in certain directions—toward greater admissions selectivity or prestige-rich research programs—when public policy considerations might favor a focus on better undergraduate teaching or admitting a larger percentage of hard-to-educate students.

We see this weakness rearing its head in the current push to raise the level of postsecondary attainment in the United States (see opportunities section). Whatever one thinks about the wisdom of this effort, only halting progress is being made toward achieving it. This slow progression is partly because truly embracing this increase in attainment would require many institutions to emphasize some priorities (better instruction and advising, financial aid) over others (research, athletics) that they are loath to deemphasize.

Mission Complexity/Conflict

Almost all colleges have multiple missions—some more than others—and while those missions often overlap and reinforce each other, they can also collide. For major universities, research, teaching, and public service are the fundamental goals; community colleges have a foundational split-focus on job training versus preparing students to transfer to four-year institutions. Consider also, as just two of many possible examples, that many four-year colleges have chosen to provide highly commercialized athletic programs that parallel professional teams, or that states have demanded that two-year institutions create adult literacy programs or transition services for immigrants, and it's easy to see that institutions may be becoming too complex and conflicted for their own good.

The reality is that colleges and universities are better rewarded for some missions than for others, such as college rankings, state funding regimes, public perception, or other sorting mechanisms. This creates a situation in which missions that might be most in the public interest, such as providing the greatest access to underrepresented students or the best possible undergraduate teaching, may get crowded out or deemphasized if institutional interests are better served by focusing elsewhere.

Opportunities

The fast-changing environment in which higher education is operating, characterized by constrained funding and digital transformation, presents opportunities for the industry (or at least for agile institutions within it) to strengthen its current position. Those that do not could struggle to thrive or even survive.

U.S. "Completion Agenda"

The last decade has seen strong unified momentum from an array of constituents—the Obama administration and many state leaders and key education foundations, among others—arguing that to meet the workforce and other needs of the U.S. economy and remain globally competitive, a greater share of the American population requires some kind of postsecondary credential. This alignment, arguably the closest the United States has come to a national higher education strategy since the Sputnik era, has created rhetorical support for (and spurred some increased financial investment in) higher education institutions and their students. The push to increase the number and proportion of credential holders strengthens the demand for higher education.

Global Democratization of Higher Education

Ironically, one frequently cited piece of evidence of the underperformance of American higher education is the United States' steady drop (to the midteens most recently) on an Organisation for Economic Co-operation and Development (OECD) list of countries based on their populations' postsecondary attainment rate. The primary driver of the United States' changed position is not American decline; it is other countries deciding to democratize their tertiary education systems in the same way that the United States did decades ago.

More countries—especially in Asia, the Middle East, and South America—want more of their citizens to have a postsecondary education, and in many of those places demand significantly outstrips local supply. Given the historical perception of U.S. higher education as the world's best—which has held firm even as internal doubts about American colleges have intensified—American institutions have remained attractive destinations for many foreign students who have the academic and (at least as importantly) financial wherewithal to come to the United States. What's more, many colleges have aggressively recruited such students as other sources of students and revenue have withered.

Innovation Technology

Excessive hype about MOOCs aside, higher education is undergoing significant transformation as a result of the spread of digital technology. Higher education joins the list of industries in which enormous potential is perceived for improving the efficiency and the effectiveness of various parts of the enterprise, from back-office operations to instructional delivery.

This terrain is contested, to be sure. For every Silicon Valley entrepreneur, think-tank pundit, and campus CIO who believes online degrees, competency-based education, and personalized learning offer ways to increase the number of students that colleges serve and lower per-student costs as a result, a dozen professors and others fear such "efficiency" gains will surely come at the price of quality (and quite possibly their jobs). But a growing middle ground recognizes that higher education institutions need to more fully embrace the digital age, and these groups are working together to make it happen. The potential upside is significant, especially in the realm of producing better data about how students learn and arming professors and advisers with it so they can better help students reach their educational goals.

Threats

Just as the current environment offers opportunities for institutions with the vision to recognize them, it also presents perils that could sink those that fail to adapt.

Changing Demographics I

Most states (and the United States as a whole) are in the early stages of a decadelong decline (or flattening, depending on the region) in the number of traditional college-age residents. This trend has intensified competition among the many enrollment-dependent colleges that still rely mainly on 18- to 22-year-old undergraduates, one of several factors putting downward pressure on their revenue.

Changing Demographics II

Traditional-age students may be in decline for now, but the aforementioned completion agenda is striving to expand the definition of who can and should benefit from a postsecondary education. (The reality is that who we call "traditional" students long ago stopped dominating higher education enrollment.) This development is ultimately positive for colleges and society, making it likelier that higher education will deliver on its promise of being an engine of social mobility. But the populations that are growing now and likely to continue to expand in higher education are those—often academically underprepared, financially struggling, culturally unaccustomed to going to college—who historically have been least well served by colleges and universities. Educating these students is therefore more difficult and more expensive, which puts more pressure on colleges to perform well with them.

Taxation Trends

Higher education has always both benefited and suffered from a boom-and-bust cycle of state support. Funding increases when times are good and declines when the economy suffers. But the historical trends have been altered—and not in a way that helps public colleges or postsecondary students—by the political trends that have led many Americans and some of their elected representatives to prefer lower taxes and smaller government. Because higher education is one of the biggest parts of most governments' discretionary budgets—budgets in which funding is not locked in and are manipulable year to year—state funding for colleges and for student financial aid has not kept up with enrollments in the last two decades, and federal funding for research, student aid, and other programs important to colleges faces regular threats. The Obama administration made higher education a relative priority over the past seven years, but the landscape could change dramatically depending on the outcome of the 2016 election.

Doubts About Value

Politicians or others have not simply concluded that higher education is not worth supporting with public funds, but the issue has been raised in a much more significant way than a decade or two or three ago. Much of this change is the result of disconcerting facts and numbers: college prices have risen much faster than inflation for the last 25 years; student loan debt hit the startling $1 trillion mark in 2013; and the federal financial investment in higher education has soared, leading critics to question the return on taxpayers' investment. The 2008 recession, and the perception that it led to many recent graduates living in their parents' basements or working as baristas, increased doubts about the value of a postsecondary education generally (in coffee shops despite data showing lifetime gains) and the desire to try to understand the value of particular colleges and programs.

Because the value of a higher education has historically been taken for granted, the industry doesn't have much of a track record of proving itself and lacks tools for measuring efficacy. (See the aforementioned weakness relating to evidence and performance.) This is especially true for the quality and amount of learning for students, but applies also to areas such as university research. The bottom line is that doubt is growing about the value that colleges provide to their students and to society.

More Accountability

Doubt about value, combined with increased federal government spending on colleges and student aid and the heightened competition for state funds in the last decade, has intensified calls for more government regulation of higher education and has emboldened some government officials to venture into once off-limits realms. Most of the accountability activity is focused on those issues most directly tied to affordability and value, often by linking funding to various performance measures. But government agencies aren't stopping there, increasingly questioning colleges' judgments about everything from the quality of their credentials to their policies on sexual violence. Colleges clearly have been knocked off the pedestal on which they perched comfortably for decades.

The Changing Instructional Workforce

For many years, a faculty position was seen as a relatively cushy job with a guarantee of lifetime employment. The image of Mr. Chips was never precisely representative, but as recently as 25 years ago, the bulk of college-level instruction was provided by professors who either had tenure or reasonable hopes of earning it. Over the last two decades, however, the proportion of instructors working on the tenure track has eroded from about three quarters to roughly a fourth, a trend that is unlikely to be reversed. Colleges and universities, like employers in other industries, have increasingly embraced a contingent model, bringing contract workers and part-time adjuncts into the mix. Most lack health insurance and other benefits, and many struggle financially.

While the approach has reduced many colleges' labor costs and given them added flexibility, it has also created an increasingly unhappy faculty and, arguably, hurt students—not because the adjunct instructors are less capable, but because they lack the resources (offices, time, professional development, etc.) that many people believe that instructors require to do their jobs effectively.

Tenure may or may not have been purposefully under attack, but it has eroded. No one is really happy with the model of faculty employment that has evolved, and yet meaningful discussion about how to improve it is rare. It's a third-rail issue on most individual campuses—presidents or provosts examine it at their peril—and the associations, foundations, and other groups that drive national discussions about higher education largely ignore the difficult problem. (It is complex because it involves not just campus employment policies but the nature of graduate education and the likelihood of success for many campus innovations, since few if any changes in instructional delivery can work without faculty buy-in.) Discussions about "flipping the classroom" and other new models of instruction provide an opportunity to reassess who faculty members are, what they do, and how they are compensated. A serious, sustained conversation about the role of instructors in the future is desperately needed but is little in evidence.

Alternatives

Just as technology can stimulate innovation within existing colleges and universities to their benefit (see the earlier section on opportunities), technology can also spur competition to challenge the established players. Industry after industry, from journalism to music to healthcare, has been disrupted in recent decades, and in higher education the biggest threat comes from potential alternative providers that might be able to more affordably provide comparable or better training. Influential foundations and Silicon Valley investors are pouring money into new providers and the creation of pathways to other credentials that could undercut the traditional stranglehold that colleges and universities have had on postsecondary education and training. Technology has helped lower the barriers to entry in ways that have threatened other sectors. Prognosticators seeking to sell books or their products often overstate this threat, but it is real.

Conclusion

What's the upshot for those of you about to dive into this book on university leadership?

It's hard to read what's discussed in the analysis and fail to notice that the list is heavier on weaknesses and threats than on strengths and opportunities; that essentially sums up my view. If you throw all of the SWOT variables into a blender, you end up, I believe, with an industry that is under significant pressure from many angles, but that is not nearly in as vulnerable a state as many commentators and futurists would suggest. The strain on higher education as a whole and many institutions individually is significant, in ways that are different from previous periods of economic distress, largely because of the alternatives made possible by technology and other innovations. And I do believe we will see more colleges and universities—particularly the undifferentiated, less wealthy private and public institutions without a clear niche—struggle and close or be merged.

Unlike those predicting massive dislocation of traditional higher education institutions, some of whom envision only a few hundred colleges left standing in a decade or two, I see the number of shuttered colleges rising from the handful we have typically seen in a year (five to seven) to two to three times that over the next decade. Do the math, and that's not a small number—as many as 200 or 300 over a decade or two. But that's a small percentage—5% to 10%—of all institutions, and some may die so that others may live. That conclusion may sound heartless to students, alumni, and employees of the colleges that might close, and I feel for them. But it's the reality I foresee.

This is where leadership comes in. Many factors contribute to institutional success or failure—some of which are largely beyond a college's or university's (or certainly an individual leader's) control, such as geographic location, underlying wealth, historic reputation, and the like. But I would argue that in an era of significant transformation and potential threat, leadership is more important than ever. Navigating through turbulent seas is harder than sailing in smooth waters, and a good versus a poor leader may be the difference between the chances of survival for similarly situated colleges.

What makes a good versus a poor leader—a successful versus an unsuccessful one? I'm neither sufficiently wise nor enough of an expert on leadership to be able to answer that question. But the question must be answered, to the extent possible, by those who care about American higher education, and the answers must guide the work of those who wish to train a new generation of leaders who will be charged with helping their institutions, and higher education, find their way.

Doug Lederman
Editor, *Inside Higher Ed*

PREFACE

This book is intended to be a useful resource for academic and administrative leaders in higher education, including those who aspire to hold positions of leadership and those already in such positions seeking help and guidance. It is also designed to be helpful for the many faculty and staff members who serve in informal leadership roles within their departments, disciplines, or institutions. Additionally, the book can be a useful resource for those responsible for the design and implementation of leadership development programs, which are growing in frequency across institutions of higher education.

Given the differences in mission and circumstance across colleges and universities of various types in the United States, the specific profile of effective leaders varies among institutions. All leaders, however, need a broad understanding of higher education as a sector, including contemporary challenges and opportunities. In addition to being knowledgeable about various concepts related to organizations and leadership, there are also a host of competencies, strategies, and tools that are increasingly critical for effective academic and administrative leadership in colleges and universities. Accordingly, the book is organized around the following themes:

- Part One: Leadership in Higher Education: A Critical Need in a Complex and Challenging Landscape (Chapters 1–4) presents an overview of the specific issues, challenges, and opportunities facing institutions and their leaders.
- Part Two: Leadership Concepts and Competencies (Chapters 5–10) explores a series of theoretical topics and presents brief reviews of literature and perspectives on key concepts that inform leadership practice, such as those related to the leadership theories, models of effective communication, and behavioral competencies that we believe are foundational for success in formal and informal leadership.
- Part Three: Applied Tools for Leadership and Organizational Effectiveness (Chapters 11–18) presents a number of applied models, strategies, and tools for personal, professional, and organizational assessment and improvement, focusing broadly on a wide array of topics, including leadership during times of change, strategic planning, crisis, and leadership succession. The odd-numbered chapters in this

section address individual leadership effectiveness, and the even-numbered chapters focus on organizational effectiveness, recognizing that both dimensions are inextricably intertwined.

- Part Four: Leadership Development Models (Chapter 19) highlights issues, programs, and approaches related to leadership development in higher education.

Each chapter concludes with a series of case studies and guiding questions in a section labeled "For Further Consideration." Several of the tools and worksheets referenced throughout the text are included in the appendices for the reader's convenience. The references section of the book also offers a resource for readers interested in pursuing specific topics in greater depth.

The content and format of this book reflect our view that leadership development works best when it is an intentional, reflective, and systematic experience. The core concepts, competencies, and tools offered in this volume are intended to contribute in all three areas. We hope your experience with this book is beneficial as you navigate the increasingly tumultuous and complex landscape of American higher education—a sector that is surely in need of effective leadership at this period in its history and evolution.

ACKNOWLEDGMENTS

We are indebted to the many individuals who contributed to this book. We would specifically like to acknowledge the following:

- Dick Edwards, Rutgers–New Brunswick chancellor, and Barbara Lee, senior vice president for academic affairs, for their dedicated and continuing support of leadership development and the work of the Center for Organizational Development and Leadership.
- Karen Stubaus, Vivian Fernández, and Brian Strom, and other senior administrators, colleagues, and participants in various leadership programs including the Leadership Academy, the Academic Leadership Program, and the PreDoctoral Leadership Development Institute, each of whom have contributed to the ideas presented in this book.
- Rutgers University colleagues Barbara Bender, Susan Lawrence, and Kate Immordino and Fordham University colleague John Fortunato for their formal contributions to specific chapters within this text.
- Doug Lederman, editor of *Inside Higher Education*, for his encouragement and for writing the foreword to this book.
- Colleagues in the Center for Organizational Development and Leadership—Sherrie Tromp, Barbara Corso, Kimberly Davis, and Brittani Hudson—for their encouragement and contributions to many aspects of this project.
- Martha Lansing, associate professor and vice chair of family medicine and community health at Robert Wood Johnson Medical School, for reviewing our text for connections to medical education audiences.
- Big Ten Academic Alliance senior staff members Barbara McFadden Allen, Amber Cox, and Charity Farber for their contributions to the leadership programs chapter.
- Liaisons and Fellows of the Big Ten Academic Alliance Academic Leadership Program and Departmental Executive Officers Program for their contributions to and support of this work.
- David Ward, former president of the American Council on Education and former chancellor of the University of Wisconsin–Madison, for his contributions to the succession planning chapter.

- Elyne Cole, associate provost for human resources at the University of Illinois–Urbana-Champaign, for her contributions to the communication strategy chapter.
- Mike Gower, executive vice president for finance and administration and university treasurer at Rutgers for his review of the budget-related content in the higher education landscape chapter.
- Karen Verde, of Green Pelican Editorial Services, and McKenzie Baker, associate production editor from Stylus Publishing, for their careful editorial review of all aspects of this project.
- John von Knorring, president of Stylus Publishing, for his enthusiastic support of this project and his commitment to the study of leadership in higher education.

PART ONE

LEADERSHIP IN HIGHER EDUCATION

A Critical Need in a Complex and Challenging
Landscape

I

LEADERSHIP AND LEADERSHIP DEVELOPMENT IN HIGHER EDUCATION

Time for Change

In This Chapter

- Why is there an increasing need for attention to leadership within higher education?
- How have colleges and universities traditionally prepared leaders for their roles, and why is this approach problematic?
- In what ways is higher education appropriately viewed as a sector or an industry?
- What are the cross-cutting pressing issues with which higher education leaders must contend?
- Why is collaboration between administrative and academic leaders essential in addressing these challenges in higher education?

The idea that leaders and leadership are critical factors in organizational success, mediocrity, or failure is widely accepted in modern Western society (Collins, 2001; Feiner, 2004; March & Weil, 2005). In general, we believe that this proposition also holds true for American institutions of higher education. College and university leaders can and do make a difference in organizational excellence, mediocrity, or failure. Since so much has already been written about leadership, it is reasonable to ask why we embarked on this project.

We have written this book because we believe that although higher education leadership is similar in many ways to other sectors, such as business, government, healthcare, or pre-K–12 education, it is also different. A great many of the principles of effective leadership proven to be of value in other sectors receive little emphasis in higher education. Properly applied, these

3

principles can be crucial for advancement of colleges and universities.[1] At the same time, special attention is also needed to take account of the unique characteristics of a higher education context. Higher education engages numerous internal and external stakeholders; has nonsingular, complex, and sometimes contradictory missions; and employs an academic workforce that enjoys a unique status in organizational governance and decision-making within a culture that situates individual autonomy and creativity near the top of its value system.

Individual autonomy and creativity are needed for faculty to conduct excellent and innovative scholarship in teaching and research. In a similar way, individual autonomy and creativity allow staff to manage complex multicultural living arrangements and student affairs issues more broadly, to keep up with technology innovations and new social media environments, to develop and implement state-of-the art environmental sustainability practices, and to manage complex revenue and expense systems, among other issues. Placing a premium on personal autonomy and creativity is a core value at the heart of the American higher education system, which has yielded many benefits. At the same time, these values have resulted in the creation of organizational cultures that present special challenges for those charged with the responsibility of leading. Our aim in this book is to focus on concepts, competencies, and tools that allow leaders to blend and benefit from these tensions.

Another aspect of higher education that motivated the compilation of this volume is the need for increased attention to leadership development within most colleges and universities. We believe that institutions of higher education would benefit greatly from a heightened focus on leadership development in a number of respects, including fostering enhanced skills in the assessment of organizational and corresponding leadership needs at particular points in time (see Chapters 12 and 16), and creating additional options for effective succession planning (Chapter 18).

Leadership competencies—the knowledge and skill sets required for effective higher education leaders—are a central focus within this book. In our view, the time has passed when disciplinary or technical excellence plus on-the-job leadership experience are sufficient to prepare outstanding leaders. The leadership model we propose recognizes disciplinary and technical expertise and experience as the *vertical dimension* of leadership, a dimension that is considered critically important in navigating the unique higher education context (Chapters 7–9). This dimension includes training and degree attainment in a specific field or discipline, accomplishments and mastery of aspects of that discipline, and demonstrated accomplishments in and contributions to the organization. We acknowledge the value and benefit that this vertical approach to higher education leadership has provided.

As Doug Lederman (2015a, 2015b), editor and cofounder of *Inside Higher Education*, points out, higher education prospered and soared to new heights in the latter half of the twentieth century without having to be overly concerned about excellence in leadership or leadership development. Arguably, individuals with distinguished careers as thought leaders in their fields, who personified the virtues of higher education and were articulate spokespersons and role models, possessed essential leadership attributes for advancing the work of the academy. However, as noted by Lederman and discussed in some depth in Chapter 2, American colleges and universities now face a threat in the area of leadership, largely because the landscape has shifted dramatically since the end of the twentieth century. Leaders today need a more expansive, cross-cutting set of competencies to maintain and advance their institutions—competencies that have long been valued in other sectors. We consider these competencies to be the *horizontal dimension* of leadership and believe that this dimension has taken on critical importance for institutions of higher education in the twenty-first century (Chapters 7–9). What is needed now among leaders, we believe, is a way of thinking broadly about contemporary institutions of higher education—a way of thinking that involves a sophisticated understanding of the organizational and leadership challenges facing colleges and universities at all levels, a competency- and communication-based approach to leadership and leadership development, and a practical guide for current and aspiring leaders that builds on traditional competencies but expands to take account of radical changes in the higher education context.

A Snapshot of the Higher Education Landscape

To a large extent, the dramatic changes in the landscape of higher education are what have affected the nature of requirements for college and university leadership. Many of the key factors that were in place in the golden age of the latter half of the twentieth century have shifted dramatically. These factors include the following:

- Dramatic declines in state investments have been accompanied by significant tuition increases at public higher education institutions.
- Large increases in the investment of public monies by the federal government have been accompanied by greater federal oversight and regulation of a sector that now includes for-profit institutions as well as traditional nonprofit institutions.

- Families view postsecondary degrees as critical for attainment of the American Dream, but the size of the student/family financial investment needed to attain an advanced degree is viewed as extremely burdensome, if not unattainable.
- The racial-ethnic-linguistic diversity of the student body and the need to assure both diverse and inclusive student bodies are increasing, and the challenges to realizing these outcomes are substantial.
- Evidence is growing that many high school graduates in the United States are neither college- nor career-ready.
- Fundamental changes have occurred in long-standing classroom teaching and learning processes, partly due to the rapid infusion of technology into the teaching-learning-assessment process.

This list only begins to skim the surface of the issues facing leaders in higher education. To an increasing degree, such issues pose challenges for leaders at all levels and types of institutions and require a knowledge and skill set that technical or disciplinary preparation alone does not adequately provide. Consider these questions: How many of these contextual factors have touched your work in higher education? How are you and your colleagues affected by and adjusting to these changing circumstances? Do you feel that your unit and your institution are dealing effectively with these and other emerging challenges? Has leadership communicated a clear vision for paths forward? Is progress in vision realization measured and communicated? Do you feel that you are part of the solution and understand your role and responsibilities in anticipating and addressing the emerging challenges of the new higher education landscape?

We want to emphasize this last question. We think it is extremely important for those who work in higher education to view these sector-wide issues as highly personal and relevant to their everyday work. This is true not only for those who occupy formal positions of leadership but also for those whose influence as leaders occurs in more informal ways at all levels. To a greater extent than in other institutions, "informal" leaders play a fundamental role in American higher education's ability to adapt to a changing landscape. The nature of this critical role is the focus of Chapter 10.

We intend for the concepts and tools presented in this book to contribute to the emerging literature on leadership and leadership development in higher education. We are well aware of the excellent resources for leadership development in higher education that already exist (e.g., Bolman & Gallos, 2011; Buller, 2014; Gmelch & Buller, 2015). Somewhat uniquely, this book is designed to be relevant for administrative as well as academic leaders. We do not focus on specific academic leadership positions, such as department chair (Buller, 2012), academic dean (Gmelch, Hopkins, & Damico, 2011; Krahenbuhl, 2004), or president (Pierce, 2011). Instead, whenever possible we consider and discuss together both academic and administrative leadership issues. We chose this blended approach based on the belief that the cultural divide between faculty and staff is a long-standing and pervasive tension within higher education. In our view, the lack of a common vision and complementary commitment to addressing the challenges confronting institutions of higher education is quite often a significant source of organizational dysfunction, as discussed in Chapter 5. And, for both types of employees—faculty and staff—the transition to a formal leadership position presents its own set of issues, many of which are explored in Chapter 6.

This text does not offer specific treatment of leadership issues and challenges faced by women and by men and women from underrepresented racial-ethnic minority groups. Insufficient representation by gender and by racial-ethnic status in academic and administrative leadership positions is a long-standing issue in higher education. The sector has made some advances, but White men continue to be overrepresented in leadership positions relative to employee (faculty and staff) and student diversity. Given this history, women and colleagues from underrepresented groups face special challenges when they occupy leadership positions in higher education. These special challenges are not specifically addressed in our book. We believe the concepts and tools presented can be extremely useful to all leaders, perhaps even more so for those who face special challenges. The final chapter of the book highlights several leadership programs specifically designed for women and underrepresented groups.

In general, this text aims to emphasize common principles, strategies, and tools for leadership in higher education for leaders in a variety of roles, at a variety of levels, in a variety of institutional types. This stems from our view that many of the most critical leadership competencies are cross-cutting and applicable across a range of positions, roles, and institutions. We address this idea throughout the book, but especially in Chapters 7 through 9. Whether you are a formal or informal leader, serving in an academic or administrative role, we intend this book to be a useful guide for improved understanding, self-reflection, and continuing personal and professional development.

Higher Education as a Sector

For most faculty and many staff, their primary professional identification is field-based or discipline-based (e.g., "I am a historian," or "I am a human resources professional"). These affiliations are sometimes as strong as or stronger than one's connections with one's institution, and both are often more extensive than identification with higher education as a sector. Not surprisingly, then, many faculty members have a more detailed understanding of trends in their field—both in teaching and in research—than they do of what is going on in their home institutions and in higher education more generally. A similar pattern is often present for many staff, whose knowledge of issues in their own field may well surpass their familiarity with issues related to the teaching, research, or outreach mission of their institution or broader concerns within higher education on a national level.

Consistent with this point, many of us have not generally thought of ourselves as being part of a sector or industry, preferring instead to consider that we are engaged in unique, specialized, and highly differentiated roles. Many staff and especially faculty members have been particularly uncomfortable with characterizing higher education as a business; however, the days in which this posture might have made sense seem now to have come to an end. Derek Bok (2013), former president of Harvard University, acknowledged the following in his book, *Higher Education in America*:

> America's venture in the realm of higher learning gave no hint of future accomplishments. Nor could the handful of young men who arrived in Cambridge, Massachusetts, in 1638 to enter the nation's first college have had the faintest idea of what the future had in store for American universities. . . . From these modest beginnings, higher education in the United States has grown to become a vast enterprise comprising some 4,500 different colleges and universities, more than 20 million students, 1.4 million faculty members, and aggregate annual expenditures exceeding 400 billion dollars. Within this system are schools ranging from tiny colleges numbering a few hundred students to huge universities with enrollments exceeding 50,000. (p. 9)

As Jon McGee (2016) puts it, "Colleges and universities today must be understood for what they are: large-scale business enterprises" (p. 5).

Data provided by the U.S. Office of Education's National Center for Educational Statistics substantiate this point (National Center for Educational Statistics, 2013). Table 1.1 presents a snapshot of changes in degree-granting institutions in the United States from 1989 to 1990 and 2011 to 2012. Inspection of the middle two columns of the table reveals remarkable growth in American higher education from 1989 to 2012. The numbers of degree-granting institutions, faculty, students, degrees conferred, expenditures, and endowment market values have each shown significant increases during these years. If there was ever a question as to whether higher education should be considered an industry in its own right, data such as

TABLE 1.1
U.S. Higher Education Snapshot

	1989–1990	*2011–2012*	*Change (%)*
Degree-Granting Institutions	3,535	4,706	33
Total Faculty	824,220	1,523,615	85
Faculty per Institution	233	323	39
Fall Enrollment	13,538,560	20,994,113	55
Enrollment per Institution	3,830	4,461	16
Expenditures	$134,655,571,000	$488,444,000,000	*See note*
Market Value of Endowment	$67,978,726,000	$424,587,666,000	525
Degrees Conferred			
Associate	455,102	1,017,538	124
Bachelor's	1,051,344	1,791,046	70
Master's	330,152	754,229	128
Doctoral	103,508	170,062	64
[Total Degrees]	[1,940,106]	[3,732,875]	92
Degrees per Institution	549	793	44
Degrees per Faculty Member	2.35	2.45	4
Enrollment per Faculty Member	16.4	13.7	–16

Source: National Center for Educational Statistics, 2013.
Note: Faculty reflects head count and does not include graduate assistants. Expenditure for 1989–1990 is current-fund only; 2011–2012 is total expenditure. Expenditures are in current dollars.

presented in this profile answer that question. Clearly, American higher education qualifies as a sector or industry, and individual colleges and universities function as businesses in many important respects.

Higher education is characterized by considerable breadth and variability within the industry. Institutions vary in terms of their history, size, populations served, and a variety of other factors, as summarized in Table 1.2. The mission—and in many cases, the multiple missions—of colleges and universities is a further significant source of differentiation among institutions in

TABLE 1.2
Structural Diversity of American Institutions of Higher Education

Degree Granting:	Yes/No
Taxpayer Subsidized:	Public/Private
Tax Status:	Not-for-profit/For-profit
Program Design:	Four years/Two years/Less than two years
Program Delivery:	Physical classrooms used/Online only
Housing Arrangement:	Residences on campus/No residences on campus

Note: Not all combinations of these structural dimensions exist.

higher education, as we explore in more detail in Chapter 3. As noted earlier, this book is intended for faculty and staff leaders and aspiring leaders who work in a wide array of institutional types—recognizing that increasingly skilled and effective leaders are essential in order to maintain and advance the position of prominence in the world that has traditionally been the hallmark of American institutions of higher education.

A Sector Under the Microscope

Many recent publications—from inside and outside the academy—are highly critical of or bemoan the current state of affairs in American higher education. The attention being afforded to higher education is, itself, part of the critical leadership challenge that leaders in higher education institutions face. We explore this issue in Chapter 4 and present information that points to dramatic increases in the numbers of articles and books written about higher education in recent years. While any attempt to summarize the various perspectives provided in these writings is beyond the scope of this chapter, it is interesting to note that critiques of higher education have been authored by those within as well as those outside higher education. Perspectives vary, but those outside the academy often describe institutions of higher education as in need of change and largely unresponsive to external voices pointing to this need. Writers from within the academy, while acknowledging the need for improvements in some areas, express concerns about threats to the traditional autonomy of colleges and universities that external forces pose, and note the many self-initiated improvements that institutions of all types have made. Clearly, both the external and internal perspectives play a pervasive role in framing the work of higher education leaders at all levels, in all institutions, in all types of positions. The increased attention paid to institutions of higher education from both internal and external stakeholders represents the new normal. Higher education is a sector or industry that is now under the microscope. In part due to the lack of answers they perceive to be satisfactory, stakeholders continue to ask questions such as the following:

- How well is a particular institution of higher education fulfilling the teaching aspects of its mission, especially for undergraduate students?
- Why is there a noted disconnect between the skills that employers demand and the type of training that enrolled students receive at the collegiate level?
- In what ways are colleges and universities creating safe and inclusive environments for student success, particularly in light of ongoing and recent controversies related to hazing, alcohol abuse, sexual violence, and racial-ethnic tensions?
- How is the institution attempting to control costs and increase revenue streams other than through increases in tuition and fees charged to students?
- Why do so many students take more than two or four years to attain an associate or bachelor's degree, respectively?
- What is the evidence that attainment of associate or bachelor's degrees is worth the investment from a dollars-and-cents perspective?
- Can more students participate and be educated through distance learning? Is distance learning equivalent to classroom-based learning?
- Why produce so many doctoral degree graduates each year, especially in fields in which gainful employment is scarce? (The same question is asked about certain graduate-professional degrees, such as the Juris Doctor [JD] degree.)
- Why should the public invest in basic research to support faculty who then conduct less classroom teaching? Are the faculty members at research universities committed to the teaching aspects of their mission?
- What is responsible for the growth in administrative positions in higher education?
- What is the future of tenured faculty in higher education?
- Are the compensation packages of top-level leaders justified?
- How are big-time athletics consistent with higher education's historic mission?

Such issues are systemic, cross-disciplinary, and cross-functional. Today's higher education leaders need a deep understanding of these cross-cutting issues, how they intersect, and how they affect many functional areas at all levels. Training and accomplishment in one specific discipline or specialty are necessary components in preparing for leadership in higher education, but a narrow band of knowledge and expertise is no longer sufficient in preparing today's leaders for the expansive array of challenges and opportunities that confront colleges and universities. People charged with the responsibility of leading institutions of higher education must see the big picture. Such a perspective helps to create a climate in which cooperation and collaboration replace individual achievement and competition.

Although most of our discussion relates to the full spectrum of American colleges and universities, some issues faced by non-degree-granting institutions are unique. Smith (2015) provides a cogent summary of the status of for-profit institutions of higher education, including declining enrollments and increasing government regulation. We do not offer in this book special treatment of the business models underlying for-profit colleges and universities; however, the concepts and tools presented here should also be useful to leaders in this sector. Additionally, professional disciplines in colleges and universities face a number of unique issues. For example, specific issues and challenges arise from peer reviews as part of accreditation in medicine, nursing, engineering, business, or education, among other professional fields. While the particulars of these professional contexts are fine-grained and discipline-specific, many of the leadership challenges, concepts, and tools that are effective in preparing for accreditation (or, more broadly, accountability) in a range of professional fields and disciplines are cross-cutting in nature and are presented throughout this text, particularly in Chapters 12, 14, and 16. In sum, we believe that the ideas, concepts, and tools presented in this book have wide applicability and utility across the spectrum of American higher education. Our approach is intentionally broad, for the challenges facing institutions of higher education require the collaboration of a community of well-prepared leaders—faculty and staff, unit leaders and institutional leaders, in both private and public institutions.

Expanding the Value Proposition to More Centrally Recognize Leadership

For faculty members, service to communities (local, national, or global) is often an explicit part of the mission of institutions of higher education. In contrast, service to the institution through participation on committees and in faculty governance (e.g., department or school-wide meetings) may be viewed as a wasteful distraction from activities that are more central to the teaching and research mission, and hence more likely to be recognized within the academic reward structure. This view of institutional service as peripheral and unessential is much less the case with administrative staff, whose attention and sources of reward and recognition are typically tied more directly to operational accomplishments. This so-called cultural divide complicates matters considerably for academic and administrative leaders who must engage both faculty and staff in organizational decision-making and governance. We discuss higher education's cultural divide and its numerous implications in Chapter 5, but we want to close this chapter with a brief discussion of this issue, given its importance for leaders and leadership development.

While the assumption of leadership positions typically represents career advancement for staff members, many faculty members ask why they should aspire to leadership positions. After all, if routine governance obligations are regarded as burdensome, taking time away from other pursuits, and undervalued by the institution, then formal leadership roles are likely to be viewed as even less attractive. In most institutions, recognition and incentives for serving in roles such as program director or department chair are limited. Often such contributions are not regarded or acknowledged as a significant component of one's professional contribution as an academic—certainly not to the same extent as other components of teaching and scholarship. A further difficulty is that many institutions of higher education lack clear markers and methods to assess excellence in leadership. In all these respects, the lack of value ascribed to leadership in higher education is quite unique in comparison to other sectors.

Since organizations value what they measure and measure what they value, failure to assess leadership contributions systematically is telling, as is the absence of systematic attention to leadership development. Both features contribute to the "Why should I care about leading?" culture that is so prevalent in contemporary American institutions of higher education.

We hope and believe that these patterns are changing. It seems to us that they must change if we are to attract and retain colleagues who are willing and able to help institutions of higher education navigate the vast and growing array of fundamental challenges confronting the industry. This book seeks to encourage and assist colleges and universities in expanding their value systems to include a focus on measuring, rewarding, and developing excellence in academic and staff leadership.

For Further Consideration

1. Focusing on Your Institution

- Which of the factors listed in Table 1.1 are particularly significant for your unit or institution?

- What issues might you add to the list of stakeholder questions (p. 11) based on your experience and perspective?
- How do faculty and staff in your unit or institution regard leadership and leadership roles?
- What mechanisms for assessing, recognizing, and rewarding leadership excellence are in use in your unit and institution?

Note

1. Our use of *colleges and universities* throughout the text is meant to describe community colleges, colleges, and universities more broadly. The following definitions distinguish these three types of institutions.

Community college connotes a nonprofit, two-year public institution that offers associate degrees to students who live locally and commute to campus. Community colleges might offer certificates as well as degree programs.

College connotes a nonprofit, public, or private baccalaureate degree-granting institution using a four-year program of study with at least some students residing on a campus. Colleges might offer certificates as well as degree programs.

University connotes a school that offers graduate degrees in addition to baccalaureate degrees. Some colleges and universities have the creation of new knowledge as central to their mission and are considered to be *research universities*.

THE HIGHER EDUCATION LANDSCAPE

Navigating the Organizational and Strategic Leadership Terrain

---

In This Chapter

- What are the four major categories of cross-cutting challenges and opportunities facing higher education leaders today?
- Why is higher education receiving such intense scrutiny at this period in its history?
- What implications does this heightened attention to higher education have for leaders?
- Why are distinctions between centralized and decentralized strategies and broad and narrow stakeholder engagement helpful for addressing leadership challenges and opportunities?

Chapter 1 introduced the idea that academic and administrative personnel from all types of higher education institutions are confronted with common issues as they assume informal and formal leadership roles. Regardless of one's leadership role, a familiarity with the modern landscape of higher education is essential. Attempting to provide a map of this landscape is a risky undertaking, because the terrain that leaders navigate can shift dramatically from year to year, and sometimes even from month to month or week to week. Indeed, the presumption that change is rapid and pervasive in higher education is a fundamental tenet of the book and viewed as basic to the nature of contemporary higher education leadership. Even in the time that has passed while preparing this manuscript, the list of hot topics has evolved. A recent search of headlines from higher education news outlets captures the many challenges facing leaders, such as: "A University Softens a

Plan to Cut Tenured Faculty, but Professors Remain Wary" (Brown, 2016), "Endowments Fall to Earth" (Wexler, 2016), "College Completion Rates Decline More Rapidly" (Fain, 2015), "Get Ready for More Protests" (New, 2016), and "Divided Over Diversity" (Flaherty, 2016).

The issues and topics selected for discussion here are particularly prominent in the present period, recognizing that not all of them will be as salient or relevant down the road. At a more general level, a number of core issues are likely to be critical facets of the landscape for some time to come. We examine these issues in some detail in this chapter. We also present a general framework that leaders should find helpful in thinking about and effectively addressing the array of landscape challenges and opportunities they will confront—now and in the future.

Challenges and Opportunities in the American Higher Education Landscape

In the foreword to this book, Doug Lederman offered a high-level summary of the current landscape of American higher education organized in terms of strengths, weaknesses, opportunities, and threats (SWOT). As his analysis suggests, the challenges and opportunities are both complex and very much interdependent. Other authors have grappled with the task of categorizing the array of issues facing higher education, and a list of the themes they have identified is presented in Table 2.1. These perspectives overlap in many ways with several others offered by Carey (2014); Ebersole (2014); Hirsch and Weber (1999); and Montez, Wolverton, and Gmelch (2002). They also complement the view provided by Gittleman (2015).

TABLE 2.1
Three Perspectives on Higher Education Challenges: Striving for "As"

"As"	Source
• Access • Accountability • Affordability • Attrition	Altbach, Gumport, & Berdahl, 2011
• Assessment • Alignment	US DOE, 2008
• Adjuncts • Affirmative Action • Athletics	Bok, 2013

Four Cross-Cutting Themes

While differences among these frameworks exist, the following four cross-cutting themes relate directly to resources, student demographics, the teaching-learning process, and workforce issues:

1. *Limited financial resources*: Issues related to affordability, generating revenues, resource management, student loans and debt, declining investments in basic and applied research by the U.S. government, and costs of athletic programs, among others.
2. *Changing nature of the college student population*: Issues related to increasing access to courses and programs, affirmative action, creating diverse and inclusive living and learning environments, international student enrollments, growth of nontraditional college students, and diversification in leadership, among others.
3. *Improving teaching-learning processes and outcomes*: Issues related to individualizing instruction via technology-based distance courses and programs, assessment of student learning, time to degree and disaggregated degree completion rates, and career development, among others.
4. *Shifts in the higher education workforce*: Issues related to adjunct faculty, internal resistance to change/reform, managing complex cultures, the faculty tenure system, recruitment and retention of top faculty and staff, leadership compensation, and leadership support and development, among others.

These issues—which can be viewed as challenges as well as opportunities—rarely operate in isolation, and almost always interact and affect one another. Limited financial resources challenge institutions and their leaders in numerous ways. In addition to day-to-day pressures placed on leaders to exercise great care in resource allocation, financial constraints require leaders to be increasingly entrepreneurial and innovative in identifying possible sources for generating new revenues. Limited financial resources encourage the utilization of more efficient options for college-level teaching and learning environments and lead many institutions to hire part-time faculty members to deliver instructional programs.[1] Resource constraints also inhibit the ability to provide financial support for all students who qualify for admission. While these and other chains of events, are understandable, they are also problematic. More efficient approaches to teaching and learning—such as the use of technology and more flexible practices in hiring teaching personnel—can be a positive development, but not always. Bok (2013) believes, for instance, that the trend toward having part-time instructors, including graduate students, deliver large segments of the undergraduate curriculum undermines public credibility in colleges and universities and is therefore one that leaders can and must reverse. We also know that students and large segments of the public think first and foremost about the educational role of colleges and universities, and understandably so. This focus leaves little room for a full appreciation of the research and knowledge creation aspects of institutional missions that research universities emphasize, particularly when an emphasis on research is perceived to come at the expense of attention to teaching and learning.

The changing nature of the undergraduate student body also illustrates the interactive nature of these four dominant themes. One aspect of the undergraduate student population that is changing is the increasing number of college students who are older, employed while enrolled, and looking to complete degrees on a part-time basis (Ebersole, 2014). Many colleges and universities cannot afford to ignore this growing customer base as the need for sustainable revenue streams has become urgent, especially for public institutions that have experienced significant declines in public monies over the past decade. One approach thought to be useful in attracting and retaining this new student constituency has been technology-based online instruction that affords the possibility of course completion in the students' spare time. For this reason and others, a great deal of interest and activity now concerns distance education. In addition to increasing access via conversion of traditional courses to small-enrollment distance formats, some colleges and universities are experimenting with massive open online courses (MOOCs) as a means to increase access to higher education on a large scale. Beyond facilitating access, technology is seen as having promise for improving teaching-learning processes by providing students with tools that permit individualized pacing, as well as flexibility that nurtures discussion, argumentation, and other social processes known to foster content mastery and retention. These approaches also have the potential to provide greater access and learning opportunities to students who might otherwise be far less able to benefit from higher education.

However, whether conducted on a large or small scale, offering courses and degrees in technology-rich distance formats is complex work. These methods of instruction raise issues about the capability and willingness of the faculty to design and deliver high-quality courses and programs in virtual formats. Remote teaching and learning approaches also can have limitations when it comes to assuring quality education in certain content and skill areas and in assessing and verifying student learning outcomes. Encouraging more seasoned and experienced resident faculty members to change their manner of teaching from face-to-face to virtual classrooms is a promising strategy but would solve only part of the problem, since fewer than 50% of college and university faculty (including non-tenure-track) are full-time employees (see Table 2.2). Another option, providing training and professional development for part-time teaching faculty, is not without its difficulties, because online instruction is complicated to organize, deliver, and assess. The shift in course and program delivery to online formats can provide new learning opportunities for students who might otherwise find it impossible to enroll in college or university courses or programs. The use of online approaches to instruction also raises the issue of the equivalency of teaching and learning outcomes in distance versus face-to-face college classrooms.[2]

A host of additional issues need to be considered: Are sufficient resources available for staff training or hiring new faculty who may already have the needed proficiencies? What are the intellectual property rights and concerns for faculty who develop courses that are presented in distance formats? What federal government requirements govern a college or university in one state gaining student enrollments in other states via distance learning? Who in the college is responsible for ensuring compliance with new federal regulations for distance courses and programs, including providing required accommodations for students with disabilities? Can a college's information technology infrastructure support a robust distance program? Finally, failure to collect evidence on these points might raise problems in accreditation reviews. The key point is that pursuing any of these potentially promising options comes with a number of interconnected leadership and operational issues—academic as well as administrative in nature—for the individuals, departments, and institutions involved. In sum, the changing nature of the undergraduate student population presents an array of complex and

TABLE 2.2
Instructional Faculty by Rank and Institution Category, 2013

	Primarily Instructional (%)	Instructional/Research/ Public Service (%)	Combined (%)
Full-Time Tenured	14.5	26.5	19.5
Full-Time Tenure Track	5.9	8.8	7.4
Full-Time Non–Tenure Track	14.0	8.8	14.3
Part-Time Instructor	51.3	11.3	46.7
Graduate Teaching Assistant	14.3	44.7	12.2

Source: Barnshaw and Dunietz, 2015.

intertwined challenges for current academic and administrative leaders. If, for example, colleges and universities retain their focus solely on traditional-age college students, the institutions run the risk of appearing unresponsive to changing societal demands and denying the benefits of higher education to an important and neglected segment of the population. Alternatively, if colleges and universities decide to view changes in undergraduate student body demographics as an opportunity to expand their mission and impact, they have much work to do in order for these efforts to be successful. These issues raise broader questions: What is the ultimate rationale for attempts to accommodate part-time undergraduate students? What are the particular needs of part-time undergraduate students, how are these needs different from those of traditional students, and how can these needs be accommodated? How will programs, departments, or schools determine what teaching and learning formats are best suited to the needs and expectations of nontraditional undergraduates? A shift toward more online courses and programs might well be a strategic initiative considered, but this transition brings with it the range of issues noted in the previous section, especially for colleges and universities with faculty, staff, and facilities historically organized around a commitment to the needs of residential education. Answers to these types of questions relate back to mission considerations. Ultimately, as we discuss in Chapter 3, considerations of mission should guide decision-making as these types of questions are raised and addressed.

In addressing the four identified thematic areas, concerns about the way institutions define and balance elements of their missions and manage associated costs are now prevalent within all U.S. institutions of higher education. This drumbeat seems to be increasing in volume with each passing academic year and is a context that leadership can neither ignore nor escape. This particular challenge demands attention from academic and administrative leaders at all levels—and calls for adopting a sector-wide perspective.

Issues of the Day

In addition to the fundamental and enduring challenges and opportunities presented previously, any number of other topics have risen to the level of national attention and demand the attention of academic and administrative leaders. Issues are highly varied, including fraternity hazing; scandals associated with revenue-generating Division I athletics programs, such as players' academic standing, coaches' and players' behavior, and other matters; policies governing free speech, civility, and inclusion (e.g., see Brown, 2015); and preventing and reporting sexual assaults or sexual violence. Student protests and demands for action by governing boards and leaders relating to ethnic and racial diversity issues have also been a particularly notable concern on a number of college campuses (see Berrett & Hoover, 2015), as have the leadership styles or actions of current presidents or chancellors, and decisions by several institutions to appoint nontraditional candidates to these positions. The concerns that some of these issues raise and the media attention they attract tend may be episodic in nature, but they are nonetheless significant to affected constituencies, leaders, and governing boards at all levels.

American Higher Education: A Sector Under Intense Scrutiny

The themes just presented and the ever-present array of other issues facing colleges and universities help to explain why higher education is arguably under the microscope to a considerably greater extent than at many other times in its history. That said, we believe that, even more fundamentally, this high level of scrutiny is the result of two pervasive and interacting public perceptions—one related to criticality and the other related to cost. To put it somewhat differently, we believe that the intersection of the following factors is primarily responsible for this intensified focus on American higher education at this period: (a) Higher education is of critical importance, and (b) higher education is unreasonably expensive. First, there is an almost universal perception that education beyond high school in the twenty-first century is critical. Second, there is a widely shared view that higher education costs have escalated unreasonably and have become unaffordable for many American families. A companion critique related to affordability is the view that students have to take on an unreasonable amount of debt to attain postsecondary degrees.

The American Public's View of Higher Education: Critical but Unaffordable

The widespread belief that postsecondary education is essential for a successful life as an adult in the United States was recently confirmed in a Gallup-Lumina poll (2014). The poll found that 96% of adults thought it very important or somewhat important for adults in this country to have a degree or professional certificate beyond high school. When asked, "How important is it to increase the proportion of Americans with a degree or professional certificate beyond high school?" 94% of those surveyed answered "very important" or "somewhat important." Fully 69% of respondents indicated that it will be more important in the future to have a degree or professional certificate beyond high school in order to secure a good job. Finally, 78% of those polled either agreed or strongly agreed with the statement that "a college degree or a professional degree leads to a better quality of life." These survey results indicate that the American public views education beyond high school as absolutely essential for both economic and personal well-being. Taken by itself, this view is extremely positive and affirming for leaders, faculty, and staff working in higher education.

A comprehensive report by Baum, Ma, and Payea (2013) indicates that this public perception about the importance of a college education has an empirical basis in reality. College graduates have greater earnings, less unemployment, higher levels of job satisfaction, are less likely to smoke cigarettes, less likely to be obese, more likely to exercise, and more likely to vote in general elections than those with a high school degree or less. Table 2.3, taken from Baum, Karuse, and Ma (2013), shows a direct positive correlation between median earnings and education levels in the United States in 2011. As the data reported in Table 2.3 clearly show, any amount of education beyond high school is associated with higher earnings relative to high school graduates for those aged 25 and older. These and other findings from Baum,

TABLE 2.3
Median Annual Earnings and Employment Status of Individuals Ages 25 and Older by Education Level, 2011

Education Level	Median Earnings			Percentage (%) Employed	Of Those Employed, Percentage (%) Working Full-Time
	Full-Time Year-Round Workers	*Full-Time and Part-Time Workers*	*Employed and Unemployed Members of the Labor Force*		
Less Than a High School Diploma	$25,300	$20,400	$17,700	85	64
High School Diploma	$34,400	$28,700	$26,200	89	72
Some College, No Degree	$40,300	$33,400	$31,200	90	73
Associate Degree	$44,600	$38,500	$36,400	93	75
Bachelor's Degree	$58,400	$50,600	$48,600	95	78
Advanced Degree	$76,000	$66,900	$65,500	96	77

Sources: Data from Baum et al., 2013 based on U.S Census Bureau 2011.

Ma, and Payea (2013) indicate that education beyond high school pays both financial and other dividends for individuals as well as for American society as a whole (Alger, 2015).

Unfortunately, this affirming perception and accompanying evidence related to the criticality of American higher education is only part of the story. The public and other external stakeholders also hold a strong perception that the costs of higher education are unreasonably high and unaffordable for a great many students and their families. According to the same Gallup-Lumina poll (2014) cited earlier, 79% of respondents replied "no" to the question, "Do you think education beyond high school is affordable for everyone in this country who needs it?" A more recent poll of 30,000 college alumni found that only half of those surveyed strongly agreed that their higher education was worth the cost (Gallup-Purdue Index, 2015). The statistics for recent graduates were even more troubling, with only 38% of those graduating from 2006 through 2015 strongly agreeing that higher education was worth the cost. In short, although the value of a college education is still held in high regard, pressing affordability issues counteract, to some degree, the perceived importance of higher education.

A detailed analysis of the factual basis of the affordability of higher education for American students and their families is exceedingly complex and beyond the scope of this book. However, a few trends are important for

TABLE 2.4

Change in State Appropriations to Higher Education, 2008–2009 to 2012–2013

States Increasing Appropriations	
Number	9
Range for Appropriation Increases	1.03%–26.15%
Average Appropriation Increase	10.79%
Range in Net Price Tuition Change	−9.78 (% decrease) to +15.10 (% increase)
Average Tuition Change	+5.41%
States Decreasing Appropriations	
Number	41
Range for Appropriation Decreases	−1.12% to −61.77%
Average Appropriation Decrease	−19.84%
Range in Net Price Tuition Change	−14.49 (% decrease) to +32.61 (% increase)
Average Tuition Change	+7.24%

Source: Barnshaw and Dunietz, 2015.

leaders to keep in mind. First, state support for public colleges and universities has declined for the past 20 years. Table 2.4 reports trends from 2008 to 2013. For the period in question, the costs of attending state college (tuition, fees, room and board) have increased. In nine states that increased state appropriations (by almost 11%, on average), tuition charges increased, on average, by almost 5.5%. For the 41 states that experienced reduced public support (almost 20% on average), tuition increases averaged more than 7.2% (Barnshaw & Dunietz, 2015). In many states, these recent increases were preceded by tuition increases in the previous decade. Since 2013, state appropriations for higher education are slowly rising, but there is wide variability among states (Baum & Ma, 2014).

The increase in the sticker prices of public and private nonprofit colleges is only part of the story concerning affordability. Increased costs for participation in higher education need to be understood in relation to changes in average family income during this same time. Baum and Ma (2014) report that family income increased for all income levels (by quintiles) from 1983 to 1993, and from 1993 to 2003. In the most recent decade, 2003 to 2013, inflation-adjusted family income actually remained constant or declined for all quintile income levels (except the top 5% of earners). Thus, in the past decade, tuition has continued to rise while family incomes have remained constant or decreased. Taken together, these two trends have rendered college less affordable for all but the top 5% of families in the United States. In short, the public perception and concerns about affordability and student debt are consistent with recent trends in college costs as well as family incomes. For many students and their families, higher education has become considerably more difficult to afford.

Other Considerations

One more piece of the affordability puzzle needs to be mentioned. What remains largely unacknowledged in expressions of concern about affordability and student debt is the fact that higher education leaders have been sensitive to—and have taken steps to respond to—these recent trends. Figures 2.1, 2.2, and 2.3, taken from Baum and Ma (2014), show that because of subsidies of various kinds, net costs (published sticker prices discounted by need-based and merit aid) to students have remained constant for four-year private nonprofit schools (Figure 2.1) and have actually fallen for two-year public schools (Figure 2.2) during the past 10 years. For four-year public schools, net tuition and fees have increased slightly from 2005 to 2015, but total costs that include room and board have increased by almost 20% (Figure 2.3). While not attributable to actions by colleges or universities, analysis also indicates that tax deductions available to families that pay tuition costs have helped to defray the net costs of a college or university

Figure 2.1. Average published and net prices in 2014 dollars for full-time undergraduate students at private nonprofit four-year institutions, 1994–1995 to 2014–2015.

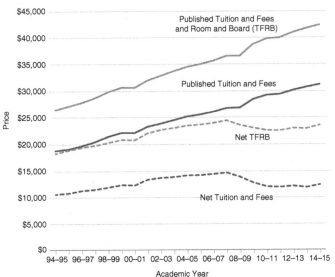

Source: Trends in College Pricing 2014 © 2014. The College Board (www.collegeboard.org). Reproduced with permission.

Figure 2.2. Average published and net prices in 2014 dollars for full-time in-district undergraduate students at public two-year institutions, 1994–1995 to 2014–2015.

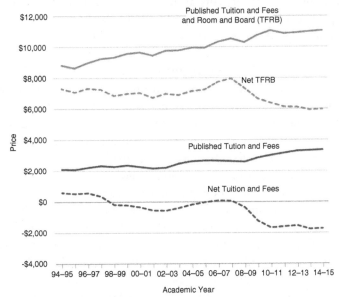

Source: Trends in College Pricing 2014 © 2014. The College Board (www.collegeboard.org). Reproduced with permission.

Figure 2.3. Average published and net prices in 2014 dollars for full-time in-state undergraduate students at public four-year institutions, 1998–1995 to 2014–2015.

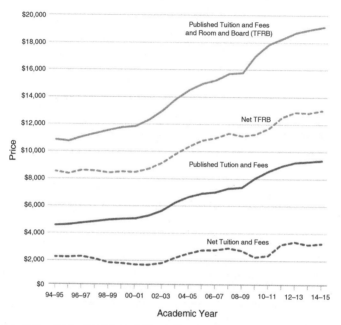

Source: Trends in College Pricing 2014 © 2014. The College Board (www.collegeboard.org). Reproduced with permission.

education. Also, at virtually all institutions, efforts have been undertaken to improve operating efficiency, identify new sources of revenue, and adopt outsourcing and shared services strategies—all in an effort to control costs.

Thus, for the past 10 years, leaders in higher education have worked to lower net costs for students and their families as average family incomes have fallen. (Four-year public colleges and universities have been least successful in doing so.) These efforts to contain costs for students and their families—largely by adopting modest tuition increases—have not found their way into public perceptions. The public may not understand the difference between published sticker prices and net prices, may not see the direct benefit of efficiency-enhancing initiatives, and may not consider government-sponsored tax benefits to families in calculating net prices.

There is no question that the public perception that higher education degree attainment is both absolutely critical but also unaffordable has placed higher education in the spotlight for the past 10 years or more and generated a great deal of critical scholarly (e.g., Arum & Roska, 2010; Bok, 2013; Fleirscher, 2015), journalistic (e.g., Bruni, 2015), and media attention. In fact, college affordability is so pressing an issue for American citizens that it rose to the level of a plank in the 2016 presidential candidate platforms. If higher education was viewed as too expensive but not seen as critical for life success, we believe the industry would likely not be as heavily scrutinized. Conversely if higher education was seen as essential and easily affordable, scrutiny would most certainly decrease. The combination of these two perceptions creates a dynamic tension in the minds of external stakeholders—students and their families, alumni groups, government officials, and potential donors, among others. These cost components are important for faculty and staff leaders to understand and communicate as they engage in what are often difficult conversations with external constituents about the financial realities associated with higher education, as well as innovation and efficiency measures in colleges and universities.

Issues of Finance and Budgeting

Leaders charged with the responsibility of obtaining and managing financial resources are caught between two contextual currents. The public wants reduced higher education costs and believes that institutions could function more efficiently. Those working inside the academy see a need for increased revenues to keep salaries and benefits competitive, maintain and upgrade classrooms and laboratories, pay for in-demand student life programs and services, and fund important research, among other needs. This debate is taking place just as colleges are receiving increased criticism for not fully preparing graduates for their professional roles (Jaschik, 2015). Understanding public perceptions and their factual basis is a necessary first step in positioning leaders to bridge the gap in expectations between external and internal stakeholders. In so doing, leaders have to be realistic and candid with external and internal stakeholders, which requires a general understanding of finance and budgeting issues—nationally, and more particularly, within one's own institution and at a department/program level.

Here we present a brief overview of the most popular budget models in use across institutions and highlight key considerations associated with each one.[3] The four most popular types of finance models are as follows:

1. *Incremental.* Traditionally the most common budget model in higher education, an incremental approach "is characterized by central ownership of all unrestricted sources" (Curry, Laws, & Strauss, 2013, p. 2). Allocations to units and departments are based upon the funding levels of the previous year and are often increased by a set percentage annually. In institutions that adopt a zero-based budgeting model, where budgets are created from scratch, the tendency is still to fall back into an incremental approach.

2. *Formula-based*. Also referred to as *performance-based budget models*, budget allocations in this approach are based on predetermined formulas. According to Curry, Laws, and Strauss (2013), when using this model, budget decisions are "made centrally but on the basis of policy formulas or metrics that relate inputs such as enrollment or research volume or outputs such as graduation rates to budget expenditure levels" (p. 4). Resources typically flow to units based on (a) the pooling of funds and the allocations based on a predetermined formula (e.g., a division teaching 10% of the credit hours received 10% of the pool), or (b) the application of an agreed-upon rate (e.g., $100 per credit hour).

3. *Responsibility center management (RCM)*. Also known as *revenue-centered budgeting*, RCM is a model in which each unit is financially responsible for its individual activities and accountable for direct and indirect expenditures. According to Curry, Laws, and Strauss (2013), entrepreneurial activities are incentivized by this approach, which "transfers revenue ownership and allocates all indirect costs to units whose programs generate and consume them respectively" (p. 5). Through the use of centralized resource redistribution, also known as *subvention*, senior academic leaders are responsible for the balance of local optimization and strategic investments that are meant to benefit the university as a whole.

4. *Every tub on its own bottom*. A budget model associated with Harvard University and Johns Hopkins University, among others, this model treats each school within the organization as an independent entity responsible for its own management and funding with minimal linkage to the university as a whole.

More decentralized approaches to financial management, as described by Strauss and Curry (2002), "attempt . . . to couple academic authority with financial responsibility; college and departmental ownership of their revenues is coupled with the responsibility of paying both the direct and indirect costs, maintaining adequate financial reserves for the applicable unit, and funding annual debt service requirements on attributable debt" (as cited in Scarborough, 2009). An exploration into the internal economic factors might also consider how the money is distributed in a department or unit and to what extent a unit or department relies on students—or in the context of professional education, patients or clients—for revenue.

Although these four models can be described as separate budget types, a number of institutions use a combination of these approaches. For example, in a 2011 *Inside Higher Education* survey, over half of the surveyed institutions indicated the use of more than one of the models noted previously, particularly the more popular incremental (60.2%), zero-based (30%), formula-based (26.1%), performance-based (14.2%), and responsibility-centered (14.2%) models (Inside Higher Ed, 2011).[4]

In a presentation delivered for the National Association of College and University Business Officers (NACUBO), Becker, Bianchetto, and Goldstein (2012) noted that an institution's character dictates the most appropriate type of budgeting. The effective allocation of resources, according to the authors, implements plans, responds to assessment data, combines top-down guidance that is informed by bottom-up knowledge and realities, and uses measures consistently. In considering the budget model that your unit, department, or institution uses, consider whether the following ideal characteristics are met throughout the budgeting process:

- Driven by strategic, infrastructural, and operational plans;
- Relies on a broadly participative process;
- Integrates resource allocation with operational planning and assessment; and
- Emphasizes accountability versus control (Becker, Bianchetto, & Goldstein, 2012).

There was a time when an understanding of budgeting models was only necessary for leaders on governing boards or in the business and finance areas of colleges and universities. Increasingly, knowledge of budgeting assumptions and practices is also becoming vital for all leaders, especially given their importance in planning, resource allocation, and organizational assessment activities. As we have seen, budgeting models vary based on institutional traditions and present circumstances; they also vary as a function of institutional size and type—public versus private, and nonprofit versus for-profit, for example. The leadership implications of particular approaches depend on one's position and level, and whether one serves in an academic or administrative function. Challenges and opportunities at a presidential or provost level are considerably different from those associated with the role of dean, department chair, or program coordinator. Additionally, because of the shifting landscape, changes are frequent in terms of the way these approaches are conceptualized and implemented by and within institutions. Given this context, leadership challenges associated with these developments often vary from year to year, sometimes month to month. That said, across a variety of institutions, a number of general strategies are being considered or pursued to control costs and increase available funds (see Box 2.1).

BOX 2.1
Available Financial Strategies

Typical Options for Reducing Expenses

- Combining programs or services within different levels, organizations, or locations
- Implementing shared services models
- Introducing new technological alternatives for staffing
- Increasing class size, and increasing the size of groups for which other programs and services are provided
- Identifying new instructional delivery models
- Reducing the size of programs and services that have decreased in popularity
- Increasing responsibilities of particular departments, staff, or faculty
- Streamlining and eliminating programs and services

Typical Options for Increasing Available Resources

- Increasing tuition and fees
- Initiating new programs for new constituencies, leading to new revenues
- Expanding popular programs and services for which fees are charged.
- Increasing marketing and recruitment of potential students who pay premium fees (e.g., international students, continuing education students)
- Identifying new ways to use existing facilities (e.g., rentals of facilities to outside groups on weekends or summer or winter breaks)
- Encouraging entrepreneurial thinking across units, departments, and the institution

---

Each change in financial strategy has any number of consequences, not only for institutions, departments, and programs but also for leaders and various stakeholders. And, to a greater or lesser extent, each strategy involves planning and change—often at multiple levels within the institution. In such situations, individual leaders may need to initiate these changes, or they may find themselves in more passive and reactive roles where their responsibilities involve adapting to changes introduced elsewhere within the institution.

Navigating the Higher Education Landscape: Plotting Your Course

Given the complexity of the higher education landscape and the intense scrutiny from internal as well as external audiences, it is no surprise that academic and administrative leaders at all levels in all types of institutions confront a broad range of issues requiring their attention. Fortunately, prescribed policies and procedures are in place to guide many operational and decision-making processes such as resource expenditures and personnel actions. However, in other areas, leaders have a considerable degree of freedom in thinking about and approaching their role. Two important and strategic areas of flexibility are centralizing or decentralizing control of various functions and determining how best to engage colleagues and external constituencies in planning, priority setting, resource allocation, and decision-making and problem-solving processes.

Most faculty and staff have experienced situations where an organization's direction and priorities were very centralized and tightly controlled by the leader or leadership team. The converse situation is where responsibility for control over decisions was decentralized and diffused to a large extent. To those who have been in organizations that exemplified one or the other approach, the benefits and liabilities of the two extremes are likely quite memorable. Leaders can use the lessons learned from these experiences as a foundation for defining leadership philosophy and an approach that is not simply reactive to one's past organizational experiences or the instincts of the moment.

The final section of this chapter introduces a framework designed to be helpful in this way—to assist leaders in analyzing situations and making informed decisions as to the best organizational and engagement strategies to address the various challenges and opportunities they confront. But before getting into the details of the framework, a few more general comments related to leadership in higher education are appropriate. There are, indeed, many important decision-making areas over which individual leaders generally do not have authority, including shifting to a new budget model, adopting new human resources tracking and reporting procedures, or modifying the faculty tenure and promotion review process.

However, to a greater degree than in most other sectors, leaders in higher education typically have a substantial degree of authority in initiating and implementing decisions that affect activities within their departments or divisions. Exercising formal authority without consultation can be an attractive way to set a new institutional or departmental course, because a leader adopting this strategy is not confronted with an array of different and often conflicting perspectives during decision-making. However, comfort and efficiency during the early stages of problem-solving and decision-making may ultimately result in more discomfort—and more time and money spent along the way—than would have been expended had a more collaborative-consultative process been used in the first place.

In thinking about high-level approaches to leadership practice, consideration of two dimensions in particular can be quite helpful: organizational strategy and engagement strategy. Each represents a continuum, as Figure 2.4 illustrates.

- *Organizational strategy* defines a continuum with end points representing two contrasting approaches for exercising control in addressing challenges or opportunities from highly centralized leader control to highly decentralized leader control.
- *Engagement strategy* defines the range of approaches available to leaders when it comes to limiting or broadly engaging faculty, staff, and other relevant stakeholders in communication activities relative to thinking through challenges or opportunities from broad engagement to limited engagement.

Figure 2.4. Addressing challenges and opportunities: Organizational and leadership options.

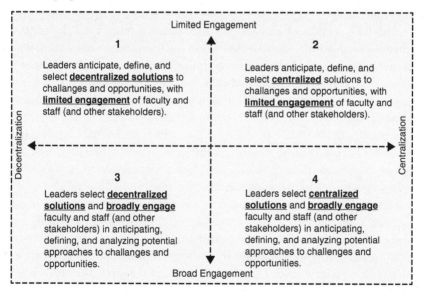

When combined, these two continuous dimensions create four quadrants—each of which describes actions available for leaders in confronting sector and institutional challenges and opportunities. This general framework consists of an organizational control axis (centralization-decentralization) and can be thought of in terms of how a leader chooses to employ the control and authority as vested in him or her by the institution. For example, leaders typically have a great deal of formal authority in dealing with personnel matters, management of revenues and expenses, setting goals and priorities for future directions, and moving forward on organizational initiatives, among many other issues. In developing and implementing a new initiative, a leader might choose to retain control of the effort, vest control of the process with a centralized executive committee, delegate oversight to one or more committees or task forces across the institution or department, or create a new structure to develop and implement the initiative.

Closely related and equally important in higher education are leadership decisions about the extent of communication and engagement of stakeholders. Distinct from centralization/decentralization decisions are decisions about how broad or narrow the communicative engagement will be in developing and implementing initiatives. Efforts to solicit input from stakeholders may be broad or narrow. Leaders decide how extensively to engage the perspectives of the various stakeholders in the design, implementation, review, and evaluation of ongoing activities or new initiatives. Leadership decisions about the extent and richness of engagement, as with those of related loci of control, have important substantive and strategic implications about which leaders need to be extremely thoughtful. As an example, when planning communication regarding a new initiative within a unit, a leader must decide whether and how to involve faculty or staff who are strong informal leaders. In thinking about this decision, a leader would want to consider not only the substantive value of opinions and advice received in arriving at the best decision but also the impact of this strategy on broadening perspective. As an example, engagement with respected informal leaders (the focus of Chapter 10) often heightens support and commitment to work toward the success of an idea or project among other stakeholders as well, when they learn that respected colleagues were consulted and have endorsed the new direction.

Clearly the decisions that leaders make relative to organizational strategy and engagement strategy up, across, and down the organizational hierarchy can be extremely critical. In using this framework, it is therefore helpful to consider one's particular leadership position and location in the institution's organizational chart. Although leadership control is vested with the individual leader and his or her department, in some instance, direction might be provided from those to whom you report (e.g., a project leader administrator in charge, chair-dean, dean-provost, manager-director, or director-vice-president). According to Figure 2.5, when you receive an assignment from a superior, it is useful to understand whether he or she has expectations as to how control of the effort is to be vested and whether there is a particular expectation of broad or narrow engagement as you execute the task. In fact, initiating a discussion about control and engagement is often useful as the assignment is under consideration; indeed, it is an example of strategic engagement. In many cases, there may be no external guidance, constraints, or even suggestions about control or engagement. Here, the decision as to how to proceed rests with you as the leader. When you are the person with primary leadership responsibility for initiating or implementing a project, or when you serve as the prime mover behind an initiative, you need to decide whether, how, and when to consult your superiors, and whether broader or narrower control and engagement of others is optimal. Figuring these things out is an extremely important part of the leaders' work, an aspect that depends on knowledge of the task at hand, the members of the unit, inclinations of other stakeholder groups, the cultural traditions of the institution or department, your leadership style and your personal preferences as leader, the time available, and the importance of shared commitment, all of which are discussed in some detail later in the book. Regardless of the specifics involved, the framework is useful in helping you think in general terms about costs and benefits of strategic approaches that are available for addressing specific challenges and opportunities.

As illustrated in Figure 2.5 each quadrant involves trade-offs; each comes with particular assets and liabilities. Some circumstances are particularly well-suited to the approach defined by a particular quadrant. Occasionally, several good options with reasonable alternatives are situated in more than one quadrant; in some cases, an approach that crosses over or blends the approaches of more than one quadrant is most appropriate. Leaders need to weigh the available options and associated trade-offs and select the most appropriate options for the circumstances and goals at hand. It's also possible that the best options depicted within the grid will vary from one phase of an initiative to another.

Figure 2.6 provides examples of various challenges and opportunities and where they fall within the four quadrants. Any number of other illustrations could have been chosen. Some opportunities, such as strategic planning (discussed in detail in Chapter 14), might be appropriately initiated within any one of the four quadrants. The same is true for integrating technology solutions for operations or for academics, as in distance coursework and program delivery. For these and other issues, decisions about where to locate initiatives

Figure 2.5. Assets and liabilities of organizational and leadership options.

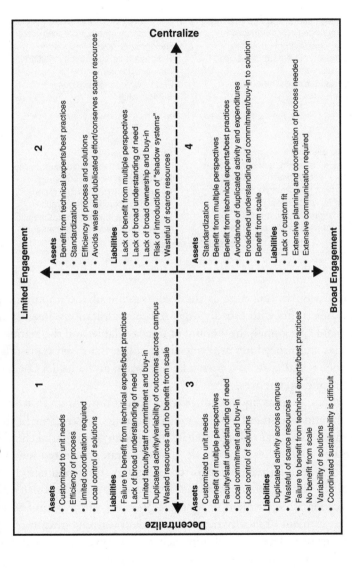

Centralize

Limited Engagement

1

Assets
• Customized to unit needs
• Efficiency of process
• Limited coordination required
• Local control of solutions

Liabilities
• Failure to benefit from technical experts/best practices
• Lack of broad understanding of need
• Limited faculty/staff commitment and buy-in
• Duplicated activity/variability of outcomes across campus
• Wasted resources and no benefit from scale

2

Assets
• Benefit from technical experts/best practices
• Standardization
• Efficiency of process and solutions
• Avoids waste and dublicated effort/conserves scarce resources

Liabilities
• Lack of benefit from multiple perspectives
• Lack of broad understanding of need
• Lack of broad ownership and buy-in
• Risk of introduction of "shadow systems"
• Wasteful of scarce resources

3

Assets
• Customized to unit needs
• Benefit of multiple perspectives
• Faculty/staff understanding of need
• Local commitment and buy-in
• Local control of solutions

Liabilities
• Duplicated activity across campus
• Wasteful of scarce resources
• Failure to benefit from technical experts/best practices
• No benefit from scale
• Variability of solutions
• Coordinated sustainability is difficult

4

Assets
• Standardization
• Benefit from multiple perspectives
• Benefit from technical experts/best practices
• Avoidance of duplicated activity and expenditures
• Broadened understanding and commitment/buy-in to solution
• Benefit from scale

Liabilities
• Lack of custom fit
• Extensive planning and coordination of process needed
• Extensive communication required

Decentralize

Broad Engagement

Figure 2.6. Fitting challenges and opportunities to the organizational-leadership framework.

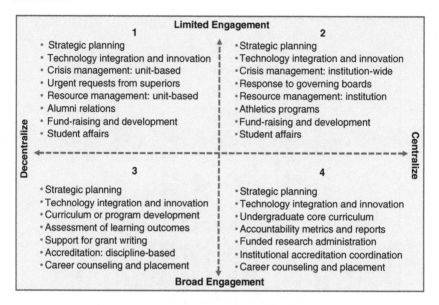

might be based on factors such as the leader's sense of the importance of the activity; how it fits with broader organizational aspirations, institutional culture, available personnel, the amount of time available, and the manner in which policies and procedures are typically handled; perceived trade-offs in terms of benefits and costs of a particular approach; and a leader's personal competencies and preferences.

Other issues, such as undergraduate core curriculum for an institution, development, and assessment of institutional learning objectives are likely to be addressed with a centralized approach involving many campus stakeholders, although other approaches are possible, and the strategy selected may vary from one stage to another in design, coordination, implementation, and follow-through. By way of contrast, the development of a particular major within an academic department or a degree program within a professional school and assessment of faculty-developed student learning outcomes typically benefit from a decentralized approach and involve those faculty and staff who will be asked to deliver the program in question.

Some issues—such as a crisis arising within a program, department, or one area of an institution—might become a crisis for the entire campus, college, or university, requiring blended and sequenced approaches involving all quadrants over time. In such instances, leaders have important and often time-sensitive choices to make about how to approach the circumstance and what role they should play relative to control and communication. While a program or department leader might have the formal authority to resolve the crisis, strategic communication with and engagement of superiors, colleagues, faculty, and staff are crucial. For example, your superiors would not appreciate learning first from the local press or media or about an issue about a faculty or staff problem within the unit that you were unable to resolve. (Chapter 17 discusses crisis leadership in considerable detail.)

In all contexts, leadership decisions have consequences, and process issues quite often override matters of substance. Adopting approaches that fail to take account of and appropriately engage stakeholders beyond one's unit may not be as immediately consequential for a leader, but resentments can build over time and can undermine confidence in, and the ability of, a leader to be fully effective within the institution or unit.

The main value of this framework is that leaders need to be methodical in their decision-making about the appropriate locus of control for the many activities and initiatives over which one has some discretion—and to know how, when, with whom, to what extent, and in what sequence to engage particular stakeholder groups as issues emerge. Attention to communication is also key to the effective implementation of any strategy and can soften the impact of missteps, unanticipated problems, or less than desirable outcomes.

The framework presented in this chapter is intended as a general guide for leaders to use as they think through these issues and trade-offs. Devoting time to consider the locus of organizational control and the strategic engagement of internal and external stakeholders is time well spent when vexing challenges or new opportunities within the higher education landscape arise.

Conclusion

The cross-cutting challenges that confront leaders in higher education in the United States pertain to the overall landscape, organizational issues, and specific leadership concepts and approaches. This chapter has presented an overview of the higher education landscape, with a particular focus on the scrutiny that arises because higher education is seen as critically important (no longer optional) but increasingly unaffordable. This view has led to demands for greater transparency and accountability relative to higher education finance. As growth in tuition revenues has declined, internal stakeholders view resource constraints as obstacles for higher education delivering on its mission, promises, and obligations. Leaders need to be mindful of this dynamic tension as they work with internal and external stakeholders. How can it be that college costs are already viewed as "too high," but institutions claim they need even more financial resources?

Several complex issues arise from this dynamic tension, and leaders confront them almost daily. On the other hand, leaders should not lose sight of the fact that there is still a strong perception that the American system of higher education is among the best in the world. Our ideas and approaches to educating students are a source of envy.

As Lederman pointed out in the foreword, leaders in American higher education have a great deal of autonomy to innovate as they approach challenges and consider opportunities, which can be both a blessing and a curse. We have used—and will continue to use—the terms *challenges* and *opportunities* extensively to characterize the external environment with which leaders are confronted. In practice, the distinction between the two is very much a matter of how leaders conceptualize and address situations. Enacting a leadership role without an informed perspective on the higher education landscape, a thoughtfully crafted leadership philosophy, an understanding of interpersonal and organizational dynamics, and a clear sense of the mission and aspirations of one's program, department, or institution is a prescription for seeing overwhelming challenges and problems everywhere. Indeed, plenty of events can be viewed in that way. If, however, one is prepared appropriately, has a clear sense of purpose, employs relevant concepts and tools, and is able to blend the perspectives of faculty and administrative staff, it is possible for a leader to be proactive in transforming challenges into opportunities. While this description is not the classic definition of a *transformational leader*, about which more will be said later, it is an apt description of the kind of leadership that is very much needed right now within higher education. Subsequent chapters in this volume provide concepts and tools for leaders to employ as they work with faculty and staff—taking account of other relevant stakeholders—to advance their units, departments, and institutions.

For Further Consideration

1. Money, Money, Money

Which of the four budget models (or combination of models) described in this chapter is used at your institution? Do you understand the relative contribution of the institution's various sources of revenues? For example, what percentage of students pays the full tuition sticker price; what percentage of operating revenue comes from public monies, such as federal loans to students or state aid; what percentage of operating revenue comes from gifts and endowments; and so forth? Name one step that leaders have taken to control costs in the last five years and one step taken to increase revenues. How were these ideas received when they were introduced? Did you personally support these steps? Why or why not? To what extent did they have the desired impact?

2. Prepare Your Elevator Speech

At a dinner party with neighbors and friends, most of whom work in the private sector, you are asked to justify the rising costs of higher education tuition and fees and the financial burden this places on families and students. What is your response? Develop a short (five minutes or less) defense of higher education as a sector.

3. Developing Distance Education Courses and Programs

Dean Williams is under pressure from the provost to increase revenues for the College of Engineering. The dean is well aware that the faculty have responsibility and authority to approve courses and programs of study offered by the college. However, the university and college policy manuals do not address whether faculty members need to approve conversion of existing courses and programs from classroom-based to fully online formats. Using the framework presented in Figures 2.4 through 2.6, analyze the benefits and pitfalls for Dean Williams as she considers how to move the college forward to offer existing courses and programs in fully online formats. How might you advise Dean Williams to proceed?

Notes

1. Many additional issues flow from inadequate resources.

2. A growing body of literature discusses the advantages and limitations of online education as it relates to student learning, instructional goals, course quality, and institutional resources. See Anderson and Ellouimi (2005), Allen and Seaman (2008), and the Online Learning Consortium (onlinelearningconsortium.org) for further reference.

3. A comprehensive review of higher education budget models is beyond the scope of this book. Visit www.nacubo.org/research/html for additional readings and resources on budgeting and finance.

4. Total exceeds 100% due to combination of models at some institutions.

COLLEGE AND UNIVERSITY MISSIONS

Purposes, Principles, and Perspectives

Barbara E. Bender

In This Chapter

- How do institutions of higher education vary in structure, purpose, core values, and mission?
- In what ways does the institutional mission influence an organization's leadership practices?
- What role does mission play in the accreditation process, and how does this process underscore the importance of mission clarity?

The Importance of Mission

How do leaders within colleges and universities decide how to allocate their resources? What underlying principles and values guide an institution's operational practices? For each of the approximately 5,000 institutions of higher education in the United States, the answers to these questions are shaped by the institution's mission. A college's or university's mission provides a foundation for all that the school does and aspires to do.

Typically, the mission is embodied in a statement of purpose that serves as a guide for determining the programs and services an institution will offer. The stated mission guides leadership decisions related to its operations, including planning, resource allocation, the development of new programs and services, and day-to-day practices and procedures. While mission statements of colleges and universities often have some common characteristics, they are also unique in various ways as a function of the type of institution, primary sources of governance and funding, their history, the populations they serve, and their distinctive aims.

Most often, these distinctive purposes are captured and formalized in a mission statement. Such statements typically include language describing *core values*, defined as the philosophical underpinnings or principles that guide the way leaders of particular colleges and universities implement their goals. In some instances, mission statements also make reference directly or indirectly to their aspirations—their vision for the future of the institution.[1]

As there are many different types of institutions, so, too, are there a wide variety of mission statements. The four statements listed in Table 3.1 illustrate the broad range of institutional missions of U.S. higher education institutions.

For leaders—ranging from members of governing boards to academic and administrative leaders throughout the institution—the mission statement ideally provides a blueprint and a touchstone for organizational decision making.

TABLE 3.1
Examples of College and University Mission Statements

Public Research Institution	*University of Michigan* "The mission of the University of Michigan is to serve the people of Michigan and the world through preeminence in creating, communicating, preserving, and applying knowledge, art, and academic values, and in developing leaders and citizens who will challenge the present and enrich the future." (president.umich.edu/about/mission)
Private Four-Year Institution	*Kalamazoo College* "The mission of Kalamazoo College is to prepare its graduates to better understand, live successfully within, and provide enlightened leadership to a richly diverse and increasingly complex world." (www.kzoo.edu/catalog/?id=1364)
Public Two-Year Institution	*Westchester Community College* "Westchester Community College provides accessible, high-quality, and affordable education to meet the needs of our diverse community. We are committed to student success, academic excellence, workforce development, economic development, and lifelong learning." (www.sunywcc.edu/about/about-the-college/mission-and-goals-of-the-college)
Medical School	*Georgetown University School of Medicine* "Guided by the Jesuit tradition of Cura Personalis, care of the whole person, Georgetown University School of Medicine will educate a diverse student body, in an integrated way, to become knowledgeable, ethical, skillful, and compassionate physicians and biomedical scientists who are dedicated to the care of others and health needs of our society." (som.georgetown.edu)

The statement should be a source of guidance when creating strategic plans and goals, designing curriculum, teaching courses, developing programs, and preparing budget models. If leaders fail to act in ways that are consistent with the established mission or drift from stated organizational principles, it may confuse faculty and staff; alienate alumni, donors, and other external stakeholders; compromise a leader's credibility; jeopardize the tenure of the leader; or, at an extreme, threaten an institution's survival.

While the importance of consistency of purpose may seem obvious and easily complied with by leaders, the numerous internal and external forces and pressures that influence higher education can complicate planning, decision-making, allocating resources, and other leadership actions. Consistency is important, and formalized mission statements also need to be living documents that can guide institutional growth and change as leaders consider new ways of meeting their goals while adapting to the many changes taking place in higher education. These changes may include demographic changes of enrolled students, evolving pedagogical approaches, shifting workforce needs, and advances in technology. While the focus of discussion thus far has been on institutional-level missions and mission statements, the same assets and leadership challenges pertain to statements of purpose developed to provide guidance at the campus, department, or program level.

Although an institution's mission may have evolved or been purposefully modified over the years, the history and original purpose of the institution's founders generally continue to have great influence on the school's mission and practices over the years. In the case of a hypothetical multipurpose university with an exceptionally strong college of education, for example, knowing that the school started as a small teachers' college that grew into a state university can help to explain why, a century later, a particular university has a college of education that is prominent within the institution and serves as a benchmark for other universities across the country. While promoting the strength of its original "teacher training" mission and expanding its school of education into one of the finest education centers in the world, this formerly small college broadened its mission, opened new schools, and created a strong, comprehensive, research-intensive university. In this example, the school of education was able to leverage its long history of alumni giving, a strong endowment, numerous graduate fellowships, a superb faculty, and the resources it needed to evolve. A school's history makes a difference.

Leadership and Mission

The responsibility for interpreting, shaping, promoting, and implementing an institution's mission begins with the governing board and the president.

The mission informs daily decisions that need to be made as well as the short- and long-term strategic planning processes that guide the institution. While a concept such as *embracing the mission* may seem simplistic, fully understanding and supporting a mission is quite often a critical factor in helping to determine the success of an academic or administrative leader. Because of this, search committees are well-advised to be especially mindful when listening to presidential candidates as they explore mission-related issues.

The overall mission should guide institutional decision-making and, concomitantly, resource allocations. Equally important, every division and unit within the institution should have its own specific mission developed in support of the overall purposes of the college or university. Maintaining a consistency of purpose throughout an institution can be a significant challenge for academic and administrative leaders who may find themselves championing a mission for their particular unit, department, or division that diverges from the institution's broader mission. Ultimately, the responsibility of the senior leadership is to work with leaders at all levels to create alignment throughout the institution. Without such a complementary and integrated approach, an institution could easily evolve into a shopping mall of courses, programs, and administrative functions with no overarching institutional distinctiveness or shared sense of identity among faculty, staff, and students.

The financial environment of most colleges and universities is particularly challenging for leaders. Pressures to operate with increasing efficiency, reduce costs, and increase available funds may pose specific difficulties for leaders as they strive to adjust to contemporary economic realities while preserving—and ideally, strengthening—the core mission or missions of their institutions and programs. Another challenge for leaders is maintaining the kind of living and learning environment that appropriately supports that mission.

Keeping Missions Current

Maintaining one's core mission does not mean that changes can never be made to the curriculum or to the institution's goals. Having a solid foundation based on a stated mission that provides for institutional dynamism allows colleges and universities to thrive and adapt to change. For example, as Bender (2002) noted,

> With the ever present demand for accountability and competing pressures from multiple constituencies, . . . effective and prudent academic leaders need to be thoughtful visionaries who can develop feasible solutions

to institutional problems. The most important factor in effecting change, ultimately, is the courage of the leaders to identify an institution's short-comings, then convey the findings, with potential solutions, to an audience that will include both proponents and adversaries. (p. 114)

Residential liberal arts colleges, for example, would never have considered including computer game design courses in their curriculum 25 years ago, while today such offerings help provide important educational experiences for their students. Similarly, institutions with a strong residential component offering distance learning courses would have been heresy just 15 years ago. But now, the great majority of institutions provide opportunities for students to learn via both traditional and online and hybrid offerings. In a parallel manner, statements of institutional purpose also provide a rationale for designing and planning new administrative, student life, and campus-related programs and services, and for reviewing, renovating, or eliminating administrative and operational programs and services that are no longer relevant.

As noted earlier and implied in the preceding examples, mission statements should not only be firmly rooted but also be adaptable to the evolving trends that impact institutions of higher education. These may well include broader demographic changes in the local community, state, and region. Despite knowledge of these trends and even with careful strategic planning, an institution might fail to attract enough students to remain viable. An appropriate response to this situation may prompt a shift in mission as a way of addressing changing demographics. In Chapter 2, for example, we noted that a college or university might decide to extend its academic, educational support, and student life programming to accommodate increasing numbers of older and employed students who seek to complete four-year degrees on a part-time, nonresidential basis. A failure by leaders to take note of a risky institutional trajectory and adapt the mission to the changing landscape in a timely fashion can, in extreme cases, have dire consequences. For example, the National Center for Education Statistics (2014) reported that in 2012–2013, 21 "degree-granting postsecondary institutions closed," including a public institution and 20 private institutions in the nonprofit and for-profit sectors.

The announcement in spring 2015 of the board of trustees' decision to close 114-year-old Sweet Briar College is, perhaps, an instructive example for at-risk colleges whose missions no longer meet the interest of contemporary students. In cases such as this, one may wonder whether there were possibilities for adapting the mission that would have created options for sustainability. Elizabeth H. S. Wyatt, a member of the board of trustees, noted, "The things that made Sweet Briar indispensable in the eyes of many alumnae—its intimate campus, its remote location—did not seem to move prospective students" (Kolowich, 2015). In June 2015 a tentative agreement was reached to keep the school open for at least another year. As part of the plan, the president and many members of the board of directors would be replaced (Stolberg, 2015).

As these situations demonstrate, it may be that one of the most critical capabilities necessary for senior leaders is balancing their attention to continuity and tradition with maintaining an awareness and responsiveness to critical changes in the higher education landscape.

Accreditation

In addition to other functions discussed in this chapter, an institution's mission provides the foundation for the accreditation process, and there is nothing quite like an upcoming decennial visit from a regional accreditation association to encourage an institution and its leaders to review its mission and assess whether its activities are in keeping with its own aims and goals. In the *Standards for Accreditation* of the New England Association of Schools and Colleges Commission on Institutions of Higher Education (2011), the first standard covers, in a very detailed fashion, the considerations related to mission.

> The mission of the institution defines its distinctive character, addresses the needs of society and identifies the students the institution seeks to serve, and reflects both the institution's traditions and its vision for the future. The institution's mission provides the basis upon which the institution identifies its priorities, plans its future and evaluates its endeavors; it provides a basis for the evaluation of the institution against the Commission's Standards.

While the language differs between regional accrediting associations, all consider the importance and centrality of an institution's mission when reviewing the extent to which the school meets accreditation standards. The Higher Learning Commission (HLC) (n.d.) includes the following in its statement titled *The Criteria for Accreditation: Guiding Values*:

> HLC understands and values deeply the diversity of its institutions, which begins from the diversity of their missions. Accordingly, mission in some degree governs each of the Criteria. The Commission holds many expectations for all institutions regardless of mission, but it expects that

differences in mission will shape wide differences in how the expectations are addressed and met.

The Southern Association of Colleges and Schools Commission on Colleges (2012) specifies that colleges and universities need to consider whether "the mission statement is current and comprehensive, accurately guides the institution's operations, is periodically reviewed and updated, is approved by the governing board, and is communicated to the institution's constituencies."

From the point of view of accreditation, everything flows from the mission, with the critical overarching question being, "Is the institution doing what it says it is doing?" Additional questions related to mission that might be considered during the accreditation process appear in Figure 3.1.

Figure 3.1. Accreditation questions related to institutional mission.

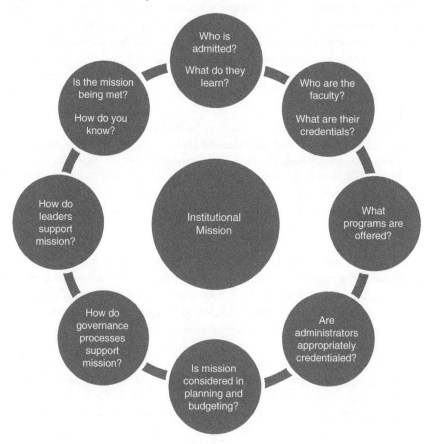

Mission Connections

Instruction and Faculty

For all institutions of higher education seeking accreditation, the most fundamental elements in executing institutional goals related to institutional effectiveness and educational outcomes address how the mission guides the instructional process and the expectations placed on the faculty for providing instruction. Certainly the curriculum, course offerings, and breadth and depth associated with these courses will be determined by the school's goals, the reasons for student enrollment, and the primary academic interests of the institution at large. Additionally, the work of the faculty will be influenced by the nature of the mission. Those expectations will also translate into workload determinations; how faculty members spend their time; and the specific indicators relating to tenure, promotion, and contract extensions for the institution. At two-year institutions, for example, the faculty teach more courses than their colleagues at research universities. Similarly, faculty at four-year colleges are expected to teach more than faculty at research institutions. Educational support services and student life functions are also a focus in the process, and these, too, are expected to mesh with and support the institution's overall mission. Within the context of institutional effectiveness, administrative, financial, and planning issues are a focus, and again, attention is placed on how these functions align with and contribute to the overall mission of the institution and its constituent programs and departments.

The image presented in Figure 3.2, while not fully representative of all institutions, provides an overview of some of the basic differences in faculty duties based on a school's mission.

The central role of faculty as it relates to an institution's mission is self-evident. Administrative and staff members play a critical role relative to the core mission and a variety of essential support programs and services; these, too, should be reflective of the institution's mission.

Student Affairs and the Cocurriculum

As with formal curricular offerings, the design, planning, and implementation of student life programs through the cocurriculum should be in keeping with an institution's mission. The various programs and activities in which students engage outside the classroom should complement and enhance the academic experience and include learning goals and assessment plans. Without a clearly defined purpose, and methods for assessing the effectiveness of these programs from both an educational and administrative point of view,

Figure 3.2. Teaching responsibilities per semester.

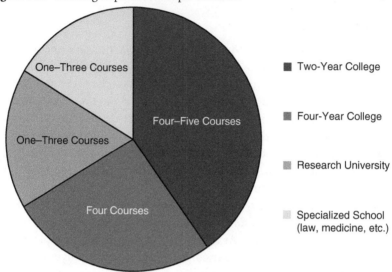

it is hard to evaluate the value of the dollars, time, and human resources devoted to the multitude of out-of-class activities that occur at most colleges and universities.

Staying true to the mission informs policy and leadership decision-making at all levels within student affairs. A student affairs administrator who is struggling with students' requests to charter a new organization, for example, can be guided by the institution's mission when examining the goals of a proposed new student group. The mission will serve as a guide for leaders when determining which aspects of the cocurriculum to support.

It is especially important when evaluating the cocurriculum that administrators, faculty, and students consider the programs in light of their learning goals and outcomes in the same fashion that they would assess a class or curriculum. Learning goals in student affairs should further the institution's mission as well as the mission of the specific unit within the student affairs organization. For example, residence life, student activities, recreation, and even the health centers will want to carefully enumerate their goals, mission, and activities in support of those goals, and then assess whether the goals are met on a regular basis.

The nature of the cocurriculum is such that there will always be some raised eyebrows when people wonder why a particular club or activity is being sponsored or a specific group is invited to a campus, and leaders may find they are called upon to explain these decisions to various internal or external audiences. But if the cocurriculum is aligned with the larger goals and values of the institution and developed in a collaborative fashion with faculty and staff, the proposed activities are far more likely to be successful, and leaders are more likely to find support from various constituencies.

In an effort to create a welcoming environment, leaders at many colleges and universities encourage the development of programs that promote collaboration between faculty and staff. Orientation programs for newly admitted students, for example, can serve as a successful and collaborative mission-driven effort between student affairs and academic affairs. There is a similar effort to bridge the connection between student affairs and academic affairs in the design of residential learning communities, service-learning programs, and honors colleges within the framework of an institution's mission. Initiating such programs benefits students, faculty, and staff.

Communication

Clear communication about the mission of an institution and its many departments is one of the vital responsibilities of senior administrators and leaders at all levels. Moneta and Kuh (2005) discussed the importance of students having accurate information about the colleges in which they enroll. When students have one set of expectations and the expectations do not materialize, the dissonance can result in failure. As Moneta and Kuh (2005) note, "This discrepancy between what students expect and subsequently experience can have a significant influence on student success and desired college outcomes" (p. 65).

Leaders must also address ethical considerations when advertising colleges and universities. Recognizing that typical families still spend more time gathering information for the purchase of a new car than in studying the details of the institution to which they are applying, leaders of higher education institutions must make the moral commitment to inform applicants accurately about what it means to enroll in their schools. After studying 100 private nonprofit colleges, Morphew and Taylor (2009) reported that the majority had multiple versions of their mission statements, using one for official purposes and another for the mass media. Morphew and Taylor commented, "A prospective student assumes that a mission statement reflects the essential nature of the organization as a whole." Studying the mission statements submitted to USNews.com, they further reported that "only six of 100 colleges submitted an official mission statement . . . while 52 submitted a document that we classified as entirely dissimilar to the official mission statement." For faculty and staff, the mission statement serves as a compass for leadership and organizational advancement.

Conclusion

The central theme of this chapter is a simple one: The mission and goals of a college and university are of paramount importance in all aspects of the planning and operation of an institution. Leaders throughout the organization, representing both its academic and administrative functions, need to keep the mission in the forefront of their planning, resource allocation, and day-to-day decision-making.

In the same way that they are critical as guides for an institution's leaders, a clear sense of purpose and aspiration are of major importance to each initiative, program, or department within an institution. These statements are also important in defining, pursuing, and regularly reviewing purposes, aspirations, goals and plans within the institutional and its various units, as we discuss in more detail in Chapter 14.

Using mission as a touchstone for decision-making is an important habit for leaders in higher education to develop. Transparency in communication about mission and the anticipated impact of decisions (e.g., resource management and allocation) on mission elements is important for leaders as they work with internal and external stakeholders. Keeping the mission in the forefront and referring to that mission in both routine and critically important matters will help an institution and its academic and administrative units maintain a constancy of purpose in pursuing its goals.

At the same time, institutional leaders need to recognize that these missions are not written in stone. Mission statements, whether for an institution, a unit, or a department, require review on a regular basis. If such reviews are performed regularly, leaders will be better able to adapt programs, make informed decisions, and guide their colleges and universities in an environment where there are growing tensions between history, tradition, and contemporary marketplace pressures—particularly as a consequence of changing student demographics economic realities, and, as we discuss in the next chapter, to the multiple and often conflicting needs and perspectives of multiple stakeholders.

For Further Consideration

1. A Mission-Centered Assessment of Your Unit, Department, or Institution

1. In your opinion, is the mission of your institution clearly defined and widely understood?

2. Thinking in terms of your academic or administrative unit, is there a clear and agreed-upon mission?

   - Is this captured in a specific mission statement?
   - Has this statement been reviewed or revised in recent years?
   - To what extent does this statement serve as a guide for leaders in decision-making, allocating resources and developing new programs and services?

3. Is there any sense in which the traditions embodied by the mission serve to hinder innovation and change?
4. Thinking in terms of your institution or your academic or administrative unit, can you identify specific examples of decisions being made that could be seen as mission drift?

   - What was the nature of these decisions?
   - Why were these decisions made?
   - Would you regard these decisions as problematic? If not, why not? If so, what leads you to this conclusion?

5. How can the leader of your unit, department, or institution leverage the mission statement to advance policies, influence behavior, or inspire others around the development of new programs, initiatives, and services?

2. Liberal Arts Case Study

You are a faculty/staff member in a small residential liberal arts college. Consistent with its historical mission, the emphasis of programming within the institution has been on arts and humanities. Departments that offer programs and services in these areas have always been priorities in the allocation of resources. Unfortunately, enrollments in particular majors and courses within the college have dwindled in recent years. Foreign language enrollments are down, as are enrollments in history, religion, and art. Programs that began as small units with very limited professional offerings—among them business, communication, human resources management, and computing—have experienced considerable increases in demand, roughly corresponding to the decreases in the liberal arts fields. Surveys of prospective students, along with preference patterns of incoming students, are consistently favoring the professionally oriented fields. You have become quite aware that it is impossible to meet this growing demand in these more professionally oriented fields unless faculty and staff resources are taken away from the traditional arts and humanities fields.

- What options are available to cope with this situation, and what are the trade-offs associated with each?
- How do these options square with the framework presented in this chapter?
- Are there mission-preserving options that might be considered? Or is a change of mission now necessary and appropriate?
- What role can communication play in responding to this complex situation?

Note

1. A detailed discussion of the nature and purpose of mission statements; the distinctions among mission, vision, and values statements; and the role of each in the planning process is provided in Chapter 14.

4

HIGHER EDUCATION'S MULTIPLE STAKEHOLDERS

Perspectives and Pressures

Susan E. Lawrence

You can please all of the people some of the time, and some of the people all of the time, but not all of the people all of the time.

—Attributed to Abraham Lincoln and others

In This Chapter

- Who are the primary internal and external stakeholders of the modern college or university?
- What missions do various stakeholders view as central?
- How can leaders understand and use stakeholder information to strengthen communication about the mission of a unit, department, or institution?
- What sources of information about stakeholder views are available to leaders?

Perhaps no other institution besides government has as many constituencies and beneficiaries—or *stakeholders*, as defined in R. Edward Freeman's (1984) influential work—as the modern college or university. This chapter identifies the widely varied groups that believe they have a stake in higher education today and provides a framework for understanding the challenges created for higher education leaders from stakeholders' competing beliefs and divergent expectations about mission. Identifying what various stakeholder groups understand as the central mission of a particular college or university, or higher education overall, is critical to effective leadership.

Higher Education on the Public Agenda

Whether higher education ever actually lived in the fabled ivory tower or not, there is no question that it has achieved an unusually high place on the public agenda in recent times, as we discuss in some detail in Chapter 2. The data presented in Figure 4.1 track this rise by reporting the number of articles indexed as "university" or "college" in *The New York Times* over the last 50 years. Even discounting for the inclusion of items such as reviews of the animated film *Monsters University* in these totals (Dargis, 2013; Rae, 2013),[1] the increase in media attention is evident. One cause and effect of this increased media attention is an expansion in the scope of who believes they have a stake in higher education and its mission. They may be called audiences, constituents, or beneficiaries,[2] but regardless of the label used, many individuals and groups clearly are paying attention to higher education.

The economic downturn of 2007–2008, coupled with the information technology revolution, has accelerated the urgency with which attention has turned to colleges and universities over the last 10 years. Government looks to higher education to fix a broken economy of displaced workers and income inequality. Individuals confronting socioeconomic difficulties may view higher education as the potential solution to their circumstances. The healthcare industry, Silicon Valley, and the business community depend on universities' commitment to basic and clinical research but often argue that higher education is not producing the educated workforce that is needed.

Tuitions climb while parental worry is fueled by reports that college graduates find it difficult to get jobs. Faculty members face escalating research expectations up and down the hierarchy of colleges and universities. Online courses and degrees seem to offer a way to hold down tuition, free research faculty from distracting teaching loads, and standardize the quality

Figure 4.1. Increased public attention to higher education.

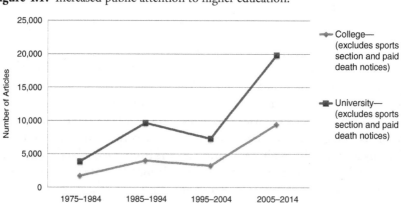

of instruction that students receive; consequently the virtual learning environment is seen as the door to economic opportunity for the disadvantaged as well as the elite. But, as discussed in Chapter 2, these issues are complex, seemingly lacking simple solutions.

Each of higher education's stakeholder groups appears somewhat unhappy. None of these constituencies seems to think they are getting what they want, deserve, or are paying for from higher education.

Stakeholders and the Higher Education Mission

While a general consensus exists on what higher education institutions and their various programs, services, and activities actually do, as shown in Figure 4.2, specifics, priorities, and weightings vary across schools to create particular types of institutions of higher education and particular brands.

Figure 4.2. What universities and colleges do.

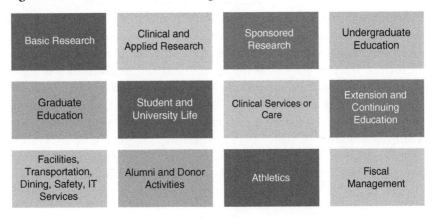

One may look to a variety of sources in determining how a particular school crafts its identity, including the following items:

1. Mission statement
2. Strategic plan(s)
3. Public face (e.g., speeches, major pronouncements, press releases, admissions and recruiting materials, web pages)
4. Recruitment, promotion, and tenure criteria (staff, administrators, and faculty)
5. Composition of top leadership bodies and "kitchen cabinets"
6. Spending/budget priorities.

As discussed in the previous chapter, a key task of leadership is to ensure that a consistent mission is conveyed and reinforced in and across each of these six forums.

Stakeholders

Examining the mission statements, strategic plans, public image, personnel criteria, inner circle membership, and spending and budget decisions provides information on a university's or college's mission priorities. These broader institutional documents do not, however, provide specific information about the individual stakeholder views of higher education (see Jaschik, 2015; Labaree, 1997; Rothman et al., 2010).

A significant leadership challenge results from the fact that there is often a fair amount of variance in understandings of a university's or college's mission among external constituencies. Table 4.1 lists and categorizes the multiplicity of internal and external stakeholders. As Ruben (2004) pointed out, higher education has been remarkably ineffective at developing the concise descriptions and explanations that would make all aspects of the academy's mission intelligible to laypeople. The expectations of external stakeholders have often reflected the current concerns of society, whether they were the agricultural and mechanical arts added by the Morrill Act, the expansion of federal grants to STEM disciplines due to Cold War concerns, or the civil rights agenda and the expansion of access to higher education through tuition grants, student loans, and affirmative action (Thelin, 2011). Recently, the governors of Florida, North Carolina, Texas, and Minnesota pitted the need to address workforce concerns against continued investments in traditional liberal arts

TABLE 4.1
Internal and External Stakeholders

Internal Stakeholders	External Stakeholders
• Administration • Faculty • Clinicians • Staff/employees • Students, prospective and current • Extension divisions • Patients/clients • Governing boards	• Political arena • Donors/taxpayers • Federal, state, and foundation funders • Employers and corporate sector • Parents • Alumni/advisory boards • Patients'/clients' family • Disciplinary/professional organizations • Local community

curricula (Bruni, 2013; Ruiz, 2011) and against the service mission of improving people's lives through teaching, research, outreach, and public service (Associated Press, 2015). A broad range of external stakeholders repeatedly point to the importance of return on investment, prioritizing lower tuition, shorter time to degree, and higher graduate employment rates. Many stakeholders have an expectation that higher education can decrease social and economic inequality, and they therefore prioritize access and affordability.

Differences in the expectations of external stakeholders may be quite familiar, while differences among internal stakeholders frequently go unnoticed or unaddressed, leaving individuals and groups working at cross-purposes, feeling undervalued by each other, and adding complexity to the role of academic and administrative leaders at all levels. Among the most common areas of academic disagreement are the relative importance of undergraduate teaching versus graduate teaching, basic research versus applied research, athletics versus academics, student life versus classroom instruction, professional schools versus liberal arts and sciences, and—more generally—academic versus administrative activities. The job of the leader is further complicated by the fact that while perceptions of the importance of personnel and budgetary decisions can vary from person to person, they are objectively critical components.

Between internal and external stakeholders, governing boards occupy a middle ground; they are "of" the university, but not "in" the university, as Table 4.1 shows. By definition, the *governing board* oversees the institution. The distinguished men and women who serve on boards are often successful leaders in business or government, institutions with procedures and norms that are very different from those of higher education (Bolman & Gallos, 2011). Generally, their fiduciary responsibilities and their responsiveness to alumni shape their understanding of the institution's mission.

Table 4.2 depicts these multiple stakeholders under the categories of research, teaching, and service/care—common elements in the tripartite mission of most four-year institutions. Different stakeholders emphasize not only the different parts of the triad but also their comprehension of how each part varies and invites misunderstandings. For example, particularly in the current budgetary situation, senior administrators tend to emphasize funded research and the ability of faculty to secure federal research dollars, leaving many faculty members in the humanities and social sciences—where support funds are often limited—feeling that their research is underappreciated. Similarly, students, parents, taxpayers, employers, and increasingly those in the political arena think of the teaching mission as

TABLE 4.2
Diverse Stakeholders' Mission Emphases

Research	Teaching	Service/Care
Adminstration: Funded and High Profile	Students: Undergrad and Professional/Career	Taxpayers, Donors, Alumni
Faculty: Pure	Parents: Undergrad and Professional/Career	Patients/Clients and Family
Doctors and Clinicans: Applied	Taxpayers and Donors	Political Arena
Extension Divisions: Applied	Political Arena: Undergrad and Professional: Access, Graduation, Employment	Disciplinary and Professional Organizations
Corporate Sector: Applied Leading to Profit-Making	Employers and Corporate Sectors: Undergraduate and Professional	Specific Constituency Groups for Extension Divisions or Service Missions
Political Arena: Applied (especially defense, STEM, and economic development)	Faculty: Cultivation of Life of Mind and Reproduction of the Profession	
Taxpayers, Donors, Alumni: Applied		

closely tied to career preparation, while some faculty may see it as cultivation of the life of the mind, development of self-actualized young adults, or reproduction of the professoriate. Faculty in professional schools may welcome greater attention to their role in improving society by producing well-trained professionals in health services, education, business, and so on.

Of course, the descriptions presented in Table 4.2 are to some extent stereotypes, and even within the categories of stakeholders identified here, views are not monolithic. Similarly, Figure 4.3 provides a graphic sketch of the constellation of stakeholders and working hypotheses about what appear to be their prominent mission expectations. This graphic highlights the 360-degree vision that higher education leaders need to have. Together, Table 4.2 and Figure 4.3 illustrate the many opportunities that exist for misunderstanding, miscommunication, and disappointment—all of which challenge leaders.

Figure 4.3. Stakeholders' mission priorities.

Communicating Mission and Vision

None of the foregoing analysis is meant to suggest that leaders in higher education must let stakeholder visions and expectations define the mission of higher education or particular universities and colleges. But communicating and realizing an institution's or unit's particular mission and its unique brand requires careful attention to implicit and explicit beliefs of beneficiaries and constituents, attentive listening for these beliefs, and an openness to learning from them. Figure 4.4 provides a simple formula for addressing the challenge presented by discordant visions of the mission of higher education.

These thought steps are probably quite obvious to leaders when composing messages that specifically address the unit's or institution's mission, but the argument here is that leaders must ask themselves the five questions found in Figure 4.4 every time they represent their institution in writing, in

Figure 4.4. Communicating mission and vision.

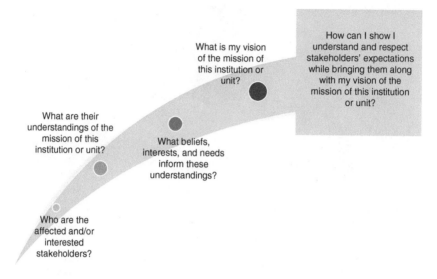

How can I show I understand and respect stakeholders' expectations while bringing them along with my vision of the mission of this institution or unit?

What is my vision of the mission of this institution or unit?

What are their understandings of the mission of this institution or unit?

What beliefs, interests, and needs inform these understandings?

Who are the affected and/or interested stakeholders?

conversations, in committee meetings, and of course, in speeches and other public profiles. Trying to imagine how others might have addressed these questions can be quite helpful as well.

Take, for example, Barack Obama's SUNY–Buffalo speech (2013) on higher education. It does not take deep textual analysis to see that President Obama was talking to students and higher education's external constituencies. The vision of mission that permeates the speech is one of access, social mobility, and workforce development. There was virtually no evidence of concern for the value that traditional faculty and administrators put on the scholarly mission achieved through the cultivation of students' intellectual skills nurtured in fields not oriented in obvious ways toward career preparation or their own scholarly research. Indeed, the speech had much to worry many faculty and administrators, perhaps needlessly.

As discussed in Chapter 2, a significant segment of higher education stakeholders cares deeply about decades of implicit and explicit promises of employment security and social mobility through education, and they find current costs crippling. Higher education can be an easy scapegoat for high unemployment, declining wages, and growing inequity in wealth distribution. For internal stakeholders, these concerns are often seen as overstated and sometimes misdirected. Helping more students get an education and succeed in college without mountains of debt will not create more jobs or

Figure 4.5. Sources of information on stakeholder views of higher education's mission.

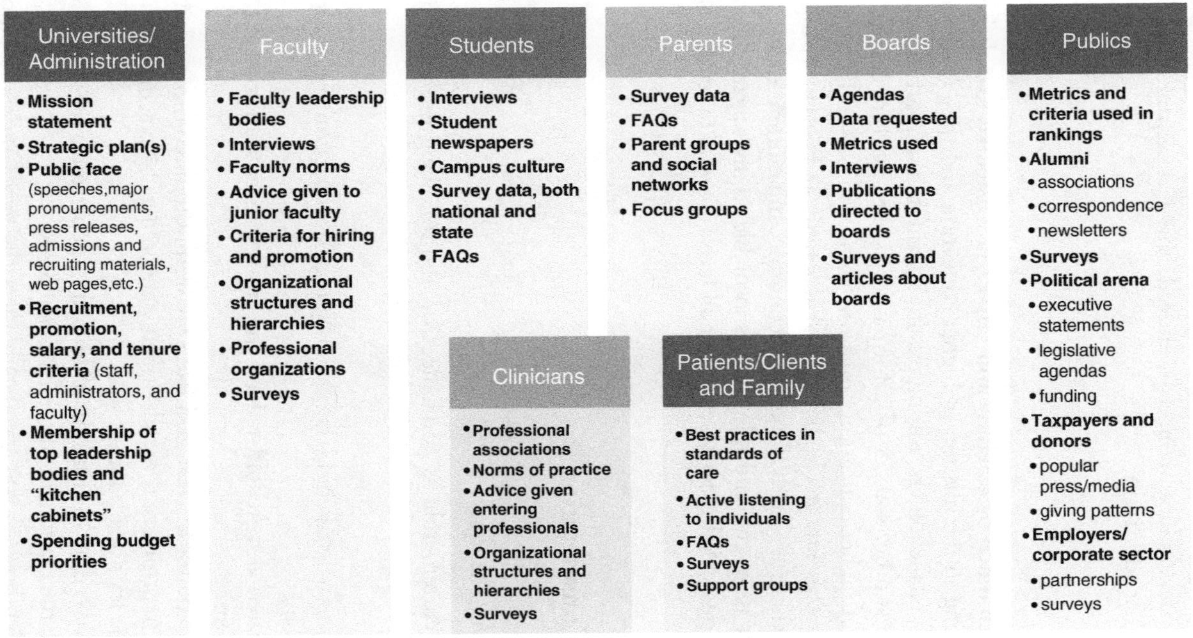

Universities/Administration

- **Mission statement**
- **Strategic plan(s)**
- **Public face** (speeches, major pronouncements, press releases, admissions and recruiting materials, web pages, etc.)
- **Recruitment, promotion, salary, and tenure criteria** (staff, administrators, and faculty)
- **Membership of top leadership bodies and "kitchen cabinets"**
- **Spending budget priorities**

Faculty

- **Faculty leadership bodies**
- **Interviews**
- **Faculty norms**
- **Advice given to junior faculty**
- **Criteria for hiring and promotion**
- **Organizational structures and hierarchies**
- **Professional organizations**
- **Surveys**

Students

- **Interviews**
- **Student newspapers**
- **Campus culture**
- **Survey data, both national and state**
- **FAQs**

Parents

- **Survey data**
- **FAQs**
- **Parent groups and social networks**
- **Focus groups**

Boards

- **Agendas**
- **Data requested**
- **Metrics used**
- **Interviews**
- **Publications directed to boards**
- **Surveys and articles about boards**

Publics

- **Metrics and criteria used in rankings**
- **Alumni**
  - associations
  - correspondence
  - newsletters
- **Surveys**
- **Political arena**
  - executive statements
  - legislative agendas
  - funding
- **Taxpayers and donors**
  - popular press/media
  - giving patterns
- **Employers/corporate sector**
  - partnerships
  - surveys

Clinicians

- **Professional associations**
- **Norms of practice**
- **Advice given entering professionals**
- **Organizational structures and hierarchies**
- **Surveys**

Patients/Clients and Family

- **Best practices in standards of care**
- **Active listening to individuals**
- **FAQs**
- **Surveys**
- **Support groups**

change the proportion of people in the top 10% of the income distribution. Doing so, however, is consistent with higher education's commitment to the transfer of knowledge, so it should be possible to find common ground and satisfy multiple stakeholders' concerns. Indeed, this is a central leadership challenge in higher education.

Conclusion

Leaders can learn much by carefully and respectfully listening to stakeholders' beliefs relating to the mission of higher education and the expectations that influence the stakeholders' willingness for continuing support. But leaders can also access other sources of information as they work to bridge the multiple views of higher education's mission. Some will be specific to each institution; others operate at a higher level of generality and pertain to higher education as a whole as a critical societal, economic, and cultural entity. Figure 4.5 reminds us of the multiple sources available to investigate the perspectives of various stakeholders. Leaders at all levels are wise to remain alert to these.

For Further Consideration

1. A Stakeholder Analysis

Consider your current role as you reflect on the following questions and considerations:

- Which internal stakeholders have the greatest impact on your unit or department?
- Which external stakeholders have the greatest impact on your unit or department?
- Using the power interest grid from www.mindtools.com provided in Figure 4.6, prioritize these identified stakeholders by placing them in one of the four quadrants.
- In what ways does the mission of your unit, department, or institution influence the placement of these stakeholders?
- As a leader, how do you specifically meet the needs and expectations of these diverse stakeholders?

Figure 4.6. Power interest grid.

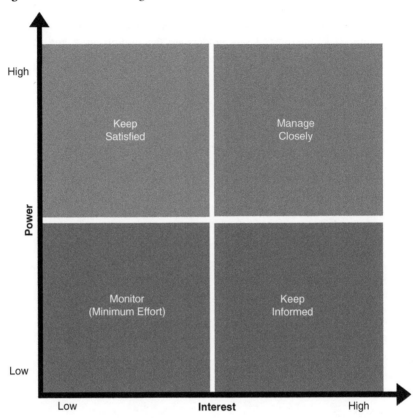

Source. Retrieved from www.mindtools.com

Notes

1. But even that is not completely spurious, as indicated by commentaries related to the movie in the *Chronicle of Higher Education* (Hoover, 2013) and *Inside Higher Ed* (Kiley, 2013).

2. As Ruben (2016) has noted, depending on the particular higher education institution, the list may include faculty, staff, current and prospective students and parents, law or medical school clients/patients, alumni, advisory boards, academic associations, disciplinary and professional communities, graduate and professional schools and organizations, potential employers, businesses and industries, state and federal funding agencies, private foundations and donors, local and state government, the citizens of the community or state, disciplinary and administrative opin-

ion leaders at other institutions, and other groups. For administrative departments that serve other departments within the institution—such as facilities, computing services, faculty/administrative councils or assemblies, and other administrative and service units—relevant internal stakeholders are the administrative and academic units for which the organization provides services or that influence or are influenced by the organization.

PART TWO

LEADERSHIP CONCEPTS AND COMPETENCIES

5

CAMPUS CULTURES
AND INTERCULTURAL
TENSIONS

The Leader as Organizational Ethnographer and
Cross-Cultural Communicator

In This Chapter

- What is an organizational culture, and why is an understanding of this topic important for leaders?
- How can the skills of an ethnographer enhance the work of higher education leaders?
- What are the distinctive cultures within colleges and universities?
- What differences between academic and administrative cultures lead to predictable intercultural tensions?
- What does it mean to become a bilingual or bicultural leader, and what intercultural communication competencies are helpful in attaining this goal?

Higher education institutions are incredibly complex organizations. Each of the major divisions, disciplines, and departments within the institution has its own distinctive history and distinguishing patterns of behavior—that is, its own organizational culture. One of the keys to leadership effectiveness is to become aware of and adept at observing and understanding these cultural practices, through a process described in this chapter as becoming an organizational ethnographer. In this chapter, we explore the concepts of organizational culture and ethnography, and their relevance for effective leadership in higher education.

Organizational Culture

There are a number of definitions of *culture*, including one by noted anthropologist Clifford Geertz (1973): "[Culture] denotes an historically transmitted pattern of meanings embodied in symbols, a system of inherited conceptions expressed in symbolic forms by means of which men [*sic*] communicate, perpetuate, and develop their knowledge about and attitudes toward life" (p. 89). Another definition posited by Edgar Schein (2015) also reflects these shared patterns of meaning:

> [Culture is] a pattern of shared basic assumptions learned by a group as it solved its problems of external adaptation and internal integration, which has worked well enough to be considered valid and, therefore, to be taught to new members as the correct way to perceive, think, and feel in relation to those problems. (p. 287)

Within the context of organizations, we describe cultures as consisting of those qualities that make the entity distinctive. One very basic description calls attention to the importance of an organization's history, language, stories, rules, traditions, customs, and preferred practices (Ruben & Stewart, 2016). Approaching culture from a communication perspective, Joann Keyton (2011) describes the phenomenon as "the set(s) of artifacts, values, and assumptions that emerges from the interactions of organizational members" (p. 28). Each of these cultural elements manifest themselves in the day-to-day workings of an institution and often come into play in quite significant ways as leaders endeavor to guide the organization in new directions or undertake new initiatives.

The cultural perspective highlights a number of characteristics associated with colleges and universities, including values and assumptions, subcultures, history, tradition, context, storytellers, language, organizational sagas, symbols, and architecture. These elements of colleges and universities play an important role in shaping the experience of all organizational stakeholders. Hence, culture is not something that an organization *has*; rather, culture *is* the organization (Smircich, 1983). For the purpose of this chapter, we understand culture to be the very fabric of an organization, and it is therefore an important area of attention for leaders. As Biz Stone (2015), the cofounder of Twitter, noted in an article in the *Harvard Business Review*, "A culture is going to form whether you like it or not, and if you pay attention to it, you can craft something that makes the . . . organization stronger" (p. 41).

Like other types of cultures, the cultures of organizations develop and evolve over time, are taken for granted, and often go unnoticed and unanalyzed. As Ruud (2000) suggests, "The concept of culture . . . [is] a resource for describing and analyzing organizational life. . . . [It] provides a way of understanding how members within the organization make sense out of their everyday interactions" (pp. 118, 119). They are not "right" or "wrong," but there is a logic to why they developed in the way they did and why particular groups value the things they do.

Cultures are stable and naturally resist change, much as our human immune systems resist irritants—intrusions that are often regarded as threats and often met with a natural fight-or-flight response. Not surprisingly, then, the more groups that are affected directly or indirectly by a leader's decisions in a particular circumstance, the more resistance a leader may encounter, and the more attention, creativity, and persistence may be required for successful outcomes. For this reason, more generally, it is often the case that organizational cultures are likely to shape the actions and behaviors of leaders as much as or more than leaders shape cultures.

Leader as Organizational Ethnographer

To be successful within organizations, the skills of ethnography are extremely helpful. According to Spradley (1979), "Ethnography is the work of describing a culture. The essential core of this activity aims to understand another way of life from the native point of view" (p. 2). A systematic study of people and culture(s), ethnography seeks to describe the culture and lived experience of members of a specific group.

From our perspective, the benefits of these ethnographic techniques extend beyond anthropological and social science research and into the domain of applied leadership practice. Academic leaders, as organizational ethnographers, can develop a deep and nuanced understanding of the subcultures within the college or university, and this knowledge can be invaluable as leaders strive to adapt to and influence units, departments, and institutions. To do this, leaders need to become students of the various cultures they encounter within the institution—focusing thoughtful attention on observation, listening, and analysis of the behavior and actions of the groups and organizations with whom leaders must work.

How and where can an individual who is new to an organization or a leadership role undertake his or her work as an ethnographer? Observations might take place during formal meetings, lunchroom conversations, or chance encounters within the hallway, coffee shop, or water cooler. In the case of meetings, for example, attention might be given to patterns of arrival, attendance, and departure. What time do individuals arrive for a meeting set to start at 10:00 a.m., for instance? How are meetings begun? Are there formalized agendas? If so, how are agendas constructed, and when are they distributed? Do members contribute items to the agenda? How is meeting time allocated among activities such as leader announcements, group discussion and analysis, group decision-making, and the development of action plans? How fully do members seem engaged? What are the typical patterns of interaction? Do some, most, or all members speak? How do patterns of participation relate to gender, race, area of expertise, rank, or seniority? Is attendance expected of all? Are explanations expected from those who miss a meeting? How are meetings ended?

Communication patterns may also be observed. For instance, what themes, analogies, and metaphors are commonly used? Do the content and tone of discussion tend to emphasize collaboration and cooperation within the unit and with other units, or are competition and individual pursuits more common themes? Do some terms have predictably positive or negative connotations? Is the *administration, faculty,* or *staff* talked about in predictably positive or negative ways? Is business language commonly and comfortably used, or are these associations avoided or negatively regarded? How candid are colleagues with one another about views and opinions? Do members openly question or challenge leaders or one another? When challenges or questions occur how do leaders and colleagues respond? Are postmeeting and back-channel conversations among colleagues a common practice? What function do such discussions seem to play? Are some colleagues predictably involved in these discussions, and others not?

Other topics of focus might include the following: Who are the formal and informal opinion leaders? What approaches to problem-solving and decision-making are common to the organization? What role do informal leaders play? To what extent is control for various functions distributed within the organization? How broadly engaged are members of the unit or institution? Are the views of external stakeholders typically sought and used? Are comparisons to other organizations a common strategy in problem-solving or decision-making?

Operationally, one can also devote attention to conventions regarding e-mail practice within the unit. For what purposes are e-mails used? Is it customary for all department members to respond to each e-mail that solicits information or poses a question? Are "CCs" and "BCCs" typically used? In what instances, and for what purposes? Are there topics that are less often discussed through e-mail?

Beyond gaining a deeper understanding of these particular groups, organizations, and subcultures, the skills of careful observation, listening, and analysis allow a leader to gain insights to help him or her predict approaches that are likely to fit with the culture and those that will not. They also can help to differentiate particular leadership styles that will be familiar and well-received from those that will likely create turbulence. Clearly, knowledge about an organizational culture and how members of that culture typically act and operate is of great value in adapting to the organization and functioning effectively as a leader. None of this discussion is intended to imply that it will always be a leader's intention to adapt behaviors or actions that will be consistent with cultural traditions of the organization or institution. Those strategic choices should be made on a case-by-case basis, depending on one's broader goals. But in all cases, one hopes to make *informed* choices reflective of a good understanding of the culture and with a sense of likely responses, rather than random or arbitrary choices made without forethought and planning. We might borrow and adapt Alice Goffman's (2014) observations in her ethnographic study of life in an urban neighborhood in Philadelphia as we think through the intersection of leadership, organizational ethnography, and culture: "To survive . . . [and succeed as a leader] . . . [one] learns to hesitate when others walk casually forward, to see what others fail to notice, to . . . [carefully analyze] what others trust or take for granted" (p. 25).

Organizational Climate

One additional idea related to organizational culture that deserves mention is organizational climate. Climate is an expression of the underlying culture. A wide range of factors may be considered as elements of an organization's climate, as is well illustrated within the "Great Colleges to Work For" framework summarized in Box 5.1. How do faculty and staff treat one another? How are students treated? Is the tone one of genuine interest, supportiveness, and respectfulness, or does a sense of disinterest, disregard, and disrespect come through? A visitor may get a feel for the climate of a college or university, or of the programs or departments within it, by walking around campus, stopping in an office to meet with staff or faculty, or reading campus-wide e-mails from the administration. Conversations among faculty and staff may also convey a sense of how people working in an organization feel about their work, their workplace, and the services that they provide. Even micro-behaviors, such as whether and how colleagues respond to routine e-mails or the tone of conversations among colleagues, are other manifestations of *climate*, which may be defined as "the feeling that is conveyed in a group by the physical layout and the way in which members of the organization interact with each other, with customers, or with other outsiders" (Schein, 2015; Schneider, 1990; Tagiuri & Litwin, 1968).

BOX 5.1
Great Colleges to Work For

In 2008 the *Chronicle of Higher Education* and ModernThink LLC created the Great Colleges to Work For program. Annually they report the results of employee surveys at participating colleges and universities. The 2015 results are instructive for formal and informal leaders in higher education. Employee satisfaction is highest in the following contexts:

- Leaders are
  - Credible
    - Leaders engage in interactions that build trust and behaviors that are consistent, reliable, and reflect integrity.
  - Capable
    - Leaders demonstrate that they have the knowledge, skills, and experience to effectively lead the institution.
- Communication is
  - Transparent
    - Leaders are open concerning both good and bad news, provide the context and rationale for decisions, and ensure that the campus community receives regular and timely updates.
  - Interactive
    - Leaders foster interactive communication that creates opportunities for two-way exchanges.
- Alignment between goals and people emphasizes
  - Collaboration
    - Leaders support faculty and staff members and require faculty and staff to support each other, solicit input from one another, and pay little attention to who gets credit for what.
  - Contribution
    - Leaders position people to contribute at their highest level by putting the right people in the right jobs and providing them with the training, tools, and resources to succeed.
- Respect is demonstrated through
  - Fairness
    - Leaders treat employees fairly, regardless of personal attributes or position.
  - Acknowledgment
    - Leaders provide specific and regular rewards, recognition, and feedback designed to motivate faculty and staff members to treat one another well and do their best work.

Source: Edmunds & Boyer, 2015.
Acknowledgment: Synthesis by Susan E. Lawrence.

Organizational climate is an important topic for leadership attention. Climate is significant to the effectiveness of a unit or institution and the fulfillment of its mission and critical to the satisfaction of faculty, staff, and others who interact with members of the institution or unit.

The Organizational Climate Inventory[1] offers a useful listing of common elements of an organizational climate, and can be used as a tool to assess the climate of your current department or institution. The benefits of using this inventory, or other inventories that allow you to systematically explore culture or climate, are expansive. These tools allow leaders to identify areas of cultural improvement, encourage a commitment to employee well-being and cultural excellence, and demonstrate a concern for improving the workplace experience for all involved with the organization.

Higher Education: A World-Class Leader in Cultural Complexity

In a classic ethnographic study of a community symphony, Ruud (2000) discovered two distinctive and competing cultural perspectives within the organization: Musicians tended to embrace an artistic code while managers embraced a business code, and each code competed with the other for organizational prominence. He illustrated how a person's responsibility in the organization had a significant influence on that person's organizational identity—with administrators taking on a business orientation and musicians attending to the more performance-oriented components of the symphony. As Ruud goes on to suggest,

> The artistic and business codes, analyzed individually or in opposition, are meaningful in that they express, in a culturally specific manner, the way in which performers and business personnel experience and evaluate organizational life. Each code . . . suggests a particular set of . . . premises that guide organizational members as they assess past, present, and future organizational actions. (p. 124)

These communication codes shape the reality for members of the organization. After 400 hours of ethnographic fieldwork, Ruud found that "certain groups [those with a business orientation] wield more power [than the performers] and . . . have more opportunity to ensure that their interests are maintained" (p. 138). We present this compelling research study here as a way of introducing the cultural complexity of higher education.

In a number of ways, the competing goals, values, expectations, and language codes of the symphony musicians and managers parallel those of the academic and administrative subcultures of higher education. In addition to the administrative-academic divide, in colleges and universities with professional schools (e.g., medical schools and law schools), the many internal subcultures add to the complexity of these organizations. For example, one might consider the critical differences among physician cultures, patient cultures, and the hospital culture for a particular medical school. The community symphony seems instructive as a way of thinking about the potentially influential role of a college or university leader as an organizational ethnographer and cross-cultural communicator.

When it comes to the number, complexity, and variety of cultures within a single organization, higher education institutions lead all others. A very large number of groups with distinct cultures are directly involved with the work of higher education institutions. Although these subgroups may remain united around some loosely shared goals of higher education, for each there are any number of differing culture views of the nature and priorities of higher education, and each group tends to privilege different interpretations.

As discussed already in some detail previously, there is no shortage of internal and external stakeholders with an interest in the work of American colleges and universities. Internal stakeholders include the various departments within the institution, which represent a broad cross-section of disciplines and administrative and technical specialty areas. Within each of these are numerous subgroups, each of which has its own nuanced cultural identities reflecting differences in discipline, rank, seniority, technical area, source of funding, tenure status, union status, and a variety of other factors (Snow, 2012; Tierney, 1988). These cultural groups include those with formal leadership roles and those who influence from untitled positions, both of which can have a great deal of impact on organizational functioning. Furthermore, one may also consider the diverse array of student stakeholders who maintain an interest in the organization, including full-time, part-time, residential, commuting, and the growing number of distance-learning students. Each of these student subcultures maintains a particular loyalty to its respective department, campus, or discipline. For example, just as faculty of a large research institution tend to identify more with their primary discipline and staff with their primary unit or department, students often demonstrate a loyalty to their primary major or campus residential community.

Academic and Administrative Cultures

The two largest and most important employee groups within higher education institutions are the staff/administrators and the faculty, each of which is a vital and distinct cultural group. A large percentage of the plans, decisions, and initiatives undertaken by higher education leaders involve both of these cultures in some way, and differences between the administrative (administrator/staff) and academic cultures in most colleges and universities create significant challenges. Each culture tends to be distinctive because of the unique makeup of the group's members, including differentiating roles and responsibilities, education and training, incentive and reward structures, and professional backgrounds. It is critically important for leaders to understand these cultures and the nuances that define and differentiate one from the other. For example, one might identify the following traditional core values of the academic culture:

- Freedom of expression
- Collegial decision-making
- Creating, advancing, and imparting knowledge
- Primary loyalty to discipline rather than institution
- Higher education as unique and special—not a business
- Students as learners—not customers
- Self-determination (individual and institutional).
- The faculty as the university—particularly in terms of input and influence
- Customization of processes and procedures
- Aversion to board, state, national, accrediting, and Department of Education perspectives as important in decision-making

These core values often clash to a lesser or greater extent with the primary values of the administrative culture, which include the following:

- Operational effectiveness
- Hierarchical decision-making
- Efficiency
- Cost-effectiveness/cost-savings
- Service orientation and loyalty to institution
- The university as a business
- Return on investment
- Compliance with regulations as a critical concern
- Valuing standardization of processes and procedures
- Attuned to board, state, national, accrediting, and Department of Education perspectives as important in decision-making.

These lists are suggestive of some of the traditional values associated with the two subcultures. Of course, these lists are cultural stereotypes and generalizations, and their validity varies from campus to campus depending on many factors. That said, these lists capture some important and generally predictable differences between the cultural values of academics and administrators that leaders need to understand and take into account in their work. These differences in core values can play out in the ways that work is structured and accomplished and in the ways that members view one another. One interesting illustration of the ways in which cultural values can affect leadership initiatives is provided in the Skyline State Travel case study at the end of this chapter.

Differences between these two cultures become evident in any number of areas, including the way in which these groups think about and approach meetings, how they think about their organizations and work activities, and in their language preferences and usage. Generally speaking, within the administrative culture, attendance at scheduled meetings is assumed to be mandatory unless a major problem arises. In that case, notification is expected, and if possible the individual who has to miss a session sends a substitute. Within the academic culture, attendance at most meetings is viewed as desirable but not necessarily mandatory. If a faculty member has a research, teaching, or service activity that is regarded as important, it may take precedence over attendance at a meeting.

In general, timely arrival to the meeting is more valued in the administrative than the academic culture, whereas academic meetings often will begin when it seems that a critical mass of participants have arrived, even if that is later than the scheduled start time. Members of the administrative/staff culture are also generally more likely to regard preparation for a meeting as essential; faculty, on the other hand, place greater importance on the discussion that takes place at the meeting. The same relative rules of formality and informality that relate to meeting start times apply to the ends of meetings, and to whether and how attendees follow up afterward. Not surprisingly, each group is somewhat puzzled, and sometimes frustrated, by these different patterns of behavior. For a leader who must organize, conduct, and follow up on meetings that involve individuals from both cultures, the task can be daunting. At least during initial meetings, it may be necessary to prepare for, accept, and work around the deep-seated cultural differences that may present themselves—and to have understanding and patience as you work to establish shared expectations within the group.

Cultural differences between administrators and academics may also be significant among work patterns and styles. While faculty work on projects at varying locales and at all hours of the day (or night), staff responsibilities are generally performed in their offices in the nine-to-five window. For staff—and sometimes students and visitors—it can be frustrating that faculty are not always in their offices during "regular" working hours; they may fail to realize that for many faculty members there really are no regular working hours. Conversely, it's sometimes a bit troubling to faculty that staff members may not be inclined to respond to e-mails in the evenings or on weekends—although, increasingly, this distinction does not necessarily hold. While the faculty work style is often characterized by greater autonomy, in fact, regular, three-year, tenure, and post-tenure reviews provide many accountability points. These may be less apparent to staff who are likely to have more frequent and sometimes more formalized performance reviews. Accountability exists for both groups, though the form and timing differ. That said, differences between these accountability models can be a source of misunderstanding and resentment.

As noted, differences between the two cultures also relate to the way they each think and talk about organizations. Faculty members are likely to describe their department, school, or university as *unique* and often talk about issues as if they are particular to their organization. Administrators, on the other hand, are more likely to use generic language, such as "organizational issues," "process issues," or "leadership issues"—reflecting a perspective that focuses more on similarities across units than on differences.

Another difference in language reflects how administrators and faculty communicate about the business operations of colleges and universities. In an article in *Inside Higher Education*, for example, Kellie Woodhouse (2015) explores the different sets of vocabulary used by faculty and staff. She quotes Margarita Rose, chair of the faculty leadership at King's College, who presents the difference as follows: "There's an expectation . . . that the financial officer will have the same language and understanding as the academic administration and faculty. Perhaps that's an unfair expectation since we don't always use language the same way." However, as Richard Kneedler, president emeritus of Franklin & Marshall College, suggests, "It's important that faculty have a willingness to learn some terminology with which they might not be familiar, because the institution where they find themselves very likely needs to have skills in a variety of areas where they might not have been necessary 15 or 20 years ago, but they are absolutely vital today" (Woodhouse, 2015). The debate as to whether the university is a business is but one example of the underlying tensions between these two dominant subcultures.

Other variations in language use and interpretations can also be a challenge. Sometimes academic words and phrases are subject to criticism—and sometimes evoke sarcastic responses—from administrators. For example, when academics say "collegial decision-making," administrators may interpret the phrase to mean, "A time-consuming process that results in no clear outcomes, and by the time this becomes clear, the time to act has probably passed." The term *tenure* may be interpreted by some staff as "immunity to accountability and organizational responsibility." The phrase *faculty participation* may well be understood by some to mean, "Lots of talking, not many tangibles/deliverables." Conversely, when faculty hear that "consultants have been hired to assist with strategic planning, branding, marketing, or process reengineering," their translations are often equally unflattering. A reference to "strategic planning" by administrators may be interpreted by faculty as, "Here we go again—a great investment of time developing a list of priorities that have been predetermined by administrators to be published in a brochure that will likely accumulate dust on the bookshelves when that time and money should be spent on teaching and research." Furthermore, the language of "efficiency," "higher education as a business," and "standardized processes and procedures" is sometimes viewed by faculty as an implicit attack on academic freedom, autonomy, and the core academic values of higher education.

One quite predictable language pattern is particularly troubling to staff and is, therefore, worth singling out for special mention. Often in discussions of the mission of a unit or institution, emphasis is placed on the role of the faculty, research, and classroom or laboratory instruction. Inadvertently, this representation marginalizes the essential contributions of administrators and staff—stakeholders who play mission-critical roles throughout the institution.

Of course, these translations are simply generalizations—they do not hold for all individuals, in all such cultures, nor at all institutions. Where they are present, differences in meanings often get in the way as administrators and academics attempt to collaborate for the collective good of the institution.

Higher Education Leaders as Cross-Cultural Communicators

What are the important practical insights to be gained from this discussion of cultures? As Harold Silver (2008) suggests, "In terms of . . . shared norms, values and assumptions, as well as symbols, myths or rituals, universities do not have a culture. [Universities are] . . . a system of subcultures in perpetual, erratic, and damaging tensions" (p. 167). There is no such thing as a unified culture, and there exist a number of competing ideas within the academic and administrative subcultures (Martin, 1992; Silver, 2008).

Individuals in formalized positions within their unit, and more broadly across the campus, often define another set of unique cultures—each with their own, often unique, perspectives, expectations, and cultural traditions that may or may not align with one another. In addition to the formal leadership structure of the unit and campus, higher education is unique in that informal leadership cultures can be incredibly influential forces. Individuals who have developed long-standing relationships and have established personal credibility—perhaps because they have previously occupied formal leadership roles—often function as what have been termed *opinion and thought leaders* in political science (Katz & Lazarsfeld, 1955), or what sociologists have referred to in other contexts as *public characters* (Duneiere, 2000; Jacobs, 1961). Individuals serving alone or with others in these capacities are potential sources of wise counsel or detractors and disruptors to the work of formal leaders. In any case, within higher education, informal leaders and individuals are an important source of influence and often a necessary focus of attention by unit leaders. We discuss this topic further in Chapter 10.

To a significant extent, success as an academic or administrative leader hinges on the ability to identify, understand, and work productively with and among these various cultures within institutions of higher education. Another, equally important key is to become skilled at intercultural communication—to translate the results of your ethnographic insights to effectively pursue leadership goals in a way that acknowledges and leverages the cultural insights gained.

As leaders navigate the often competing subcultures within the academy, it is helpful to realize that they are essentially operating in an intercultural environment. Cross-cultural communication offers a very useful frame for understanding leadership in higher education. Even though all parties often speak the same language, work in the same place, and share many traditions, differences in work practices, career aspirations, and the incentive and reward system can lead to quite a set of cultural barriers. The implication is that a leader must be not only an organizational ethnographer but also an adept cross-cultural communicator.

For leaders grappling with cultural differences, the issue at stake is typically not whether particular perspectives are right or wrong. All perspectives have a historical explanation and logic and are generally regarded by members of the cultural group as valid and correct ways to operate (Ruben & Stewart, 2016). Once formed, the elements of culture take on a reality of their own—one that reflects the norms of a culture that are understood to be "right," whereas others might seem wrong. New members of the culture, including new organizational leaders, must learn and adapt to cultures in order to be accepted. Organizational leadership requires working with and through existing cultures. Effective leadership requires skills in predicting and detecting culture differences, demonstrating sensitivity to them, and finding creative ways to utilize and leverage the strengths of each perspective.

In higher education, and in other contexts, communication across cultures often presents major challenges. These situations typically demand patience, care, and critical thinking. Some examples of intercultural communication include those encounters between a doctor and patient, teacher and student, and staff and faculty. Communication in these situations can best be thought of as instances of "cross-cultural communication" and recognized as contexts that benefit greatly from, and sometimes demand, bicultural understandings and skills.

Some of the most challenging cross-cultural communication situations in higher education are those that involve crossing the business-academic cultural divide. Janet Mason Ellerby (2009), professor of English at the University of North Carolina Wilmington and former interim director of the Women's Studies and Resource Center, acknowledges this divide:

> Having had the opportunity to look at academe from both sides now—as professor and administrator—I'm disillusioned. The divide I had always suspected between faculty and administration seems quite real, and any ideals I might have entertained of mutual respect have been tarnished. . . . What I can see from both sides now is what could have happened, what still could happen. Administrators need to work harder to raze the divide between administration and faculty, to construct sturdy bridges of mutual respect that encourage communication, consultation, and collaboration. Is it too facile to say, "We're all in this together?"

Strategies to Increase Cross-Cultural Communication Competence

Cross-cultural situations call for academic leaders to value outcomes and process equally and to emphasize shared goals. There are a number of specific strategies that can be helpful in anticipating and responding to cultural differences, including the following:

- Remind yourself that while you are likely to have your own opinion of the merits of a particular initiative, project, change, program, or activity based on your experience as a faculty or staff member, your personal opinions may not be all that critical when you are in a leadership role. Bluntly stated, as a leader, the task is often less about advocating your own point of view and more about creating constructive dialogue, developing high-quality decisions that are informed by multiple perspectives, and cultivating buy-in and support for the directions to be pursued. Multiple perspectives generally heighten the probability of sound decisions, and the act of engaging others greatly increases the likelihood that the chosen directions will have traction and sustainability.

- Identify the perspective that varying groups have—and the array of assets, liabilities, risks, and opportunities each is likely to see—and develop plans and process strategies that take account of the varying cultures and relevant cultural differences.

- Work to develop solutions that take account of your goals and the cultural realities of others whose support will be critical to your success as a leader in this instance and over time.

- Whenever possible, identify and engage individuals who have a stake in an initiative, project, change, program, or activity being contemplated, planned, or implemented.

Over the longer term, it becomes imperative for leaders to commit to becoming multicultural. In particular, a leader might develop a network of friends and acquaintances from a variety of cultural groups within the institutions and invest in understanding their cultures and perspectives. If you're a faculty leader, some of your best friends really do need to be administrators; and conversely, if you are a staff administrator, you need to be able to count faculty members among the friends who you know and appreciate. The same need for multicultural competence extends to students and external stakeholders. Simply put,

> [There is] the need to be alert and sensitive to the needs, orientations, values, aspirations, and . . . communication styles of other persons with whom one interacts. One needs to know how respect, empathy, non-judgmentalness, turn-taking, orientation to knowledge, and group and organizational roles are *regarded* and *expressed* in a given culture. Of equal or greater importance to effectiveness at transfer of skills is the willingness to be introspective, and committed to see, to examine, and to learn from one's failures and weaknesses as well as one's successes and strengths. Only in this way can one's behavior be brought into congruence with what one believes and intends. (Ruben, 1977)

A description of the behavioral components of this cross-cultural communication effectiveness may be found in the Intercultural Communication Behavior Scales offered in this book's appendices.[2]

Influencing Organizational Culture

Perhaps the greatest test of a leader's ethnographic and multicultural communication skills is provided in situations where the goal is to influence existing organizational cultures or shape the culture of a new organization. While there is clearly no simple set of strategies that assure success in such instances, the following suggestions can be helpful:

- Create and articulate a vision of an alternative or desired organizational culture, being specific as to how and why it would differ from the present culture.
- As a new leader, identify, recognize, and validate the good work done by predecessors (leaders and units), particularly emphasizing accomplishments that exemplify dimensions of the desired new culture.
- Recruit employees who embody the desired aspirations and values of the new or modified culture.
- Disseminate an alternative organizational vision to internal and external constituencies.
- Be visible and associate yourself personally and behaviorally with the values and principles embodied in the new or modified culture (e.g., role modeling and finding ways to visibly "walk the talk").
- Identify previous and present leaders, including thought leaders, who are talented, and make an effort to engage them fully in the new directions.
- Commit to making decisions that are transparent and consistent with the alternative organizational vision.
- Establish goals and strategies for both the short and long term that are consistent with the desired culture.
- Align organizational rhetoric with organizational practices (e.g., in decision-making and resource allocation).
- Hire and promote in ways consistent with the institution's vision and values. For example, take professorial criteria and peer review processes seriously for external hires and internal promotions, and do not use promotions as a strategy to move weak leaders out of their present positions, because doing so sends precisely the wrong message to colleagues.
- Give visibility to exemplary projects and outcomes.
- Create reward and recognition systems that encourage movement toward the new cultural vision, including public forums and

communication mechanisms to publicize changes that exemplify the desired new directions.

- Work with and through leaders at all levels.
- Maintain alignment between what is said and what is done, and ensure that this consistency is apparent to internal and external stakeholders.

Conclusion

Attention to organizational culture and climate may well help to shape one's legacy as a leader. Indeed, an individual's success as an academic or administrative leader will often depend on his or her success at entering and navigating among the many subcultures of higher education. It is through thoughtful ethnographic observation and analysis that one can understand the values and practices of the many cultures of higher education institutions—and through effective cross-cultural communication, differences can be negotiated and reconciled.

For Further Consideration

1. A New Leader's Cultural Discovery

As the newly appointed leader, you invite members of your department to discuss plans for the upcoming academic year. You are committed to setting the right tone in your new role, a leader who is both inclusive and enthusiastic. Rather than impose a set of goals upon the department, you invite the members of your team to complete an anonymous survey of their top priorities for the new year. You intend to use this feedback as part of your first planning meeting. Four of 12 team members respond to your initial request. After sending a reminder e-mail to the group to complete the survey, one more person responds. Upon entering the room for your first meeting, you are surprised to see that only a handful of members are on time. You begin to observe that meetings typically start 10 to 20 minutes after the designated start time. In addition to not starting on time, engagement throughout the department meeting is quite low as members check their e-mail and work on personal projects throughout the meeting.

Do you find these various factors to be problems? If so, what do you see as problematic about this situation? What does the lack of response to your survey and the lack of engagement within the meeting communicate to you about the unit's culture? How might you respond to this situation? At a deeper level, is it possible for the new leader to change the culture of a unit—or should you even attempt to address this issue at the outset of your formal tenure as leader?

At the conclusion of your first three months in this position, you determine that the existing administrative structure within the unit needs to be revised. Additionally, some of the individuals currently occupying various roles need to be replaced. How should you proceed with the proposed restructuring? Should you formally or informally consult with others in the unit? If so, who? Is three months in the role too soon to consider structural changes? Would different timing make more sense? Finally, how might the decision to consider a new structure affect the culture of the unit, and how do you best respond to those who resist the idea?

2. Skyline State Travel

To illustrate the ways in which cultural values can come into play in leadership initiatives, let's suppose that a university with a tradition of decentralized and collegial decision-making wanted to embark on a new approach to faculty and staff travel. Imagine that the new approach would include the establishment of a single university travel service, through which all faculty, administrator, and staff travel would be booked. Imagine further that a joint committee of faculty, administrators, and staff was formed to consider this idea and make recommendations as to the advisability of moving in this direction.

Think first about the administrative/staff perspective. Given the cultural values discussed in this chapter, what would likely be some of the predictable questions or concerns on the minds of administrators and staff members serving on the study committee? Next, let's consider the academic and faculty perspective. Based on the values outlined in this chapter, what would be some of the predictable questions or concerns on the minds of faculty and academic administrator members serving on the study committee? What other cultural issues might arise in discussions of the proposed policy change if this idea were to be considered at your institution?

3. Leadership Development as a Culturally Embedded Phenomenon

Thinking about the larger culture of your institution, what individual attributes, attitudes, and behaviors are important to selection, promotion, and success as a leader? In what respects could these characteristics be seen as positive in your opinion? As negative?

Notes

1. More information regarding this inventory can be found at www.nacubo.org/Products/Organizational_Development_Series/Organizational_Development_Series_Organizational_Climate_Assessment.html

2. Additional information is also provided in Ruben (1976, 1977, 1988, 1989, 2015b) and Ruben and Kealey (1979).

6

THE CHALLENGING TRANSITION FROM PILOT TO AIR TRAFFIC CONTROLLER

Leadership in Crowded Skies

In This Chapter

- What are the fundamental differences between the role of a faculty or staff member and that of a formal leader?
- What are the positional cross-pressures that leaders must understand and balance?
- How do you balance positional cross-pressures with personal and professional goals, and what strategies are most helpful during this balancing act?

Becoming a leader in higher education moves individuals into roles that are fundamentally different from the technical or academic positions for which they were trained and into which they were socialized. As an individual faculty or staff member, one learns to focus on what is needed for one's own personal and professional success; what each of us most values; and what is of greatest personal concern about the way the department, school, or institution functions. Individual professional aspirations, plans, and goals are front and center in each faculty member's thinking—essentially, "It's mostly about me—what I need, believe, think, and value—and what I must do as an individual to have a successful career." As an individual faculty member or staff member with highly developed technical expertise, one develops a competence and confidence in the mastery of the role—a sense of personal efficacy, and an operating style that is regularly rewarded. Functioning in an individual role within a college or university—particularly as a faculty member—one is able to exert a high degree of control over the way one

86

allocates time to various tasks, chooses which colleagues in the department with whom one wants spend the most time, and focuses energies on issues that are of greatest personal and professional interest.

The transition from being an individual member of a unit to a position as leader of that or another unit is likely to be a significant experience and, as a result, can be quite a turbulent one. A shift in frequently used pronouns is only the beginning. For successful leaders of a unit, "we," "us," and "our" become far more relevant than "I," "me," and "my." Key issues are now what *others* think and believe, what *others'* motivations and concerns are, what *others* expect and need. Even more critical are considerations about the unit, including what the unit wants to do, what the unit aspires to become, and what resources and recognition are needed—that is, what can be done with and for the unit to help facilitate its collective effectiveness. Gone is the freedom to make personally oriented choices as to who in the department should receive the most attention and with whom to spend the most time. Gone also are the times when one can share an opinion without thinking of its precedent-setting or policy implications. These are key elements in the necessary, but often discomforting, shift in one's identity within the unit or department—a shift from an emphasis on individual accomplishments and personal efficacy to a focus on the collective accomplishments of the group and collective efficacy. With the transition comes the recognition of the need for equity, equality, and consistency in dealing with all members of the unit. For most incoming leaders, one's previously established senses of competence and mastery are challenged by the demands of the new role.

The role of leader also requires one to understand a much broader landscape and to appreciate the perspectives of multiple stakeholders within and outside the institution (topics covered in Chapters 1 to 5). In many respects, our training and socialization as faculty and technically focused staff members prepare us for individual success. As implied in the foregoing paragraph, many of the capabilities and skills that are essential for individual success are unrelated—even antithetical—to those necessary for effective leadership, a topic we explore in subsequent chapters. The preparation and socialization of faculty members, in particular, often promote a focus on an individual's own career and an identity linked more to one's discipline or professional specialty than to one's institution. Individual staff—and particularly faculty—are well prepared to become skilled self-entrepreneurs who are highly adept at advancing and promoting their own professional advancement. Highly effective leadership—whether in academic or administrative positions—requires sublimating one's own interests in favor of those essential to the success of the group. The shift of responsibility from advancing and promoting oneself, alone, to advancing and promoting the work of others and the accomplishments of a team requires dramatic changes in outlook and behavior.

Higher Education Leader as Air Traffic Controller

As a staff member, and to a greater extent as a member of the faculty, you are the pilot of your own plane. As self-operating pilots, faculty in higher education are largely responsible for planning their own trips, establishing flight plans, and taking off and landing when and where desired—all within the agreed-upon rules and boundaries of an institution, or a shared space for air transportation. This characterization is no doubt less accurate for some staff, who are given a plane, but are also likely to receive considerable guidance as to where and when to go and when to come back. These differences represent further examples of the challenges presented by the multiple cultures of the academy. That said, the transition for the role of individual faculty member or staff member is equally daunting. As a leader, the individual pilot takes on the role of an air traffic controller, concerned not only—or even primarily—with his or her own plane, but also with all the planes and pilots for whom one has responsibility. The safety of aviation hinges on the role of the air traffic controller, leading many to classify it as one of the most stressful occupations (Brown, 2011; Costa, 1993; Zeier, 1994). The leadership responsibilities of an air traffic controller are significant and include the following:

- Helping to establish flight plans
- Tracking weather conditions
- Overseeing runway movement and gate departures/arrivals
- Establishing takeoff/landing sequences
- Coordinating departures and arrivals
- Monitoring flight trajectories
- Assuring the safety and well-being of all

In order to effectively manage the extensive responsibilities of an air traffic controller, one must demonstrate proficiency in a number of leadership competencies (Ruben, 2012). Position-based requirements include experience with the role, familiarity with the work, baseline knowledge of planes and the work of pilots, an understanding of the air traffic control language, and a general comprehension of the challenges facing the airline industry. A number of *personal* capabilities are also needed in the role of air traffic controller, including energy, integrity, enthusiasm, high standards, and self-discipline, among many others.

Communication skills are critical to the success of an air traffic controller, including a proficiency with listening, observation, and explanation, along with the ability to build credibility, trust, and positive interpersonal relationships with colleagues. Maintaining the flow of aircraft in and out of airports and in flight is no easy feat, and the needed *organizational* competencies are extensive, including expertise in the areas of visioning, management, planning, crisis and conflict management, and technological capability. Finally, a number of *analytic* competencies, including problem-defining, problem-solving, situational analysis, and self-assessment, are needed for an air traffic controller's successful performance.

Pilots *and* air traffic controllers have a thorough understanding of aviation, and both roles are essential to the work of the airline industry. Despite the similarities between these positions, great pilots do not necessarily make great air traffic controllers. In particular, the competencies necessary for piloting and those necessary for the role of air traffic controller often have limited overlap. The International Civil Aviation Organization (2005) suggests, for example, that the pilot is responsible for the operation and safety of the aircraft during flight time. The focus of the pilot in command is limited primarily to his or her specific aircraft. Air traffic controllers, on the other hand, must develop and maintain a wide-ranging awareness of the broader environment in which the aircrafts operate.

A shift in roles is often difficult, and an individual's approach and actions often making a substantial impact on the nature of the work itself. For example, as noted earlier, decisions and actions made as an individual seldom set precedents within a department. As a leader, however, any decision about what individual actions to endorse, encourage, allow, or censure have a far greater significance for the organization as a whole. Each such action becomes part of the developing culture and history of the organization and is often precedent-setting for colleagues within the unit. Moreover, each action by a new leader becomes an element of his or her developing legacy.

The role of air traffic controller—or leader in higher education—challenges one to think and act strategically, to consider the totality of the "friendly skies" rather than just one's own flight trajectory. This shift in focus and behavior is not easy and may not come naturally, as exemplified in Box 6.1. Outstanding faculty or staff members must become much more reflective, and must set aside familiar habits and routines, in order to transition successfully to a leadership role.

Navigating at the Crossroads

Part One of this book laid out a number of foundational ideas for the practice of leadership in higher education—a shifting and increasingly tumultuous landscape, a diverse array of institutional types with unique mission(s), a host of external pressures and perspectives that reflect the diversity of stakeholders with an interest in our institutions, and a blend of distinctive

---

BOX 6.1
A Message From the Chair

A recently appointed department chair sent the following e-mail to all faculty and staff in her unit:

Hey Everyone, I usually just delete the University Faculty and Staff Newsletter that comes each week, but today I happened to notice—and wanted to let you know—that the news about William's new appointment was noted in today's edition.

—Jamie

The opening of this e-mail might be fairly routine and unremarkable for an individual faculty member to send to colleagues. This same message, however, coming from a formally appointed institutional leader may take on quite a different significance. One can imagine potentially unanticipated and undesirable consequences when such a message is sent to new full- and part-time faculty or staff, or is inadvertently forwarded by colleagues around the university. This simple example highlights the potentially different responsibilities of an individual faculty or staff member acting as a free agent—a solo pilot—in comparison to that same individual's responsibilities upon assuming the role of unit leader.

---

cultures and subcultures that influence the routine experiences of the members of our institutions. Leaders in higher education are positioned at the crossroads of these influences and pathways. The path that each of us chooses for ourselves—and the priorities we define and balance at the crossroads—are all critical. The final section of this chapter presents a set of practical considerations for developing a road map for decision-making at the crossroads. We believe that effective academic and administrative leadership involves working at the intersection of what matters to others and what matters to you, as depicted in Figure 6.1. Working at this crossroads involves everything from the strategic decisions that have a lasting impact on a department or academic unit to the choices made about which e-mail to respond to first as the inbox continues to fill up. These leadership choices made at the crossroads of multiple, divergent, and often competing paths can be a critical component in shaping and defining a leader's role. Each decision matters, provides a statement of values and priorities, sets precedent, shapes the organization's culture, and contributes to your legacy as a leader. The daunting challenge is to attend to, prioritize, and balance the distinct purposes, aspirations, values, expectations, needs, requirements,

Figure 6.1. Leadership: Working at the intersection of what matters to others.

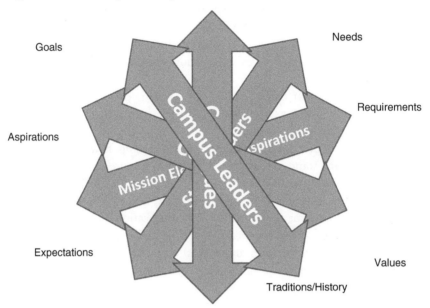

traditions, and histories of others while remaining focused on one's own leadership aspirations.

Following is a set of practical suggestions for planning and evaluating the choices you make in balancing priorities:

- Develop an understanding of the implications of the personal role you will be playing as the leader. What changes does it imply?
- Assess your personal skills and behavioral strengths and limitations. How can you leverage your strengths while striving to bolster your weaknesses?
- Invest time to study and gain a deeper understanding of the perspectives, values, needs, and leadership expectations of stakeholders, colleagues, and campus leaders who will be critical to your success in your role. What are the key issues to keep in mind relative to each group?
- Give careful consideration to what matters to you as a person assuming a leadership role. Why did you agree to pursue this role? Where do you hope the organization will be in five years? What would you like your legacy to be?

- Prioritize your leadership responsibilities. Give careful consideration to the development of a framework for prioritizing and balancing.
- Recognize the importance of having a collaborative and supportive leadership team. Determine what strengths need to be represented on the team, where those exist, and how individuals who possess them can be engaged.
- Remember that every decision or action is precedent-setting when you are in a leadership role. Consistency, principle, and transparency are extremely important.
- Develop criteria for leadership success, using new indicators and unlearning some past behaviors. This may require some new language or new metaphors—for example, an air traffic controller rather than pilot of a small plane. Develop unit- or system-level ways of thinking about important functions like communication and leadership, and make use of concepts such as "leadership architecture" (i.e., the design of leadership structures and teams) and "communication analytics" (i.e., clarifying strategy, goals, audience, and communication implications).
- Structure time and methods for reflecting on your performance and success in achieving the purposes and aims of all.
- Solicit and carefully consider feedback from members of your team and from those to whom you report.

Conclusion

Within the context of higher education, it is only appropriate that we would privilege a commitment to learning. Do not assume that you know everything you need to know coming into a leadership role. Strive to be open to new concepts, new language, and new metaphors; these ways of thinking can shape the insights and behaviors of leaders in very powerful ways. Furthermore, as an aspiring or new leader in higher education, commit to reflective practice. Recognize that years as a faculty or staff member developing technical expertise may actually be an impediment to leadership. Finally, work to understand the nature of leadership and the ways in which higher education leadership may be unique. Having an understanding of the higher education concepts presented up to this point in the book provides an important foundation upon which subsequent chapters build. As the book proceeds, we further examine the idea of leadership, exploring the connections between leadership and communication, and proposing a variety of models, lenses, and ways of thinking about social influence—all of which are useful items to bring as one approaches the many intersections that lie ahead.

For Further Consideration

1. Shift in Focus

Identify an issue that might arise within your unit or institution that demonstrates the conflicting expectations, needs, or perspectives of internal or external stakeholders.

In what ways would this issue challenge you, as a leader, to shift your focus from pilot to that of air traffic controller? Identify the strategies that you would take to balance the perspectives of internal and external stakeholders in responding to this issue. Which concepts from this chapter are most useful as you think through your response?

2. Blogging Dean Case Study

As a faculty member in your institution's management department, you have developed a number of personal concerns about the growth of online education within the School of Business, a school that offers an array of online and hybrid courses, along with two fully online degrees. Your personal philosophy of education leads you to place great value on your interpersonal interactions with your undergraduate and graduate students—and you believe that online education mechanisms compromise the mutual learning that happens inside of the physical classroom. After years of notable accomplishments as a management teacher-scholar, you apply for and receive the position of dean of the school of business. One of your goals in the new role is to openly communicate with your internal and external stakeholders through a monthly blog. You decide to launch your blog with a candid post on your concerns about online education in undergraduate and graduate business programs.

- What are the benefits of writing a blog on this topic—for you or your institution?
- What are the likely upsides and downsides of your decision?
- What type of reaction might a blog on this topic elicit from the faculty, students, and alumni of your school?
- Might there be a better format for sharing your concerns on this subject with your internal and external stakeholders?
- How does this example capture the conflicting responsibilities and expectations with which one must contend when making the transition from the role of faculty member to dean—from an individual pilot to an air traffic controller?

7

WHAT IS LEADERSHIP?

In This Chapter

- Why is it important to think about the nature of leadership?
- Why is there such a diverse array of views about leadership and leadership practice?
- What makes leadership "effective" or "successful"?
- What are the major concepts, approaches, and theories of leadership?
- In what ways does an individual's conceptualization of leadership influence that person's approach to leading others?
- Can leadership theory provide a useful foundation for leadership practice?

*L*eadership is widely discussed and studied, and the term is used with increasing frequency in settings ranging from business and politics to sports, education, and religion. For all of the interest that exists in the topic, there is considerable ambiguity over how to conceptualize and define *leadership*, and substantial difference of opinion exists as to what constitutes effective leadership practice. Texts abound that address the subject, presenting a myriad of strategies presumed to be relevant for effective leadership, and news and feature articles regularly capture the accomplishments (and, more often, the failures) of contemporary leaders. Clearly, the diversity of theories, approaches, models, and guides that offer practical advice is expansive. In this chapter we aim to provide an overview of core concepts that are central to the study and practice of leadership.

Competing Perspectives on Leadership

Given the attention paid to the term *leadership*, it is not surprising that there are many folk theories related to the topic. On the one hand, these underscore the importance attached to understanding leadership, yet they also reveal and contribute to what are often overly simplistic ideas concerning leadership dynamics and practices. One such notion is the belief that some individuals are natural leaders while others are not. This view is sometimes accompanied by the presumption that leadership traits are an inherent part of an individual's personality rather than the product of experiences; therefore, efforts to become more adept as a leader are not likely to have much influence. While this idea was quite common in early theoretical conceptions, the general view now is that a person's natural leadership capacities are honed through experience, and that any of us can acquire enhanced leadership capability if we dedicate ourselves to that goal (Northouse, 2015; Parks, 2005; Velsor, McCauley, & Ruderman, 2010).

Another common notion is that, in order to be influential, one must be outgoing and highly verbal. There are certainly instances where this style is associated with those in highly visible leadership positions, and it is easy to see how these skills can be helpful in many settings. However, these behaviors may also be associated with the tendencies to be overpowering and domineering, thereby causing a backlash and increasing resistance to intended outcomes and, over time, diminishing the respect and influence the leader may enjoy. Conversely, being skilled at selective communicative engagement and careful decision-making about with whom and when to assert one's views can be a very important leadership quality in a range of situations.

The view that those with advanced degrees are inevitably more effective leaders than those with less education is also commonly held. While intellectual capability—often associated with educational attainment—certainly can contribute to a person's knowledge and analytical skills, possessing these capabilities provides little assurance of an ability to apply them effectively in practice in a manner that leads to effective leadership. Also, in many situations, technical expertise and advanced education may actually impede the ability to engage successfully with others—particularly with those who lack that background and capability.

The term *leadership* is often associated with formal positions or titles, and we assume that those who occupy these roles represent the essence of what *leadership* means. While this way of thinking is certainly familiar and understandable, informal roles also afford excellent opportunities for leadership influence. We explore this issue in detail in Chapter 10.

Another concept that provokes opinions is whether there is one single constellation of leadership knowledge and skills that, if possessed and applied, will lead to consistently positive outcomes across a broad range of settings, situations, and cultures. We examine this topic at greater length later, but suffice it to say here that some leadership capabilities are important across situations, sectors, and cultures. But there are also situation- and context-specific knowledge and skill sets that can be vital to producing desired outcomes, such that there is no simple or single profile of *the* successful leadership approach. Perhaps the greatest challenge, as we note later in this text, is to know which cross-cutting capabilities are most essential and when setting- and position-specific knowledge and skill are critical—and how to determine and apply the appropriate blend from a leadership perspective.

Defining Effective Leadership

One additional issue deserves mention. There frequently is a blurring of distinction between "good" or "effective" leadership practices, on the one hand, and "good" outcomes, on the other hand. Clearly, an individual can exercise what would be considered effective and successful leadership, even when the outcomes of those efforts may be negative or undesirable, either by intention or default. There is no shortage of historical or contemporary organizational examples of such situations.

Quite aside from the ethical issues that these situations raise, when the goal is to learn about leadership, it is important to differentiate between how we value a leader's intentions, strategies, and practices, and how we value the outcomes of their efforts. We can often learn a great deal about leadership from those who are successful in achieving outcomes—regardless of how we might feel about the value or appropriateness of those outcomes or their motives. By the same token, much can be learned from those whose aims are worthy and desirable, but whose efforts to achieve these ends are not successful.

Our View of Leadership

Prior to presenting an overview of central leadership concepts, we want to highlight several propositions about leadership that undergird the ideas presented in this book. Traditionally, the term *leadership* has been associated with intentional and generally planned efforts to persuade and motivate others to accept particular ideas or adopt particular behaviors. However, not all actions that persuade or motivate others in particular ways are intentional or planned. Most fundamentally, we view leadership as the process of social influence—a process that involves both verbal and nonverbal communication. The term *social influence* subsumes those situations not only where leadership is planned and intentional but also where it may be unplanned and unintentional. As we explore in detail in subsequent chapters, we also believe that the process and outcomes of social influence are defined by followers as much as by leaders. Moreover, as will become apparent, our perspective on leadership draws heavily on communication theory, and the framework and strategies in this text reflect a communication-centered understanding of the leader-follower relationship.

What Makes a Great Leader?

Traditional approaches to leadership tend to focus on those traits or attributes that are characteristic of effective leaders, including confidence and extroversion, yet libraries are filled with the biographies and narratives of individuals who are born into poverty, have introverted personalities, and are powerless by most formal measures, yet who have gone on to excel as leaders. Conversely, a number of individuals who would seem to excel as leaders based on their credentials, attitude, and position in the organization may ultimately fail as leaders. In some instances, a particular critical incident and highly visible leadership moment may create a leadership impression that becomes emblematic of an individual leader's legacy. What then are the necessary qualities for a great leader?

A list of attributes of effective leadership that are sometimes mentioned in popular writings on the subject include the following:

- Natural ability
- Experience
- Forcefulness
- Knowledge of leadership theory and concepts
- Skilled at personal relationships and networking
- Good at leveraging the talents of others
- Being in the right place at the right time
- Persuasiveness
- Quick learner—able to adapt quickly to a situation

A number of scholars have addressed the important question, "What makes a great leader?" One prominent author, Warren Bennis (2007), for example, offers the following view:

Great leaders
1. Create a sense of mission
2. Motivate others to join them on that mission
3. Create an adaptive social architecture for their followers
4. Generate trust and optimism
5. Develop other leaders
6. Get results (p. 5)

Another noted author, Peter Northouse (2015), defines *leadership* as "a process whereby an individual influences a group of individuals to achieve a common goal" (p. 6). For Northouse, leadership involves influence, relates to leader-follower interactions, occurs within the context of groups, and addresses a common or mutual purpose. As we discuss in greater detail in the next chapter, social influence and effective communication lie at the core of these various definitions of *leadership*, and both are central to our conceptualization of leadership.

In his synthesis of the common definitions, Ruben (2006) captures a variety of approaches to defining *leadership* in the following list:

- Attracting people (Maxwell, 1999)
- Building community (DePree, 1999)
- Creating and sustaining culture (Schein, 1999)
- Change management (Kanter, 1983)
- Influencing individual or group behavior (Hersey, 1984; DuBrin, 2004)
- Pursuit of mutually beneficial purposes (Hackman & Johnson, 2013)
- Problem-solving (Luke, 1998)
- Vision plus action (Useem, 1998)
- Vision plus strategy (Ruben, 2006)

The literature on leadership includes many other attributes as well.

Dichotomies: The Yin and Yang of Leadership

In efforts to capture the essence of leadership and leadership effectiveness, a number of dichotomies are common, among which are the following:

- Management versus leadership
- Leadership versus followership
- Science versus art
- Theory versus practice
- Transparent versus opaque
- Authentic versus calculating
- Planning versus execution
- Servant versus master
- Incremental versus strategic
- Great influence versus influence often overstated
- Formal versus informal leadership
- Directing versus role modeling

- Transactional versus transformational concepts
- Leadership as decision-making versus leadership as process facilitation
- Context specific versus context general

Three of these dichotomies are worthy of some additional considerations, for they frequently inform the ways in which leadership is both studied and practiced. The first and one of the most popular dichotomies considers the presumed differences between management and leadership. The current literature tends to identify the manager's role in maintaining order and consistency through the demonstration and accomplishment of activities and routines. Leaders, on the other hand, focus on articulating a vision for the future that both privileges and produces change and movement (Bennis & Nanus; 1985; Kotter, 2012; Rost, 1993; Zaleznik, 1992). This separation between leadership and management highlights a useful distinction; however, the distinction sets off leadership as the more glamorous role and seems to suggest that attention to detail and routine work are not required for effective leadership performance. In practice, a closer look would often reveal that these two images are blurred in the work of successful individuals. Leaders often have many management responsibilities and vice versa.

The second dichotomy, leader versus follower, is commonly identified in the leadership literature. Much of the literature presents a clear distinction between *leaders*—those who exercise power (make critical decisions, supervise, influence, create vision, direct activities, manage resources, etc.)—and *followers*—those who are led (carrying out the directions of leaders, receiving guidance and supervision, "reporting to," etc.). It may also be the case that leaders are responsible for initiating the relationship, creating communication linkages, and carrying the burden for maintaining the contact. Clearly, this delineation has value in some respects, but as we discuss in greater detail in the next chapter, we see leadership and followership—and the distinction between them—as being quite fuzzy and fluid, and potentially oversimplified. For one thing, leaders have an ethical responsibility to attend to the needs and concerns of their followers. Also, many authors note that leaders are not above or better than followers, despite the implied power and importance ascribed to leaders. Moreover, as with the distinction between leaders and managers discussed previously, in practice, leaders often follow, and followers often lead. In fact, in the ongoing dynamics of group and organizational life, it may be quite difficult to discern who is leading and who is following at any moment in time, and the roles are dynamic. Recent scholarship goes so far as to suggest that leadership itself is coconstructed through interactions between leaders and followers via communication

(Barge & Fairhurst, 2008; Ruben, 2006; Smircich & Morgan, 1982; Witherspoon, 1997), a topic we discuss more in Chapter 7. The simple test of notions about the interdependency of leaders and followers can be found in the recognition that unless there are people who follow, the concept of leader has little or no value.

The third dichotomy is leadership as science versus art. From a scientific or scholarly perspective, there exist a number of generalizable theories and concepts that are useful in informing our understanding of leadership. The application and implementation of leadership, however, is ultimately an art (Grint, 2000)—a personalized, subjective, and creative action that is subject to individual strengths, weaknesses, and idiosyncrasies that are in play as scientific and scholarly theories are translated into practice. Each of the various leadership dichotomies listed adds to the richness of the leadership concept, but also introduces additional tensions and complexities that further challenge the ability to arrive at a simplified understanding.

Multiple Approaches to Leadership

One primary reason for the many concepts of leadership is that it can be approached from personal, professional, and scholarly perspectives, and definitions of *leadership* emerge from all three: personal/native theory (e.g., autobiographies and biographies of famous leaders), professional theory (e.g., current practices/policies and case reports of leadership in an applied context), and scholarly theory (e.g., qualitative and quantitative research studies that are descriptive, explanatory, and predictive). The perspectives on leadership advanced in this book are primarily informed by traditions within the scholarly approach and include the following major categories:

- Classical approaches: Traditional approaches to the study of leadership that include trait, skills, style, and situational theories
- Contemporary approaches: Modern approaches to the study of leadership theory and practice, including transformational, authentic, and servant leadership
- Communication approaches: An approach to leadership that explores the topic through a communication-oriented lens, highlighting the importance of communication for leadership success, including communication theory, dynamics of social influence, the negotiation of meaning, and the language of leadership and framing
- Competency approaches: Approaches to leadership that focus on the ability of successful leaders to acquire a portfolio of knowledge and skills that they are able to apply strategically

Much of the classical literature on leadership focuses specifically on the traits, skills, or styles of leaders in a multitude of situations. More contemporary theories seek to explore charisma, influence, and the soul of leadership, particularly transformational, authentic, and servant leadership theories. The communication-oriented approach suggests that leadership and communication are inseparable phenomena, with a relationship that, when understood, provides very useful insight into the nature of social influence and the role of leadership in that process. A competency approach builds on other approaches and focuses on the combined knowledge and skills that successful leaders may apply strategically in a variety of settings. Finally, many of the ideas within the classical, contemporary, communication, and competency approaches to leadership overlap with one another, but this taxonomy still provides a useful summary of the primary perspectives.

The following section provides an overview of major classical and contemporary leadership theories based on work by Peter Northouse (2015). For each, we offer a summary that includes an overview of key concepts advanced by the theory, and a brief discussion of key strengths and criticisms associated with each theoretical perspective.[1] Each section concludes with a brief explanation of the linkage to the work of higher education leadership—applications that are meant to showcase ways of using the theories to inform and think through leadership in higher education contexts.

Trait Approach

The trait approach to leadership captures the thinking of many of the early classical theories, including the so-called "Great Man" and "trait" theories. In this perspective, leaders are viewed as possessing innate leadership qualities that differentiate them from nonleaders (e.g., intelligence, self-confidence, determination, integrity, sociability) (Northouse, 2015). Historically, this approach has been appealing because of its simplicity and the substantial body of research that it has generated. The perspective suggests that specific traits may be measured and matched to specific jobs. A major weakness of this approach is its assumption that only individuals with particular fixed traits can be effective leaders, and despite extensive research, an exclusive list of traits that would differentiate leaders from nonleaders has not been identified.

The literature has tended to move away from the idea that certain individuals possess personality traits that make them effective leaders, while others lack this potential. That said, various writers and studies continue to find evidence to suggest that certain traits are associated with leadership effectiveness. In a study on leadership in corporations as compared to higher education, for example, the executive search firm Witt/Kieffer (2013) found that some traits were common to leaders in both groups, while others were more likely to be present in one than the other. The traits that were more prevalent among higher education leaders were initiative, tact, creativity, and self-expression.

Skills Approach

The skills approach to understanding leadership reflects a shift in focus from those innate and generally fixed traits to individual skills that are cultivated and developed over time (Northouse, 2015). Various taxonomies of leadership skills have been presented, including the three-skill approach, which highlights the technical, human, and conceptual skills required for effective leadership (Katz, 1974). This leader-centered model indicates that leadership skills are accessible to all and suggests that anyone can learn the necessary skills for influencing others. A key limitation of this approach, however, is its lack of predictive value. In particular, the skills approach fails to explain how variations in skills affect overall leadership performance or effectiveness. Within the context of higher education itself, leaders must develop the technical, human, and conceptual skills needed to lead these complex organizations effectively. To illustrate, this approach to leadership would focus on the cultivation of particular skills—in public speaking or strategic planning, for example—that would be important to successful leadership within a program, department, or institution.

Style Approach

A style approach to leadership focuses on common leadership behaviors in a variety of contexts. Unlike the previous two approaches to leadership, a style approach considers the needs of subordinates in determining leadership effectiveness (Northouse, 2015). Seminal studies conducted at The Ohio State University and the University of Michigan point to the various styles that leaders may typically exemplify, distinguishing those task-oriented behaviors from more relationship-oriented behaviors. Blake and McCanse's (1991) Leadership Grid (formerly Blake and Mouton's Managerial Grid) is one of many tools available for leaders to use to self-assess, change, and improve upon their leadership style. Another benefit of the style approach is its emphasis on leadership behavior in a broad range of situations and contexts. Similar to a skills approach, however, no consistent link exists between task and relationship behaviors and outcomes, and thus the approach is not particularly helpful in identifying a "best" leadership style. A democratic approach to leadership in higher education appears to be most effective within the context of shared governance. As Lewin, Lippitt, and White (1939) found in their seminal research, followers exhibit more commitment and cohesiveness under democratic leaders, but one might also think of situations in higher education that demand a more authoritative leadership style.

Situational Approach

One explanation for why it is difficult to identify a "best" leadership style relates to the dynamic and evolving context in which leadership occurs. Taking account of this dynamic, the situational approach, based on research by Hersey and Blanchard (1969), suggests that the traits needed for effective leadership vary based on circumstances. Different situations call for different approaches to leadership, including, for example, directing, coaching, supporting, and delegating. According to this perspective, leaders must adapt their style to adequately meet the demands of the situation (Northouse, 2015). This approach is intuitive and prescriptive, yet it lacks a strong body of empirical research.

The situational approach calls attention to the need for leaders to be able to demonstrate an awareness of the nature of the situation in which they are leading. For example, colleges and universities experiencing a reputational or financial crisis call for a different approach to leadership from that needed during times of prosperity or tranquility. More generally, quite different leadership capabilities may be required when dramatic change is needed within a program, department, or institution, compared to a time in that same organization when calming and reinforcement are needed, such as after major changes have been instituted.

Contingency Theory

Building from the situational approach, contingency theory focuses on the match between a leader's style and the context in which that person is leading (Northouse, 2015). Contingency theory identifies specific styles of leadership that may be best or worst for a particular organizational context. For example, Fiedler's (1967) contingency model offers a series of preferred leadership styles based on the leader-member relations, task structure, and position of power of a particular situation. This theory is supported by empirical research and allows for fairly accurate predictions to determine the probability of success for a given person or style in a given situation. A key criticism of this theory, however, is that it is cumbersome to apply in real-world settings. Moreover, it lacks explanatory power for why certain styles are more effective in some situations than others. Through environmental scanning strategies, leaders in higher education can develop a more sophisticated understanding of the situation and can adapt their behaviors accordingly. Academic leaders often receive little preparation when assuming leadership responsibilities at the unit, department, or institutional level. In many instances, as this book dissects in greater detail, the behaviors and competencies required for effective performance as a faculty or staff member do not always align with the characteristics of effective leadership at an administrative level. Contingency theory allows one to focus attention on the match (or mismatch) between style and context as an important dimension when an individual assumes leadership responsibilities.

Path-Goal Theory

Path-goal theory seeks to explain the ways in which a leader motivates followers to accomplish desired goals. Based on this theory, subordinates will be motivated if they think they are capable of performing the work, if they believe efforts will result in a specific outcome, and if they trust that the payoffs for doing the work are worthwhile. Leaders can motivate followers by clearing the path to the goal (Northouse, 2015). This theory deals directly with motivation in a way that other theories do not. Furthermore, by exploring the relationship between style and goal, this theory instructs leaders on ways of choosing a particular style based on both the demands of the task and the goals of the subordinate. Path-goal theory is often criticized for being overly complex and for lacking conclusive research findings. Additionally, this theory treats leadership as a one-way event that fails to fully recognize the significance of the abilities of followers. Path-goal theory allows one to consider the ways in which academic leaders motivate others to accomplish particular tasks for the overall benefit of the institution by clearing the path for others to succeed. For example, how might a college or university leader remove obstacles that obstruct innovative thinking? As the competition for resources continues to increase, in what ways can academic leaders encourage others to think creatively about work in order to maximize institutional resources, collaborate across units, or seek new avenues for outside funding sources? The path-goal perspective focuses attention on these approaches to leadership.

Leader-Member Exchange Theory

Leader-member exchange theory considers leadership as a process, paying particular attention to the interaction between leaders and followers. According to Graen and Uhl-Bien (1995), the quality of leader-member exchange is related to positive outcomes for leaders, followers, groups, and the organization in general. One classification to emerge from this theory is the distinction between in-group and out-group leader-member relationships, whereby managers sort team members (often unintentionally) into one of these two groups (Northouse, 2015). In-group members maintain the trust of the leader and often receive challenging and meaningful work, unlike the out-group members who have limited access to the leader and are often restricted to less challenging work responsibilities. This approach to understanding the leadership process explores how leaders use some subordinates more effectively than others to accomplish goals. The leader-member relationship is the focal point of this approach, yet some suggest that this approach gives insufficient attention to the role of subordinates. Furthermore, the theory does not adequately explain how leaders might create high-quality exchanges with followers.

This theory lends itself well to an exploration of higher education leadership. Much of the work of higher education is accomplished through a committee structure. The leader-member exchange theory allows us to consider the ways that leaders select, organize, motivate, recognize, and reward the members of the committees. Committee members far too often receive little direction, support, or recognition for the important work they do, and the quality of leader-member interactions has the potential to influence the work of current and future committees. Furthermore, this theory may allow for a deeper understanding of the in-group and out-group relationships developed within the committee structure.

Transformational Leadership

Transformational leadership focuses on the ability of leaders to create change in the lives of those they lead. A concern with the collective good is central to this leadership approach (Northouse, 2015). As described in the framework, transformational leaders demonstrate an exceptional influence that moves followers to accomplish more than would normally be expected of them. Four factors of transformational leadership include idealized influence, inspirational motivation, intellectual stimulation, and individualized consideration (Bass & Avolio, 1994). This approach is intuitively appealing because it is possible to identify a number of noted leaders who embody this approach. It also provides an expansive view of leadership that demonstrates utility across a variety of situations. Despite the wealth of research on this approach, it has been criticized for its breadth and lack of conceptual clarity. Furthermore, by focusing so heavily on individual leaders and their impact, some see the approach as elitist and unduly marginalizing the role of followers.

With an emphasis on the leader's vision, questions are often raised as to who determines the ultimate value of this vision—in particular, which followers? There is often a widely shared admiration for individuals who exhibit the qualities of transformational leadership, particularly those who have the special ability to envision and inspire individuals and groups to move in new, bold directions. However, these capacities may not be matched by the interest and skills needed to manage the more routine and less glamorous aspects of academic life, aspects that are often critical to following through on a vision, and to successful implementation, whether of a new degree program, a new school, or a new service for users.

Servant Leadership

According to Robert Greenleaf (1977), who coined the term, *servant leadership* "begins with the natural feeling that one wants to serve, to serve first. Then conscious choice brings one to aspire to lead" (p. 13). This approach to leadership suggests that servant leaders are those who place the good of followers ahead of their own self-interest. Servant leadership extends beyond the act of doing and reflects a specific way of being (Sendjaya & Sarros, 2002). One model of servant leadership outlines a series of antecedent conditions, behaviors, and outcomes associated with this other-oriented approach to leadership (Liden, Wayne, Zhao, & Henderson, 2008). Servant leadership is unique in making altruism the central component of the leadership process, and it presents a provocative, counterintuitive approach to the use of power and influence (Northouse, 2015). Some criticisms of this approach include the lack of a consistent theoretical framework, the contradictions between principles of servant leadership and other principles of leadership, and the perceived moralistic tone of this leadership approach. One of the tensions related to the implementation of servant leadership lies in the ways that academic leaders balance individual, interpersonal, group, and organizational commitments. Specifically, a leader who privileges service to the university above all other values appears to offer extraordinary benefits. In many situations, however, commitments to self, other, group, and institution often come into conflict with one another. One example might be the challenges that department chairs face when preparing the academic course schedule. Should they prioritize the needs and expectations of the students, other faculty members, the dean, or the institution? Despite best efforts to exemplify and embody the principles of servant leadership, how might such leaders respond to the conflict that arises from these competing sources of attention and others that involve a conflict in needs for resources?

Authentic Leadership

Authentic leadership calls for an approach to leadership "that is consistent with our personality and character" (George, 2003, p. 13). In an exploration of whether leadership is genuine or real, authentic leadership consists of four components: self-awareness, internalized moral perspective, balanced processing, and transparency in relationships. A more practical approach to authentic leadership identifies the following characteristics: purpose, values, relationships, self-discipline, and heart (George, 2003). Similar to servant leadership, authentic leadership calls for leaders to do what is right and good both for followers and society. Being true to one's self and forthright with others is fundamental to this approach. Trustworthiness is understood to be critical for effective leadership. Some of the other concepts of authentic leadership, including the moral component, are not fully substantiated, and the specific connections between authentic leadership and positive organizational outcomes remain unclear (Northouse, 2015).

This perspective emphasizes the idea that "knowing thyself" and behaving in a way that is consistent with one's true self is a positive aspect of social influence. Authentic leaders have a clear sense of who they are, and their behaviors reflect this self-perception. Yet in her article on the "authenticity paradox," Herminia Ibarra (2015b) casts authenticity in a different light. She notes that all of us have multiple identities and approaches, potentially calling into question the existence of one, true authentic self. Being preoccupied with a single authentic identity as a leader can create an inflexibility and "can be a recipe for staying stuck in the past" (p. 59). Fear of acting in an inauthentic manner serves as an "excuse for sticking with what's comfortable" (p. 54). Ibarra points to the value of leaders recognizing and experimenting with their multiple identities and different leadership styles and behaviors. Although some may label these actions as inauthentic, Ibarra considers this adaptive approach to create opportunities for learning and leadership development. In the course of a leader's daily responsibilities, a number of situations present themselves where candor, disclosure, and transparency are appropriate and highly valued; but there may be circumstances involving personnel or human resource matters where one is obligated to maintain confidentiality and where the commitment to transparency and authenticity can present challenges for all involved. These different pressures are characteristic of higher education contexts.

Team Leadership

A team leadership model explores the ways in which interdependent members of groups coordinate activities and accomplish common goals (Northouse,

2015). The leader of the team is responsible for the effectiveness of the group. This demands a behavioral flexibility in which leaders match their behaviors to the complexity of particular situations. Team leaders, according to McGrath (1962), play a critical role in diagnosing group deficiencies, taking remedial action, forecasting environmental changes, and preventing deleterious changes. Considering how much work in higher education is accomplished in teams, this approach to leadership strikes a relevant chord for leadership scholars and practitioners alike. Furthermore, it addresses the dynamic and evolving roles of leader and follower in a team setting. A criticism is that the list of skills needed for effective team leadership, as presented by this model, is somewhat limited and fails to fully address the specific problems associated with team dynamics. As useful as teams can be for sharing expertise, and as important as it is for academic leaders to have the skills necessary to cultivate teams as a way of heightening engagement and solving collective problems, by their very nature teams often require more time and effort to arrive at decisions—time and effort that academic leaders might not be able to devote to particular decisions.

Leadership Theory Summary

The ongoing research on these theoretical perspectives is expansive, and the brief summaries offered previously are inherently limited and cursory. (For a more thorough summary of each theoretical perspective, see Northouse, 2015.[2]) As is apparent from the foregoing review, approaches to leadership have evolved from those focused solely on the individual's inherent capabilities to include theories that acknowledge the importance of developmental influences in the acquisition of leadership capabilities. In the evolution of leadership theories, an increasing emphasis has been placed on the choices leaders are able to make, and the importance of situation, timing, goals, followers, and the interactions between and among these factors in explaining the success or failure of a particular leader.

Each theoretical approach has strengths and weaknesses; each is a way of seeing and *not* seeing. By understanding and using a number of theoretical lenses, one may gain a more thorough understanding of leadership and the factors that are important to leadership outcomes in practice. As Hackman and Johnson (2013) suggest, "Sometimes the approaches overlap; other times they contradict one another. No single approach provides a universal explanation of leadership behavior, but each provides useful insights" (p. 73). The communication and competency approaches that are emphasized in the approach to leadership advocated in this book are described in the next two chapters.

A Comprehensive Leadership Megamodel

As a way of making sense of the voluminous leadership literature, Hernandez, Eberly, Avolio, and Johnson (2011) offer a comprehensive "megamodel" of the leadership system that integrates diverse theoretical perspectives. Their review of the literature leads to the development of a common language across theories—the loci of leadership (where leadership comes from) and the mechanisms of leadership (how leadership is transmitted). Based on their findings, the authors identify five dominant loci, or sources from which leadership is thought to arise according to various theories, including the leader, context, followers, collectives, and leader-follower dyads. These points of origin for leadership do not exist on a fluid continuum; rather, they represent distinct and independent sources for leadership The authors identify four common mechanisms of leadership—what they describe as the means by which leadership is transmitted. These mechanisms are traits (personality characteristics), behaviors (actions), cognition (thoughts and sense-making processes), and affect (emotions and moods). Similar to the loci, the mechanisms are not ordered in a continuum but rather stand alone as independent categories.

This comprehensive model represents an inclusive way of thinking about leadership, and it offers a common language for understanding the complex leadership system. As noted in the article,

> By way of analogy and for ease of use, the two dimensions can be compared to grammar: the locus of leadership is the subject of the sentence (that which acts) and the mechanism is the verb (the action). It follows that combining the two will result in a complete sentence such as "The leader behaves" or "The follower feels." To push the analogy further, a substantive analysis of leadership is not possible unless both dimensions are considered, and we posit that the loci and mechanisms of leadership can be used as fundamental building blocks to understanding what constitutes leadership. A list of nouns and verbs, however, is of little use unless one combines them into a coherent story. Hence, while we started with a simple sentence employing only a noun and verb, we tell the story of leadership theory through a combination of multiple loci and mechanisms that we suggest form a more comprehensive leadership system. (Hernandez et al., 2011, pp. 1168–1169)

The locus-mechanism imagery captures the evolution and expansion of leadership theory from the Great Man perspective to a view of leadership that is interactional. This perspective also makes the point that context—for our purpose, a higher education context—can be an important factor in understanding leadership dynamics.

In their model, the authors (Hernandez et al., 2011) locate a number of dominant leadership theories within the two-dimensional framework based on the mechanism and locus of leadership. This framework presents a useful structure for understanding the theoretical constructs and connections between the aforementioned leadership theories.

Despite the many contributions of this megamodel, a few limitations may be noted. First, their comprehensive model focuses on purposeful or intentional leadership efforts, or both, and it overlooks or diminishes the relevance of informal, unintentional, or unplanned leadership processes. If leadership is understood to be about social influence, as we and a number of authors suggest, then it seems important to recognize that social influence is often intended, but not always. While the usual leadership focus is on intentional acts, in our view it is quite limiting to overlook the broader view of social influence and leadership. For instance, an administrator's choice to respond to an e-mail in a particular way clearly would fit the classical definition of *leadership*. But a decision not to respond, whether an active choice or not, also constitutes a potential leadership act. Whether such an action was a planned attempt at social influence or an oversight may matter very little to the outcome.

Second, the authors choose to talk about mechanisms for *transmitting* leadership. One might argue that *interaction* would be a more appropriate word for understanding the ways in which leadership is accomplished. The idea of transmission reflects a mechanistic view of the influence process— one that is associated with early views of the communication and influence process, but a perspective that has evolved significantly. As we discuss in Chapter 8, in more contemporary theories, communication is understood to be meaning-centered rather than transmission-centered. Moreover, influence outcomes are seen as coconstructed, resulting from interaction, and inherently a collaborative act. We discuss these concepts more fully in upcoming chapters.

Conclusion

What is the value of being familiar with classic and contemporary concepts and theories of leadership for the current or aspiring higher education leader? How might this knowledge be useful in everyday leadership situations, such as recruitment and hiring, making and communicating decisions, dealing with interpersonal conflict or other sensitive matters, or evaluating one's own or others' performance as a leader? Quite often, the recruitment and hiring process for new leaders begins with identifying the desired academic or technical qualifications and credentials. Generally, the assumption is that these academic or technical qualifications are the most critical attributes necessary for effective leadership. We would argue—and we explore this topic in greater depth later in the book—that an individual's leadership philosophy and approach are as important, and sometimes more important, to the individual's success as a leader. Each of the perspectives discussed in this chapter provides a particular way of thinking about what leadership is, and by implication what a leader does—or should do. Reviewing the concepts and approaches presented in this chapter offers a reminder of the range of ways of enacting leadership roles, the potential strengths and limitations of various approaches, and the potential match or mismatch of these approaches to the particular context and needs for which a leader responds.

In the case of hiring a leader, attention to conceptualizing leadership provides an important complement to attention focused on disciplinary or technical needs. Each of the perspectives on leadership reviewed in this chapter can provide practical guidance for the recruitment, interviewing, selection, and retention processes. When it comes to describing the leadership capabilities desired in a director, chair, dean, or vice president, the trait approach points to quite different characteristics than does an authentic leadership approach. Similarly, distinctions between the skills or situational approach might well suggest a different line of questioning during the candidate interview process than would be implied by the transformational or servant approach.

Likewise, in many other typical leadership tasks—such as making and communicating decisions, dealing with interpersonal conflict, or deciding whether and how to evaluate the performance of leaders—there would likely be considerable variation depending upon the theory of leadership that guides one's thoughts and behavior. The approach suggested by the path-goal theory, for example, would likely be quite different than that implied by the authentic leader framework or that of the servant leader.

These theories are lenses—ways of seeing and thinking about the nature of leadership and the roles and practices of leaders. The more we understand their underlying assumptions and can see their principles in action, the broader will be the array of insights and choices available to make sense of and address the full range of leadership challenges that arise. These theories, or lenses, matter to the interpretation, evaluation, and refinement of leadership performance in higher education.

For Further Consideration

1. Critical Incidents in Leadership

- Think back and identify an experience in higher education in which you were a participant or an observer that provided an example of exceptional or very poor leadership. The situation could be one that was quite recent or in the distant past, one that occurred in your current organization or elsewhere.
- Describe the situation, taking care to change the names of individuals, institutions, departments, or other identifiers. Be prepared to briefly describe the vignette and to share your thoughts on the following questions:
    - What made this a memorable and significant leadership example?
    - What do you believe to be the reason for the leader's actions?
    - What were the interpersonal or organizational consequences of the leader's behavior?
    - What could and should have been done differently?
    - Can any general leadership principles be drawn from this scenario?

2. Case Study Analysis

Choose two of the theories discussed in the chapter. Analyze the case study scenarios in this section through these two distinct theoretical perspectives. If theories are understood to be both a way of seeing and not seeing, what do each of these leadership theories allow us to see, and in what ways do they limit or restrict our vision in the selected case? What are the implications for leadership action based on each theory? What are possible positive and negative consequences from each course of action?

1. You have been asked to head a committee whose task is to identify, recruit, and interview candidates for the senior administrator role in a new department within your institution. Considering each leadership theory you've selected, what characteristics would be judged to be particularly important? Would the two theories point to the same or different criteria? What guidance might these theories offer in terms of how to describe the new position in job ads, and how to assess candidates who apply for the position?
2. You are a department head and are called to a confidential meeting with the person to whom you report. At the meeting, you and a number of

other leaders are told in confidence that a hiring freeze and institution-wide budget cut will be announced in three weeks. You have a search under way, are scheduled to meet with the leadership team of your department this afternoon, and have a full department meeting scheduled the next day. What would various leadership theories advise you to do relative to sharing or acting on the information you have with colleagues? What are the consequences of those choices?

3. You have a growing dissatisfaction with the work of a long-serving and highly regarded member of your administrative team. In your mind this person should be thinking about retirement. Your frustrations are building on a weekly basis as you note a growing number of errors and what seems like decreasing motivation. You are getting increasingly convinced of the need to do something to improve the situation. You have been keeping extensive notes on the problems, but you have not discussed your concerns or any of the particulars with the individual in question or with the person to whom you report. What are your options for dealing with the problem, and what are the potential benefits and liabilities of each option? What types of guidance are provided by the various leadership theories reviewed in the chapter?

Notes

1. The summary of theories was created by Kate Immordino and Ralph Gigliotti, based on the framework provided by Northouse (2015). The overview of theoretical perspectives, including the summary of strengths and critiques, reflects many of the central ideas from Northouse's work.

2. A number of other texts offer additional summaries of these seminal leadership theories, including, but not limited to, Gill (2012), Hackman and Johnson (2013), and Yukl (2012).

8

LEADERSHIP-COMMUNICATION CONNECTIONS

In This Chapter

- In what ways does the study of communication intersect with the study of leadership?
- What are the various approaches to understanding communication theory, and which of these approaches makes the most sense for understanding the process of leadership?
- Why are the concepts of leaders and followers inseparable? In what ways do followers define *leadership*, and what implications does this have on the ways that social influence is accomplished?
- Which communication concepts are particularly important to the study and practice of leadership, including leadership in colleges and universities?

I n this chapter we focus on the communication process and its contribution to leadership knowledge and practice. Fully understanding communication and its relevance requires that we leave behind many of the assumptions we make based on our everyday experience. Historically, discussions of leadership communication—which imply that the leader and his or her message have a direct and controlling influence on message receivers—have reinforced a misleading, "romanticized" view of leadership (Meindl & Ehrlich, 1987). A more nuanced understanding of communication theory leads to a considerably more expansive view of leadership—a view that envisions leadership within the context of social influence (Ruben & Gigliotti, 2016). This approach to leadership communication thinking focuses on the instrumental role of followers in making leadership work, so much so that, in many respects, leadership and followership are inseparable concepts. This chapter examines the leader-follower relationship in detail from a communication-centered perspective.

Human Communication

As Thayer (2003) and others have noted, *communication* is one of the two fundamental activities of all living things (Miller, 1965; Ruben, 2003; Ruben & Kim, 1975). Indeed, it can be defined as the *sine qua non*—an essential condition—of the behavioral sciences (Thayer, 2003). Thayer (1968) further notes, "The essence of being human is thus communicating-to and being communicated-with" (p. 18). Ruben (2005) extends this perspective to define *communication* as "the process through which the social fabric of relationships, groups, organizations, societies, and world order—and disorder—is created and maintained" (p. 294). To be human is to engage in communication—and, perhaps even more relevant to this current project, to lead is to communicate. Communication, a "universal human experience," is critical to social behavior (Thayer, 1968, 2003).

In everyday ways of thinking about communication, it's quite natural to assume that the process involves the creation and transmission of verbal messages to intended receivers, thereby bringing about shared understanding. However, as Watzlawick, Beavin, and Jackson (1967) noted, "One cannot *not* communicate" (p. 49), which indicates that the study and practice of communication extends beyond talk-in-interaction and must also take into account that which is *not* said and messages created by accident as well as by design. Further study leads one to recognize that communication involves a complex array of messages—planned and unplanned, verbal and nonverbal, intentional and unintentional. Moreover, messages received are seldom interpreted by listeners or viewers in precisely the same ways as intended by those who sent them. This idea suggests that a shared understanding is one of many possible outcomes of communication—and actually quite an unlikely one in many instances. This more complex and nuanced perspective has evolved over many years, and as we explain in this chapter, it has important implications for how one thinks about the connections between communication and leadership.

Leadership Communication Models

Classical Linear Model

In popular and classical writings on the subject, leadership is thought about and described in terms of the intentional creation of messages with particular influence outcomes in mind. As Figure 8.1 shows, this view suggests that if a leader intends to accomplish a particular goal or communicate a specific message, he or she creates and transmits the message, and the process seemingly plays out in a very predictable manner.

Essentially, such a view reflects a linear, one-way, cause-and-effect-oriented characterization of the communication and influence process. In their synthesis of the literature, for example, Michael Hackman and Craig Johnson (2013) define *leadership* as "human (symbolic) communication that modifies the attitudes and behaviors of others in order to meet shared group goals and needs" (p. 11). Based on this understanding, leadership failures may be directly associated with communication failures. This approach to human communication is very intuitive and easy to understand—which helps to explain its popularity over many years—yet it has many limitations when it comes to understanding the dynamics associated with social influence. The most fundamental problem with this model, as suggested previously, is the implication that a message sent equals a message received. Neither communication nor social influence operates in such a predictable manner.

Figure 8.1. The classical linear perspective.

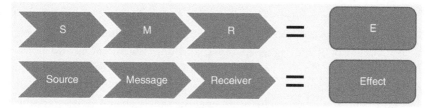

Implications for Conceptualizing Leadership

Classical models describe communication as consisting of a source/sender conveying a message to a receiver through a one-way process that results in the receiver being influenced. This paradigm provides a view of leadership communication, how leaders bring about influence—and more generally, what leadership is and how it works.

Interactional Model

Researchers who study communication recognize that the classic view has a number of limitations as it relates to describing communication, leadership, and the relationship between the two. An interactional perspective, such as that depicted in Figure 8.2, attempts to capture more of the complexity and two-way influence between a sender and receiver—or, for the purpose of this text on leadership, a leader and follower. Unlike the linear model that affords

Figure 8.2. The interactional perspective.

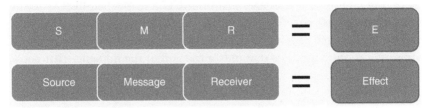

Implications for Conceptualizing Leadership

Interactional models describe communication as consisting of an ongoing process of negotiation between sources and receivers through messages. Influence is understood to result from interaction and the negotiation of meanings, providing the basis for a more collaborative view of what leadership is and how leadership functions.

all control to the sender, the interactional model credits the receiver with having some influence in this reciprocal process.

Indeed, many of the messages that make a difference in communication and influence situations are unplanned and unpredicted, nonverbal as well as very verbal and the product of ongoing dynamics rather than a single message-sending/message-receiving event. It becomes clear that the linear classic model does not capture these key points well. Unlike the most traditional view, the interactional model expands the focus to a more complex two-way interchange between sender(s) and receiver(s). Just as the sender communicates with the receiver, the receiver is communicating reciprocally, sometimes simultaneously, with the sender. This transactional communication exchange may include both verbal and nonverbal messages. For example, a speaker's messages may include verbal elements (e.g., sentences, cheers, applause, laughter) as well as nonverbal components (e.g., yawns, tears, crossed arms, a uniform). Despite its more expansive approach, the focus of the interaction model is still on the intentional exchange of messages. The model maintains a focus on communication as exchanging, sharing, or transmitting information. Even with various improvements associated with the interactional model, the complexity of communication and the critical issues for understanding the dynamics of leadership and influence are not fully explored.

Systems Model

A systems view of communication, as depicted in Figure 8.3, overcomes many limitations of the linear and interactional models and more adequately captures the complexity of leadership communication and social influence. This view of communication focuses directly on the way people create, convey, select, and interpret the messages that inform and shape their lives—viewing communication as a basic life process rather than an exchange of information or meaning between people (Ruben, 2011). This more contemporary view of communication reminds us that only a fraction of the influence that occurs in communication situations is the result of these kinds of purposeful and intentional acts. A multiplicity of factors are at play in even the most basic situation, and the net result is that the communication process associated with influence is far more complex and unpredictable than linear and interactional models suggest. The contemporary perspective recognizes that some of these messages are intentionally created; others are produced accidentally. Some messages—such as a speech, written text, bumper sticker, or terrorist attack—are constructed to achieve specific influence goals or intentions; others may be unconsciously created by their initiator through their behavior or actions with no specific communicative purpose in mind but may be quite influential for others nonetheless. Some messages are created in the moment in face-to-face settings; others occur at remote times and places and are conveyed into a particular setting via print or electronic media (Ruben & Stewart, 2016). What's more, some messages that can be very important to communication outcomes have inanimate sources—a natural disaster, for example.

This characterization of communication takes into account the fact that throughout any message-sending/message-receiving event, each individual brings his or her own unique maps and personal luggage to the

Figure 8.3. A systems perspective on communication and social influence.

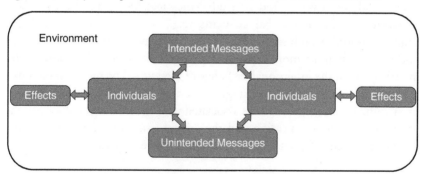

Implications for Conceptualizing Leadership
Many factors are at play in even the most basic situation, resulting in multidimensional, multidirectional, and extremely complex influence-associated process. These involve some messages created and sent intentionally, and others that are unintentional.

interaction—each individual's unique needs, values, attitudes, goals, aspirations, styles, education, cultures, physical and emotional abilities and disabilities, life history, and present life circumstances. These belongings travel
with an individual and influence every aspect of the way messages are created (or not), made sense of (or not), and reacted to (or not). As Thayer
(1968) describes the process, "Needs, values, expectations, attitudes, and
goals are brought to every communication encounter. These predispositions,
susceptibilities, and take-into-account-abilities influence the outcome of the
interaction and are equivalent to our individual make-meaningful-abilities"
(p. 36). This luggage guides the individual to notice and attend to certain
messages while ignoring others, prompts certain kinds of interpretations and
not others, and influences what will be retained and remembered. Often the
communication luggage of one individual does not align all that well with
the expectations, attributes, outlooks, states, and orientations of others with
whom they are engaging. Generally speaking, the greater the extent of mismatch, the less the likelihood that message-sent will equal message-received
(Ruben, 2015a; Ruben & Stewart, 2016).

The more expansive representation of communication underscores the
inadequacies of the linear exchange views of communication and reminds
us that single messages and single message-sending events seldom translate
simply into message-reception outcomes. Rather, communication and social
influence are parts of an ongoing process through which messages wash
over individuals—somewhat analogous to waves repeatedly washing upon
a beach. Over time these messages shape the sensibilities and responses of
receivers, much as waves shape a shoreline. The exceptions to this subtle
process are those rare, life-changing messages that can have a tsunami-like
impact on message reception.

Leader-Follower Communication

From a systems perspective, followers play an instrumental role in making
leadership work, so much so that, in many respects, leadership and followership are inseparable concepts, and the outcomes of communication are
defined as much by followers as they are by leaders.

The implication of this view of human communication is that, at any
moment in time, an individual is being bombarded with messages of varying sorts, intentions, and origins—including even intrapersonally sourced
reflective messages generated by the individual. All of these messages in some
sense compete for one's attention (Ruben, 2003). The act of selecting a particular message, making sense of that message, and responding in specific
ways is a complex, personal, and subjective process, and quite difficult to

predict, let alone control—even in the case of what would seem to be very simple messages with straightforward intentions. A profound consequence of this perspective is that outcomes of communication are not easily shaped or controlled by leaders, but rather are guided by the followers' predispositions, susceptibilities, and take-into-accountabilities (Thayer, 1968).

Thus, a communication-systems perspective provides an alternative way of understanding the dynamics of social influence. It helps explain why many leadership and social influence outcomes are often unplanned, unintentional, unpredicted, and unpredictable. It also helps to explain the reasons why observers of leadership dynamics could well conclude that the impact of leadership activity is often overstated and romanticized. The systems way of understanding communication focuses less on the leader's intentions or message-sending acts and more broadly on the array of factors and dynamics associated with communication and social influence.

Another way to talk about the leader-follower relationship is in terms of *cocreation* (Barge & Fairhurst, 2008). This phraseology suggests that the nature of leadership and influence outcomes are the result of the leader-follower relationship. Indeed, it is the decisions of "followers" to attend to, support, endorse, follow, reinforce, or work for an individual that allows the individual to be a leader. No followership implies that there is no leadership. The profundity of this notion is captured succinctly by a quotation that John Boehner (2015) used in his resignation speech as Speaker of the U.S. House of Representatives: "A leader without followers is simply a man taking a walk." In a very real sense, *leaders* and *leadership* are defined more by the actions of followers than leaders. Drawing on Fairhurst (2007), Barge and Fairhurst (2008) view leadership "as a co-created, performative, contextual, and attributional process where the ideas articulated in talk or action are recognized by others as progressing tasks that are important to them" (p. 232). So fundamental is this relationship—in theory and practice—that these two concepts become inseparable.

Leader as Docent Analogy

The systems view of communication, and the notion of the cocreation of leadership and influence outcomes, offers a radically different view than other perspectives, which imply that a leader exerts direct, predictable, and controllable influence on followers. The systems concept of the leader's role might be compared to the role of docent (Ruben & Gigliotti, 2016). There is no leading to be done if a gallery or museum has no visitors. The docent-as-leader takes on a potentially meaningful role only if there are visitors who come with an intention to look, listen, or learn. There is no one to lead if the museum is empty, so the fundamental leadership task may be identifying and attracting an audience. While shepherding visitors through the respective galleries of an art museum, the docent serves as a tour guide. As such, the docent has the opportunity to expose patrons to a number of messages—those present in the museum itself and those in one's formal and informal script. Depending upon the appetites, interests, motivations, and take-into-account-abilities of the patrons, this leader-follower interaction has the potential to contribute to the ways in which patrons make sense of their experience. Through communication, leaders make sense of a situation for themselves and then lead others through that environment in a way they hope will shape their interpretation of the situation—or the artwork—for those who are seeking some type of framework with which to interpret their experience. The docent—like a leader—is a guide, and despite a desire to fully share a certain vision on a tour, a broad range of factors beyond the docent's knowledge or control are at play. Some of these factors might be the knowledge and interest level of the visitors, concerns about the need to expedite the tour to arrive on time for a dinner reservation, difficulty hearing the guide's comments from where they are located in the group, distracting comments by others in the group, a preoccupying physical condition, financial pressures at home, and so on. All these messages compete with the carefully planned leadership efforts of the dutiful and dedicated docent. Understanding communication theory, particularly a systems approach to communication, allows—even compels—us to explore how to take account of the complexities of the art gallery or any context in which we aspire to be an influential leader.

Like the docent in the example, leaders may take on a number of different identities in the life of an organization, depending on the context and situation. Identities may include, but are not limited to, storytellers, agents of change, counselors, spokespeople, visionaries, impression managers, and cheerleaders. These individuals are validated as leaders, and their efforts are proclaimed to be successful to the extent that they and their messages are attended to, considered meaningful, and generally connected to the needs, aspirations, experiences, and goals of the group, organization, network, and environment. Leadership is not inevitable. Without followership, there can be no leadership, aligning with Bennis's (1997) notion that managing people is like herding cats. Those who understand these underlying dynamics recognize the irony that the effectiveness of the leadership is not a result of the leader's actions alone, nor of the needs and desires of followers, but rather exists at the intersection between the two. With this systems view in mind, two communication tools are especially useful for leaders as they interact with followers, peers, and even those to whom they report: attention and agenda setting and managing meaning and framing.

Attention and Agenda-Setting

Leaders play a potentially significant role in influencing those items that receive institutional attention. This phenomenon, also known as *agenda-setting*, is an important communication tool for leaders in higher education. In their seminal work on the subject, McCombs and Shaw (1972) studied the role of the mass media during the 1968 presidential election. As the authors concluded, "The mass media set the agenda for each political campaign, influencing the salience of attitudes toward the political issues" (p. 177). From this perspective, for its audiences, the news can shape not only *what* to think about but also *how* to think about it (McCombs & Shaw, 1993). The theory and research on the topic point to potential parallels between the mass media and leaders in higher education as those who may directly and indirectly determine the items that become prominent agenda items for their audiences.

A myriad of organizational issues often compete for attention, which presents an initial challenge. Further, the identification of an organizational problem does not necessarily imply immediate or specific action. As suggested in the public policy literature, recognizing a problem is important to attracting significant attention to it; however, recognition alone typically lacks the command necessary to place an item on the political agenda (Kingdon, 1984). In order for an issue to receive political attention, three streams of influence—a recognition of the problem, a proposed solution, and the political will—must converge to create a "window of opportunity" (Kingdon, 1984). As these three components come together in the political sphere, the window of opportunity opens for individuals to act on an agreed-upon problem. In a similar way, academic and administrative leaders in higher education must demonstrate a sophisticated understanding of the environment, the institution, and the primary stakeholders who maintain an interest in American colleges and universities. Additionally, effective leaders are able to identify the shifting windows of opportunity in their college or university, to advance items to respective agendas, and to influence the ways that others think about particular agenda items. From a systems view of communication, agenda-setting is an important device in a leader's toolkit.

Managing Meaning and Framing

As noted earlier, the transmission model of human communication neglects the role of meaning, which remains one of the most fundamental aspects of human communication (Axley, 1984). More contemporary views of communication privilege meaning, with leadership itself often being described as the "management of meaning" (Smircich & Morgan, 1982). This meaning-centered view of communication presents leadership as a product, result, or outcome of collective meaning making (Barge, 2007; Barge & Fairhurst, 2008; Parker, 2005). According to Smircich and Morgan (1982), "In understanding the way leadership actions attempt to shape and interpret situations to guide organizational members into a common interpretation of reality, we are able to understand how leadership works to create an important foundation for organized activity" (p. 260). It is through communication that leadership—and organization (Fairhurst & Putnam, 2004)—are possible.

As Gail Fairhurst (2009) suggests, "Even if leadership actors cannot always control events, they are still viewed as having the ability to control the context under which events are seen" (p. 1608). According to Fairhurst and Sarr (1996), "Leaders operate in uncertain, sometimes chaotic environments that are partly of their own creation: while leaders do not control events, they do influence how events are seen and understood" (p. xi). Leaders are seen as having the ability to cocreate the contexts, situations, and opportunities to which they and others must respond (Fairhurst, 2009). The skill of framing has the potential to cause others to accept one meaning or interpretation over another. During unprecedented and chaotic moments of organizational disruption, for example, it is often the leader's role to frame the situation in a way that builds trust, confidence, and hope. Drawing upon the work of Pondy (1978), Entman (1993), and Weick (1979), Fairhurst and Sarr (1996) define *framing* as

> the ability to shape the meaning of a subject, to judge its character and significance. To hold the frame of a subject is to choose one particular meaning (or set of meanings) over another. When we share our frames with others (the process of framing), we manage meaning because we assert that our interpretations should be taken as real over other possible interpretations. (p. 3)

The management of meaning calls for leaders who maintain a sophisticated understanding of human communication. In her call for an increased emphasis on framing, Fairhurst (2005) concludes, "For leaders who are not particularly skilled communicators, the road is not always easy. However, the possibilities of worlds yet to be imagined await those who try" (p. 179). In a similar vein, Bolman and Gallos (2011) suggest, "Whether academic leaders realize it or not, they always have choices about how to frame and interpret their world—and their choices are fateful" (p. 22). From a systems view of communication, framing is another important device for leaders in higher education, given the complex landscape, multiple missions, and multiplicity of stakeholders that leaders have to attend to on a daily basis.

Leadership Communication Principles for Effective Practice

Of the various factors identified as impediments to successful leadership, as well as in efforts to reduce those impediments, communication is a primary consideration. The following principles (Ruben & Gigliotti, 2016) represent ideas drawn from the concepts presented in this chapter—concepts that emphasize a contemporary systems view of communication and influence, highlight the critical role of both leader and follower, and align with the communication-oriented tools of attention and agenda-setting and the management of meaning/framing.

Leaders "cannot not communicate" (Watzlawick, Beavin, & Jackson, 1967, p. 49). While discussions of leadership communication typically focus on the creation and delivery of intentional, verbal messages with particular ends in mind, Watzlawick, Beavin, and Jackson (1967) remind us that human communication and human influence are best understood as far more complex and multidimensional phenomena. The words of a leader represent an effort to set an agenda or frame an event. As important as these verbal messages may be, in many cases nonverbal messages may be of greater import. Moreover, some messages may be attended to, while others are ignored; some messages are interpreted more or less as intended, while others may be interpreted in a wholly different way; some messages will be remembered, while others will be forgotten; and some messages will be acted upon and others ignored. Additionally, intentions are being imagined, motives are being attributed, and a willingness to follow is being determined. In these activities, verbal messages are important sources of potential influence; yet one must not underestimate the importance of silence and nonverbal messages. As but one example, consider the potential influences of one's actions as a leader in the context of planning and conducting a meeting. Regularly arriving on time or early as opposed to being late; distributing an agenda several days before meetings—and following the agenda—as opposed to verbally announcing the agenda topics at the beginning of the meeting and introducing various additional topics that come to mind as the meeting progresses; being visibly attentive while others are speaking, compared to frequently checking your phone; or being responsive versus being defensive when questions are asked. All of these actions may be messages of significance in the multifaceted dynamics of influence for those in attendance. In other contexts, although no words are spoken, the potential influence of a line of uniformed officers with shields and automatic weapons in hand, crowd members hurling rocks, and cameras and cell phones capturing these events can be quite influential messages.

Leadership communication is a process that involves the negotiation of—rather than the transmission of—meaning. Viewing communication in a linear fashion has the advantage of focusing influence efforts on the leader, the message, and the medium for disseminating the message. These elements are envisioned as being controllable and predictable by the leader. But this perspective, while comfortable, generally fails the test of providing either control or predictability of outcomes. Leadership communication is better understood as a coconstructed process between leader and follower that concerns itself with the way people create, convey, select, and interpret the messages that inform and shape their lives; in other words, viewing communication as a basic life process of constructing meaning to adapt to their environment rather than simply an exchange of messages between people (Ruben, 2003, 2011; Thayer, 1968).

Communication dynamics create a history that shapes and guides future influence efforts. The ebb and flow of messages, along with the interpretations that result, create a leadership-followership history that builds on itself and cannot be reversed. This relationship shapes current meanings and creates the foundation for future communication encounters—a bell that cannot be unrung, perceptions that have a potentially lasting impact and influence. Thus, even as individuals strive to shape interactions and outcomes, they are engaged in creating a communication landscape and legacy that—for better or worse—provide a backdrop and context for all that follows.

All leadership communication is intercultural. Leadership communication, like all communication, is essentially an intercultural phenomenon in which one's own cultural baggage—personal experiences, language patterns, religion, family history, work history, values, beliefs, and so on—provides a unique set of cultural filters through which all messages to and from others must flow. These differences are both predictable and unpredictable sources of infidelity in many, if not most, communication and influence contexts—interpersonal, social, organizational, and societal. This points to the necessity of adopting a more nuanced view of the dynamics and pragmatics of leadership influence efforts, recognizing the fundamental sense in which meanings and social influence are coconstructed by leaders and followers, and always in a variety of cultural contexts.

Leadership communication always has both content and relational consequences. What one says and does matters in terms of the content of the messages sent and received, as well as the leader-follower relationship that is being formed in the act of communication. While more explicit attention is typically devoted to the content of messages, and to the informative or persuasive goals one has, an awareness of the concomitant relational consequences of all communication events is an important part of leadership communication—perhaps more so than the traditional focus on message content. Content and relational functions of communication are often mutually reinforcing. Message content that is mutually affirming encourages the development of supportive relationships, and conversely, supportive relationships generally contribute to supportive outcomes relative to content. The absence of supportive relationships can be a substantial impediment to the communication process as it is viewed from a content perspective. Here, again, we are reminded of the central role of the follower in defining one's success as a leader and the importance of keeping content and the relationship dynamics of communication continuously in mind, since both are at stake in all situations.

Leadership dynamics occur in all social decision-making. Whether the decision is where to go to lunch or what the topic of hallway conversation should be at a given moment, leadership-followership dynamics are continually in play. These informal contexts can be extremely important to the attributions of colleagues, perhaps as much as or more than those taking place in meetings and formal decision-making settings. These relationships in turn provide the foundation for subsequent communication, so leaders must not take lightly the importance of cultivating these formal and informal relationships. These situations, where informal leadership dynamics are in play, also provide an important training ground for leadership theorists and practitioners wishing to better understand the dynamics of social influence, the key factors playing a role in influence outcomes, and the personal options available for influencing those outcomes.

Leadership opportunities are not something that one waits for; rather, they are situations that leaders must create (Stone, 2015). A corollary notion is that opportunities don't simply emerge and present themselves; rather, they must be identified and labelled as such, and the ability to do so may well be a necessary capability of outstanding leaders. Beyond recognizing such situations and constituencies as prospects for significant impact, as noted in Chapter 2, successful leaders must be able to seize challenges and transform them into opportunities, all the while encouraging others to do so as well. Here again, the role of communication in the practice of leadership is indispensable. Developing competencies in assessing a situation to determine with whom, when, and how one can become successful as a leader may be among the most important leadership knowledge and skill sets one needs to learn.

There is often a gap between what leaders know and intend, how they behave, and the impact of their actions. Despite one's best efforts, a gap often exists between one's intentions and aspirations and subsequent actions—between the leader you see and the leader others see. Assume that gaps are present—everyday instances where intentions will not be well displayed behaviorally or will not be received as was hoped for at the outset. A commitment to reflective practice (Schön, 1984) provides the potential for self-guided leadership theory building and personal development. Developing and using mechanisms for monitoring one's leadership and leadership/followership relationships are valuable components for increased leadership effectiveness.

If leaders want others to be committed to solutions, they need to engage those individuals in naming and framing the problem. Consistent with the notion of cocreation, shared leader-follower engagement is quite essential to a mutual commitment, a sense of shared ownership, and ultimately a successful follow-through on desired outcomes. Language and a genuine sense of verbal and behavioral engagement characterized by "we," "us," and "our" when speaking of vision, goals, projects, and accomplishments are far more likely to strengthen leadership-followership collaboration than "I," "me," or "my." By recognizing the central role that followers can play in defining problems and identifying possible solutions, leaders may be less likely to romanticize their view of leadership influence, while increasing the potential impact they may actually have in a situation. In so many of the most pressing of societal issues, shared ownership of the leadership products and processes seems essential to effective and engaged problem solving.

Initiating the learning process for the group builds stronger leader-follower collaboration than does simply describing the conclusion one has reached through one's own learning process. For those who aspire to influence others, it is important to recognize the limited knowledge or interest often present among those whom one wishes to influence. The challenge is often to use communication to lead potential followers through a process that re-creates that which led the leader to his or her position, understanding, and sense of need. The art of framing and the management of meaning remind us of the value of guiding others to replicate the leader's learning process for potential followers, rather than simply advocating for the adoption of his or her conclusions through communication efforts.

Leadership training and development efforts are subject to the same communication issues and challenges as leadership itself. Similar to the romanticization and oversimplification of popular discourse around the concept of leadership itself, there is a tendency to romanticize the value and direct impact of leadership training and development programs. This inclination reflects the limited perspective suggested by the notion that the message sent is equal to the message received. As discussed in Chapter 19, one's participation in a onetime leadership training initiative, albeit valuable for certain purposes, clearly provides no guarantee of fostering significant and lasting enhanced leadership capabilities. There is a related inclination to overvalue a specific training program because of a failure in recognizing the episodic nature of the event. Drawing on the imagery offered earlier, one wave is unlikely to dramatically shape the shoreline. Rather, the shoreline—or an individual leader's perspective, knowledge, and skills—is shaped by the influence of numerous waves over time. To this point, leaders are more likely to be socialized through the culture of their organization, learning from the formal and informal, intended and unintended influences of the leaders around them.

Conclusion

The connections between communication thinking and the study and practice of leadership are vitally important. Traditionally, the study and practice of leadership communication have focused on the leader and the specific mechanisms and strategies employed to influence others, all of which involve communication. Viewed more broadly, communication is a process through which individuals create and use information to relate to the environment and one another (Ruben & Stewart, 2016). As discussed in the previous pages, the implication is that communication outcomes and the meanings and interpretations involved are jointly created by senders and receivers, leaders and followers (Fairhurst & Connaughton, 2014a, 2014b).

This conceptualization of human communication leads us to view the process of social influence as one that is constituted through both verbal and nonverbal communication. Meaning, context, and goal setting are interwoven into this leadership transaction. Leadership and influence outcomes are planned and unplanned, formal and informal, used for good and evil. Leadership is inherently complex, and the centrality of communication should not be underestimated.

A communication-oriented understanding of the leadership process reveals the complexity in that which might otherwise be understood as a simple, commonsensical, intuitive, and taken-for-granted accomplishment. Notably, a communicative approach highlights the informational and relational consequences of social influence—consequences that are defined by followers as much as leaders. Most specifically, this approach suggests that an excessive emphasis on leader-as-source-of-influence, along with the focus on influence as a consequence of planned and formal leadership activity, requires some rethinking by leadership scholars as well as practitioners. We have more to say about the role of communication in understanding leadership throughout the remainder of this book.

For Further Consideration

1. Meeting Agenda Sequence

Provost James is developing the agenda for two upcoming meetings of the Faculty Council for the semester. There are a number of items she wants the council to discuss and, she hopes, endorse during the semester. The list includes the expansion of a university Honors College, the decision to promote a new and more ambitious post-tenure review process for all faculty, the decision to pursue advancement to a new Carnegie classification (from a regional to a national institution), a board-recommended review of faculty workload, increased attention devoted to continuing education and professional development programming, and the proposed expansion of the Alumni Services Department. As assistant provost you have been asked to propose a structure for the agenda of the two upcoming meetings. How would you sequence the agenda items listed for these meetings? How would the concepts presented in this chapter be of use in this task; specifically, what guidance might be provided by a consideration of the notions of the interdependency of leader/follower and framing?

2. Multiple Paths for Designing a New College

Bolman and Gallos (2011) provide an example of a new community college president facing a myriad of budgetary and human resource challenges. She approached these challenges with a spirit of confidence and optimism. In particular, there is extensive debate surrounding the development of a new professional college that will house all online degree initiatives. Seeking the counsel of five other new presidents at a summer institute, the community college president received the following 5 conflicting pieces of advice about how best to proceed: (a) launch the new online college as a separate unit; (b) encourage existing departments to develop their own online degree programs; (c) form a senior faculty committee to consider options and make a recommendation; (d) scale down the proposal and focus primarily on the development of part-time certificate programs; and (e) reject the proposal and enhance the in-person experience for current students.

- How might the concepts of the chapter explain the range of options suggested?
- How might these recommendations translate into next steps for the president to undertake?
- What concepts related to leadership and communication would guide those decisions?

9

THE COMPETENCY
APPROACH

A Two-Dimensional View of Higher Education
Leadership

In This Chapter

- In what ways are colleges and universities distinct from other types of organizations?
- Are special capabilities necessary for effective leadership in higher education?
- What is the competency approach to leadership?
- What are the benefits of this approach?
- What are the differences between the vertical and horizontal approaches to leadership competence?
- How do these two approaches apply to higher education? What are the critical competencies needed for effective leadership in higher education?
- In what ways does the proposed two-dimensional model best capture leadership development and leadership practice in higher education?

In his important work on the patterns and actions of leaders, Grint (2000) presents an "ensemble of arts" associated with the doing of leadership (p. 27). Suggesting that leadership is best understood as an art rather than a science, he considers "how four particular arts mirror four of the central features of leadership: the invention of an identity, the formulation of a strategic vision, the construction of organizational tactics, and the deployment of persuasive mechanisms to ensure followers actually follow" (Grint, 2000, p. 27). He classifies these central elements of leadership as philosophical arts (the who), fine arts (the what), martial arts (the how), and performing arts (the why). In this chapter we focus primarily on what Grint might consider to be the "how" of leadership, or the martial arts of leading complex organizations—the specific leadership competencies needed to effectively influence followers. As we explore in this chapter, these competencies may be unique to higher education leadership, but could also cut across other organizational sectors.

The Unique Character of Colleges and Universities as Organizations

A widely held view within the academy is that colleges and universities are unique as organizations in that they serve higher, special, and particularly noble purposes. Pursuing this line of thought further, one can identify a number of characteristics that appear to be unique to the sector of higher education, including the following:

- Structural complexity
- Loosely coupled elements, decentralization, and shadow systems, whereby individual departments and units create their own structures and services (e.g., technology and accounting functions) because the central systems are seen as providing inadequate or unnecessary services
- Extensive array of stakeholders and cultures
- Multiple, sometimes blurry purposes or missions
- Unclear bottom line
- Distinctive internal administrative and academic units with (often vastly) different structures, cultures, accountability requirements, core values, and leadership traditions and practices
- Differing core values among administration, faculty, staff, and students
- Traditions of autonomy, self-direction, academic freedom, and decentralized collegial decision-making
- Absence of attention to succession and transition planning

Can the Uniqueness of Higher Education Be Overstated?

As compelling as these perspectives seem, one can also argue that colleges and universities may not be as unique as they are often assumed to be. At a very general level of analysis, one can say that colleges and universities—and their constituent units—share a number of general features with other organizations, including the following:

- Structure—composed of component parts (programs, departments, schools, divisions)
- Stakeholders—internal and external groups and organizations that influence and are influenced by the activities of the organization
- Interactions between and among components—necessary to the functioning of the whole
- Resources—necessary to establishment and continued functioning
- Decision-making responsibilities—strategic and operational
- Traditions and culture—characteristic and unique shaping forces influenced by past practices that also shape future practices
- Leadership responsibilities—informal and formal functions necessary for guidance, cohesion, and planned change
- Operating within a larger environment—imposing constraints and creating opportunities
- Bureaucratic work structures and processes—allow for the accomplishment of routine tasks

Additionally, a number of other organizations—such as many in government or healthcare—are extremely complex, are composed of numerous subcultures, and serve multiple stakeholders that often have competing or conflicting needs. Moreover, the *loosely coupled system* (Weick, 1976) label that describes higher education may also be used to describe government, healthcare, and virtual organizations. Like democracies or republics, colleges and universities have traditions of collective governance, and the modern multiversity is particularly like government, with diffuse missions and multiple stakeholders, notes Susan Lawrence, Rutgers political science faculty member (personal communication, June 11, 2015). Also, similar to politics, the power to persuade is often more influential than the power bestowed by any type of formal constitutional authority (Neustadt, 1960). Much like cultural/artistic, government, and civic organizations, among many others, multiple missions, blurry purposes, and competing bottom lines call into question the value of traditional measures of productivity, value, and performance. All of this helps to elucidate the reasons why it is important to be cautious in concluding that the realm of higher education is unique.

It is also the case that changes in the marketplace have contributed to ways in which higher education collectively can be viewed as an industry, as discussed in Chapter 1. The existing research seems to acknowledge both sides of the argument—and it also suggests that effective leadership competencies in higher education have much in common with other sectors, yet involve some unique elements that are important to consider (Ruben & Gigliotti, under review). In the following pages, we explore both of these views, along with a competency-based framework that integrates these two perspectives as they relate to higher education leadership.

What Is a Competency?

The term *competency* is increasingly used in the higher education sector. One definition is "the ability to do something successfully or efficiently" (Oxford Dictionaries, 2015). Marrelli, Tondora, and Hoge (2005) offer a similar definition: "a measurable human capacity that is required for effective leadership" (p. 534). Note that competencies have both a knowledge and a skill component. *Knowledge* refers to leaders' understanding of a concept. *Skill* refers to leaders' effectiveness in operationalizing the knowledge they possess and their strategic ability to effectively act on this information (Ruben, 2012). An understanding of the competency and proficiency associated with the "doing" of the competency are both important. Leadership issues may arise because of the gap that often exists between theory and practice—or knowing and doing (Pfeffer & Sutton, 2000). Competency-based approaches to leadership focus on the ability of successful leaders to acquire a portfolio of knowledge and skills that they are able to apply strategically in a particular context or situation.

We believe that some leadership competencies are position-specific, but many others are cross-cutting and generic. The position-specific skills that are important for effectiveness in particular contexts and situations can be referred to as the "vertical" competencies. Additionally, an argument can be made for a "horizontal" approach that considers the general knowledge needed to help individuals understand why those skills work and allows them to translate and apply these skills across settings and circumstances. We discuss this idea later in the chapter.

Many of the most popular approaches to leadership are built around a focus on competencies, which is instructive as a way of thinking through the "how" of leadership and holds much promise for the enhancement of academic leadership practice. Writing from the higher education perspective, Smith (2007) found that the competency approach to leadership "provides a valid and relevant context for understanding the knowledge, skills, abilities, and attributes necessary to effectively lead people and organizations" (p. 27). According to Wisniewski (1999), "A competence model is a functional categorization of separate competencies that tend to occur simultaneously in situations where effective performance is demonstrated" (p. 3). In addition to understanding and mastering specific competencies, a leader must also discern which competencies are most relevant to a particular situation.

Attributes of the competency approach that help to explain its popularity include the following:

- Integrates varying concepts and approaches to leadership
- Focuses on factors over which leaders can exercise influence
- Accommodates connections between communication and leadership
- Recognizes the need for leaders to have an array of capabilities
- Presumes leadership abilities can be developed and learned
- Provides the basis for self-assessment and personal development
- Offers a foundation for leadership development programming
- Can be applied with varying situations/sectors and levels of generality

These characteristics point to the value of the competency approach as a conceptual framework and its utility as an applied guide for leadership practice and leadership development.

The Vertical and Horizontal Views of Competency

As noted earlier, the literature on the topic of competencies casts two distinct views. The *vertical* view focuses on those leadership competencies that are specific to a particular sector, setting, context, work environment, or position. This perspective emphasizes the importance of silo-based, context- and position-specific experience, knowledge, and skill as the critical ingredients for effective leadership. The *horizontal* view highlights those general leadership competencies that transcend sectors, settings, contexts, work environments, and positions—capabilities that are essential to outstanding leadership regardless of sector (Ruben, 2012; Ruben & Fernandez, 2013). Advantages and limitations are associated with adopting either view in the context of higher education leadership.

The Vertical View

The vertical approach begins with the assumption that a unique set of competencies is needed for effective leadership in higher education. In particular, this approach may presume that effective academic leadership requires knowledge and skills specific to higher education and to a particular discipline or technical area and position. According to this view, outstanding leadership is provided by individuals who have superior technical, disciplinary, and job-specific knowledge and skill. This view plays out regularly in higher education. For example, when considering candidates for program director, department chair, dean, or provost, the outstanding teacher or scholar is a likely candidate for academic leadership based on the vertical view. In information technology, the most technically knowledgeable are the best candidates for roles in leadership, just as those individuals with the most expertise of issues in student affairs are often considered the best prepared for the role of senior student affairs officer.

An early example of the vertical approach was provided by Gilley, Fulmer, and Reithlingshoefer (1986), whose work focused on the following competencies that college and university presidents need:

- Work well with board members
- Exhibit dogged persistence in pursuit of goals
- Keep antennae extended
- Demonstrate a sixth sense about opportunities
- Take unexpected actions (as cited in McDaniel, 2002, p. 80)

In consultation with university presidents and vice presidents and former American Council on Education (ACE) Fellows, Texas A&M University established the Center for Leadership in Higher Education in 1994, which Donathen and Hines (1998) evaluated. In selecting specific core competencies to teach in their newly designed leadership program, Donathen and Hines found the following competencies to be closely associated with effective academic leadership:

- Communication
- Decision-making
- Use of systems
- Professional ethics
- Team development
- Supervision
- Planning
- Teaching and counseling
- Creativity and innovation (as cited in McDaniel, 2002, p. 80)

There have been a number of additional efforts to identify competencies associated with particular higher education contexts and roles (Agnew, 2014; McDaniel, 2002; Smith, 2007; Teniente-Matson, 2013; Wisniewski, 199). As these studies might suggest, the list of competencies associated with effective academic leadership is diverse and multifaceted. Figure 9.1 depicts the vertical approach to higher education leadership competencies.

A vertical approach to exploring leadership in higher education is appealing for a number of reasons. First, the perception that each position and each department has its own knowledge and skill requirements is intuitive for the work of higher education, particularly as it relates to the often siloed separation of college and university departments. In addition, familiarity with a particular (often, one's own) area, along with the ability to focus in-depth in a given area, makes the vertical approach an attractive model for leadership development efforts. Credibility among peers and followers in colleges and universities requires relevant technical/disciplinary experience and knowledge—again, competencies that represent a vertical orientation. Finally, the ease of access to study leadership in a particular area, along with the corresponding difficulties associated with studying leaders across disciplines and areas, adds to the appeal of this approach.

Despite the aforementioned benefits, a number of limitations are associated with the vertical competency approach. Most notably, a vertical perspective inherently fails to benefit from the extensive, potentially relevant leadership literature from other sectors. Furthermore, the vertical approach may reflect a time when higher education was typified by the detached, ivory-tower model, as compared to the increasingly dominant marketplace model,

Figure 9.1. The specialized (vertical) approach to higher education leadership competencies.

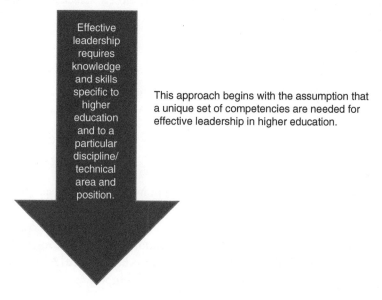

Effective leadership requires knowledge and skills specific to higher education and to a particular discipline/technical area and position.

This approach begins with the assumption that a unique set of competencies are needed for effective leadership in higher education.

which recognizes the importance of a broad range of competencies beyond academic excellence in higher education leadership. It is also interesting to consider whether the functions and competencies that seem to be specific to higher education may be manifestations of more generic leadership characteristics (Smith & Wolverton, 2010). Additionally, the focus on current leaders and practices in higher education may reproduce those leadership approaches that have come under increasing scrutiny and criticism. Finally, a vertical approach to leadership competencies may fail to identify those leadership behaviors that are not job-, position-, or sector-specific—that is, horizontal competencies.

The Horizontal View

The horizontal view, a generic approach to understanding higher education leadership competencies as depicted in Figure 9.2, begins with the assumption that a general set of competencies is needed for effective leadership across a range of sectors, positions, and settings, of which higher education is but one example. Based on this view, effective academic leadership requires generic knowledge and skills that transcend particular disciplines, technical areas, or positions. In this section, we describe three examples of horizontal research—studies that explore the diverse, non-sector-specific competencies needed for effective leadership; however, one could draw on a myriad of additional leadership studies that reflect this approach.

The first example of a horizontal leadership approach is John Maxwell's (1993) 10 leadership qualities that distinguish managers from leaders. These competencies are as follows:

1. Creating positive influence
2. Setting the right priorities
3. Modeling integrity
4. Creating positive change
5. Problem-solving
6. Having the right positive attitude
7. Developing people
8. Charting the vision
9. Practicing self-discipline
10. Developing staff

According to Maxwell, these 10 qualities—or what we would describe as leadership competencies—may be learned and cultivated over time. Maxwell's work has inspired much research on the topic of leadership development and has further advanced the dichotomy between management and leadership (see Chapter 7).

The second example of a horizontal approach to leadership is provided in the ongoing work on emotional intelligence. A number of scholars have contributed to current thinking about emotional intelligence, many building upon Salovey and Mayer's (1990) and Goleman's (1998) work in this area. According to Goleman, emotional intelligence is "the capacity for recognizing our own feelings and those of others, for motivating ourselves, and for managing emotions well in ourselves and in our relationships" (p. 317). Others have defined *emotional intelligence* as "the ability to perceive and express emotion, assimilate emotion in thought, understand and reason with emotion, and regulate emotion in the self and others" (Mayer, Salovey, & Caruso, 2000, p. 396) and "the ability to purposively adapt, shape, and select environments through the use of emotionally relevant processes" (Gignac, 2010). These three definitions begin to capture why emotional intelligence may be labeled a horizontal competency. In order to excel as a leader, this perspective asserts that, regardless of context, one must demonstrate an understanding of self, other, and context in order to effectively manage and express emotion.

Emotional intelligence is seen as an important competency for leaders in a variety of organizational settings—a competency that can be learned and developed over time (Goleman, 2004). In his important work on the topic, Cherniss (2010) acknowledges that success in work and life often depends on more than one's cognitive abilities. As Cherniss indicates, "It also depends on a number of personal qualities that involve the perception, understanding, and regulation of emotion" (p. 184). Related to the process of social influence, Goleman (1998) describes emotional intelligence as "the *sine qua non* of leadership. Without it, a person can have the best training in the world, an incisive, analytical mind, and an endless supply of smart ideas, but he still won't make a great leader" (p. 5). Intellect alone does not predict effective leadership, which is an important idea to consider as we think through the development of leaders in American higher education—a context that

Figure 9.2. The generic (horizontal) approach to higher education leadership competencies.

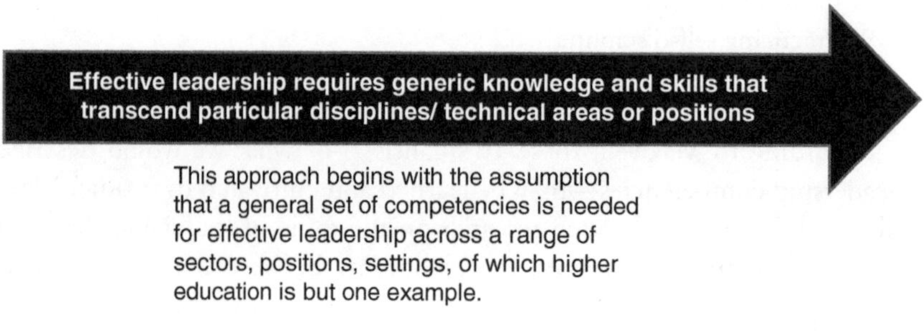

Effective leadership requires generic knowledge and skills that transcend particular disciplines/ technical areas or positions

This approach begins with the assumption that a general set of competencies is needed for effective leadership across a range of sectors, positions, settings, of which higher education is but one example.

contains some of the world's best thinkers, scholar-teachers, and subject matter experts.

Much writing exists on the topic of emotional intelligence, and a comprehensive review of this literature lies beyond the scope of this chapter. For our purposes, however, it seems useful to identify the primary skills needed to demonstrate proficiency in the area of emotional intelligence. Goleman (1998) presents four primary skills that constitute emotional intelligence: self-awareness, self-management, social awareness, and relationship management. These four components each include a host of related competencies, as shown in Table 9.1. Once again, the characteristics associated with emotional intelligence represent a horizontal, or generic, approach to leadership competencies regardless of unit, department, institution, or sector.

The third example of a horizontal approach is provided by Ruben's (2012) leadership competency framework (see Figure 9.3). Based on a review

TABLE 9.1
Emotional Intelligence Competencies

Four major skills make up emotional intelligence, with competencies in each quadrant:
1. Self-awareness
2. Self-management
3. Social awareness
4. Relationship management

	Self (Personal Competence)	*Other (Social Competence)*
Recognition	**Self-Awareness** • Emotional self-awareness • Accurate self-assessment • Self-confidence	**Social Awareness** • Empathy • Service orientation • Organizational awareness
Regulation	**Self-Management** • Emotional self-control • Trustworthiness • Conscientiousness • Adaptability • Achievement drive • Initiative	**Relationship Management** • Developing others • Influence • Communication • Conflict management • Visionary leadership • Catalyzing change • Building bonds • Teamwork and collaboration

and thematic analysis of approximately 100 academic and professional writings on the topic of leadership, Ruben created a competency framework and scorecard that identifies five thematic areas, or leadership competency clusters, each composed of a number of more specific competencies (see Table 9.2). This framework incorporates the vertical and horizontal perspectives, reflecting the assumption that the two knowledge sets and skill sets are complementary in thinking about leadership effectiveness.

As illustrated in Table 9.2, one competency cluster captures the specialized, vertical view of leadership. Termed *positional competencies*, this area refers to knowledge and skills related to the particular type of work, discipline, setting, or context. As noted in the section on the vertical view, these positional competencies include field-, discipline-, and sector-specific education, training, experience, expertise, and knowledge, as well as organizational knowledge, familiarity with the work, and professional involvement. Positional competencies are viewed as necessary elements for leadership excellence but generally are insufficient in and of themselves.

The four additional thematic competency areas depicted in Figure 9.3 and Table 9.2 reflect the generic, horizontal view of leadership and include personal competencies, organizational competencies, communication competencies, and analytic competencies.

Personal competencies refer to standards, character, and expression of values, including ethics, personal character, cognitive ability, creativity, enthusiasm, maintenance of high standards, personal conviction, persistence, self-discipline, self-confidence, and role modeling.

Figure 9.3. Leadership Competencies Scorecard major competency themes.

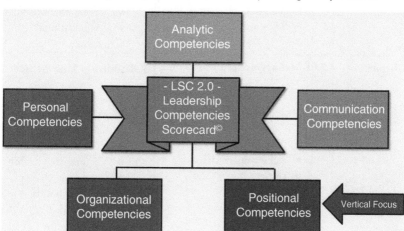

TABLE 9.2

Specific Competency Areas Within Each Theme

Analytic	Personal	Organizational	Positional	Communication
Self-assessment	Character, personal values, and ethics	Vision setting, strategy development, goal setting	Education	Credibility and trust
Problem definition	Cognitive ability and creativity	Management and supervision	Experience	Influence and persuasion
Stakeholder analysis	Enthusiasm	Information/knowledge management and boundary spanning	Expertise	Interpersonal/group relations and team building
Systems/organizational analysis	High standards	Technological capability	Knowledge of sector	Listening, paying attention, questioning, and learning
Analysis of technology to support leadership	Personal conviction and persistence	Collaborative decision-making and empowerment	Knowledge of organization	Writing and public speaking
Problem-solving	Self-discipline and self-confidence	Teaching and coaching	Familiarity with work	Diversity and intercultural relations
Review and analysis of results	Role modeling	Change, risk, and crisis management	Professional involvement	Facilitation, negotiation, and conflict resolution

Organizational competencies are the administrative capabilities that are necessary for leadership in organizations of varying purpose, function, and size. They include vision setting; strategy development; goal attainment; management and supervision; information and knowledge management; boundary spanning; use of appropriate information and communication technologies and strategies; collaborative decision-making; empowerment; teaching and coaching; and change, risk, and crisis management.

Communication competencies include the knowledge and skills necessary for effective interaction in interpersonal, group, organizational, and public settings. Among them are credibility and trust; influence and persuasion; interpersonal relations and team building; listening and paying attention; asking questions and learning; writing and public speaking; diversity and intercultural relations; and facilitation, negotiation, and conflict resolution.

Analytic competencies refer to thoughtful reflection on one's own and others' behaviors and careful consideration of the consequences of alternative leadership options and strategies, including self-assessment, problem analysis and problem-solving, stakeholder analysis, organizational and situational analysis, analysis of technology, and review and analysis of outcomes.

The horizontal approach is appealing for a number of reasons. First, although sector- and position-specific knowledge and skills may be helpful, more general competencies may better distinguish truly exceptional leaders across contexts. Second, general competencies are often cross-cutting, and a focus on these competencies allows for the identification and development of leaders who can be successful in a number of areas. Third, a horizontal approach allows leaders in higher education to benefit from the vast leadership literature available in other sectors and, in some instances, allows leaders coming from other sectors to excel in higher education leadership roles.

Similar to the vertical approach, however, this generic and potentially abstract approach to identifying effective leadership competencies across sectors runs the risk of oversimplifying or overlooking the subtleties of a particular sector. In particular, by casting a wide net across organizational types, the horizontal approach may miss those critical vertical competencies that are most relevant for a particular sector or job.

A Two-Dimensional Competency Approach for Effective Leadership

Conceptual and practical advantages and disadvantages are associated with both competency approaches. What is most useful, we think, is a two-dimensional competency framework that accommodates both the general and unique nature of higher education organizations and higher education leadership. A vertical *and* horizontal approach allows one to explore those leadership competencies that may be uniquely important within a particular sector or specific positions, while recognizing the value of cross-cutting competencies that are characteristics of leadership across diverse sectors and positions.

Leaders in colleges and universities face a number of challenges that are in some sense unique to higher education and to various positions within higher education. At the same time, we believe that cross-cutting competencies such as those identified in the generic leadership models discussed previously are vital to understanding and developing leaders, because these models identify characteristics of leadership excellence that are common to all outstanding leaders, regardless of the sector, role, or position. A two-dimensional competency model, as illustrated in Figure 9.4, offers a way of integrating both perspectives. Indeed, this two-dimensional model offers a framework for leadership development that lies at the foundation of this text. Effective leadership often relies on an understanding of the specific qualities and characteristics of higher education and the particular position, unit, or department, as well as the terrain of American higher education. At the same time, an array of horizontal competencies—such as interpersonal, analytic, organizational, and personal knowledge and skills—are vitally important for outstanding leaders, regardless of their specific roles or the sectors in which they work.

Figure 9.4. A two-dimensional competency approach for effective leadership.

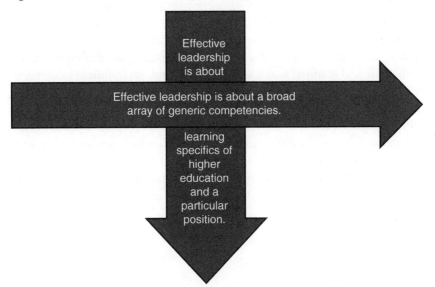

Conclusion

Competency-based models have the capability of highlighting specific knowledge and skill sets needed for effective leadership within a particular position and industry. At the same time, because these models highlight generic and cross-contextual leadership attributes, they permit comparisons and benchmarking both within and beyond sectors. As this chapter has noted, the term *competency* is used with varying levels of generality. It has been used to refer to very specific capabilities, like *student affairs competencies* (Smith & Wolverton, 2010). More commonly, and more usefully, the term refers to knowledge and skill sets, such as *analytical competencies*, that are seen as applicable in a broad range of leadership contexts (Ruben, 2012).

We believe that the practical implications of the topics explored in this chapter are incredibly important. Higher education is *not* wholly unique as an organization, and neither are the requisite capabilities for leadership excellence. There may have been a time when an argument for uniqueness could be made in a compelling manner, but that is no longer true. Based on existing theory, research, and current practice, we believe it is detrimental to higher education if our idealized conception of leadership focuses too much attention on disciplinary and technical competence in the selection, preparation, and recruitment of leaders—if that attention comes at the expense of attention to horizontal capabilities.

Without dismissing the important role of disciplinary and technical knowledge and skill, cross-cutting competencies—such as those necessary for communicating and collaborating effectively with a broad array of internal and external constituencies, dealing effectively with colleagues representing an array of interpersonal and multicultural styles, building effective teams and fostering successful teamwork, anticipating and dealing effectively with crisis and conflict, and fostering hiring and development efforts—are increasingly essential. To the extent that this characterization is accurate, a recalibration in our ways of thinking about leadership is needed, along with changes in the way we recruit, develop, and prepare leaders. Further research—focusing on differences and similarities between leadership competencies needed in higher education and other sectors, as well as among types of higher educational institutions and departments—will greatly contribute to the advancement of theory as well as effective practices.

For Further Consideration

1. Hiring and Promotion

What leadership competencies are emphasized in the hiring and promotion processes within the local unit and the institution with respect to positions that have formal leadership responsibilities? In research-intensive institutions, for example, how are competencies other than scholarly accomplishments considered in the selection of a department chair or dean?

2. Search Committees

Faculty and staff are asked to serve on a search committee for the next provost of the institution. How do members of the committee decide on the needed competencies of the position? What specific competencies do you look for in senior academic leaders? In what ways might members of the committee take account of these competencies throughout the search process?

3. Training and Development

As director of a specific unit, Jackie encounters an issue with office morale. Which of the competencies presented in this chapter will likely be most useful in addressing the morale within her department? How might she use the proposed two-dimensional approach to best address the needs of her specific department?

4. An Admirable Organization

Identify a noneducational organization or institution that you greatly admire. It could be, for example, a large corporation, a mission-centered nonprofit, or a government-related association.

Drawing on the ideas from this chapter, consider the following questions based on this exemplary organization:

1. What, in your opinion, makes this organization excellent?
2. How would you describe the leaders and leadership within this organization?
3. Which of these characteristics does the organization share with your college or university?
4. What can colleges and universities learn from the best practices of this organization?

FORMAL AND INFORMAL LEADERSHIP IN HIGHER EDUCATION

Roles and Responsibilities

Susan E. Lawrence and Richard De Lisi

In This Chapter

- What is informal leadership?
- What differentiates formal and informal leadership?
- How does the higher education context facilitate informal leadership?
- What are the assets and liabilities of informal leadership?
- How do formal and informal leadership function in committee and group work?
- In what ways can faculty and staff members benefit from taking on informal leadership roles?
- What strategies might one implement to exert influence as an informal leader in higher education?

Previous chapters proposed that leadership roles require cross-cutting or horizontal competencies and that higher education presents some unique challenges and opportunities that require special consideration when thinking about effective leadership. These ideas are particularly relevant as we consider informal leaders in higher education.

Informal Leadership Defined

We define *informal leadership* as social-organizational influence exercised by individuals who do not occupy a position of authority within a particular context. The impact of informal leadership is especially profound in college and university settings. The academy encourages discussion and debate both in the classroom and beyond. Within the context of colleges and universities, internal stakeholders feel free to challenge the opinions and decisions of leaders. Moreover, the traditions of shared governance in the academy delegate powers to members of the faculty and staff working within committees, departments, senates, and other faculty and staff bodies. For example, in higher education, faculty members evaluate colleagues' teaching for the purpose of merit, retention, and promotion decisions. In most other sectors, some of these powers and responsibilities are reserved for managers, directors, and other types of formal leaders. In the K–12 sector, for example, teaching evaluations are only conducted by those with formal leadership positions. These norms spill over into other realms in higher education as well, with committees and task forces being enlisted as policy changes are considered. Given the cultural values and governance structures of institutions of higher education, a complete account of leadership in higher education requires consideration of informal leadership.

Informal leadership includes a broad range of behaviors, from being an exemplary role model to being a purposeful and strategic opinion leader or change agent. For example, highly capable individuals whose work products are excellent (Collins, 2001) and who model helpful behaviors that advance organizational efficacy may be considered to be one class of informal leaders. These good citizens of the academy lead by example. Another class of informal leader includes those who wield influence behind the scenes or in assigned committee work. These informal leaders show particular skill in working with others (Collins, 2001). Their opinions are valued and sought out by colleagues. Those who chair standing committees, college senates, and so forth may be considered both informal and formal leaders depending on their sphere of influence and on the roles and responsibilities conferred by the chair position at a particular institution. Particularly respected senior members of a department, program, or unit often function as underground leaders. Such leaders may have acquired their influential status through professional accomplishments, seniority or tenure, former formal leadership positions, personal relationships, or personal style. The presence of a very powerful leadership underground is one of the particularly interesting and unique features of higher education. These informal leaders can facilitate or disrupt, focus or defocus, support or stall the efforts of those in formal leadership roles.[1] Finally, those with formal leadership roles, such as directors, department chairs, or deans, serve as informal leaders when they exercise influence among their peers within the institution more generally.

Focusing on informal leadership serves as an important reminder that many opportunities for participation are available to all members of a campus community. In higher education, leadership is often the result of personal choices in addition to institutional appointment. Stincelli and Baghurst (2014) note that, even in the business sector, "leadership, the process of influencing individuals to work jointly toward common goals, is carried out by both formal and informal leaders within an organization" (p. 1). The structure of a college or university, with its norms of faculty governance and individual autonomy, and multiple discrete administrative units, makes higher education particularly open to, and in need of, informal leadership. Bolman and Gallos (2011) explore this idea further:

> [The university's] loose coupling is essential for the *autonomy* that is typical of campus units and academic work—and [is] vital to an ambiguous mission like the discovery and dissemination of knowledge or the creation of educated and responsible citizens for today's and tomorrow's organizations. There's a reason that everyone on campus often seems to be going off in different directions or crashing into one another—they are. Higher education has evolved an architecture of disconnection. (p. 52)

Informal leadership, or *distributed leadership* as it is termed in the United Kingdom (Bolden, 2011; Bolden, Petrov, & Gosling, 2009; Macfarlane, 2011), naturally emerges in a culture that values collaboration, collegiality, and shared governance, as does higher education. Structurally, perhaps more than any other modern institution besides legislatures, higher education delegates much significant decision-making power to committees, weaving informal leadership opportunities into the daily operation of the university. As summed up by one of the respondents in Juntrasook's (2014) study on the contested meanings of leadership in higher education, "You can lead from wherever you are" (p. 27). All faculty, administrators, clinicians, and staff throughout the university have many occasions to exercise leadership behaviors during the course of their careers, quite apart from whether they ever occupy official leadership positions.

Informal leadership is deployed not only by individuals without a formal title but also by titled formal leaders. Few formal leaders are successful when they rely only on the influence that comes from their title and formal authority without also deploying the skills and methods of social influence used by informal leaders. Further, formal leaders often rely on the leadership skills of informal leaders as they work with other formal leaders who may be their peer colleagues or superiors. Finally, formal leaders need to be aware of the forms of social influence exercised by informal leaders. As noted in Chapter

5, an understanding and engagement of various cultures and subcultures—and the informal and well as formal leaders within these networks—call for college and university leaders who are expert organizational ethnographers and also skilled in cross-cultural communication.

Informal Versus Formal Leadership

At the opening of this chapter, we defined *informal leadership* as forms of social-organizational influence exercised by individuals who do not occupy a position of authority within a particular context. In practice, the distinction between formal and informal leadership is typically more a matter of degree than a rigid dichotomy. At the extremes of the continuum, we find that formal leadership positions are organizationally specified, whereas informal leaders are behaviorally identified. Formal leaders hold officially designated and titled positions of power and authority at a specific location in the institutional hierarchy. Informal leaders gain their influence from credibility, respect, and interpersonal relationships (Peters & O'Connor, 2001; Stincelli & Baghurst, 2014). Informal leadership is often exercised among lateral peers or within interpersonal networks that may cut across formal unit divisions and status hierarchies in the university. While formal leaders are officially and explicitly accountable for their actions and are required to discharge administrative and managerial tasks, informal leadership roles are not generally associated with specific responsibilities or administrative duties.

The informal leader has no portfolio for which he or she is accountable and no formalized metrics in terms of which to assess effectiveness. This is not to say that informal leaders may not be held accountable when disruptive, or credited when constructive, but rather that they typically lead at their own pleasure and set their own standards for success. This freedom, though, comes with a price. Unlike the formal leader who controls tangible and intangible resources that can be used as carrots and sticks, the informal leader has nothing to dispense beyond the intangible social rewards and sanctions deployed within social networks. Table 10.1 summarizes these distinctions between formal and informal leadership.

Among the approaches to leadership, some are based on formal authority and control over resources and as such are only available to formal leaders. Others are open to informal leaders as well as formal leaders and are essential to the effective enactment of formal leaders' official authority and power. Even the power held by the president of the United States has been described as dependent on the power to persuade rather than constitutional grants of authority (Neustadt, 1976). Moreover, formal leaders must often rely on the same leadership tools as untitled informal leaders when seeking

TABLE 10.1
Organizational Characteristics of Formal and Informal Leadership

Formal Leadership	Informal Leadership
Organizationally defined; carries a title Officially designated position with specified responsibilities and authority	Behaviorally defined; no official title
Part of hierarchy within the organization	Credibility and respect in the context of interpersonal relationships; typically exercised among peers within committees or interpersonal networks
Accountable to higher levels of authority; must ensure that routine administrative tasks are completed	Does not carry specific responsibilities or administrative duties; no specific accountability*
Controls tangible and intangible resources; can use carrots and sticks as means of influence	Does not control tangible or intangible resources; influence is embedded within peer networks, interpersonal rewards, and sanctions

*Informal leaders might serve as chairs of committees or task forces and therefore have a committee chair title and the responsibility to work with others to complete a specific charge. Committee chair roles have elements of both informal and formal leadership.

to influence equals, such as on a council of chairs, or when leading up by influencing those with greater formal authority (Bolman & Gallos, 2011). Because the leadership skills used by those without titles are also quite important for leaders formally in the administrative hierarchy, informal leaders are an important pool of potential formal leaders (DeZure, Shaw, & Rojewski, 2014; Downey, Parslow, & Smart, 2011).

Colleagues' Perceptions of Informal Leaders

Heider's (1958) classic work shows that people tend to explain other people's behaviors in terms of stable, internal traits and characteristics and downplay the role of contextual and situational factors. Subsequent work in social psychology on attribution theory showed that this tendency was reversed for explanations of one's own behavior. We tend to see our own behavior as largely determined by situational factors that are beyond our control. Research on explanations of other people's behaviors due to stable, internal factors such as beliefs, personality traits, and motivations now includes work that seeks to identify the specific areas of the human brain that are responsible for these socially based attributions (Spunt & Adolphs, 2015). In Chapter 8 we briefly discussed the trait approach to leadership. This approach endures, in part, because it stems from this basic human tendency to account for others' behaviors in terms of stable, internal characteristics.

Pielstick (2000) extended this approach to contrast perceptions of formal versus informal leaders by asking respondents to complete a 5-point Likert scale on 161 leadership characteristics for one formal and one informal leader at their institution. Table 10.2 presents the top 10 characteristics for formal versus informal leaders identified in the study. Characteristics that facilitate social influence dominate the list for informal leaders, while attributes of professionalism dominate the list for formal leaders. Among the total list of 161 characteristics, 46% showed no significant difference in how respondents rated their importance for formal and informal leaders. Pielstick's research suggests that it is important to demonstrate positive leadership traits in order to be identified as an informal leader.

At times, formal leaders may be suspicious of the influence of informal leaders who seem to be outside of their control and a threat to their own leadership, but informal leadership can also be exercised in support of formal leaders, not just in opposition. Many informal leaders are dedicated individuals who deploy informal leadership in ways that are supportive, constructive, and supplemental in pursuing institutional missions and goals. These individuals are great assets to an institution's formal leaders. It is also the case, as noted earlier, that higher education is full of very smart and independent thinkers, and not surprisingly, conflicts sometimes arise about how to best achieve the department, school, college, or university missions

TABLE 10.2
Characteristic Perceptions of Formal and Informal Leaders

Formal Leaders	Informal Leaders
Intelligent	Display honesty and integrity
Self-confident	Credible
Committed	Fair
Professional expertise	Sense of humor
Persevering	Treat everyone with dignity and respect
Strive for excellence or quality	Like to have fun
Understand complexities	Promote gender equity
Personable	Ethical
Positive spirit	Caring
Use critical thinking	Principle-centered

Source. Pielstick, 2000.

and how those missions should be prioritized. At times, informal leaders are those who generate, mobilize, and organize dissent. Such dissent is often not meant to be obstructionist, and the most influential leaders promote constructive conversations and listen closely to the explicit and implicit messages conveyed. Often the final outcome is better because of the contributions of dissenters. Even dissent that seems less constructive provides leaders with important information about the concerns of stakeholders within the university and should not be dismissed too quickly.

Sometimes, however, informal leaders are indeed oppositional. These oppositional informal leaders may simply be bent on obstruction, perennially suspicious of administrators and formal leaders, or unwilling to give up battles that were lost long ago. Formal leaders must develop strategies to address the challenges this type of informal leader presents. Finally, the autonomy that the academy promotes allows opposition based on individual self-interest to emerge. When policies seem to similarly threaten the autonomy or self-interest of a category of individuals, an oppositional informal leader may emerge. Despite the encouragement of the free exchange of ideas on college campuses, faculties and career staff and administrators are often conservative when confronted with pressure to change long-standing policies and practices (Tagg, 2012).

Exercising Informal Leadership: Processes of Social Influence

As a process of social influence, there are many ways to exercise informal leadership, especially in colleges and universities. Contexts, objectives, and personalities in one's unit, department, or institution influence which informal leadership approach is most appropriate at a given point. One of the simplest—and perhaps, therefore, most overlooked—leadership behaviors is to become a supportive follower and opinion leader. Leadership is always an interactive process; consequently, in practice the follower may exercise as much power as the leader, as discussed in Chapter 8. Supporting and mobilizing others in support of the vision or a decision of a formal leader can be a decisive exercise of social influence. Similarly, modeling the kind of behavior and speech you would like to see your colleagues engage in can also be a powerful leadership strategy that is open to formal and informal leaders. This approach is particularly effective in changing underlying attitudes and climates. For example, if one wants to maintain a commitment to the undergraduate educational experience and cultivate a culture of respect for these students, it is essential to take care in how students, their needs, and the problems or challenges they present are talked about. People who align their behaviors with what they say demonstrate integrity and understanding.

These types of informal leadership activities generally require loyalty to the institution and taking ownership of its missions. Informal leaders see opportunities in their multiple roles as colleague, ambassador, teacher, researcher, steward, opinion leader, and change agent to further the university's mission and particular policy objectives.

Building dense social networks within the university can be an extremely successful strategy for formal and informal leaders. Being an active mentor and supportive colleague across rank, role, status, and culture builds social capital, trust, and influence. Institutions of higher education are well known for silos—multiple distinct cultures and reporting lines—as well as the obvious faculty-staff divide, yet all units have important interconnecting roles to play in furthering the university's missions. Developing cohesive networks that build bridges of mutual understanding and reciprocal respect across faculty-staff lines and between disconnected groups creates a space for compromise, cooperation, and compliance. Informal leaders often have more freedom to work across silos and potentially help foster connections among them, since it may be easier for informal leaders to appear to rise above their formal affiliation with a particular group or unit. Formal leaders brought in from outside the university are often at a disadvantage precisely because they are new and therefore do not have cross-silo informal leadership networks throughout the institution upon which to draw. Such outsiders would generally do well to connect with local informal leaders who already have developed such wide-ranging networks. For informal leaders, offering such assistance to new leaders and colleagues is in itself an important strategy to advance the institution.

Informal leaders are also able to employ more visibly proactive approaches. The open nature of higher education allows change to percolate up from the grass roots as well as to be mandated from the top. For example, new programs training graduate students in pedagogy may begin in departments, and initiatives to support transfer students may be launched in advising offices. What's more, new strategies for using information technology and social networks for student support may start as an individual faculty or staff member initiative, and activities promoting nutritional health on campus may grow out of the efforts of line employees in dining services. The operation of most colleges and universities allows informal leaders to develop new initiatives. Mobilizing support for a policy change and lobbying those with the formal power to implement it is a strategy open to those aspiring to informal leadership. While the endorsement of new initiatives by formal leaders should be cultivated, success usually requires informal leaders to follow through with close attention to implementation, perhaps doing the implementation work themselves.

Exercising Informal Leadership in Small Groups

In sectors other than higher education, informal leadership has most often been studied in groups, teams, and committees as individuals take on roles as task, social, and opinion leaders (Benne & Sheats, 1948; Luria & Berson, 2013; Neubert & Taggar, 2004; and Zhang, Waldman, & Wang, 2012). These roles also can be exercised in multiple sites within the loosely coupled structure of the university (Birnbaum, 1988), including academic departments, intraschool administrative initiatives, forums of faculty governance, and broad committees that include academic and administrative personnel. Academic and administrative leaders need to consider specific strategies for effective social influence at an informal level. The next section explores some of these strategies, with a focus on behaviors in groups, teams, and committees, drawing upon seminal studies by Benne and Sheats (1948), Katz (1957), and Tuckman (1965).

The legacy of commitment to faculty governance and the need to work across reporting lines in key activities make small groups an especially important aspect of the leadership landscape in colleges and universities. On the academic side of the house, committees are called upon to conduct searches and review candidates for reappointment and promotion. At times, this practice is carried over into hiring for other high-level positions. Standing committees review curriculum, monitor the status of diversity initiatives, and review admissions and academic standing policies, for example. Councils of department chairs and executive committees are formed to advise deans, provosts, and chancellors. Academic departments themselves and some smaller units may function as small groups. Ad hoc committees are established to review policy questions or carry out new initiatives. Task forces are convened to develop strategic plans or address specific problems. Work is done in teams or small groups in labs, clinics, hospitals, and living-learning communities. Academic integrity and student conduct disciplinary processes often include small groups of faculty and staff acting in a jury-like role. Common tasks done by multiple units—such as school-specific student advising and work processes that involve multiple units, such as registering students for classes—are discussed and decided on in group meetings. Within administrative and business offices, the private business sector's penchant for teams has become increasingly popular in higher education.

These multiple variations on small groups provide a wealth of opportunities to exercise informal leadership. Here the literature on group processes and informal or emergent leadership can be especially instructive. Some of these groups are made up exclusively of like-rank peers, such as faculty curriculum committees or deans' councils. Others are made up of senior or mid-level administrative officers from across units. Task forces and other types of working groups may pull people from across ranks and units. At times, a clear hierarchy of leadership exists within the committee, but most often a range of informal leadership roles will be open to everyone in the group. Across these variations, predictable patterns of development and assumptions of roles have been identified in the research literature.

In 1965 Bruce Tuckman published a classic article outlining four stages of group development, as depicted in Figure 10.1. Informal leadership behaviors play a role in each stage. Tuckman labels the first stage *forming*, during which group members establish relationships and identify the boundaries of the task before them. This stage is characterized by processes of "orientation, testing, and dependence" (p. 396) on authority figures. The second stage is *storming*, during which conflict arises around relationships within the group and the requirements of the task with which the group is charged. It is a heavily emotional stage in the group process. The third, *norming,* stage occurs as the group begins to coalesce and members begin to identify as part of the group. Standards and roles emerge as individual opinions are expressed. Finally, in the fourth stage, having developed a functional interpersonal structure, the group's attention and energy are more clearly focused on *performing* the task at hand. Roles are now viewed as more flexible, and shifting occurs as necessary for functional effectiveness (Tuckman, 1965). In 1977, based on several additional studies, Tuckman and Jensen added an *adjournment* stage characterized by dissolution of the group, often with members experiencing some sadness and self-reflection.

Figure 10.1. Tuckman's four stages of group development.

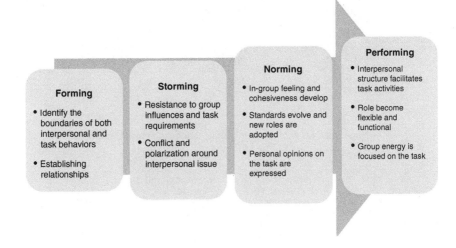

Each of these stages of group development provides opportunities for informal leadership as members adopt different roles within the group. Writing in 1948, Benne and Sheats argued that improving group functioning could not rely solely on improving the skills of the formal leader of the group, but also must attend to membership roles. They identified 27 functional roles open to people in groups, providing many opportunities for informal leadership of several types. Benne and Sheats classified these roles as group-building and maintenance roles, "individual" or self-centered roles, and group task roles. In examining how committees and other groups on campus function, it may be more helpful to group the 27 functional roles into three categories and a fourth "disrupter" category. Functional roles in small groups allow individuals to act as social leaders, opinion leaders, and task leaders. Figure 10.2 presents these roles and re-presents them in terms of informal leadership activities.

All of these roles are avenues for social influence and can be adopted as strategies of informal leadership by individuals with and without formal leadership titles. Within any group, these roles may be centralized with a single leader or small group of leaders or disbursed widely throughout the membership. Social leadership roles include acting as an energizer, encourager, gatekeeper and expediter, harmonizer, follower, or coordinator. As shown in Figure 10.3, they are especially important during the forming stage and again during the norming stage. Disrupter roles, such as aggressor, dominator, blocker, recognition-seeker, loafer (or playboy, in the 1948 typology),

Figure 10.2. Functional roles in groups.

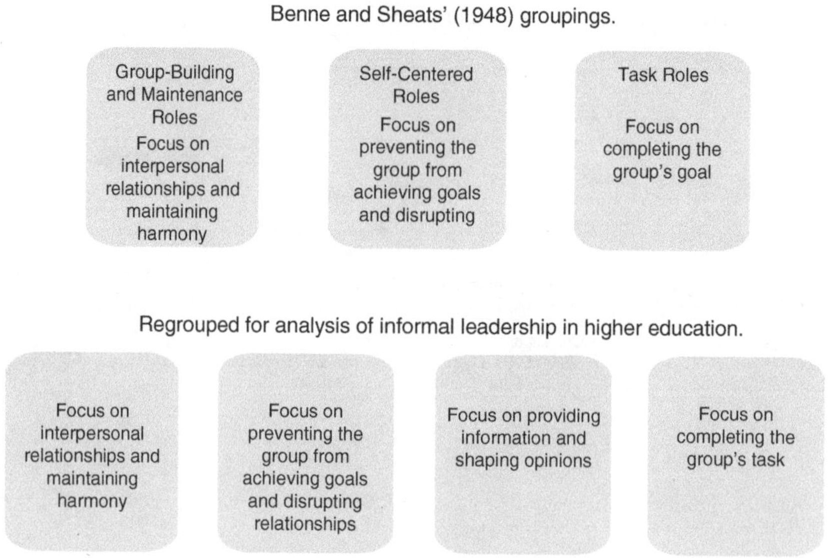

Benne and Sheats' (1948) groupings.

Group-Building and Maintenance Roles	Self-Centered Roles	Task Roles
Focus on interpersonal relationships and maintaining harmony	Focus on preventing the group from achieving goals and disrupting	Focus on completing the group's goal

Regrouped for analysis of informal leadership in higher education.

Focus on interpersonal relationships and maintaining harmony	Focus on preventing the group from achieving goals and disrupting relationships	Focus on providing information and shaping opinions	Focus on completing the group's task

special-interest pleader, help-seeker, or self-confessor, are manifested prominently during the storming stage and can derail the group if not balanced by other members. Even though elements of these roles can be frustrating, as noted earlier, dissent, debate, and challenge contribute to better solutions and processes—sometimes in spite of the motives of those who enact those roles. Opinion leader roles include initiator-contributor, elaborator, information giver, opinion giver, information seeker, opinion seeker, and compromiser. These roles are crucial during the norming stage. Task leader roles—including orienter, coordinator, recorder, procedural technician, observer, evaluator-critic, and standard setter—are essential during the performing stage. Social leadership roles are likely to come to the fore again during the adjournment phase. Individuals can move in and out of each of these roles at different stages of the group's work and can engage in several simultaneously. Disaggregating and labeling common postures and roles that members take on in a group and identifying them with particular stages provides a language and framework for understanding and influencing group processes. A great deal of frustration can be avoided and strategic advantage gained by recognizing certain behaviors as typical parts of the process of group work.

Exercising Informal Leadership as a Change Agent

Beyond working as a social, opinion, or task leader in group settings, there are opportunities to be a change agent on campus within roles such as colleague,

Figure 10.3. Exercising informal leadership in groups.

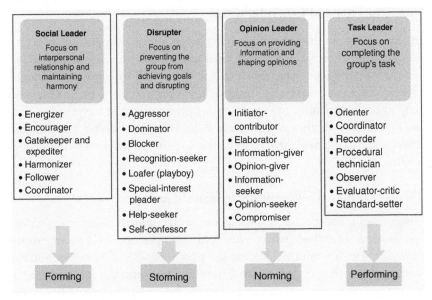

ambassador, teacher, steward, and opinion leader. Volunteering for committees or providing other forms of assistance is one way to move change forward. People without formal leadership positions may nonetheless be able to float new initiatives and seek grants and other outside support for initiatives they think important. Stepping up to take on the implementation of policies provides another opportunity to move change forward and may not require a formal charge to do so. When initiating change, recruiting the support of formal leaders may be important; at least one should make sure they are not opposed to your goals.

It is nearly always easier for people to continue in their established patterns, and change can be frightening in a number of ways (Tagg, 2012). It is especially important to explain why and how change is needed, particularly stressing how it addresses a need of those who adopt it or how it can make things easier for them. It is important to identify and cultivate like-minded people in order to build teams and coalitions in support of change. If a relevant committee does not exist, create a group for advice and guidance, always beginning with coalitions of the willing. This approach can develop momentum for the change by providing small wins that demonstrate the feasibility of the change and cultivate ambassadors who support it. Likewise, it is important to be sensitive to constraints under which others are working across role, rank, status, and culture. Things are the way they are now for a reason. Knowing what those reasons are and addressing them gives the informal leader credibility and makes it easier for others to follow.

Practical Tips and Considerations

In this section we discuss the implications of informal leadership in higher education for those who occupy formal leadership positions. In general, we believe formal leaders have much to gain from informal leaders and much to lose if the perspectives of informal leaders are ignored or unaddressed. Relying on formal authority alone is a risky proposition in higher education. We also discuss whether an individual should choose to become an informal leader and, having made that choice, how to gain effectiveness and influence in that capacity.

Formal Leaders Working With Informal Leaders

Given that higher education is fertile soil for the growth of informal leaders, it is important for those with formal leadership positions to be aware of the powerful role that informal leaders can play, especially if one is an outsider who is new to the campus. Leaders need to know who the informal leaders are within their unit, which can be learned by being an astute listener and observer, applying the concepts and tools of an organizational ethnographer, as discussed earlier. It is also important to minimize the tendency to classify informal leaders as generally supportive or oppositional as they offer advice and perhaps even advance their own initiatives. Leaders need to consider the ideas and opinions of informal leaders on the ideas' merits, not based on personal relationships. Leaders also need to examine their own contributions to dysfunctional patterns before blaming others (Feiner, 2004). Informal leaders can provide invaluable feedback in this regard.

It is important to cultivate informal leaders among the administrators, faculty, and staff who share your vision and commitment to the institution. Those who function as good citizens of the academy are prime candidates for nurturing as informal leaders. As a rule, cultivation efforts are more successful when leaders create a governance culture in which debate and discussion are encouraged. As decisions are made and implemented, those who had voiced opposition should not feel permanently disenfranchised. It also helps to have key members of the faculty and staff work together where possible. The staff may not initially appreciate the role of informal faculty leaders, and faculty members also should understand the role of key staffers who exercise considerable leadership influence. As a formal leader, the example you set will help with these cultural considerations. For example, maintaining one's equilibrium and professionalism when votes do not go your way is an important behavior to model.

Titled leaders also should fully understand the governance limitations on their formal authority. Campus policies and procedures must be adhered to with fidelity. On issues that require faculty approval, faculty governance policies and procedures should be faithfully followed in letter and spirit. As a formal leader, the more radical your proposals, the more important it is to solicit the views of informal faculty and staff leaders prior to formal processes (e.g., committee fact-finding) and discussions. Sharing the rationale for your ideas about new paths and directions early on with informal leaders can be critical step in the governance process. Often, the ideas of informal leaders— whether pro or con—can be accommodated to the benefit of the institution. Whenever possible, avoid unrealistic deadlines or perpetual states of crises as an excuse to trample on faculty governance procedures or institutional policy. Without also winning the hearts and minds of informal leaders, successes may be short-lived, reflecting compliance without commitment and leading to an abandonment of the idea or initiative once you no longer hold the formal position of authority. Disregard for established procedures and cultural norms is likely to create an oppositional culture in which even routine completion of everyday operations is met with resistance and foot dragging.

Choosing to Become an Informal Leader

As we have seen in this chapter, there are numerous opportunities in higher education for those who do not exercise a position of formal authority within a particular context to exercise social-organizational influence on issues about which one feels passionate. Some informal leadership behaviors, such as being an exemplary role model or effective committee member, present themselves naturally. Others, such as change agent or strategic opinion leader, may take more time and commitment. Decisions about how active to become as an informal leader are contextual and personal. Such decisions may reflect the level of passion one has for a particular issue. They may also reflect individual career stage and the professional and personal resources one has to devote to engaging in proactive informal leadership. At times, informal leadership may require putting the needs of the institution above one's own individual advancement. Faculty members often see informal (and formal) leadership opportunities in this light since advancement in faculty rank generally depends on individual accomplishment in the classroom, in scholarship, and in the profession. For others, especially staff and those who aspire to formal leadership positions, informal leadership may be an important way to advance one's career. Both groups should consider their own need for formal approval or recognition. Informal leaders often work behind the scenes and receive little recognition for their work in advancing the university's mission. Indeed, the most frequent reward for being an effective informal leader and getting things done might be more assignments of a similar nature in the future. That said, nearly everyone, whether content to exercise social influence through being a model citizen or aspiring to be a widely recognized opinion leader, can follow the practical advice offered in the final section of this chapter.

Gaining Respect and Influence

Much of what has been discussed here as strategies for informal leadership applies equally to those holding formal leadership roles, particularly because the decision-making structures in higher education are often fluid among groups of people of various ranks and positions. As a process of social influence, everyone can develop the potential for leadership through some practical everyday activities that also, along the way, make the university a more pleasant place to work for all involved (Edmunds & Boyer, 2015). It is crucial, however, that these behaviors not be adopted simply as instrumental strategies; rather, they should emerge as a genuine outgrowth of one's own personality and commitment. Not all of these will fit every personality, and inauthentic displays are often met with enough skepticism to make them ineffective.

- Earn a reputation for integrity, discretion, genuine interest, helpfulness, and reliability.
- Follow through on promises, big and small.
- Model hard work and dedication to the common good.
- Become an asset to those above and an assistant to those below. Cultivate the support of the people doing the day-to-day, on-the-ground implementation, and get the support of whomever the various implementers and stakeholders report to in the organization.
- Develop a broad network across rank, role, status, and culture.
- Express gratitude by thanking people for their contributions and being genuinely appreciative. It can be especially powerful to recognize those contributions that many others overlook. Praising those who contribute to others, particularly to their formal leaders, earns loyal friends.
- Know your peers and cultivate goodwill among them.
- Know the relevant formal and informal leaders and their views; cultivate their support.
- Make the lives of formal leaders easier by getting buy-in from those who report to them so that your project is not their problem.
- Always show up prepared, and provide appropriate information.
- Ask strategic questions or questions that reframe the issue.
- Volunteer for tasks and follow through on completing them.
- Frame the debate by introducing drafts or other materials to use as starting points for discussion; this makes following your lead easy.
- View the situation from other participants' points of view and in light of their various interests.
- Be open to other views; accept suggestions that improve the outcome; compromise when it will get to "the good," even if not to "the perfect."
- Share the credit. Be more concerned with getting good ideas adopted or the task completed than getting credit for it. Patience may be required. You are often planting seeds that may take a while to germinate.
- Mentor, and be mentored.
- Be humble and have a sense of humor.

Conclusion

Institutions, especially loosely coupled ones like higher education, run better when multiple members exercise formal and informal leadership in support of the organization's missions and goals. Informal leaders are frequently among the most passionate about the goals and missions; they contribute because they believe, not because it is their job. People follow because of the social capital the informal leader has built. Informal leaders thrive in group decision-making structures, and such leaders can be especially important in creating networks across siloed reporting lines. The most successful formal and informal leaders use many of the same strategies and tools. Given the limited powers of titled leaders in higher education, formal leaders would be well served to hone the tools of informal leadership and to cultivate the support and assistance of those around them on whose effectiveness as informal leaders they can rely.

For Further Consideration

1. Your Experiences as an Informal Leader

As you reflect on your own leadership experiences, select two instances where you exercised an informal leadership role. Were you successful as an informal leader? How would you define *success* in these instances? Which of the informal leadership strategies presented in this chapter did you use during these experiences? What might you do differently next time?

2. The Influence of Informal Leaders

Identify two informal leaders in your department, unit, or institution. In what ways do these individuals demonstrate informal leadership? How would you characterize their behaviors and attitudes? In what ways do these leaders—who do not occupy a formal position of authority—influence others in your organization?

3. Anticipating Informal Leadership Roles in Group Settings

You have been appointed to a task force composed of a range of formal leaders of various ranks drawn from a range of academic and service units. Your task force has been charged with developing a series of interdisciplinary programs to commemorate your institution's centennial. The task force, made up of 15 leaders, includes vocal individuals, many of whom are interested in advancing their own department or unit in the centennial programs. Reflecting on the four informal leadership roles in higher education presented in this chapter—social leader, disrupter, opinion leader, and task leader—describe how you would attempt to influence the group's decisions based on these four roles. Which of the roles do you believe would be most advantageous in influencing the group to design a schedule of programs that are truly illustrative of the institution's many units and departments?

Note

1. Our use of the phrase "underground leaders" draws on the concepts of the opinion leader developed and widely applied in political science and mass communication studies (Katz & Lazarsfeld, 1955), and public character used in sociology and ethnographic studies to describe informal leadership roles within urban communities (Jacobs, 1961; Duneier, 2000).

PART THREE

APPLIED TOOLS FOR LEADERSHIP AND ORGANIZATIONAL EFFECTIVENESS

II

BECOMING A BETTER LEADER

Self-Assessment and Leadership Development

In This Chapter

- How does one translate theories of leadership into personal leadership practice?
- What roles do learning and change play in the leader development process?
- What differentiates personal leadership development from organizational leadership development?
- Why is personal leadership development important for the individual leader as well as the unit, department, or institution?
- How can the five-step model for becoming a better leader presented in this chapter be useful to your own growth and development?

The pursuit of leadership excellence is a personal matter, one that must begin with a personally defined and personally relevant sense of purpose. Becoming a better leader is always possible, and this developmental process is ongoing. A continuous improvement perspective applied to the self can be helpful, especially when situations are challenging and desired outcomes are elusive.

The two critical aspects to personal leadership development are learning and change (Day, Zacarro, & Halpin, 2004). Leadership development, as described by Kegan (1982) and Luthans and Avolio (2003), is a process of human development that occurs throughout one's life. An individual's commitment to development as a leader requires a continuous process of learning, discovery, and self-awareness. The metaphor of a journey best captures the processes of personal leadership development. Like many journeys, the terrain is often rough, the conditions are often unpredictable, and the final destination is often uncertain. Despite variables that are not under the leader's control, the decision to develop as a leader must be made with intention and purpose and requires a deliberate commitment. The challenge of leadership development is not necessarily identifying a specific plan of action; rather, the more significant challenge is maintaining the momentum of the journey through the varied challenges that lie ahead. With this framework in mind, this chapter lays out a series of concepts and guides for personal leader development. Our hope is that the tools presented, along with the many strategies and models offered, are useful for academic and administrative leaders in strengthening their overall leadership performance and sense of leadership efficacy.

Personal Leadership Development

In this chapter we discuss individual or personal leadership development (sometimes called *leader development*)—not to be confused with the more expansive concept of institutional or organizational leadership development, addressed in Chapter 19. *Leader development*, as defined by McCauley, van Velsor, and Ruderman (2010), is "the expansion of a person's capacity to be effective in leadership roles and processes" (p. 2). In leader development, emphasis is placed on cultivating human capital, or the "individual-based knowledge, skills, and abilities associated with formal leadership roles" (Day, 2001, p. 585). We focus here on self-assessment and self-improvement for individual leaders in higher education, with a goal of having readers reflect on how well they understand the important dimensions required of academic and administrative leaders and their current level of effectiveness related to these dimensions.

As noted throughout this text, leaders in higher education at this point in time face complex challenges and intriguing opportunities. Leadership roles require proficiency in a wide array of leadership competencies, and in many instances the decisions of those leaders directly affect the future of the institution. Indeed, an investment in personal leadership development is an investment in the very future of the organization. McCauley, van Velsor, and Ruderman (2010), editors of the *Center for Creative Leadership Handbook of Leadership Development*, outline the following items that leadership development might positively influence:

Leading Oneself

- Self-awareness
- Ability to balance conflicting demands
- Ability to learn
- Leadership values

Leading Others

- Ability to build and maintain relationships
- Ability to build effective work groups
- Communication skills
- Ability to develop others

Leading the Organization

- Management skills
- Ability to think and act strategically
- Ability to think creatively
- Ability to initiate and implement change

Each of these topics is relevant to the work of higher education, and institutional investments in leader development are an important component of efforts to improve a college or university.

The Path to Becoming a Better Leader

As noted, developing one's skills as a leader occurs over time and can be thought of as a continuous (self-)improvement process. The model presented in Figure 11.1 outlines key dimensions for individual leadership development over the course of one's career.

Figure 11.1. The path to becoming a better leader.

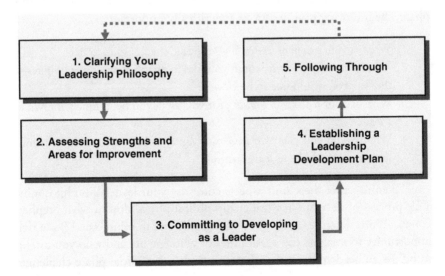

The first step in the learning and change process is to set your leadership philosophy and the standards to which you aspire. The second step is determining where you stand relative to those standards. Gaps between your current performance—in general or in particular situations—and the standards you have set for yourself represent potential areas for improvement that can only be addressed through the third step, which is a genuine commitment to change. The fourth step is to translate that commitment to action into plans and strategies for improvement, and the fifth step is to ensure follow-through on those plans. As the dotted line in the figure implies, the learning and change process is ongoing and involves a recursive cycling through the steps. This model of learning and change is applicable to a wide range of contexts, including personal, social, and organizational situations, and it is particularly relevant for leadership development. Existing leadership styles and skills should not be regarded as permanent fixtures of one's life. On the contrary, it is important to continue to be aware of and refine one's leadership style throughout one's career. The learning and change model presented in Figure 11.1 provides a tool that outlines the process by which that can occur.

Clarifying Your Leadership Philosophy

A sound approach to leader development begins with gaining clarity in terms of personal and professional aspirations. Step one begins with identifying and clarifying your leadership philosophy. By thinking about the type of leader you want to be, you engage in a process that allows you to move forward with intentionality and purpose. Identifying role models and reading the leadership literature—including professional and practical advice and biographies of respected leaders—are helpful actions in this stage. For this phase, the following four questions are critically important:

1. What is your *vision of leadership*—the leader you aspire to be?
2. What *leadership identity* would you like to establish among colleagues— the way you would like to be viewed?
3. What is your *leadership brand*—for what will you be uniquely known as a leader?
4. What would you like your *leadership legacy* to be—the lasting contribution you would like to leave behind?

Taken together these four aspects comprise your leadership philosophy. This process of developing a leadership philosophy is akin to what Stephen Covey (1989) describes as "beginning with the end in mind" (p. 97)—a rich opportunity to imagine the possibilities of who you are and who you intend to be. As an academic or administrative leader, this initial phase challenges you to think about your own leadership goals and aspirations while considering the expectations, perceptions, and attitudes of the many stakeholders with whom you might engage in your work in higher education. Self-awareness and self-discovery are intricately connected to this important first step. Despite the complexity and multiplicity of leadership concepts, roles, and strategies, you can consider some fundamental questions to help clarify your personal leadership philosophy and vision, and these can serve as personal guideposts that are useful across settings. Perhaps the most basic of these questions are described by Lance Perez (2015), associate vice chancellor and dean at the University of Nebraska–Lincoln, as follows: "Before you take a job as an academic administrator, know what issues you are willing to resign over and what you are willing to be fired for. If you don't know the answers to these questions, you shouldn't take the position." Consider the various guideposts to leadership presented in Box 11.1. Rating yourself on each can help you to define aspects of your leadership philosophy.

BOX 11.1

Formulating Your Personal Leadership Guideposts

How does your rating of these various leadership dimensions help to shape your aspirations and guide your actions as a leader? What are you known for, and what would you like to be known for, in your unit, department, or institution? How would you rate the following in importance to you personally?

(very important: "1"; somewhat important: "2"; not important: "3")

___ Thought of as an honest and candid colleague

___ Respected for your intellect and insight

___ Admired for your contributions to your discipline or professional area

___ Remembered for your contributions to the department and institution

___ Thought of as a competent leader

___ Known as a supportive and accommodating leader

___ Seen as someone who is forceful in voicing your opinions

___ Thought of as someone who is forceful in saying what needs to be said

___ Seen as an inspirational, transformative leader

___ Building a reputation among senior administrators as an effective leader

___ Leaving a significant legacy

___ Regarded as a champion of student rights

___ Respected for your dedication to teaching/learning

___ Developing the next generation of leaders

___ Admired for your dedication to the well-being of your colleagues

Assessing Strengths and Areas for Improvement

Step two on the path to becoming a better leader involves assessing your strengths as well as areas that need improvement. This step allows you to understand where you stand relative to the aspirations and philosophy identified in step one. Leaders in higher education come from many disciplines and technical areas, often with little familiarity with the issues in higher education beyond their own areas and with little or no background in leadership concepts, practices, or tools. Entry into a formal leadership role in colleges and universities requires a candid assessment of the strengths that can be leveraged and of those areas most in need of improvement.

One approach to self-assessment might involve consideration of the various competencies needed for effective leadership, using a tool such as the Leadership Competencies Scorecard (see Appendix B), which outlines the various competencies required for leadership excellence, including positional competencies, analytic competencies, personal competencies, communication competencies, and organizational competencies (Ruben, 2012). The self-assessment process using this model involves the following:

- Identifying competency areas of strength via self-reflection
- Identifying competency areas in need of improvement via self-reflection
- Asking colleagues to complete the inventory with you as the target
- Based on a comparison of self- and colleagues' assessment, identifying specific competencies that must be enhanced to attain your stated leadership philosophy
- Crafting an assessment technique to keep track of progress in developing competencies you identified as in need of improvement (e.g., keep a journal, ask for feedback from members of your leadership team, your peers, or your superiors)

This competency approach to personal assessment is one of many that are available in the leadership literature. For a sample of other leadership inventories, descriptions of the tools as offered on their websites, and the various metrics that they seek to assess, see Table 11.1.

A more extensive summary of these inventories, along with other leader and leadership assessments, is beyond the scope of this chapter; however, a number of important themes cut across these various self-assessment tools. To start, all of the inventories encourage honest self-awareness in responding to the various inventory questions. The very act of completing these inventories may enhance one's understanding of self, other, and context. Next, the

TABLE 11.1

Summary of Relevant Behavioral and Leadership Inventories

Inventory Tool	Description	Key Metrics	Website
Campbell Leadership Descriptor	A self-assessment designed to help individuals identify characteristics for successful leadership, recognize strengths, and identify areas for improvement	Vision Diplomacy Personal styles Management Feedback Personal energy Empowerment Entrepreneurialism Multicultural awareness	www.ccl.org/leadership/assessments/CLDOverview.aspx
DiSC Personality Test	A self-assessment of personality and behavioral style intended to improve work productivity, teamwork, and communication	Dominance Influence Steadiness Conscientiousness	www.discprofile.com/what-is-disc/overview
Emotionally Intelligent Leadership Inventory for Students	A 57-item evidence-based assessment that measures how often students engage in behaviors that align with emotionally intelligent leadership	Nineteen emotionally intelligent leadership capacities categorized into the following domains: ● Consciousness of self ● Consciousness of others ● Consciousness of context	www.wiley.com/WileyCDA/WileyTitle/product Cd-111882l661.html
Leadership Competencies Scorecard 2.0	A competency-based framework that identifies and integrates a diverse array of characteristics described in scholarly and professional writings as being important for effective leadership	Analytic competencies Personal competencies Communication competencies Organizational competencies Positional competencies	www.nacubo.org/Products/Publications/Leadership/What_Leaders_Need_to_Know_and_Do_A_Leadership_Competencies_Scorecard.html

(Continues)

TABLE 11.1 *(Continued)*

Inventory Tool	Description	Key Metrics	Website
Leadership Practices Inventory (LPI)	A 30-item self-report measure that assesses leadership behaviors based on the five practices of exemplary leadership model	Model the way Inspire a shared vision Challenge the process Enable others to act Encourage the heart	www.leadershipchallenge.com/leaders-section-assessments.aspx
Leadership Style Inventory (LSI)	A tool designed to assist in the reflective learning process, to help people explore and better understand their own approach to leadership by distinguishing two leadership style preferences	Directive style Consensual style	www.nacubo.org/Products/Organizational_Development_Series/Organizational_Development_Series_The_Leadership_Style_Inventory.html
Myers-Briggs Type Indicator (MBTI)	A self-report questionnaire that indicates personality types based on the psychological preferences identified by Carl Jung. These preferences are indicative of how individuals perceive the world and make decisions	Sensation Intuition Feeling Thinking	www.myersbriggs.org/my--mbti-personality-type/mbti-basics
Clifton Strengths Finder	A language of the 34 most common talents based on a 40-year study of human strengths, Gallup developed the assessment to help people discover and describe these talents	Thirty-four strengths, including but not limited to the following: • Achiever • Belief • Consistency • Empathy • Includer • Strategic • Win others over	strengths.gallup.com/default.aspx
True Colors Personality Test	A self-assessment of personality traits identifying individual strengths and challenges across four personality types	Green = independent thinkers Gold = pragmatic planners Orange = action-oriented Blue = people-oriented	truecolorsintl.com

potential leadership inventory findings are broad enough to be made relevant to the leadership work needed in higher education. For example, admissions counselors, associate professors, and public safety professionals, despite their different work requirements and institutional responsibilities, may use the findings from these inventories to inform their leadership approach in college settings. Finally, the listed inventories present a series of metrics for what is understood to be effective leadership practice. All have the potential to be useful for encouraging reflection, which is arguably more valuable than the score or descriptive profile that any inventory provides. Tracking your scores on these various inventories over time may help to further clarify your strengths and areas of improvement. Note that inventories and self-ratings are always subject to the limitations of our self-report and self-perception. The way we see ourselves and the way we intend to behave are often inconsistent with how others may see us. For this reason, there is value in gaining the perspectives of others on our leadership performance, needs, and strengths. Mentoring and assessment methods that allow for colleagues or friends to constructively share their perspectives—methods like 360-degree feedback—can be most helpful in this regard.

Committing to Developing as a Leader

Step three is committing to developing as a leader. As described in Chapter 9, the idea of enhancing one's leadership competencies is particularly compelling because of the relationship between knowledge and behavior. Competencies have both a knowledge and a skill component. *Knowledge* refers to leaders' understanding of a concept. *Skill* refers to leaders' effectiveness in operationalizing the knowledge they possess and their strategic ability to effectively act on this information (Ruben, 2012). Both an understanding of the competency and a proficiency associated with effectively carrying out the competency are important. Leadership issues may arise because of the gap that often exists between theory and practice—or knowing versus doing (Pfeffer & Sutton, 2000). Note that an understanding of a leadership theory or concept does not naturally translate into action. It is also often the case that in our self-assessments, we blur the distinction between knowing and doing. In fact, without input from others, it's very difficult to separate knowledge and good intentions as we see them from the way these play out in practice from the perspective of others.

Reflective practice is essential to connecting knowledge and behavior. Simply put, reflective practice involves a commitment to consciously monitor and review your actions as a leader, the understandings that guided those actions, and the outcomes that result (Dewey, 1933; Lewin, 1952; Schön, 1984). Schön describes this practice as follows:

> The practitioner allows himself to experience surprise, puzzlement, or con-
> fusion in a situation which he finds uncertain or unique. He reflects on
> the phenomenon before him, and on the prior understandings which have
> been implicit in his behavior. He carries out an experiment which serves to
> generate both a new understanding of the phenomenon and a change in
> the situation. (p. 68)

In essence, the idea is to apply the scientific method to your own performance as a leader—to become, in effect, a leadership researcher—where your
own understanding and behavior and the outcomes that result from those
understandings and behaviors are the focus of the study.

However knowledgeable you are about your understanding and skills,
becoming a better leader is a lifelong process. Continuous improvement
requires continual experimentation and reflection, much as is the custom in
the research traditions of higher education. Through reflective practice, one
can revisit both the leadership philosophy and self-assessment findings as a
way of assessing continuing gaps, tracking progress on these areas that will
benefit from improvement, and identifying new areas in need of attention.
Part of this process includes receiving feedback from those who observe
your actions and reactions in specific contexts and situations, which provides a check on self-assessments that may be overly self-critical or self-
congratulatory.

Committing to reflective practice implies that time will be spent debriefing at the end of interactions, meetings, or events—that is, rethinking the
leadership concepts that guided one's actions, reexamining the way those
understandings were put into practice, and reflecting on those outcomes.
The following are some key questions to use in the reflective process:

- What was I trying to accomplish?
- What understandings—theories or concepts—guided my actions?
- How effective was I at translating my understanding into practice?
- Was the outcome what I expected or hoped for? If not, why not?
- What options should I have considered?
- What refinements should I consider for the future in my understanding
  and my actions?

A commitment to reflective practice will help you as a leader to translate the findings from self-assessment inventories into an applied and realistic plan for practice. Furthermore, by focusing on individual leadership
behaviors as a specific unit of analysis, demonstrating a commitment to
solicit and use feedback, and treating every leadership situation as a learning

opportunity, one can continue to experiment with and learn from various approaches to leadership that best address the needs of the unit, department, or institution.

Establishing a Leadership Development Plan

The three previous steps eventually lead to step four, where you begin to establish a clear, realistic, thoughtful, and action-oriented leadership development plan. Such a plan might involve any number of steps, which include the following:

- Become a student of leadership theory and practice
- Identify role models from whom you can learn
- Make every situation a learnable moment and an opportunity to become a better leader
- Look for informal and formal opportunities to lead and learn both within and beyond your unit, department, or institution
- Establish goals and a plan in every influence situation
- Monitor your behavior
- Debrief to assess your effectiveness (compare your goals and plan the outcome)
- When possible, seek third-party assessments from others

McCauley, Kanaga, and Lafferty (2010) offer a wide array of approaches to individual leadership development, organized into five broad categories:

Developmental Relationships
- Mentors
- Professional coaches
- Manager as coach
- Peer learning partners
- Social identity networks
- Communities of practice

Developmental Assignments
- Job moves
- Job rotations
- Expanded work responsibilities
- Temporary assignments
- Action learning projects
- Leadership roles outside work

Feedback Processes
- Performance appraisal
- 360-degree feedback
- Assessment centers

Formal Programs
- University programs
- Skill training
- Feedback-intensive programs
- Personal growth programs

Self-Development Activities
- Reading (books, articles, online resources)
- Speakers and colloquia
- Professional conferences and trade shows
- Fireside chats, town hall meetings, all-staff meetings (p. 45)

Your college or university may offer any number of these opportunities for leader development, often depending upon the organization's "climate for development" (McCauley, Kanaga, & Lafferty, 2010, p. 50). This idea reappears in the final chapter on collective leadership development initiatives. For now, it is most important to recognize the need for articulating a plan for development—one that bridges the theories, concepts, and ideas to emerge from self-reflection and self-assessment with the concluding step of following through.

Following Through

The fifth step on the leadership development journey is following through on the identified plan. The plan and the various methods of self-assessment and self-reflection are only worthwhile if they are put into action to enhance one's own leadership practice and to strengthen the project, unit, or department that one leads. This emphasis on action is consistent with what Herminia Ibarra (2015a) offers in her recent text, *Act Like a Leader, Think Like a Leader*. In discussing what she identifies as the outsight principle, Ibarra states, "The only way to think like a leader is to first act: to plunge yourself into new projects and activities, interact with very different kinds of people, and experiment with unfamiliar ways of getting things done" (p. 5). These new ways of acting change not only how we think, according to Ibarra, but also who we become along the way. She continues by acknowledging the following important point about leadership development, one that is especially relevant to leadership in higher education:

Who you are as a leader is not the starting point on your development journey, but rather the outcome of learning about yourself. This knowledge can only come about when you do new things and work with new and different people. You don't unearth your true self; it emerges from what you do. (p. 5)

For Ibarra, it is through action—and what we would describe as following through on the plans that you initially set for yourself as a leader—that you can begin to learn how to lead. As she suggests, "Knowing the kind of leader you'd like to become is not the starting point on your development journey, but rather the result of increasing your outsight" (p. 186). The value of following through and acting upon these leadership plans cannot be underestimated.

A commitment to personal leadership development—like any personal change—is challenging. Behavior change relative to leadership practices can be particularly difficult for higher education faculty and staff. As mentioned throughout this text, education and socialization as faculty and technically focused staff members provides preparation for *individual* success. The preparation and socialization of faculty, in particular, often teaches members to be independent, candid, defensive, and assertive. While these characteristics may well be important for individual success, they are generally unrelated—sometimes even antithetical—to characteristics necessary for effective leadership. Furthermore, as faculty learn to defend their work, argue on behalf of specific claims, and develop an independent point of view, these same behaviors may pose potential liabilities for leadership development, where careful listening; encouraging feedback, negotiation, and compromise; asking for help; cultivating interdependent relationships; and developing engaged followers are critical.

Finally, trained as creative thinkers, faculty and technical professionals tend to be very effective at developing plans—which is certainly an important capability for leaders. However, given faculty's training and socialization, implementing those plans with others can often be very challenging. Without effective implementation, our actions can easily contribute to stereotypes associated with the slow pace of change within higher education.

Conclusion

The most proactive and constructive approach to refining leadership competencies and behaviors is much the same as it would be for improving musical or athletic competency: Continue the commitment to further development and broadening of your knowledge and skills, devote serious attention to reflective practice, look for opportunities and helpful tools to aid in genuine self-reflection, solicit others' evaluations and improvement suggestions, identify and learn from others who possess the desired knowledge and skills, look for opportunities to practice and improve, and stay the course. The lifelong leadership development journey may seem arduous, unpredictable, and complex, yet by maintaining a commitment to continually develop one's skills as a leader, there will be opportunities to enrich and enhance one's overall leadership experience.

For Further Consideration

1. Leadership Competency Scorecard

Complete the Leadership Competency Scorecard presented in Appendix B (self-assessment), and ask a friend or colleague to complete the same inventory with you in mind (other-assessment). Focusing on the results for effectiveness in practice, compare the findings of the self-assessment and other assessment to develop a profile of leadership strengths and leadership areas that can be improved.

2. Personal Leadership Plan

Complete one of the self-assessment inventories described in this chapter. Develop a personal leadership plan that aligns with your personal and professional goals. Based on the findings of the self-assessment, identify your core strengths and areas that would benefit from improvement. What specific actions can you take to enhance your leadership effectiveness? Place these intended actions on a timeline that you can revisit periodically as part of your personal leadership plan.

12

ENVISIONING AND ACHIEVING EXCELLENCE

A Rubric and Practical Tool for Organizational Review and Improvement

---

In This Chapter

- What is organizational excellence, and how does it differ from and relate to academic excellence?
- What are the characteristics of outstanding organizations?
- What best-practice models or rubrics are applied to the design, assessment, or improvement of organizations in sectors other than higher education?
- What is the Excellence in Higher Education framework, and how can it be useful as a rubric for leadership in higher education?

The pursuit of excellence is a fundamental aspiration of all leaders. But what, exactly, do we mean by the term *excellence*, and what tools are available to help leaders imagine and pursue this vision? Particularly for those who work in higher education, mention of the word *excellence* typically evokes images of academic and professional distinction, along with a group of outstanding faculty, staff, students, programs, and facilities. The importance of academic excellence is widely acknowledged and always a cause for recognition and celebration. A somewhat less obvious—but no less important—sense of excellence in higher education relates to the way institutions and departments are organized and led and how they operate.

In thinking about excellence, one can easily overlook the fact that in higher education, as in other contexts, organizational and leadership excellence provide the necessary foundation for enabling and sustaining excellence of the core mission. In colleges and universities, for instance, the foundation necessary for achieving academic excellence is effective organizational and leadership practices. Such practices help to recruit and retain outstanding faculty, staff and students, and create and sustain the kinds of organizations in which individuals are able to do great work.

Unfortunately, within higher education, there are few, if any, models available to help leaders envision the components of organizational excellence. Missing also are rubrics to guide in their development, and practical tools for leaders to use as they pursue these aspirations.

Assessment, planning, and improvement are critical elements of organizational effectiveness. These are three familiar concepts within higher education, and every campus has administrators, faculty, and staff who are committed to engaging in these activities within their units. What is often lacking, however, is a systematic and integrated approach to assessment, planning, and improvement that is applied consistently within the varying units of the institution and is also appropriate for bridging the cultural gaps among academic, administrative, student life, and service organizations. In much the same way that rubrics have been recognized as being useful to systematic course design and assessment across multiple disciplines, comparable templates can also be extremely valuable for designing, planning, assessing, and improving organizations. *Excellence in Higher Education* (EHE) (Ruben, 2016a)—a framework for organizational design, assessment, innovation, and continuous improvement—is one such tool. A description of the rationale and the steps involved in implementing the EHE model are the focus of this chapter.

When would a leader consider using an approach such as EHE? In fact, the framework can be a very helpful tool for addressing a variety of challenges. For instance, EHE would be applicable in any of the following situations:

- You were recently appointed leader of your department, and you feel the need to get a quick but comprehensive sense of your leadership team and staff and to identify organizational strengths and areas in need of improvement.
- You have been asked to conduct a full review of your administrative unit with an eye to considering where significant improvements might be made in the services offered.
- You and your unit are thinking about launching a new master's program, and you lack a framework to evaluate the merits of idea and to guide the design process.
- In anticipation of accreditation, you want to begin a systematic review of your department and its programs.
- The student affairs unit has undergone a number of evolutionary changes over the past several years in response to changing environmental demands. There is now a need to step back and take stock of where

the department stands, how well the division is functioning, whether current programs and services are effectively serving their intended constituencies, and if there are unaddressed needs for change.

- You are on the leadership team of an interdisciplinary initiative that was launched three years ago with participants from multiple disciplines and services. You feel it is time to take stock of where things stand and to develop a list of priorities for strategic planning in the future.

The Baldrige Framework

Of the various approaches to systematic organizational review, planning, and improvement designed to address precisely the kinds of organizational situations in the preceding list, none has been more successful or more influential than the Malcolm Baldrige model (Baldrige National Quality Program, 2015a).[1] The EHE (Ruben, 2016a) approach and framework were inspired by the Baldrige framework and adapted specifically to the context of higher education. In the first sections of this chapter we describe the basic tenets and approach of the Baldrige framework and provide background to a detailed discussion of EHE as a valuable tool for helping leaders envision, pursue, and enact a systematic approach to organizational assessment, planning, and improvement at all levels within colleges and universities.

Named after U.S. secretary of commerce Malcolm Baldrige, who served from 1981 until his death in 1987, the Malcolm Baldrige National Quality Award (MBNQA) program was established by the U.S. Congress in 1987. The intent of the program is to promote U.S. corporate effectiveness. To do this, the Baldrige model provides a systems framework for organizational assessment that blends scholarly concepts of organizational theory and behavior, principles from the professional literature, and successful organizational and leadership practices. The Baldrige organizational quality framework and program accomplishes the following: (a) identifies the essential components of organizational excellence; (b) recognizes organizations that demonstrate these characteristics; (c) promotes information sharing by exemplary organizations; and (d) encourages the adoption of effective organizational principles and practices. As such, the program provides a useful conceptual framework and helpful guide for leaders as they envision and pursue organizational excellence in a variety of contexts and settings.

The following core concepts and values are central to the model:

- A clear and shared sense of purpose (mission) and future aspirations (vision)

- Effective leadership and governance processes
- Strategic planning processes, plans, priorities, and goals
- Excellent programs and services
- Strong and reciprocally valued relationships
- Qualified and dedicated employees and a satisfying work environment
- Systematic review processes for the assessment of outcomes
- Comparisons with peers and leaders
- Gathering and sharing information
- Documenting outcomes and achievements

The Baldrige view is that these values are essential for organizations to function effectively. Those who work in colleges and universities recognize that these concepts are especially pertinent to the work of college and university leaders reviewing the quality of our organizations, collecting and using data to assess and improve organizational effectiveness, and more generally, responding to the numerous challenges posed by the rapidly changing higher education landscape.

Baldrige Categories

The Baldrige framework covers seven categories that are illustrated in Figure 12.1. Although the language and definitions used to describe the framework

Figure 12.1. Baldrige view of organizations: A systems perspective.

The Malcolm Baldrige framework consists of seven categories or themes that are viewed as critical to the effectiveness of any organization—small, large, manufacturing, service, healthcare, or education.

Source. From Baldrige Performance Excellence Program. 2015. *2015–2016 Baldrige Excellence Framework: A Systems Approach to Improving Your Organization's Performance.* Gaithersburg, MD: U.S. Department of Commerce, National Institute of Standards and Technology. Retrieved from www.nist.gov.baldrige

have changed over the years, and vary somewhat from sector to sector, the seven categories are constant.

The model has been an extremely popular framework for organizational review in many settings. In addition to the national programs, parallel programs exist in many states, and versions of the Baldrige program are available for the healthcare and education sectors, as discussed later. In addition to the more than 1,500 organizations that have applied for Baldrige review and recognition (Baldrige National Quality Program, 2015a), the National Institute of Standards and Technology estimates that thousands of organizations have used the criteria for self-assessment. Consider the following example from a fast-food chain:

> Pal's Sudden Service received the Baldrige Award in 2001. Since then, the quick-service restaurant chain's founder, Pal Barger, has repeatedly shared why he considers his company's heavy investment in employee training to be cost-effective—despite high turnover in the industry. Other business leaders reportedly ask Pal, "What if you spend all this time and money training someone and then they leave?'" His response to them: "Suppose we don't, and then they stay?" (Schaefer, 2015)

There are numerous case studies, professional endorsements, and leader testimonials that speak to the benefits of the Baldrige model in advancing organizational insight and practice (Baldrige National Quality Program, 2015d). Beyond these qualitative reports, a number of quantitative studies also provide evidence of value of the process. Organizations rated highly in terms of Baldrige criteria have been shown to outperform other organizations financially and also report increased job satisfaction, improved attendance, reduced turnover, improved quality, reduced cost, increased reliability, increased on-time delivery, fewer errors, reduced lead time (customers), fewer complaints, higher customer retention rates (profitability), improved market share, and better performance in a range of other sector-specific indicators (Baldrige, 2015c; Heaphy & Gruska, 1995; Jacob, 2004; Jacob, Madu, & Tang, 2012; Przasnyski & Tai, 2002).

Baldrige in Higher Education

Recognizing its cross-sector relevance, modified versions of the Baldrige framework were developed for education and healthcare in 1999. The education criteria (Baldrige National Quality Program, 2015b) were intended to be broadly applicable to school and educational settings at all levels, public or private.

How can the model be useful for leaders in higher education? As noted in Chapter 9, higher education qualifies as a unique organizational context in degree, if not in kind, yet one can also make a strong case for the view that effective organizations and effective leaders in higher education have many of the same attributes required for successful organizations in other sectors.

The core values listed earlier provide some sense of the cross-cutting relevance of Baldrige themes, and the following list of desired organizational characteristics offers further insight into the potential applicability of the model for higher education.

- Effective *leadership* that provides guidance and ensures a clear and shared sense of organizational mission and future vision, a commitment to continuous review and improvement of leadership practice, and social and environmental consciousness
- An inclusive *planning process* and coherent plans that translate the organization's mission, vision, and values into clear, aggressive, and measurable goals that are understood and effectively implemented throughout the organization
- *Knowledge of the needs, expectations, and satisfaction/dissatisfaction levels of the groups served by the organization*; operating practices that are responsive to these needs and expectations; and assessment processes in place to stay current with and anticipate the thinking of these groups
- *Focus on mission-critical and support programs and services* and associated work processes to ensure effectiveness, efficiency, appropriate standardization and documentation, and regular evaluation and improvement—with the needs and expectations of beneficiaries and stakeholders in mind
- A workplace culture that encourages, recognizes, and rewards excellence, employee satisfaction, engagement, professional development, commitment, and pride and synchronizes individual and organizational goals
- Development and use of *indicators of organizational performance* that capture the organization's mission, vision, values, and goals, and provide data-based comparisons with peer and leading organizations; widely sharing this and other information within the organization to focus and motivate improvement and innovation
- *Documented, sustained positive outcomes* relative to organizational mission, vision, values, and goals, the perspectives of groups served, and employees, all considered in light of comparisons with the accomplishments of peers, competitors, and leaders (Ruben, 2004)

The EHE Framework

The EHE model was developed by the Center for Organizational Development and Leadership at Rutgers University specifically for use within colleges and universities. Particular attention was devoted to customizing the model to the mission, culture, and language of higher education. The first version was published in 1994 and has been revised through a number of subsequent editions.[2] The 2016 version (Ruben, 2016a) is structured to be appropriate for use by higher education institutions of various types, as well as by individual units of all kinds within colleges and universities—business, student services and administration, as well as academic.

The EHE framework has a number of attributes that make the particularly appropriate and useful:

- Integration with general organizational effectiveness frameworks and built around widely accepted standards of organizational effectiveness
- Consistency with the language and culture of higher education
- Alignment with accreditation frameworks and standards
- Application in academic, student life, service, and administrative organizations
- Appropriate for departments, programs, centers, advisory councils, governing groups of any size, or an entire institution
- Tool to inventory and integrate ongoing assessment, planning, and improvement initiatives
- Appropriate for facilitating systematic review and creating baseline measures
- Language for information and best practices sharing across institutions, departments, and programs
- Appropriate for broadening participation in leadership and problem-solving
- Useful as a method for expanding organizational and leadership knowledge and understanding

EHE Categories

The EHE model, like the Baldrige framework from which it takes its inspiration, consists of seven categories that are deemed essential to organizational effectiveness. These categories are considered to be components of excellence in any educational enterprise—program, department, school, college, or university. The seven categories are viewed as distinct but interrelated components of higher education organizations and are seen as components of an interrelated system, as shown in Figure 12.2.

While this model is similar to the Baldrige model, the framework, standards, and language are adapted to the culture of higher education and to common standards of accrediting. To a far greater extent than Baldrige, EHE uses concepts and terms that are familiar and accepted within colleges and universities.

Figure 12.2. Excellence in Higher Education: The framework and categories.

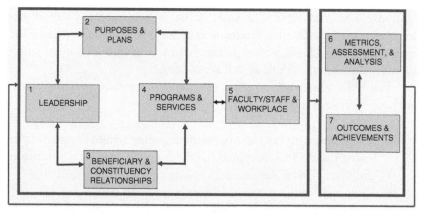

Note. This is a Baldridge-inspired framework adapted to higher education language and cultures. From Ruben B. D. (2016). *Excellence in Higher Education.* (8th edition). Sterling, VA: Stylus.

Category 1: Leadership
Category 1 considers leadership approaches and governance systems used to guide the institution, department, or program; how leaders and leadership practices encourage excellence, innovation, and attention to the needs of individuals, groups, or organizations that benefit from the programs and services of the organization and how leadership practices are reviewed and improved.

Category 2: Purposes and Plans
Category 2 considers how the mission, vision, and values of the institution, school, department, or program are developed and communicated; how they are translated into goals and plans; and how faculty and staff are engaged in those activities. Also considered are the ways in which goals and plans are translated into action and coordinated throughout the organization.

Category 3: Beneficiary and Constituency Relationships
Category 3 focuses on the groups that benefit from the programs and services offered by the program, department, or institution being reviewed. The category asks how the organization learns about the needs, perceptions, and priorities of those groups, and how that information is used to enhance the organization's reputation and working relationships with those constituencies.

Category 4: Programs and Services
Category 4 focuses on the mission-critical programs and services offered by the institution, department, or program under review and how their effectiveness is maintained and enhanced. The most important operational and support services are also reviewed.

Category 5: Faculty/Staff and Workplace
Category 5 considers how the program, department, or institution being reviewed recruits and retains faculty and staff, encourages excellence and engagement, creates and maintains a positive workplace culture and climate, and promotes and facilitates personal and professional development.

Category 6: Metrics, Assessment, and Analysis
Category 6 focuses on how the program, department, or institution assesses its effectiveness in fulfilling its mission, providing effective leadership, achieving its plans and purposes, meeting the needs of beneficiaries, offering quality programs and services, attracting and retaining excellent faculty and staff, creating a positive workplace climate, and effectively accomplishing other organizational functions.

Category 7: Outcomes and Achievements
Category 7 focuses on reporting outcomes and achievements. The category asks for information and evidence to document or demonstrate the quality and effectiveness of the program, department, or institution, which is the focus of the review.

Baldrige and Accreditation

The broadly stated purposes of Baldrige and EHE have much in common with those of the regional and program accreditation processes that are familiar in higher education. As described in the standards of one of the regional accrediting associations, the goal of the accreditation process is to "stimulate . . . evaluation and improvement, while providing a means of continuing accountability to constituents and the public" (Southern Association of Colleges and Schools Commission on Colleges, 2012, p. 2), and much the same can be said of the Malcolm Baldrige framework. As with accreditation frameworks, the Baldrige and EHE approaches emphasize the need to broadly define *excellence*; value leadership and planning; establish clear, shared, and measurable goals; create effective programs and departments; conduct systematic assessments of outcomes; and engage in comparisons with peers and leaders.[3] The frameworks also share in common the position that reviewing, planning, and continuously improving are fundamental to institutional effectiveness and should be thoroughly integrated into the fabric of every institution aspiring to excellence (Baldrige National Quality Program, 2015a, 2015b; Middle States Commission, 2014; North Central Association, 2015; Western Association of Schools and Colleges, 2013).

The most fundamental characteristic of the Baldrige, EHE, and accreditation frameworks is a commitment to an iterative process of mission-based goal setting, assessment, and improvement. By emphasizing the importance of clear purposes and aspirations, the evaluation of departmental and institutional effectiveness, and the use of this information for continuous improvement, the Baldrige and EHE frameworks integrate the core values and standards emphasized through accreditation into the day-to-day activities of the organization. While these approaches are not a substitute for accreditation, they are compatible with and reinforce accreditation values and standards in a number of useful ways. Figure 12.3 shows the common themes across these frameworks.

Figure 12.3. Core principles of Baldrige-based and accreditation frameworks.

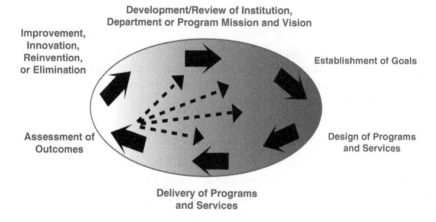

The EHE Process

The most common method for presenting the EHE program is a retreat or workshop. When used in this way, a workshop might last one or one and a half days. This approach has the advantage of generating an intensity that is difficult to achieve with other methods and providing a strong foundation for follow-up on projects to address improvement priorities in weeks and months ahead, as shown in Figure 12.4.

Figure 12.4. The EHE process.

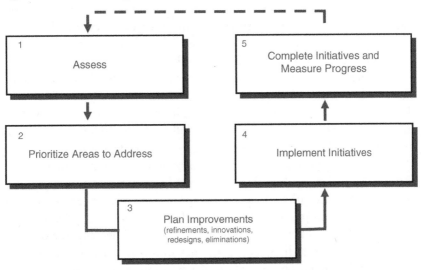

There are many other ways in which the EHE program can be implemented. For example, it can be presented in three half-day sessions, or each category can become the focus of a series of one- or two-hour sessions.

Whatever approach is used, completion of EHE consists of a step-by-step process moving through the seven categories one at a time. For each category, the steps include the following (Ruben, 2016a):

- Discussing the basic themes and standards for the category
- Brainstorming a list of strengths and areas for improvement for the unit with respect to the category
- Reviewing best practices in the category as implemented by leading organizations
- Scoring the unit in the category on a 0% to 100% scale to capture colleagues' perceptions of the extent to which the unit is fulfilling the standards of the category[4]

To illustrate, Category 2 focuses on purposes and plans (see Table 12.1). This category concentrates on developing and implementing organizational directions, aspirations, planning, and plans. It begins with the session leader or facilitator talking with members of the unit about how their institution, department, or program reviews, refines, and/or reaffirms their mission, vision, and values and how the unit develops plans and goals. The category then considers how these organizational directions are translated into priorities and action steps and implemented in a coordinated manner to foster continuing innovation and improvement. A detailed discussion of the elements of the category is provided in the *Excellence in Higher Education Guide* (Ruben, 2016a). Generally, participants are asked to review the descriptive material prior to the workshop so that they can familiarize themselves with the categories and areas to be addressed within each.

Outlines and discussion guides are provided in the *Workbook and Scoring Instructions* (Ruben, 2016c), a typical page of which is shown in Table 12.1. Slides and facilitator guidance are provided in the *Facilitator's Guide* (Ruben, 2016a). The *Facilitator's Guide* also includes additional information and structured exercises that are helpful for addressing the details of each category.

In exploring each category and assessing how thoroughly the program, unit, or institution is addressing the themes in each category, group discussion focuses on strengths and areas for improvement relative to that category, using the questions provided. Lists are made of strengths and potential areas in need of improvement—which might be minor refinements major transformations—and the discussion continues until the participants feel they have covered all questions and all excellence criteria to be considered in this category.

In preparation for scoring, a list of exemplary practices for this category is reviewed (see Table 12.2). Detailed instructions for scoring are discussed next; participants then complete individual ratings of the effectiveness of the unit in the category under discussion. In the example being considered, the

TABLE 12.1
Purposes and Plans Guiding Questions

Focuses on the planning process and how missions, aspirations, and values are developed and communicated, how they are translated into goals and action steps and coordinated throughout the organization, and how faculty and staff are engaged in these processes.
Is there a formalized planning process?
How are faculty/staff engaged in developing and implementing plans?
Does an up-to-date, written plan currently exist?
Does that plan effectively translate the mission, vision, and values into priorities, measurable goals, and action steps with specified roles and responsibilities?
How does the plan take account of current strengths and areas in need of improvement, innovation, or elimination?
Does the plan consider resource needs?
Are the plans and goals synchronized with those of the larger organization or institution?

TABLE 12.2
Exemplary Practices: Purposes and Plans

A clear and shared sense of the organization's purpose and aspirations is present.
A formal planning process is in place and understood by all.
Plans are built fully synchronized with the mission, vision, and values of the organization and institution.
Plans include short- and long-term goals.
Sufficient time and resources are allocated for benchmarking/peer review research, environmental scanning, and the development and pilot testing of innovations.
Plans include clear, measurable, ambitious goals and action steps and a strategy for monitoring progress to completion.
Plans identify possible programs and services that should be improved as well as programs and services that are candidates for major renovation or discontinuation.
Resources, climate, culture, and peer comparisons are integral to the planning process.
Plans anticipate and allow for addressing strategic opportunities and unexpected events and crises.
Plans, goals, and action plans are broadly communicated and enthusiastically supported and pursued throughout the organization.

rating is based on how fully participants believe their program, department, or institution is addressing the standards identified for Category 2, Purposes and Plans. A summary of scoring guidelines is provided in Table 12.3.

The scoring for each category is conducted anonymously, the ratings of participants are displayed, and the distribution of scores is discussed. The mean rating for the group is then calculated and entered on a chart, which is also displayed and discussed after each category, and again at the conclusion of all categories. See Figure 12.5 for an example of ratings for a hypothetical institution, department, or program.

Once these steps have been completed for all seven categories, the list of areas of strength and those in need of improvement are reviewed and discussed further. Next, multivoting is employed to rank-order the priority areas for improvement across all categories in terms of importance, potential impact, and feasibility.[5]

The four to five most highly ranked priorities for improvement become the focus of attention for the unit and its leadership. Depending on the approach being used, the next step may be the formation of committees or teams to draft action plans for addressing each of the priority areas for

TABLE 12.3
Percentage Rating Guide

100% to 90%	• A superior approach; systematically addressing *all* dimensions of the category. • *Fully* implemented without significant weakness or gaps in any area. • Widely recognized leader in the category/item. • Systematic approach and commitment to excellence and continuous improvement *fully* ingrained in the organization and its culture
80% to 70%	• A well-developed, systematic, tested, and refined approach in *most* areas, addressing *most* dimensions of the category. • A fact-based assessment and improvement process throughout *most* of the organization with few significant gaps. • Recognized as an innovative leader in the category. • Clear evidence of effectiveness, innovation, and ongoing improvement throughout *most* areas of the organization and its culture.
60% to 50%	• An effective, systematic approach, responsive to *many* dimensions of the category. • Approach well implemented in *many* areas, although there may be unevenness and inconsistency in particular work groups. • A fact-based, systematic process in place for evaluating and improving effectiveness and efficiency in *many* areas. • Clear evidence of excellence, innovation, and continuous improvement in *many* areas of the organization and its culture.
40% to 30%	• An effective, systematic approach, responsive to *some* dimensions of the category. • Approach implemented in *some* areas, but some work areas in the early stages of implementation. • A systematic approach to assessing and improving effectiveness and efficiency in *some* areas. • Evidence of effectiveness, innovation, and ongoing improvement in *some* areas of the organization and its culture.
20% to 10%	• The beginning of a systematic approach to *a few* dimensions of the category. • Category criteria addressed in *a few* programs, services, activities, and processes. • Major implementation gaps inhibit progress in achieving the basic purpose of the category. • Evidence of effectiveness, innovation, and ongoing improvement in *a few* areas of the organization and its culture.
0%	• *No* systematic approach to category; anecdotal information on approach and implementation; not part of the culture of the organization.

Figure 12.5. A sample profile.

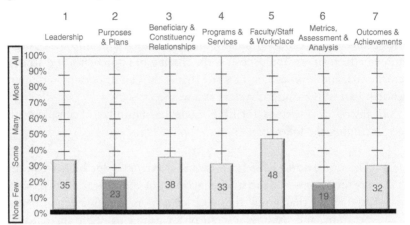

improvement. The action plan typically includes a summary of what needs to be done: the project mission, a list of key steps, identification of the individuals or roles that should be involved in the project, a proposed team leader, a project time line, estimate of resources, and identification of important outcomes and measures (Ruben, 2016a).

Members of the leadership team or other specially formed groups of faculty and staff move forward on the high-priority improvement initiatives. As these projects are completed, the group could return to the list of other areas for improvement to select the next round of needed improvements. Ideally, the process would be undertaken on an annual or semiannual basis.

The Value and Impact of the EHE Program

The applicability of a single organizational framework for reviewing and improving academic as well as administrative departments and programs is a unique and important attribute of the EHE approach. Within academic units, the process naturally focuses on how the college or department may function more effectively to fulfill its academic mission and aspirations; to evaluate its accomplishments and improvement needs; to address student learning and service needs; to identify departmental processes that can be streamlined; to address faculty and staff needs; to build its reputation on campus and beyond; and, in general, to function more effectively as a department or school for the good of all. Within administrative or service units, the focus is on mission and aspirations, the core programs and services the unit provides, ways to assess and improve effectiveness and efficiency, how to use technology to streamline work processes, how to enhance service relations with external constituencies, and so on. Using the same model within academic, student life, administrative, and service units creates a common, institution-wide vocabulary for assessing, planning, and improving organizational effectiveness. It also fosters the sharing of approaches and strategies across units, and it promotes the sense that each is an important and interdependent part of the campus system as a whole.

In any of these settings, the EHE model has a number of complementary uses, including the following:

- The framework defines a *standard of excellence* for higher education organizations—one that takes account of the variety of missions and aspirations that guide the work of any institution, department, or program, and outlines a strategy for achieving these standards in a manner that is based on the distinctive mission of the institution, department, or program being considered.
- EHE also offers a way to inventory and organize existing planning, assessment, and development initiatives into a coherent, cohesive, and integrated framework.
- EHE provides a blueprint for leaders in the creation of new academic or administrative units or programs or redesign of an existing department or program, by providing a view of the elements and considerations that should be taken into account in the design process.

For any organizational assessment or improvement program—accreditation, Baldrige, or the EHE process—the question always arises of whether the initiative has the intended value and impact. Within the higher education environment, good intentions and enthusiasm for a program's effectiveness are not persuasive. At Rutgers, two studies have been undertaken to measure the impact of the EHE assessment process (Ruben, Connaughton, Immordino, & Lopez, 2004; Ruben, Russ, Smulowitz, & Connaughton, 2007). Findings from both studies point to the impact of the EHE organizational self-assessment process in the acquisition of a knowledge and theory base, in the clarification of organizational strengths, and in the pursuit of critical improvement needs.

From our own experience and available evidence it would seem that the EHE program can be most helpful for leadership in envisioning organizational excellence, in identifying categories that are important to realizing a vision of organizational effectiveness, in identifying gaps within a particular institutional or organizational setting, and in providing a framework for leaders and colleagues to address improvement needs.

Whatever approach is used for the implementation of EHE, an invest-ment of time and energy is required. However, to the extent that the process results in identifying and addressing the most important priorities for organi-zational advancement, that investment is arguably a very good one.

To date, more than 50 academic and administrative departments at Rutgers have participated in the program. Roughly 50 other U.S. and international colleges and universities have found this program helpful in their assessment and improvement efforts. The guide has also been translated into Chinese by Wuhan University Press (Ruben, 2015c).

Conclusion

The specific aim of the EHE assessment process is to establish ways of track-ing progress, gauging effectiveness, and promoting meaningful and ongo-ing improvement in the quest for excellence. As noted, the approach can be extremely useful as a guide to organizational design, assessment, planning, and change throughout a college or university—in administrative, service, and student life organizations, as well as in academic departments and pro-grams, or entire institutions.

In addition to benefits directly associated with identifying immediate organization needs, the EHE process has demonstrated value in promoting organizational self-reflection, and increasing and enhancing communication through the establishment of a shared language for discussions of organi-zational excellence. Use of EHE also reinforces the importance of commit-ting to the use of a culture of evidence, establishing a foundation for using evidence to document and track performance, and promoting comparisons and benchmarking. Finally, participation in the EHE process contributes to leadership and professional development for faculty and staff, and enhances teamwork and a shared sense of organizational strengths and improvement priorities for both faculty and staff groups.

For Further Consideration

1. EHE Case Scenarios

Review the cases presented here and consider the questions that follow for each of the scenarios.

1. You are a new leader of your unit, recently appointed as director/dean. You see a need to get a quick but comprehensive sense of your leadership team, as well as of the strengths and areas for improvement in the unit.

2. You have been asked to conduct a full review of your administrative unit with an eye to considering where significant changes should be made in the services offered. This could include creating new initiatives or discontinuing existing programs or services.

3. You and your academic unit are thinking about launching a new master's program, and you lack a framework to evaluate the merits of idea and to guide the design process.

4. In anticipation of accreditation, you want to begin a systematic assessment of your department and its programs.

5. An interdisciplinary unit has been in existence for three years, with participants from multiple disciplines and services from collaborative roles played by multiple administrative and service units. You want to take stock of where things stand and develop a list of priorities for strategic planning in the next year.

- How would you decide whether EHE was appropriate? What questions or concerns might you have?
- How might EHE be helpful conceptually? Operationally?
- What goals would guide your thinking, and what outcomes would you hope for?
- Which criteria would you be most interested in analyzing throughout the process?
- If you chose to use the tool, who would you involve in the process?
- How would you prepare for EHE?
- How would you conduct the EHE process?
- In what ways would you follow up?
- What leadership challenges could the EHE process present?

Notes

1. For further information on the Baldrige National Quality Program, visit www.nist.gov/baldrige/

2. The first version of this model was called Tradition of Excellence and was published in 1994 (Ruben, 1994). Revised and updated versions were published under the current name, Excellence in Higher Education, in 1994, 1997, 2000, 2001, 2003, 2005, 2009/2010, and 2016.

3. For a comparative analysis of educational goals and outcomes identified by the regional and professional accrediting associations, see Association of American Colleges and Universities (2004, pp. 20–21).

4. In some instances, due to time restrictions or participant resistance to the idea of quantitative scoring of this type, the scoring component of the process can be omitted. While eliminating the scoring detracts from the precision of the rating process, the possibility of clarifying the extent of similarity/difference in perceptions among participants, and the establishment of a baseline, it does not seem to materially alter the process or its value in other ways.

5. The ranking could be done in two stages, beginning with rankings within categories, and then proceeding to an overall ranking across categories.

13

STRATEGIC COMMUNICATION

Developing Essential Habits for Effective Leadership

In This Chapter

- What is the strategic value of communication?
- What is the distinction between the informational and relational dimensions of communication, and why is this distinction important?
- What are the critical steps in translating communication understanding into effective leadership practice?
- What insights, principles, approaches, and tactics related to strategic communication and influence are particularly relevant for leaders in higher education?
- How can strategic communication be used as a general leadership tool for problem analysis and problem-solving?

The logic underlying our approach to strategic leadership presented in this chapter is rooted in an understanding of foundational principles of communication and human behavior. We have discussed a number of these core concepts previously, and in this chapter we highlight some of the most practical implications of these concepts as a foundation for understanding and applying the strategic leadership framework.

Communication Basics: The Foundation for Strategic Leadership

As discussed in Chapter 8, communication is an essential condition of the human experience—what Lee Thayer (2003) describes as the sine qua non of social life. As he observed, "The essence of being human is thus communicating-to and being communicated-with" (Thayer, 1968, p. 18). Communication takes place in many different contexts, including interpersonal, group, organizational, and community contexts. It may be accidental or intentional, planned or unplanned. Communication is so natural and fundamental—not unlike breathing—that we think of it as a very simple process, if and when we think about it at all. However, any analysis of communication dynamics and outcomes in relationships, families, organizations, and communities provides a wealth of evidence as to just how difficult it can be to make communication work well. Some might go so far as to suggest that there is no greater challenge in life—personally, professionally, organizationally, and internationally.

American colleges and universities provide myriad examples of the wonders and the difficulties of human communication and the need for more attention to strategy in human interaction. Higher education institutions bring together a collection of bright, highly educated, and independent thinkers, who come with interests and expertise in a wide variety of fields and professional affiliations. The success of the institution and fulfillment of its varying missions for its multiple constituencies requires individuals not only to work both independently and collaboratively and to maintain strong connections to their technical or disciplinary fields of training, but also to forge strong campus and interdisciplinary linkages in order to work effectively with faculty, staff, students, and outside stakeholders. Any thought that dealing with these challenges would be easier for particularly bright and well-educated people is quickly dispelled by a few months of campus life. In fact, it sometimes seems that precisely the reverse is true; one's technical and disciplinary expertise often increases the difficulty in sensegiving and sensemaking, particularly with those who lack similar goals, comparable roles, similar experience and education, or similar disciplinary orientations.

Across any number of higher education contexts, communication problems can be costly for the individual, group, and organization, leading to one or more of the following outcomes:

- Confusion and misunderstanding
- Blame and defensiveness
- Errors
- Personal conflicts
- Mismatched expectations
- Loss of confidence in colleagues and leaders
- Wasted time and resources
- Dissatisfaction of those who use the service or program
- Low morale
- Adverse consequences for culture and climate
- Disengagement

It is uncommon to go through a deliberate or methodical process when it comes to engaging in communication. In this chapter, we advocate doing just that, and we urge leaders to engage in what we call *strategic communication*. While strategic communication practices do not guarantee the absence of undesirable outcomes for leaders, such practices certainly lessen their likelihood of occurrence and their severity if and when they do occur. The discipline of a strategic approach might seem daunting at first, but when implemented regularly, it will become quite natural, less cognitively taxing, and as routine as everyday "talking."

Communication and Strategy

For these very reasons and others discussed throughout this volume, colleges and universities are excellent contexts for observing the full range of human communication dynamics at work, and there may be no more thought-provoking laboratory for those committed to learning about and mastering leadership theory and practice.

Consider the following example:

> After a yearlong search to fill one position allocated to the department by the dean, the unit is informed that it can hire two individuals from the finalist list instead of just one. Contrary to what one would expect, the dean's unanticipated sharing of this news at a department meeting is not met with delight or celebration, but rather with silence and indifference.

A seemingly ideal outcome, one that would have led the department, search committee, and chair to express gratitude, evoked quite different reactions. What might be considered an occasion for celebration over a new colleague and opportunity to move forward with a sense of cohesiveness instead became an incident that drove a deep wedge between a senior leader and other leaders and colleagues within the department. It could have been otherwise.

The explanation for this most improbable outcome can be found in the absence of attention to communication strategy by the leaders involved. Leaders are elected or selected to guide and coordinate this expansive array of interests and perspectives to create a whole that is, ideally, something more than the simple sum of the parts. But that is seldom a simple assignment, and almost never one in which the outcome can be achieved without careful planning and attention to the details of communication.

In this chapter we explore some of the factors that explain familiar results such as this one, and then revisit the example in some detail after reviewing key issues related to communication process and communication leadership strategy.

Considerations in Formulating and Implementing Strategy

Strategic, according to the *Oxford Dictionary* (2015), is defined as follows: "Relating to the identification of long-term or overall aims and interests and the means of achieving them." *Strategic,* in the sense we use the term here, refers to thoughtful, deliberate, purposeful, and future-oriented communication. A general theme implied in this definition and underlying this chapter is that effective leadership is not solely about being authentic or intuitive, acting instinctively, or simply "being yourself." No matter how small, all of the many critical leadership moments and challenges matter, and an element of strategy becomes critical to one's leadership during these moments and challenges. The way you handle each situation makes a statement about who you are and what matters to you. Each creates precedents, strengthens or diminishes the quality of relationships, and shapes the history and legacy in terms of which future actions will be judged.

The Importance of History

As discussed in Chapter 8, a leader's potential success is shaped by the ways in which messages are received by his or her followers. Strategic leadership involves formulating and implementing effective strategies that simultaneously consider the perspectives of the leader and his or her colleagues.

Communication events involve a sequence of verbal and nonverbal actions and responses. The sequential message sending and receiving between individuals creates a process, and that process, over time, creates a communication history—one that often has a profound impact on the delivery, reception, interpretation, and impact of any particular communication event. These histories have a very significant influence on the overall communication process.

Although communication histories are seldom the object of explicit focus in everyday activity, they are often more significant in shaping communication dynamics than the content of particular messages sent and received. The reason is that histories shape the way individuals attend to, interpret, and react to particular messages. Given this reality, effective leadership strategy must focus on the current communication events and challenges *in the moment,* but in a manner that also takes account of the background relevant to the situation at hand. Doing this effectively requires an awareness of the current circumstance and perspectives at play, an understanding of the relevant history, and a clear sense of how one's actions can contribute positively to the evolving history of the organization. Leaders must grapple, simultaneously, with the ways sensemaking is happening for a particular event at a specific moment in time, while also considering the long-term impact of particular communication dynamics.

Two corollary points related to the communication process are worth noting. First, while communication events are far more tangible and visible than communication histories, an understanding of the latter is essential to make sense of the former. Second, today's actions contribute to an unfolding history that will affect future encounters, and each of these actions contributes to the leader's legacy as well as the culture of a group, organization, or community with which future members and leaders must contend.

In the faculty hiring vignette described earlier, the history of interaction between the chair and department members and the dean played a central role in the sense made of the "good news" to create an extra position for the department. Very salient to that history from the perspective of the chair and department members was the fact that the candidate that the department recommended as its first choice—after an extensive search, interviews, and multiple meetings devoted to comparing candidates—was initially rejected by the dean with the explanation that he did not feel the candidate was as strong as some others. Without meeting with the search committee or department to discuss his thinking or hear the rationale for their preference, the dean went ahead and extended an offer to another candidate—the one he most favored. The department and chair were left wondering about the rationale for the dean's decision and action, and they were annoyed at not having been involved in a discussion with the dean on any of these issues. Did the dean have a vision of what was needed that differed from that of the department? Was the job description that had been collaboratively developed and approved by the dean and department now judged to no longer be relevant? Did the dean mistrust the ability or motives of the department in its analysis or recommendation process? Of significance is the fact that this series of events followed on the heels of two previous search cycles where the dean's role in the final selection process had also been viewed as mysterious, intrusive, and disrespectful to department members and its chair, and the dean had made efforts to assure the department that the process had been improved before beginning the current search. As this example illustrates quite dramatically, communication is fundamental to effective leadership strategy in a great many respects—beginning with understanding and taking account of the perspectives and relevant history, establishing and conveying clear expectations, and maintaining open lines for communication.

Communication Dynamics: Information and Relationships

It is easy to assume that one is being "strategic" in communication as long as he or she is sharing information that is relevant to the audience. Thinking of the example of the dean who conveyed the positive news about the two faculty hires, for instance, it is likely that the dean would assume his communication was appropriately strategic. However, the less-than-jubilant response from the faculty to what could have been a very positive event would suggest otherwise. A deeper understanding of strategic communication and influence reminds us of the importance of history, as well as the informational and relational dynamics associated with human communication as they operate in situations like this. As discussed in Chapter 8, in addition to the personal and organizational history that is relevant in any communication situation, both the content and relational dimensions of communication are also important to the process (Watzlawick, Beavin, & Jackson, 1967).

Every communication encounter has the potential to convey information and to shape the kind of relationships that develop. As a leader, you should continually remind yourself of the informational-relational duality in communication planning, actions, and analysis. Thinking about what to say is only the beginning; in addition, one needs to also consider how to say it, when to say it, to whom to say it, in what setting to say it, and how this communication event is likely to influence and be influenced by the relationships among those involved. These additional considerations serve as a reminder that the interpretation, and hence the impact, of leadership messages are fundamentally shaped, molded, and impacted by their recipient(s). This central underlying dynamic connects leaders and followers.

Thinking of communication in terms of its informational aspect focuses attention on striving to create desired outcomes through the management and coordination of meaning and the translation of meaning into desired actions. In general terms, this involves an iterative process of establishing goals, creating and transmitting messages, listening to and observing whether one's messages are attended to, discerning how these messages are interpreted, noting what actions result, and carrying forth this process while making necessary adjustments along the way. Thus, when a leader's purpose is to promote the sharing of knowledge, an idea, a perspective, or a point of view, the process should move through the steps depicted in Figure 13.1: Introduce/state purpose, explain, check for understanding, clarify and restate, and summarize the intended takeaways. The goal, of course, is to increase the likelihood that the message sent equals the message received, or, put another way, that the sensegiving behaviors match the sensemaking behaviors. Although this linear progression from the statement of purpose to the summary of intended takeaways may seem to be a prescriptive and tidy formula for effectively sharing new information, in practice, the dynamics and outcomes involved are complex and not nearly as predictable as one would like.

The complexity and unpredictability are magnified when the intended flow of information involves a number of individuals. This is the case, for example, when the communication chain begins with a senior leader in one part of the university and progresses to a series of other leaders in other units, such as a dean, chair, committee chair, and graduate program director. The initiator of messages in such cases may assume that information flows logically through the formal channels of the organization to those charged with letting "the troops" know about this new piece of information. Unfortunately, the flow from top level to the troops is problematic in so many cases, and the process often presents a real leadership challenge for those who initiate the original message and may well come to feel that they lose control over the process. This can be a particular problem if individuals in some units get reports while others do not. Communication across units occurs, leading some individuals to feel they are out of the organizational loop, which leads to misunderstanding and, at times, resentment. In other situations, those in the middle may communicate the initial message poorly and in ways not intended by the original source. Even when the conduit works reasonably well, the message received may be lost or distorted through negligence or by uninformed, recalcitrant, or oppositional colleagues.

Again referring back to the hiring vignette—which is emblematic of many organizational communication challenges—an important but omitted

Figure 13.1. Focusing on the informational dimension.

Informational Aspect of Communication
Primary goal: To share knowledge, an idea, a perspective, or a point of view
To increase the likelihood that sensemaking will match sensegiving

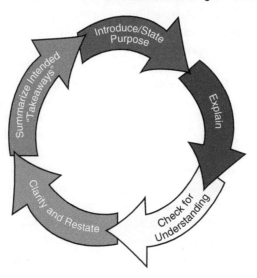

step for the dean and the department chair, the search committee, and the faculty of the department would have been to do more to be thoughtful in establishing and conveying their specific expectations for the search process, its goals, and the ultimate decision-making process that would be followed. For example: Was the expectation that the department would put forward one candidate or several? Should these be ranked in order of preference? Was the dean committed to following the department's recommendations, or did he view these merely as advisory? Particularly given the troubled history relative to recruitment and hiring, working to be as clear as possible about the process would have been a critically important goal. The department thought they had addressed these issues thoroughly—discussing and seemingly agreeing on the type of faculty member needed, collaboratively developing the job description, engaging the dean fully during campus visits of candidates, and chatting informally with the dean after each visit. In none of these information events did members of the department or chair come away with a sense that there were major differences of opinion or brewing problems.

In cases where multiple individuals are involved in the chain, the complexity is multiplied, and success requires that each member in the chain assumes responsibility for employing strategies that facilitate effective message flow and fidelity, using an approach such as that depicted in Figure 13.1. As the complexity and the number of messages and individuals involved increases, carefully crafted written messages—in the form of minutes or meeting summaries—designed with the intent of having these shared to provide a single and lasting record can be an important supplement to oral exchanges.

In addition to communicating to share information—the content dimension—there is also a relational dimension interwoven into every communicative event. With every message that is sent and received, the type of relationship between individuals involved in the communication encounter is being shaped. Relationships are critical in organizational settings; they have an influence on the interpretations of messages, reactions to new ideas, and also the establishment of trust and credibility. More generally, relation-building aspects of communication are vital to the creation of what might be termed *leadership capital*—which translates into accumulating support for a leader when things are going well and a willingness to suspend judgment and criticism in order to give a leader the benefit of the doubt when problems arise.

The relational aspect of any communication exchange is often more difficult for leaders to understand and analyze than the content—or information—dimension. Several points are helpful in this regard: First, most relationships are formed initially based on self-interest. Second, once established, relationships are often quite stable and resistant to change. Third, and perhaps most important for our present purposes, relationships must be nurtured and maintained over time. Often this nurturing occurs in subtle but significant ways through communication—an insight that leaders need to keep in mind.

The relationship cycle, like the information cycle, typically follows a sequence of steps, as depicted in Figure 13.2. The pattern includes the following elements: establishing rapport, showing interest, demonstrating empathy, respecting point of view, and acknowledging/thanking. Like the information cycle, these stages are not meant to be prescriptive strategies for cultivating strong relationships; rather, the stages capture some general areas of communication focus for creating, shaping, and reinforcing relationships. A number of other, more specific leadership behaviors can be helpful in enhancing relationships in the workplace. Such behaviors include the following:

- Listening
- Clarifying/establishing common goals
- Demonstrating mutual respect and support

Figure 13.2. Focusing on the relationship dimension.

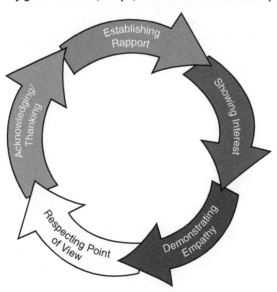

Relationship Aspect of Communication
Primary goal: To create, shape, and reinforce a relationship

- Clarifying expectations and boundaries
- Maintaining consistency
- Being transparent with knowledge, information, and ideas
- Displaying empathy
- Promoting a sense of teamwork—sharing the glory, sharing the pain
- Recognizing the accomplishments of others
- Using inclusive thought and language ("we," "us," "our" versus. "I," "me," and "my")
- Avoiding self-preoccupation and self-promotion—the "it all began when I became your leader" syndrome—and the temptations of narcissistic leadership (Chatterjee & Hambrick, 2007)

Other behaviors, such as those listed in Box 13.1, detract from and weaken relationship bonds.

In the hiring vignette discussed previously, there seems little doubt that relationship dimensions of the communication process were critical to the eventual outcomes. Absent any information on the dean's rationale or thinking about the process or candidates, and coming on the heels of other problematic search processes in previous years, faculty members felt ignored and disrespected, and the chair felt undermined—all outcomes that were quite predictable from a relational perspective. This situation led to faculty meetings and multiple e-mail exchanges questioning the dean and the dean's motives and contemplating an appropriate response. Although the hiring decision had already been made, the department decided to demand a meeting with the dean and to discuss the process and its consequences.

The dean agreed to meet after a number of requests from the chair and senior faculty. When he arrived at the meeting, he assumed the role of meeting chair and began with a short speech, explaining that a dean always knows things by virtue of his or her position that often couldn't be revealed to chairs or faculty. He then indicated that, in this case, it had been his intention all along to hire the person the department recommended in addition to offering a position to the candidate he preferred. So the "good news" was that the department was receiving an extra faculty line, and he went on to announce that he had already extended the offer to the department's preferred candidate. The dean expressed his unhappiness at the way the chair and faculty had disrespected his authority and failed to understand that he was operating in the best interests of the department throughout the entire process. The chair and faculty sat rather silently in disbelief. The chair had no prior knowledge of the decisions or the decision-making and neither did the search committee. The dean seemed quite surprised that there was anything short

---

BOX 13.1
Communicative Acts That Weaken Relationship Bonds

Just as relationships may be enhanced through communication strategies, relationships may also be weakened through communication. Porath's (2015) research on incivility in the workplace captures various communication behaviors that are regarded as rude and potentially damaging to relationships in the workplace. Porath identified the following as among the most often cited rude behaviors by bosses, in descending order of frequency:

- Interrupting people
- Being judgmental of those who are different
- Paying little attention to or shows little interest in others' opinions
- Taking the best tasks and leaving the worst for others
- Failing to pass along necessary information
- Neglecting to say "please" or "thank you"
- Talking down to people
- Taking too much credit for things

When asked to consider the rude behaviors that people most often admit to seeing in themselves, the following items were frequently cited:

- Hibernating into e-gadgets
- Using jargon even when it excludes others
- Ignoring invitations
- Being judgmental of those who are different
- Grabbing easy tasks while leaving difficult ones for others

---

of jubilation among the group. The meeting ended on a somber note. All in all, the vignette provides a classic example of a leadership failure—a failure that could have been a significant success, adding to the dean's credibility, respect, leadership capital, and leadership legacy, had the dean understood and applied basic concepts of strategy and communication.

A Rubric for Strategic Leadership

Colleges and universities, as noted throughout this text, are incredibly dynamic and complex places. The multiple missions, stakeholder concerns, decision-making processes, and potential areas of strategic focus present faculty and staff leaders with a seemingly endless number of communication choices as they endeavor to translate challenges into opportunities. For all these reasons, strategic leadership in higher education is critical. Strategic leadership extends beyond doing what comes naturally, and, as noted earlier, it is not simply about being yourself. Rather, strategic leadership—and strategic communication more specifically—involves a conscious and thoughtful analysis of one's communication-related choices.

All leaders encounter a number of challenging circumstances on a daily basis. Some are complicated and nuanced, such as the case study discussed in this chapter; others may be more routine and easily addressed. Every leadership action—no matter how significant or insignificant it may seem to be—is an important one in many respects. Each has consequences for the organization, for the leader, and for colleagues. Each action contributes to an impression of the leader and strengthens or diminishes the quality of the leader's relationships. Each decision also contributes to the foundation of how a leader's future actions will be judged, and each will ultimately contribute to one's lasting legacy as a leader.

The following rubric for strategic leadership outlines five critical steps that we believe can be extremely helpful in addressing the multiplicity of challenges associated with any leadership role. Using this framework requires conscious effort initially. Over time, however, it becomes a leadership habit—a habit that can greatly enhance one's effectiveness across a variety of situations. Each leadership situation can be viewed as a teachable moment— a moment that affords a leader the opportunity to apply, test, and further refine one's skills. The five steps are as follows:

1. Analyze the situation.
2. Define the audience(s).
3. Clarify goal(s).
4. Select a plan of action.
5. Debrief.

Analyze the Situation: Determine What Is at Stake

The first step involves a careful assessment of the circumstances confronting a leader. The critical questions one must ask are: What is at stake in this particular situation? Is the issue related to a program, department, or the institution; or to students, faculty, or staff members? Or, is the identity, credibility, or reputation of the leader at stake? How fundamental is this issue for those involved and for you as a leader? Being clear on the nature and significance of the issue(s) involved provides a necessary starting point for developing a thoughtful strategy, recognizing that a leader's handling of mundane as well as challenging situations can be important in the short run and can also shape the long-term legacy of an individual or organization. For example, the following might be at stake:

- For the program/department/institution:

  o Core purposes or aspirations
  o Critical values or principles
  o A problem to be addressed
  o Consistent practices
  o Organizational climate, culture, morale
  o Critical regulations or policies
  o Fair and equitable treatment
  o Recognition for contributions
  o Personal and professional standards and practices

- For you as a leader:

  o Clarifying your role as leader
  o Establishing your voice
  o Upholding personal values or principles
  o Setting or maintaining a precedent
  o Building your credibility
  o Defining your personal/leadership style
  o Demonstrating consistency in how you treat colleagues, students, or problems

Define the Audience(s): Who Needs to Hear From You on This If You Decide to Respond, and Why?

The second step allows the leader to determine the intended audience(s). It is far too easy to omit careful consideration of who you need to reach with a particular message, thereby missing an important stage of the strategic communication process. Possible audiences include the following:

- A specific individual or individuals
- Broader groups
  o Administrators
  o Colleagues
  o Students
  o Alumni
  o Members of advisory groups

Clarify Goal(s): What Exactly Do You Hope to Accomplish?

The third step calls for a leader to clarify goals in addressing the situation. Building on the assessment of the situation and the appropriate individuals with whom one might choose to communicate, it is essential to determine exactly what you want, need, or intend to accomplish and to define your message and methods based on these predetermined goals. Recognize that it is impossible to determine what would be an effective or ineffective strategy without knowing the goal. An interaction that is perfect for one goal can be problematic or disastrous when viewed in terms of other goals. Perhaps the most obvious examples are the potential problems that occur from a confusing goal such as listening to and learning from what others are thinking versus goals like persuading or informing. Very different approaches and messages are appropriate for each of these situations.

A myriad of communication goals may exist, including, but not limited to, any of the following:

- Provide input.
- Solicit input.
- Clarify facts.
- Demonstrate interest/concern.
- Persuade or influence.
- Demonstrate your expertise.
- Assure that your position, reaction, or perspective is clear.
- Be on the record.

Select a Plan of Action: What Do You Do?

The fourth step involves reviewing options and selecting a plan of action. At this point in the process, one must consider whether it makes sense to respond to the situation at all. This decision requires leaders to carefully identify the potential costs, benefits, barriers, and sources of resistance before selecting a course of action. This stage is often where leaders are inclined to begin, but it should be apparent why moving to action without first being clear about what is at stake, who the appropriate audience is, and precisely what the goals should be is a mistake.

During this fourth stage, leaders engage in the communication action determined to be most efficacious:

- Do nothing (e.g., not much at stake, benefits and costs of response not clear, the problem will likely take care of itself).

- Respond immediately.
  - Why?
  - How (e.g., e-mail, phone, plan in-person "spontaneous" hallway conversation, schedule a meeting)?
  - What is your message?

- Delay response (e.g., give the matter further thought, address in regular meeting, and then revisit previous options).
  - Why?
  - What might trigger further action?

Debrief: How Did It Go?

The fifth stage of this process, and perhaps the most frequently overlooked, relates to previous discussions of self-awareness and reflection. This debriefing stage leads one to consider how well the plan and execution worked, seeking and using feedback where available. The following questions can be useful during this stage:

- Did your strategy achieve the outcome you intended?
- How would those involved in the process describe how things went?
- Is further follow-up needed? (Repeat previous four steps iteratively.)
- What might you do differently in the future to address this kind of problem if it were to occur?
- What might you do differently in the future to prevent this kind of situation from developing (e.g., set clearer expectations, stay closer to the process, request periodic progress reports, assign several people to collaborate on the task)?
- What personal or professional leadership lessons can you take away from the situation?

This model for making strategic communication choices may be useful to all current and aspiring leaders in higher education. The decision to address a particular situation often carries enormous consequences. The model and stages presented call for one to move through the first four stages prior to designing and delivering a message. Like other topics presented in this book, the model and sets of questions are intended to present a simplified tool. Clearly, their application in any situation is a matter of subtlety and nuance, but the basic stages and their purposes remain constant.

Strategic Communication Insights, Tips, and Tactics

We conclude this chapter with a set of insights, tips, and tactics related to strategic communication. These thoughts align with the leadership communication principles offered throughout the text. In particular, leadership is a process of social influence that is achieved through communication that might be planned or unplanned, intentional or unintentional, used for good or for evil. Importantly, the goals, messages, and implications are shaped by the leader and also by those whom one leads. Thus, leaders must take careful account of those whom they assume and hope will be followers as they think through their own communication behaviors. Leadership is not possible without followership, and social influence is possible only with collective buy-in. These principles, like others offered in this chapter, are not meant to be a prescriptive list for influencing others; rather, they are meant to provide helpful guidance as to how leaders in higher education can improve their communication strategies.

Nothing is more important than being clear on your communication goals, your audiences, and your messages. The five-step strategic communication rubric encourages you to be clear as to what is at stake in a situation, identify and understand each of your audiences, thoughtfully select goals and messages, methodically select and implement plans of action, and complete the process by debriefing and reflecting on what transpired in order to learn from your successes, and more so from your failures. This model emphasizes the importance of clear communication goals, which we understand to be one of the most essential components of strategic leadership communication.

Colleagues won't know or care as much as you do about what you know and care about. Remember how long it has taken you to get to this point and the many experiences that brought you to your present understanding and sense of what needs to be done. To help others reach this same place, you need to create a similar process or set of experiences for them. Keeping this idea in mind, leaders must do all they can to create a compelling and descriptive vision of challenges and opportunities, what is possible, what should be done, and why, tailoring messages to the various goals and interests of the specific audience. Asserting one's authority to advance a particular position might work in the short term, but it will not build a base of trust and understanding, nor necessarily motivate action.

A single message seldom has much impact. Effective communication requires repetition. One message seldom motivates a change in behavior or opinion. Recall the metaphor offered earlier in this book related to the waves on the shore, whereby communication and social influence are understood to be parts of an ongoing process through which messages wash over individuals—somewhat analogous to waves repeatedly washing upon the shore. Over time these messages shape the sensibilities and responses of receivers, much as waves shape a shoreline. Exceptions to this subtle process are those rare, but in some instances life-changing, messages that can have a tsunami-like impact on message reception. In practice, do not count on your messages (meeting minutes, comments at meetings, etc.) flowing downward to colleagues in your organization in a logical, unadulterated way. Plan for and learn to appreciate the need for repetition. When it comes to important themes, expect that you may be bored with your messages before they get to the people you are trying to reach.

The simple message is the one that is remembered and retold. Let the elevator ride be your guide. Have a simple story about vision, benefits, and challenges at your disposal—one that could be told on an elevator ride going up or down three or four stories. The use of concise but powerful language can help to leave a memorable impact on those with whom you interact in your formal and informal leadership roles. Be prepared to elaborate if questions are asked and if you can be certain there is a genuine interest in learning more.

Do not count on getting agreement on what really happened, who did what, who was to blame, or why it was done this way and not that way. Each of us has a huge stake in our perceptions and interpretations of events and their significance. Recall that communication events maintain a history of their own, but this history can often serve as a trap or obstacle to forward movement. Effort is generally better spent going forward than arguing about history—though it is important for leaders themselves to do the debriefing necessary to learn from the past and to derive implications for future action.

In communication, less is sometimes more. More communication is not necessarily better communication. Flooding channels with too many messages—including in meetings and e-mails or engaging in too many interpersonal interactions with colleagues and others—can be problematic when it comes to ensuring that close attention is paid to what you have to say. Related to this strategy, it is essential for leaders to invest substantial time in activities that allow others to share their views and feel listened to and valued. Just as you cannot unring a bell, communication itself is irreversible. Information shared with one can become information shared with all, which often leads to problems related to sharing too much information. Finally, in some instances, clarity is not the intended goal; rather, ambiguity can be used strategically and purposefully by a leader to avoid making a definitive commitment on a particular issue or course of action (Eisenberg, 1984). All of these claims point to the potential importance of decisions about how much information to share, with whom, and when.

Process is often more important than content. In problem-solving and decision-making, it is important for leaders to keep in mind that the *process* of communication is often at least as important as the *content*. If processes are designed to provide opportunities for engagement and inclusion by relevant stakeholders, the final decisions that are reached are more likely to be accepted and supported—even when the final outcome is at odds with stakeholder preferences. As was poignantly demonstrated by the vignette discussed early in this chapter, failure to attend to process issues undermines and discredits decisions that would otherwise be embraced. Process inadequacies create a lasting legacy and diminish leadership capital with consequences that live on far beyond the recollection of the particulars of any single decision or action.

Devote particular care to problem situations, colleagues, and conversations. Leaders are periodically confronted with unpleasant or uncomfortable situations involving a colleague or student that require attention. When heading into these difficult conversations, take particular care in planning for them, addressing them, and documenting the results. In these circumstances, seeking and following the guidance and advice of more senior leaders and those experienced with such situations makes a great deal of sense. (The suggestions in Box 13.2 provide a useful foundation.)

Think carefully about the best leadership architecture in any situation. There are a variety of leadership architecture options—alternatives for structuring a leadership team for the purposes at hand of gathering and disseminating information related to planning, change, administration, team building, and changing a particular culture. Give careful consideration to the design and appropriate use of leadership architecture, taking into account the circumstances, goals, a leader's communication style, unit culture and climate, and other factors. Note the following models that one might adopt.

Mass communication (top-down, one-to-many) model: Using this model, the leader deals with everyone in public, shared forums, or through publicly shared messages to the entire organization. The advantages include that everyone has equal access to information, and the approach takes less time, less customized messaging is required, and less investment up front in communication activities is needed. However, the communication architecture can overload individuals with information that is not pertinent to all, lead to inattention to particularly important messages, and result in messages being directed to everyone when only certain individuals need to receive the information (e.g., rules pertaining to particular programs, reprimands, or new procedures).

Interpersonal (one-on-one) model: The leader communicates directly and personally with each individual on a one-to-one basis. This model, which is only viable in smaller organizations, allows for spontaneous, interactive, and customized communication. The interpersonal model allows leaders to gather personal perceptions, build coalitions, invent as he or she goes on, and plan strategy without public commitments. However, the lack of a systematic approach results in the uneven dissemination of information, leading to some individuals' perceptions and reality being privileged and others marginalized.

BOX 13.2
Difficult Conversations

Many faculty members and other university staff accept leadership positions with the noblest of goals: To move their organization forward, helping their organization make progress toward its stated mission and goals. Many of these new leaders have been very successful in pursuing their individual goals and are already acknowledged experts in their academic discipline or administrative area. They are eager to apply their skills and talents to pursuing goals that will have a broader, positive impact on their department, college, or campus. However, all their plans can be quickly derailed if they lack one crucial skill: The ability to engage effectively in difficult conversations.

The truth is, leaders at all levels find that a most fundamental part of their position involves dealing with people. In the process of pursuing the goals and reasons for which they accepted leadership roles, personal challenges arise, and some of these situations require engaging in difficult conversations—discussions with faculty members about denying promotions or tenure; talking to supervisors, employees, or union representatives about position eliminations and layoffs; or advising an employee that a grievance or other complaint has been filed against him or her. Most people view these situations as difficult, and while a difficult conversation doesn't automatically mean conflict and confrontation, most people avoid having such conversations because they fear the consequences. Handling these situations effectively is not an easy task, but the reality is that leaders will not be successful if they cannot handle the difficult conversations that confront them.

It is essential, therefore, that leaders deal with these issues immediately and effectively so that they can return to devoting their passion and energy to their original goal: moving their unit forward. Some basic guidelines that can help to achieve one's goals effectively when conducting difficult conversations are as follows:

(Continues)

Box 13.2 (*Continued*)

- Do not ignore the problem and hope that it will go away. It won't. It will grow and become more difficult to resolve.
- Don't react too quickly. Think through the situation and develop a plan. Consider applicable policies, rules, and regulations before having the conversation.
- Select an appropriate time and place. It's your job to set the stage and create the appropriate environment.
- The subject matter will tell you how difficult or uncomfortable the conversation will be. Don't gauge the effectiveness of the conversation by how comfortable you or the person with whom you are having the conversation feel.
- Be very clear about the message you want to convey. State the purpose of the meeting clearly at the opening; summarize next steps at the end.
- Establish a respectful decorum. Avoid trying to be light or humorous.
- Follow up with documentation that may be shared with the other person and appropriate others.
- Don't be reluctant to seek advice from others, including offices and individuals trained to handle difficult conversations. You do not have to do this alone!

From Elyne G. Cole, Associate Provost for Human Resources,
University of Illinois at Urbana-Champaign

Intermediary/mediated (gatekeeper) model: The leader forms and uses a layered structure. This model allows a leader to form structures based on particular needs or interests, such as program-centered or topical area committees or task forces, or the formation and utilization of an executive committee. Note that this model may be used in a way that purposefully includes or excludes influential members of the leadership underground. Considerations might include time or efficiency, effectiveness of existing structures, level of resistance or support, desire to socialize new people, the importance of validating or building a team, or opportunities for customized and topically focused information. Limitations include the potential exclusion of interested individuals from particular groups, and the challenges of sharing information across groupings. These limitations can be overcome to some extent through formalized and systematic information sharing and reporting activities.

Combinations: Any of these architectures can be used in any combination for particular purposes or for specific periods of time.

You won't be successful with everyone—or with any one person all the time.
Leadership roles in higher education can be incredibly consuming and
exhausting. To avoid burnout, always keep in mind the institution's best
interests and consider changing your strategies, approaches, and audiences
in a way that makes sense for you, your audience, and your institution.
Remain grounded in your interactions, but do not be afraid to evolve and
adapt in order to stay fresh. Moreover, be open to concluding that you have
reached a point of diminishing returns in your efforts with some potential
message recipients.

Do not underestimate the power of powerless language. Leaders are often
taught to use assertive and direct language; however, leaders must also
recognize the value of powerless language in certain situations. Expressing vulnerability, asking questions, talking tentatively, and seeking advice
are all forms of powerless language that can influence others. As Grant
(2013) notes, what is often described as powerless language can be incredibly powerful in building rapport and trust and gaining the admiration of
others.

*Plan to be pleased and surprised when colleagues acknowledge or thank
you for your work or accomplishments as a leader.* Some colleagues can be
counted on to notice and express their appreciation for your efforts on
behalf of the organization; many others cannot. Unfortunately, many colleagues will come forth to identify problems, failures, or gaps they identify
in your leadership, pointing to ways you can better meet their needs. This
is especially true for those who have not, themselves, occupied roles similar
to yours. Despite this predictable pattern, there may be useful information in the complaints and suggestions of your critics. Also, the compli-
ments and expressions of appreciation—as well as those who consistently
provide supportive communication—should be valued and not taken for
granted. It may be useful to structure a periodic organizational debriefing
session, where colleagues are asked to list and discuss "things that are going
well" and "things that can be improved." Such sessions can provide useful
information on organizational and leadership needs and can also remind
colleagues that it is important to focus on strengths as well as areas for
improvement.

Conclusion

The importance of strategic communication cannot be overstated. It is
far too easy to assume that one is an effective communicator based on life

experiences or professional or educational accomplishments. In reality, the demands of academic and administrative leadership in higher education can present a host of challenges for even the most accomplished faculty and staff leaders. For everyone, becoming a skilled strategic leader is a work in progress.

The remainder of the chapters in this part focus on various higher education functions that require strategic communication, including strategic planning, managing change, crisis leadership, and leadership transition and succession. The five-step rubric presented in this chapter, along with the related strategic leadership and strategic communication themes and tips, place a spotlight on communication behaviors that will be helpful in each of these endeavors.

For Further Consideration

1. Vignettes

Read through the following vignettes. For each, consider how the five steps in the strategic leadership rubric, and the insights, tips, and tactics discussed throughout the chapter, might be helpful in addressing, and potentially preventing, these situations.

- You have been chair of the department for three years when you learn from a colleague that several women in the department are organizing a meeting of the female faculty to discuss what some feel are gender-biased practices and inequalities.
- A particular staff member on the committee you lead is consistently resistant to points you raise and initiatives you propose at meetings. The pattern has become quite predictable. It seems to you that whenever you introduce ideas, the individual finds problems with the suggestion, and the problems are generally voiced in a manner that stalls discussion.
- A colleague in your department went over your head as chair and obtained from the dean additional resources for teaching that you denied based on equity considerations. You were unaware of the meeting between the dean and faculty member.
- A student comes to you to express confidential concerns about what he believes is a romantic relationship developing between one of your faculty members and a student in the class. He reports that

it's extremely awkward for others in the class and requests that you address the situation immediately.

- You are assigned to develop a core course for the department based on input from everyone who would like to contribute. A semester has passed, and the deadline for the approval of new courses is fast approaching. Three days before the faculty meeting at which new courses are to be reviewed and approved, the colleague assigned to the task of developing the course distributes what looks like a final draft of the syllabus. At the meeting, various faculty members complain that this was supposed to be designed with broad input to reflect the perspectives of the entire faculty, but clearly this approach was not taken. The author of the syllabus explains that he had been disappointed to have received no input or suggestions during the previous semester. No one recalls any input being sought. What should you do?

- An e-mail goes out from your office to key people with the intent of inviting them to a guest speaker's presentation, and someone writes back to point out an embarrassing typo. Your e-mail said, "You are indicted," when the intended phrase was, "You are invited." What, if anything, do you do?

- You are one of four members appointed to a committee to develop a first draft for a new program to be implemented within your department. No committee leader was appointed, and you find yourself adopting the leadership role. One of your colleagues seldom attends meetings, and when she does, she has only negative input. Clearly she is opposed to the idea of the new program and does not seem to appreciate your efforts to move the group forward. What do you do?

- Your school, composed of four departments, was formed based on some common interests and what the central administration viewed as interdisciplinary potential. To most faculty, however, the merger was seen as a matter of administrative convenience. In the four years since the unit was formed, there have been some grassroots efforts to develop a unifying rhetoric and future vision, but none of these have been enthusiastically supported. The administration believes it is becoming essential for the school to develop a unifying narrative and a more collaborative rather than divisive attitude, and you have been asked to chair a committee to address this issue. How do you respond? If you accept the invitattion what will be your approach?"

- Research and grants are the primary activities emphasized when it comes to promotion and tenure in your institution. Teaching is important, but not nearly as critical as research in the mix. Service to the department ranks a distant third. Unfortunately, much of what it takes to create a strong, cordial, and welcoming environment and effective departmental practices requires faculty engagement. Faculty are reluctant to volunteer or accept invitations to become engaged in service activities within the department, noting that it simply is not valued or rewarded within the institution. As head of the unit, what can you do?

14

STRATEGIC PLANNING

Core Concepts and Critical Steps

Sherrie Tromp, Ralph A. Gigliotti, and Brent D. Ruben

In This Chapter

- What is strategic planning?
- What purposes does strategic planning serve?
- What options exist for implementing strategic planning at the unit, departmental, or institutional level?
- What are the key steps for a successful strategic planning initiative within higher education?

With its range of missions, multiplicity of stakeholders, and distinctive shared governance structures, the realm of higher education engenders a unique setting that requires special considerations in regard to strategic planning. In his seminal work on academic planning, Keller (1983) set the stage for a new approach to planning in higher education when he pointed out the importance of such questions as, "What business are we really in?" "What is most central to us?" and "How shall we proceed?" (p. 72). As Keller explains, unlike other forms of planning, *strategic planning* focuses on determining and guiding outcomes rather than falling victim to myriad external forces that bombard organizations on a daily basis—reactions to which result in ad hoc or activity-based planning. In direct response to the host of challenges facing institutions of higher education, strategic planning is critical. This chapter describes strategic planning, discusses the multiple purposes for which it is useful, and focuses specifically on the implementation and use of strategic planning as a tool for leaders in higher education.

What Is Strategic Planning?

There is no shortage of definitions of *strategic planning*. For example, *strategic planning*, sometimes called *integrated planning*, is defined by the Society for College and University Planning (2016) as: "Integrated planning is a sustainable approach to planning that builds relationships, aligns the organization, and emphasizes preparedness for change." *Strategic planning* is defined by Allison and Kaye (2005) as "a systematic process through which an organization agrees on—and builds commitment among key stakeholders to—priorities that are essential to its mission" (p. 1). Rowley and Sherman (2001) define it as "a formal process designed to help an organization identify and maintain an optimal alignment with the most important elements of its environmental set" (p. 328). Bryson (2011) describes strategic planning as "a deliberate disciplined effort to produce fundamental decisions and actions that shape and guide what an organization (or other entity) is, what it does, and why it does it" (p. 26). Although definitions differ, most share the depiction of strategic planning as an intentional leadership tool for setting future organizational direction in a dynamic environment through a process that takes account of—and ideally engages—key stakeholders, and keeps in mind some of the following basic planning principles and practices:

- Acknowledging and taking account of the national and local contexts, as well as institutional and organizational strengths, weaknesses, opportunities, and threats (SWOT)
- Providing comparisons to peers and leaders
- Offering ideas and goals that are ambitious yet achievable
- Providing a foundation and context for decision-making, action planning, operational priority setting, and resource allocation
- Articulating a thoughtful narrative and aspirations in a coherent and compelling manner

Why Strategic Planning?

Strategic planning has value for organizational development; it also can be very useful for academic and administrative leaders as they decide how best to address a variety of challenges or opportunities within their organizations. Among these challenges and opportunities are the following:

- Complacency and low aspirations among members of the organization
- Inconsistency between the way organizational insiders and outsiders view the organization

- A lack of shared perception of organizational priorities or goals
- Individuals and groups focused on priorities that detract from the mission of the organization as a whole
- An evolving political or economic landscape from which the organization has become disconnected
- An absence of a clear or shared set of criteria or measures of progress or success for the organization
- A need to redirect the organization toward new opportunities—new programs, initiatives, or areas of focus
- Insufficient attention being devoted to innovation, change, and out-of-the-box thinking

In considering how best to address these sorts of circumstances, any number of leadership strategies come to mind, and strategic planning may not initially be among them. Perhaps the most obvious of these strategies is for a leader to take control—developing a plan, communicating that plan throughout the organization, and naming individuals or groups to oversee its implementation. A second strategy would be for leaders to search for tools to deal with the specific issue at hand—for instance, initiating team-building sessions, developing a marketing communication plan, or introducing a new incentive structure to reward innovations. A third strategy would involve waiting until an issue becomes a crisis and then using the crisis as a rationale for a quick and forceful response.

In approaching leadership and organizational difficulties, there is an understandable tendency to focus specifically on what seem to be the immediate issues at hand. In situations such as these, classic adages like, "If it ain't broke, don't fix it," or, "Don't bite off more than you can chew," come readily to a leader's mind. Often, however, what may look like a very specific and narrowly defined challenge that could easily be addressed through marketing, team building, improved internal communication, or a new incentive structure is a manifestation of a larger set of issues that would be more effectively addressed through comprehensive leadership approaches such as, strategic planning.

Strategic Planning in Higher Education

In recent years, strategic planning has become an increasingly popular tool for college and university leaders who are confronted with the types of situations described previously. The concept of strategic planning is not a new one within higher education. Dooris, Kelley, and Trainer (2004) identified a 1959 meeting of 25 campus planners at the Massachusetts Institute of Technology as an important historical marker. This meeting was centered on the need for facilities planning during an era of rapid expansion. Massive changes in the second half of the twentieth century led to the expanded adoption of strategic planning initiatives in higher education, and by the 1980s, strategic planning had emerged as an influential practice in higher education (Keller, 1983). Interest in strategic planning in higher education continued to increase, and the initial group of 25 campus planners in 1959 grew to 4,200 active members of the Society for College and University Planning by 2004 (Dooris et al., 2004). An estimated 70% of colleges and universities in the United States engaged in some form of strategic planning in 2000 (Sevier, 2000), and that number should be expected to grow steadily, in light of growing pressures for increasing efficiency and effectiveness and systematic approaches to organizational goal setting and outcomes assessment (Flynn & Vredevoogd, 2010).

In many higher education settings, two of the most common obstacles leaders face are the lack of a clear and shared sense of where the project, program, center, department, or institution should be headed and a genuine commitment to the collaboration and coordination necessary to achieve the desired outcomes. Often, the specific challenges that leaders face are easier to address if these core issues have been resolved first. An appropriately structured planning process can provide the needed foundation. More specifically, strategic planning processes have the potential to establish an agenda for advancing organizational excellence and creating a mechanism for follow-through in these ways:

- Stimulating meaningful dialogue about the units, departments, or organization's mission, aspirations, values, and priorities
- Establishing shared and energizing goals and strategies for progress toward those aspirations
- Defining necessary action steps and fostering the broader commitment required to successfully execute these steps
- Identifying critical audiences and stakeholders for the organization, developing key messages, and developing a persuasive communication, marketing, and fund-raising plan
- Analyzing the directions and approaches of peers and leaders
- Adopting effective practices that are in line with the goals of the organization

One of the attractions of strategic planning is that it may be implemented as a standalone activity or in conjunction with other institutional opportunities or requirements, such as preparation for accreditation visits (e.g., the Middle States Commission on Higher Education, 2014; Dodd, 2004), award applications (e.g., the Baldrige National Quality Program; Jasinski, 2004; Ruben et al., 2007), and other institutional initiatives. At the University of Wisconsin–Madison, for example, strategic planning was infused throughout the organization during two accreditation cycles (Paris, 2004). At Penn State University, an integrated planning approach connects strategic planning with budgeting, enrollment management, and human resource planning (Sandmeyer, Dooris, & Barlock, 2004). Another example is Northwestern University and its Feinberg School of Medicine, in which strategic planning efforts are linked with changes in the medical school's budgeting structure in order to better align activities with the institution's mission and resources (Haberaecker, 2004).

The Components of Strategic Plans in Higher Education

While various strategic planning approaches used in higher education may differ in some respects, a common characteristic is that they encourage an institution, department, or program to consider and clarify issues related to their mission, vision, and values, and then to develop and implement plans and strategies that translate these organizational attributes into a well-defined blueprint for collective action. Tromp and Ruben (2010) define *strategic planning* as "the means by which the most effective organizations establish priorities and goals and coordinate their efforts to anticipate, direct, and manage change" (p. 7). This approach to planned change in higher education may be implemented through a variety of different strategies. One model introduced by Tromp and Ruben (2010), strategic planning in higher education, is described later in this chapter.

A typical strategic planning framework for higher education consists of a series of major planning phases, as illustrated in Table 14.1 and summarized in the following list:

- reviewing—and in some cases drafting or clarifying—the organization's mission, vision, and often values;
- determining the list of key stakeholders and their perspectives;
- conducting an environmental scan, including benchmarking;
- establishing themes/goals;
- identifying and prioritizing strategies and action plans;
- drafting the planning document; and
- specifying intended outcomes and achievements.

TABLE 14.1
Creating an Effective Plan

Mission, vision, and values	Define the reason for the organization's existence, the desired future state of the organization, and the principles and perspectives that guide and influence daily work and the organizational culture.
Stakeholders' perspectives	Identify the primary beneficiaries and collaborators, along with their perceptions, needs, expectations, and concerns.
Environmental scan and benchmarking	Consider the social, economic, political, regulatory, technological, and cultural environment in which the organization functions, including assumptions and potential challenges; identify relevant peer and aspirant organizations for analysis and comparison.
Goals	Identify the organization's broad, high-level ambitions.
Strategies, priorities, and action plans	Formulate the specific, detailed ways in which goals will be fulfilled and through which the approach and concrete activities needed to transform the organization will be executed; prioritize options; develop specific action plans.
Plan creation/ implementation	Create a document that clearly articulates the organization's plan and serves to inform, influence, anchor, and guide the organization's future.
Outcomes and achievements	Translate goals, strategies, and action plans into tangible and meaningful measures that can be used to monitor outcomes and milestones and to asses the ultimate impact of the planning effort.

Mission, Vision, and Values Statements

Thoughtful mission, vision, and value statements remind members of the organization and other stakeholders of the core purpose of the organization, identify aspirations, and specify key principles and priorities. They provide an important communicative function for internal and external audiences and can offer a useful guide for day-to-day behaviors and decision-making within the organization. Of particular importance to leaders in higher education is the role these statements play in anchoring, linking, and guiding programs and services. Mission, vision, and value statements also facilitate communication with various stakeholder groups.

For all these reasons, strategic planning typically begins by drafting, refining, or reviewing existing documents that address the issues of mission, vision, and values. In many settings, statements on these themes already exist, and they may only need to be reviewed and discussed. In other cases, some refinements and updates may be necessary, and in still others, statements need to be created.

As discussed in Chapter 3, a mission statement provides a description of an organization's primary purpose and reason for its existence. It focuses on the current state and articulates what others can expect from the organization—the services and programs provided by the institution, department, or program. For example, a typical mission statement for a center for online learning within a college or university might be, "To serve as a center for training in online instruction and research for university faculty and staff, and to share information and materials with comparable centers at other institutions."

Vision statements describe the aspirations of the institution, department, or program, and are generally considered—drafted, refined, or reviewed—after the mission statement. A vision statement for the center for online learning might be, "To be a recognized center of excellence in online learning education and research within the university, regionally, and nationally."

Some organizations may also have—or wish to create—statements of values or principles. If so, they should be considered at this stage in the planning process. Organizations operate in a manner that reflects particular values—whether explicitly stated or not. These values guide and influence daily work, interactions, relationships, and the overall organizational culture. While values are not always included as a part of the planning framework, a statement that includes such principles can be an important element not only as a foundation for planning but also as a guide for the day-to-day activities of the program, department, or institution. The values for the center for online learning, for example, might include collaboration, professionalism, integrity, and tolerance for diversity in levels of knowledge and experience in technology.

It is possible to combine elements of mission, vision, and values in a single statement. One noteworthy example is provided by Johnson & Johnson's company credo. The statement, created in 1943, combines elements of mission, vision, and values, while also identifying and prioritizing the key groups the company serves.

> We believe our first responsibility is to the doctors, nurses and patients, to mothers and fathers and all others who use our products and services. In meeting their needs everything we do must be of high quality. We must constantly strive to reduce our costs in order to maintain reasonable prices. Customers' orders must be serviced promptly and accurately. Our suppliers and distributors must have an opportunity to make a fair profit.

> We are responsible to our employees, the men and women who work with us throughout the world. Everyone must be considered as an indi-

vidual. We must respect their dignity and recognize their merit. They must have a sense of security in their jobs. Compensation must be fair and adequate, and working conditions clean, orderly and safe. We must be mindful of ways to help our employees fulfill their family responsibilities. Employees must feel free to make suggestions and complaints. There must be equal opportunity for employment, development and advancement for those qualified. We must provide competent management, and their actions must be just and ethical.

We are responsible to the communities in which we live and work and to the world community as well. We must be good citizens—support good works and charities and bear our fair share of taxes. We must encourage civic improvements and better health and education. We must maintain in good order the property we are privileged to use, protecting the environment and natural resources.

Our final responsibility is to our stockholders. Business must make a sound profit. We must experiment with new ideas. Research must be carried on, innovative programs developed and mistakes paid for. New equipment must be purchased, new facilities provided and new products launched. Reserves must be created to provide for adverse times. When we operate according to these principles, the stockholders should realize a fair return. (Johnson & Johnson, 2016)

The company website describes the importance of its credo accordingly:

Robert Wood Johnson, former chairman from 1932 to 1963 and a member of the Company's founding family, crafted Our Credo himself in 1943, just before Johnson & Johnson became a publicly traded company. This was long before anyone ever heard the term "corporate social responsibility." Our Credo is more than just a moral compass. We believe it's a recipe for business success. The fact that Johnson & Johnson is one of only a handful of companies that have flourished through more than a century of change is proof of that. (Johnson & Johnson, 2016)

Johnson & Johnson's credo serves as a guiding philosophy that greets visitors and employees as they enter the lobby of the world corporate headquarters in New Brunswick, New Jersey. The statement is also prominently displayed on the company website and in other communication materials. The credo provides employees with a set of priorities to guide their day-to-day work. It is also used as the basis for periodic internal assessments through which employees provide anonymous feedback as to whether the company is living up to these standards and to identify any areas where this may not be the case. Table 14.2 provides examples of mission statements for various types of educational organizations. In reviewing these, consider how each might serve as a cornerstone for planning.

Mission statements should provide a clear and enduring description of the work of the organization, yet they can also be general enough to permit organizational change and growth. As you consider the mission statements in Table 14.2, some of which are also in the discussion of missions in Chapter 3, consider how they might be an essential cornerstone for planning at the unit, departmental, or institutional level.

TABLE 14.2
Examples of Departmental and Institutional Mission Statements

Public Research Institution
University of Michigan
"The mission of the University of Michigan is to serve the people of Michigan and the world through preeminence in creating, communicating, preserving, and applying knowledge, art, and academic values, and in developing leaders and citizens who will challenge the present and enrich the future." (president.umich.edu/about/mission)
Private Four-Year Institution
Kalamazoo College
"The mission of Kalamazoo College is to prepare its graduates to better understand, live successfully within, and provide enlightened leadership to a richly diverse and increasingly complex world." (www.kzoo.edu/k-plan/outcomes)
Public Two-Year Institution
Westchester Community College
"Westchester Community College provides accessible, high-quality, and affordable education to meet the needs of our diverse community. We are committed to student success, academic excellence, workforce development, economic development, and lifelong learning." (www.sunywcc.edu/about/about-the-college/mission-and-goals-of-the-college)
Medical School
Georgetown University School of Medicine
"Guided by the Jesuit tradition of *Cura Personalis*, care of the whole person, Georgetown University School of Medicine will educate a diverse student body, in an integrated way, to become knowledgeable, ethical, skillful, and compassionate physicians and biomedical scientists who are dedicated to the care of others and health needs of our society." (som.georgetown.edu)

(Continues)

TABLE 14.2 *(Continued)*

Academic Department
Northern Arizona University Social Work Program
"The mission of the Northern Arizona University Social Work Program, grounded in the history, purpose, and values of the profession, is to educate competent, generalist social workers for practice with diverse populations and multi-level social systems in local, regional, and global contexts. The generalist practice for which we educate is based on social work knowledge, values, and skills; geared to practice with rural and Indigenous populations of the Southwest; and focused on addressing poverty, structural racism, and oppression. This practice provides leadership in promoting human rights and social and economic justice, and service with vulnerable and underserved populations locally, regionally, and globally."(nau.edu/sbs/ssw/degrees-programs/mission-statement)

Administrative Department
Loyola University Division of Finance and Administration
"The Division of Finance and Administration is responsible for preserving, enhancing, and supporting the University's financial, physical, and human resources. The Division provides consultation, support, and services to the University. In order to achieve these goals, the Division must challenge the actions of all University units to ensure the activities proposed and resources requested reflect sound business judgment and support the overall goals and mission of the University. The Division's staff works closely with all areas of the University to • Responsibly manage the University's resources ensuring its sound financial condition for this generation and those that follow; • Deliver quality services expeditiously; • Enhance the physical infrastructure of the campus; and • Create conditions in which students and employees can do their best work." (finance.loyno.edu/about-finance-administration)

Stakeholders' Perspectives

Achieving clarity on the list of those who benefit from and collaborate with any program, department, or institution is important for organizational practice in general, and also another valuable foundational step in the planning process. The Johnson & Johnson credo, for instance, identifies doctors, nurses, patients, employees, communities, and stockholders—in that order—as the company's key constituencies. This deliberate and explicit prioritization of key stakeholders can be very helpful for defining aspirations, developing plans, and establishing specific goals and strategies. Leaders and colleagues within colleges and universities can similarly benefit from clarifying who their key stakeholder groups are and what needs and expectations exist for these groups as they relate to potential departmental, program, or institutional priorities.

Environmental Scanning and Benchmarking

Environmental scanning is another critical step in strategic planning. Also known as a strengths, weaknesses, opportunities, and threats (SWOT) analysis, this stage in planning calls for a careful consideration of the social, economic, political, regulatory, technological, and cultural environment in which an organization functions, focusing particularly on those factors that could impinge on potential plans or the planning process. Depending on the planning context, and the time and financial resources available, the extent and sophistication of data collection and analysis can vary considerably. It may involve some or all members of the organization and representatives of key external stakeholder group and require taking account of relevant regional, state, national, and perhaps international information sources. A decision may also be made to draw on external expertise to assist with this process. Regardless of how this stage is conducted, it is essential to engage a central role to members of the program, department, or institution who generally have insights and perspectives that are especially useful.

Benchmarking—gathering information from comparable organizations within and beyond the institution—is also an important step in planning. In nearly all cases, there exist relevant peer or aspirational institutions, departments, or programs to which comparisons can be extremely useful for informing plans and goals related to programs, services, or processes.

In combination, environmental scanning and benchmarking are key elements in strategic planning. Each contributes to a leader's knowledge of the potential challenges and opportunities facing the unit, department, or academic institution, and can also encourage the adoption of innovative ideas from other organizations and sectors.

Goals

Supported by a foundation of clear mission, vision, and values; a well-defined list of stakeholders and stakeholder perspectives; and pertinent information from environmental scanning and benchmarking activities, the strategic planning process focuses next on establishing goals. Goal setting is a core activity in strategic planning, and it is often the point at which people are tempted to begin the process. However, without a clear sense of purpose, aspirations, stakeholders, and comparative perspectives, goal setting could easily proceed in less-than-useful directions.

Goals should be broad and far-reaching in scope and should describe what the organization needs to do to achieve its high-level aspirations. In establishing goals, it is important to resist pressures to create a catalogue of projects that might be undertaken. While creating an expansive list of suggested projects may seem like a good place to start, it is important to first clearly formulate and articulate goals that represent the critical needs of the organization. Also, generating a list of potential projects without first carefully determining and focusing goals typically results in the creation of an unfocused, undifferentiated, and unwieldy list of activities that may fail to address key priority areas for the advancement of the organization. It is also important to express these goals in terms that allow for tracking progress and measuring outcomes (Tromp & Ruben, 2010). For the hypothetical Center for Online Learning, for example, a goal may be, "To make a high-quality, affordable education available for higher education faculty who wish to further their online education design, delivery and evaluative capabilities."

Strategies, Priorities, and Action Plans

The next step in the process is the formulation and implementation of strategies and action plans. Strategies or statements describe *how* the goal(s) will be realized. Action plans specify *what will be done, by whom*, and *when*. Together, strategies and action plans provide the details as to how the goals will be addressed. This is the stage where the many project ideas that often surface in earlier discussions can be considered and—when appropriate—adopted as specific strategies. The challenge for leaders in this phase of planning is determining which of the many possible ways to achieve the organization's goals are likely to have the greatest significant impact, are the most manageable to implement, and are likely to provide the greatest potential return on time and resources.

Consideration of potential strategies should include a candid and realistic appraisal of key influences on specific activities and a conscious, well-thought-out approach for capitalizing on people, timing, and circumstances that can further the direction of the organization and eliminating or minimizing factors that, if left unaddressed, could derail critical components of the plan. The availability of resources, potential impact, and probability of success are factors of significance in establishing final priorities. Additionally, if identifying priorities for a unit or department, one must consider the aspirations and plans of the larger college or university throughout the process.

Plan Creation

With the prior stages completed, now is the time to create a strategic planning document. The aim is to design a document that clearly articulates the organization's plan, and thereby serves to inform, influence, anchor, and guide the organization's future. The plan is, by design, a visible and public document—one intended to be a leadership tool, a communication device, and the most tangible record of the effort. Because of its physical and public nature, it is likely to be the focus for judgments of the success of the planning effort. In selecting content and format for the planning document, people involved in the planning efforts must consider the plan's primary audiences, expectations for how the plan will be used, and the role the document is expected to play in facilitating the sharing of information with multiple audiences (Tromp & Ruben, 2010). Once the planning document is completed, it is a leadership responsibility to disseminate plan progress reports and promote the value and importance of its content within and beyond the program, department, or institution.

Outcomes and Achievements

Achieving and sustaining the desired outcomes is the overriding purpose of strategic planning and the fundamental goal for organizations and leaders alike. Ironically, if there is one area in which higher education organizations generally do a less-than-adequate job, it is in measuring and documenting the achievement of stated goals, tracking progress over time, and making the necessary adjustments to ensure the intended outcomes during the implementation of the plans.

Although listed as the final step in the planning process, considerations relative to this stage should begin early and continue throughout the implementation and follow-through stages. The critical activities include maintaining focus on the institution's aspirations and plans, and tracking progress relative to each goal, strategy, and action plan. This approach requires leaders to identify the critical indicators of success for the plan as well as the planning process, to determine the appropriate methods for monitoring progress at each stage, to decide how information regarding progress outcomes will be organized and shared, and to develop an approach to using that information that will assure follow-through for the plan.

Table 14.3 highlights specific elements to emerge from the planning process for the center for online learning.

TABLE 14.3

Planning Components for a Hypothetical Center for Online Learning

Mission, vision, and values	**Mission:**
	To serve as a center for training in online instruction and research for university faculty and staff, and to share information and materials with comparable centers at other institutions.
	Vision:
	To be a recognized center of excellence in online learning education and research within the university, regionally, and nationally.
	Core Values:
	• Collaboration • Professionalism and integrity • Tolerance for diversity in levels of knowledge and experience in technology
Stakeholders' perspectives	The following stakeholders are a sample of those constituents who have an interest in the center: • Online instructional faculty and staff • Students • Partner colleges and universities • Learning management system providers • Online accreditation associations
Environmental scan and benchmarking	Strengths:
	• A strong reputation for being a national leader in online learning education and research • Highly productive research and training center
	Weaknesses:
	• Limited staff compared to other research centers • Inadequate resources for conducting advanced qualitative and quantitative data analysis
	Opportunities:
	• Predictions for extensive growth in online education nationally and internationally • Corporate donors who are interested in contributing to the work of the center

(*Continues*)

Table 14.3 (*Continues*)

	Threats:
	• Growing number of critics of online education • Potential for universal budget cuts across the university
Goals	*Goal #1:* To make high-quality, affordable education available for higher education faculty who wish to further their online education design, delivery, and evaluative capabilities. *Goal #2:* To expedite participant progress toward instructional program completion.
Strategies, priorities, and action plans	*Corresponding Strategy #1:* Seek creative funding alternatives that will expand available resources for instructional programs. Action plan: Identify current available corporate, government, and educational grant options.
	Corresponding Strategy #2: Identify areas of primary impact on completion rates compared to peers. *Action plan:* Survey current faculty in the program to determine facilitators and barriers to completion.
Plan creation/ implementation	The strategic planning leadership team for the center created a full-color document highlighting the details of the plan. The plan was printed for in-house audiences, posted on the center's website in an accessible format, and distributed to key external stakeholders who are familiar with the work of the center.
Outcomes and achievements	At the conclusion of the first year of the program, the center hosted a forum to highlight some of these notable accomplishments: • Based on survey data and benchmarking with peers, funded two new technology support people to assist with training about online platforms • Implemented a program completion audit application that allows participants to track their progress toward completion and entertain what-if scenarios about class choices • Obtained two grants used to provide additional course offerings each semester so that participants do not have to wait months for a needed course to be offered

The Success of Planning Depends on the Process

While the content of the individual phases of the strategic planning process is essential to creating the plan itself, it is no more important to a successful outcome than is the *process* by which that plan is developed. This process can often be quite challenging. While faculty and staff generally express a desire to be actively involved in developing plans, leaders often find that in practice, this may not be easy to accomplish for any number of reasons. That said, failing to meaningfully engage members of the unit or institution for which plans are being developed can have rather dire consequences when it comes to supporting and implementing the final plans. The traditions of shared governance, the customary pattern of relatively loosely coupled units, and the typical levels of autonomy in which higher education units and their members often operate all point to the importance of faculty and staff engagement. As Woodhouse (2015) notes, "As more and more faculty resolutions against strategic plans and administrative actions surface, nearly all of them have a common thread: concern over not only the proposed changes, but how those changes are communicated. Often faculty members decry a lack of transparency or consultation. Sometimes their concerns are as simple as the vocabulary administrators use."

Additional process challenges result from the need for the process to consider the perspectives of students and other key stakeholders, to draw on comparisons with peer organizations and leaders within and outside the institution, and to focus attention on relevant environmental and economic factors. There is no doubt that the multiplicity of stakeholders and traditions of shared governance in higher education present leadership challenges and opportunities. Thoughtful attention to the five process considerations listed in Figure 14.1—leadership, communication, assessment, culture, and follow-through—will help to greatly enhance the probability of a successful strategic planning effort (Tromp & Ruben, 2010).[1]

Leadership. Of the many leadership themes and capabilities that are important to higher education, several are particularly valuable in assuring a successful strategic planning process. Knowing and leveraging one's own leadership competencies is fundamental. Also critical is designing a leadership architecture that appropriately reflects the organization and its key internal and external stakeholders to guide the various phases of the planning process. This step includes identifying the subject-matter expertise needed for the planning process and creating a team of collaborative leaders and change agents to serve in critical roles throughout the various stages. Assuming personal and organizational responsibility for envisioning, supporting, and guiding change is also important, along with serving as a vocal advocate for planning and change.

Figure 14.1. Creating a plan effectively

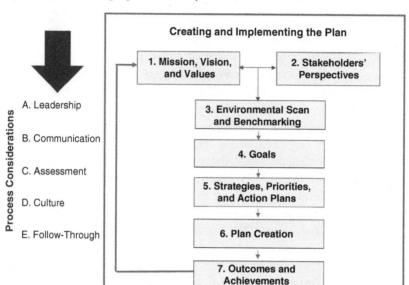

Communication. Identifying the key stakeholders of concern in strategic planning efforts is a fundamental dimension of communication, as is determining their perspectives, formulating focused communication goals, designing appropriate communication themes, framing messages appropriately, and selecting appropriate media and delivery methods for each audience and planning stage. Two-way communication with key stakeholders—supporters and critics—is also essential during plan development and implementation.

Assessment. Establishing indicators and methods for assessing progress in the planning process and of the completed plan and its implementation is another important step. Assessment allows leaders to monitor progress and outcomes related to the planning effort, the alignment of goals and strategies, and stakeholder comprehension and engagement. Benchmarking specific goals and strategies with peer and leader organizations is another component of assessment that contributes to strategic planning effectiveness.

Culture. Understanding the history, habits, traditions, and natural resistance to change, and taking account of this information in plan development and implementation, are additional elements that facilitate successful planning. Perhaps most fundamentally, leaders need to identify each of the cultural groups within the organization that have a stake in the plans being developed. This knowledge is useful in all phases of plan development and implementation, and is particularly critical for determining who needs to be engaged in the planning process, and at what stages. Cultural awareness can be extremely helpful in identifying potential facilitators and impediments to planning efforts in general, as well as in predicting and addressing reactions to specific goals, strategies, and action plans.

Follow-through. In many respects, this issue is the most difficult, yet the most important to the success of a planning effort. Faculty and professional staff are often very effective in envisioning what might be and in posing creative possibilities for the future. When it comes to following through with the details necessary to realize the planning vision and goals, the results are often less impressive. One significant leadership and communication challenge is keeping faculty and staff broadly engaged throughout the implementation stage of strategic planning efforts. It is helpful to establish the mechanisms and methods for maintaining a public focus on the goals, strategies, and action plans that are developed. A recognition and celebration of organizational achievements and those involved in helping to reach these achievements can contribute to sustained engagement. It is also beneficial for leaders to communicate consistently, to periodically review goals and plans, and to hold the team accountable for planning outcomes. Other helpful leadership actions during the follow-through phase include the following:

- Ensuring that each program, project, or initiative has an "owner" who is responsible for moving the initiative ahead and seeing it through to its completion
- Holding periodic group meetings to share information on progress and identify potential delays or problems
- Maintaining engagement of multiple stakeholder groups using their preferred communication channels
- Creating and meeting an expectation for periodic updates to critical audiences

Approaches to Higher Education Strategic Planning

Strategic planning can be undertaken in a variety of ways. Generally speaking, the ideal approach is an institution-wide effort that sequentially integrates all units of a college or university to create a unified plan—one that articulates how the current and aspirational purposes, goals, and action steps of each unit fit within the larger institutional context. The same approach is also appropriate if the planning is to be implemented within individual units—divisions, schools, departments, or programs. Here, too, the ideal is to develop a plan that defines and clarifies the overall unit directions and plans, as well as how the programs or smaller units within the larger organization align with and contribute to the larger purpose and plans.

Regardless of the level of the organization that undertakes strategic planning, the effort may proceed in a manner that is top-down, bottom-up, or a combination of the two. The planning process can begin at the highest level of the organization, and the broad framework of purposes, aspirations, plans, and goals could guide planning efforts undertaken subsequently within individual units in the organization. Alternatively, the planning sequence could begin with units that constitute the larger organization (for instance, programs or departments within a division or institution) completing unit-based plans. These plans could then be synthesized to create higher-level plans for the organization or institution as a whole. Combinations of the two approaches, where a plan is created through multiple iterations of drafting, reviewing, and fine tuning at multiple levels, has the potential to be maximally inclusive of the range of perspectives within the organization. Additionally, this approach may provide opportunities for broad engagement by faculty and staff at all levels, result in fewer surprise reactions when the final plan is completed, and ideally, lead to greater levels of commitment to implementing the plan when it is finalized. That said, it is important to achieve a balance: the more iterations in the process, the more time and effort required by leaders to complete the planning initiative and often the greater the likelihood of generating alternative—sometimes conflicting—ideas and proposals.

As there are various options for sequencing efforts, alternatives also exist regarding how to design and lead the process. One option is to assign all phases of planning to internal leaders, using the internal talent and resources of the unit or the institution. Typically in this model, a strategic planning leadership team is formed, often headed up by the senior leader of the organization, and this team has the responsibility for designing, developing, coordinating, and implementing the strategic planning initiative with others selected to participate from within the unit or institution. Another quite different approach is to procure the services of consultants who may be contracted to design and oversee part or all of the strategic planning process. Alternatively, the unit's leadership may oversee some aspects of plan design and development, while securing the support and guidance of external consultants or individuals from elsewhere in the university who have expertise in the strategic planning process. With either of these last two possibilities, the role of the external experts can be highly visible, or their role may be to offer behind-the-scenes support, essentially serving as coaches, with the unit or leaders serving as the face of the institutional planning effort.

When it comes to making choices among these varying options and approaches, there are obvious trade-offs to consider, based on factors such as the capability and experience of leaders and others who might serve as consultants or coaches, the culture and previous practices of the organization, available resources, time considerations, the benefits or liabilities of having internal or external expertise, and validation for the process and the final report. One possible strategy that provides a way to manage the trade-offs is to vary the strategy and leadership for stages in the strategic planning process. For instance, if an expansive and detailed environmental scan is required, it might be better accomplished by external consultants. External resources might also be used to conduct interviews, focus groups, or surveys of various stakeholder groups and to analyze resulting themes. Further, external expertise might be used to design and produce the completed planning document. Internal leadership, consultants, or coaches might then be utilized for reviewing and clarifying the mission and vision, developing core themes and goals, identifying and prioritizing strategies, and designing the publication of the document drafted by the leadership team, as illustrated in Table 14.4.

TABLE 14.4
A Hypothetical Approach to Facilitating a Strategic Planning Effort

Plan Component	Suggested Approach
Mission, vision, and values	Develop internally (with or without facilitation by others from outside the institution or unit).
Stakeholders' perspectives	Inventory the available information internally and develop strategies for gathering additional needed information.
Environmental scan and benchmarking	Conduct an internal SWOT analysis involving faculty and staff (with or without facilitation by someone from outside the institution or unit). Consider additional research and consulting support for gathering and analyzing national data if that is necessary to the scope of the planning process.
Goals	Develop internally (with or without facilitation by others outside the unit).
Strategies, priorities, and action plans	Develop internally (with or without outside facilitation).
Plan creation/ implementation	Develop draft internally. Consider consulting support for professional-level editing, layout, and publication of the plan.
Outcomes and achievements	Develop an internal monitoring group (with or without outside facilitation).

The strategic planning approach may also include prework and preplanning activities, including the following: meetings with leaders to establish goals for the planning process; the development, distribution, and analysis of preplanning surveys to faculty, staff, and other stakeholders that become the basis for issue identification; facilitated planning sessions or retreats with various groups; a written report providing feedback on the information developed during the retreat and any relevant outcomes; post-report debriefing with leaders; and as-needed follow-up and assistance.

Conclusion

There are a number of approaches to strategic planning, but Hunger and Wheelen (2010) posit four essential elements in the process:

1. Environmental scanning.
2. Strategy formulation.
3. Strategy implementation.
4. Evaluation and control. (p. 5)

Allison and Kaye (2005) enumerate seven phases associated with strategic planning:

1. Get ready.
2. Articulate mission, vision, and values.
3. Assess your situation.
4. Agree on priorities.
5. Write the plan.
6. Implement the plan.
7. Evaluate and monitor the plan. (p. 5)

Despite subtle differences among these and other perspectives reviewed in the chapter, all have much in common. Each identifies a number of critical steps, including the clarification of mission and vision; analysis of internal and external influences; identification of core organizational issues; assessment of internal strengths and weaknesses, and external threats and opportunities; development and selection of strategic imperatives; implementation of strategic goals; and the assessment of outcomes and achievements (Burkhart & Reuss, 1993; Pfeiffer, Goodstein, & Nolan, 1986; Roberts & Rowley, 2004; Tromp & Ruben, 2010).

Regardless of the framework chosen, the following points are important for leading strategic planning initiatives in the higher education sector:

- Planning should not be undertaken as a reaction to a crisis.
- Heading a planning process requires both *leadership* (the vision) and *management* (the details; implementation).
- The process and its stages should be clear to all from the outset.
- Meaningful engagement of faculty and staff is essential to commitment and follow-through. This engagement can take a variety of forms.
- Multiple opportunities for input and iteration are necessary, but the process should also proceed in an efficient, logical, and time-sensitive manner.
- Plans should be designed for internal use, but should also take account of external audiences for whom they will be important.

Strategic planning initiatives can be extremely useful experiences for an institution, individual departments, and stakeholders throughout the organization. Facing a myriad of environmental challenges and opportunities, colleges and universities are in need of transformative, visionary, and mission-oriented activities, programs, and initiatives—many of which can emerge from a thoughtful strategic planning process. The development and implementation of these plans requires a considerable investment of time and resources; the potential payoff, however, can be significant.

As should be apparent from the foregoing, the authors believe strongly that successful strategic planning has two distinct aspects, both of which are critical: (a) developing the *plan*, and (b) developing and implementing a methodical, inclusive, and engaging *planning process* (Immordino et al., 2016). Few models devote explicit attention to factors that are critical to the process—leadership, communication, assessment, culture, and follow-through—each of which is essential to success in plan development and implementation (Tromp & Ruben, 2010).

The success of a strategic plan can be judged not only on the quality of the document and specifics of the formal plan but also on the inclusivity of the process and the sense of engagement and ownership of the goals, plans, implementation, and outcomes that result from the effort. Strategic planning can clarify organizational purposes and aspirations, promote the development of broad and high-level goals, guide the allocation of resources, energize the organization to address key issues, and assist in the articulation of clear measures of success. Use of follow-through, periodic progress checks, and ongoing communication allows leaders to ensure that strategic plans become living, adaptive documents that serve as helpful guides in pursuing unit and institutional aspirations.

For Further Consideration

1. Strategic Planning for a New Family Medicine Residency Program

The Department of Family Medicine of Superior University Medical School, in partnership with the Regional Medical Center (RMC), wants to expand its teaching mission to include a new residency training program.[2]

RMC's mission is to provide quality healthcare to all persons within their inner-city community regardless of an individual's ability to pay for this care; to develop a primary-care network of practices that support the inpatient specialty work of the Medical Center; and to develop a workforce of physicians, nurses, and other healthcare personnel who, upon graduation from their programs, remain in the community and become both providers and consumers of the quality healthcare for which RMC is known. The vision of the RMC is to become the preeminent healthcare system in the community, regionally recognized as a center of quality healthcare that improves access to care and the overall quality of health for the larger community it serves.

The mission of the Department of Family Medicine at Superior University is to train physicians who deliver high-quality primary healthcare within the context of the patient-doctor relationship. The department aspires to become regionally and nationally known for its residency training programs and, through its faculty and graduates, become one of the top-five leaders in primary-care delivery, education, and scholarship in the nation.

Funding for the new program will be provided by the RMC through Graduate Medical Education dollars and through grants and gifts as well as with support from the RMC operating budget. The Department of Family Medicine at the Superior University Medical School will manage and sponsor the program.

The Department of Family Medicine will hire, evaluate, and supervise faculty and residents needed for the new program. These faculty and residents will be paid by the Regional Medical Center. Other faculty who will teach residents in hospital medicine and various specialties will be from within the medical staff of RMC and will be granted clinical faculty positions within the Superior University Medical School.

RMC will provide a community primary-care practice site and staff and a population of patients for the residency practice. Residents will see patients in the hospital under supervision of faculty both from the medical school and from RMC medical staff. All billing from the practice and inpatient care will be handled by the RMC, but accounting, practice billing, and quality-care issues will be available to faculty and residents for monthly review and input. Outcome measures for the residency program will include the following:

- Continued accreditation of the program by the national Accreditation Council for Graduate Medical Education (ACGME)
- Board certification of all graduates immediately upon completion of the program
- Twenty-five percent of graduating residents practice within the community served by the RMC
- At least 25% of graduates take on fellowship, regional, or national leadership positions within the community, regional, and national healthcare environments
- Patient satisfaction with the residency practice ratings at "good" to "very good" for issues of quality of care and access
- Satisfactory ratings of the Family Medicine Practice group by the Medical Center as it relates to accountability, effectiveness, and efficiency.

Imagine you are part of the leadership team of the Department of Family Medicine and you need to evaluate and plan for the new program.

- In what ways does the proposed residency training program fit the mission and vision of the Department of Family Medicine?
- In what ways does the proposed residency training program fit the mission and vision of the RMC?
- Who are the stakeholders in the project? Pick three of the stakeholders you identified and describe how the leadership team of the Department of Family Medicine might effectively involve each of them in planning for the residency training program.
- Conduct a SWOT analysis from the perspective of the RMC and from the perspective of the Department of Family Medicine. How do these analyses differ? How are they similar?
- What difficulties do you foresee arising around funding and management/sponsorship of the program? As an academic or administrative leader of the medical school, how might you approach some of the concerns that may develop?
- Which of the measurable outcomes would be most important for the RMC? For the Department of Family Medicine?

2. Residential Learning Community

Senior leaders from academic affairs and student affairs would like to design a residential learning community for undergraduate students organized around the theme of sustainability and environmental leadership. Based on your understanding of student and academic affairs, along with your commitment to the environmental theme of the learning community, you have been asked to oversee the planning process for the new community. The overarching goal of the planning process is to engage collaborative partners from various academic and student life areas to think through the mission, structure, and general curriculum of the residential learning community. You recognize that there will be many individuals with an interest in the topic; however, like many institutions, collaboration across the traditionally siloed departments is not common.

- How would you proceed with the design of this planning process?
- Whom would you engage throughout the process, and how would you facilitate sharing ideas across collaborative units throughout the process?
- What challenges might you expect to encounter—and how can you strategically design the planning process to best address these challenges?

Notes

1. For a more extensive explanation of the framework, along with worksheets for facilitation, case studies, and planning exercises, see Tromp and Ruben (2010).

2. This case study was written by Martha Lansing, MD, associate professor and vice chair of the Robert Wood Johnson Medical School.

15

UNDERSTANDING AND LEADING CHANGE IN COLLEGES AND UNIVERSITIES

In This Chapter

- What is organizational change? What makes change complex in both a personal and organizational context?
- What are the predictable sources of resistance to change in organizations—particularly change in higher education?
- Why is this resistance to change both a problem and an opportunity?
- What are the common stages associated with the acceptance or rejection of change efforts?
- Which strategies are most useful for leading change efforts in higher education?

Resolutions and Good Intentions

Each New Year's Eve, millions of people make resolutions about things they need, want, and intend to change—in their outlooks, their behaviors, and their lives. Examples include wanting to lose weight, manage finances more effectively, exercise more, spend more time with family, complete a project, take time to stop and smell the roses, and so on. These kinds of resolutions are familiar to all of us as adults. Moreover, as we think back to our early school experiences, many of us can probably remember making well-intentioned pledges to ourselves each fall. "*This* year, I'm going to be a better student. I will get new and better notebooks, be more organized, devote full attention to my studies, and pay close attention in each class. I won't put off working on assignments or studying to the last minute. *This* year will be different!"

When it comes to change, optimism reigns supreme, and bookstores sell a vast array of self-help guides that nourish our optimism. However, in so many cases—despite our resolutions, best intentions, and book purchases— we find it extremely difficult to make meaningful change. Weight control is one area in which many of us engage in change efforts, and the statistics on the success of those efforts across the population are quite revealing. Ayyad and Andersen (2000) found that in an analysis of 17 comprehensive studies including a total of more than 3,000 dieters, only an average of 15% were successful in effecting *change*, defined in that analysis as losing and maintaining a weight loss of at least 20 pounds for three years or more. So often our hopes and plans for weight control and other change efforts are dashed, as we slip back into old habits and traditions that have been, and will continue to be, very powerful shaping forces in our lives.

Our disappointments lead to frustrations, but they also teach a powerful and important lesson; hope and good intentions, in and of themselves, are not particularly effective strategies for change. This lesson provides the foundation for one of the most fundamental concepts of behavioral science—and an especially relevant topic for considering the concept of change in American colleges and universities: The single best predictor of what we are likely to do in the future is not what we say, intend, hope, or plan, but rather what we have done in the past and what we are doing in the present. Simply said, *behavior is the best predictor of behavior.*

None of this implies that people and circumstances do not change. Changes of various kinds are occurring continuously—within our bodies, our relationships, our work, and the world at large. Some changes are triggered by what are considered natural forces—health, financial, or environmental factors. Others are the result of purposeful efforts to promote planned change. No doubt we can each point to examples of successful changes in our own lives and those of friends and colleagues; in relationships, social processes, and organizations; and at national and international levels. The changes can be the result of the adoption of new ideas, innovations, technologies, structures, or behaviors. At the national level, an interesting example of successful planned change is the considerable decrease in cigarette smoking that has occurred in the past half century. In 1965, 42.4% of the U.S. adult population smoked. Through ongoing, systematic, and multifaceted change efforts, that rate has dropped consistently—to approximately 18% in 2013 (Centers for Disease Control and Prevention, 2013). Even though this decrease is substantial, the challenge continues with each new generation of potential smokers.

The challenges associated with change are inescapable; they exist at all levels of life. Immune systems resist intrusions that threaten our physical well-being, our psychological system resists perceived threats to our emotional and cognitive stability, and organizations, communities, and societies resist threats to the existing order (Bertalanffy, 1968; Ruben, 1975).

Our focus here is on planned organizational change within higher education. Organizations, like individuals, have habits, traditions, and histories—and as with individuals, all of these are powerful forces that reinforce past and present practice and impede efforts to stimulate progress and innovation. The challenges associated with guiding planned change are particularly daunting in colleges and universities, where organizations are loosely coupled, decision-making is often decentralized, and attention to the perspectives of multiple stakeholders is essential to successful change. In a recent survey conducted by the *Chronicle of Higher Education* (2015), college and university presidents were asked to consider one strategy they would use to cut costs or raise new revenues at their institutions if they did not have to worry about the consequences among their constituents. Of the survey respondents, 16% did not choose any of the options presented. As Selingo (2013) wrote, "Even when given a pass from the potential consequences of their actions, presidents remain reluctant to make major changes on their campus" (p. 12).

Whereas personal change involves only one individual, and we can arguably exercise some direct control over ourselves, organizational change involves many people, all with their own personalized agendas, hopes, fears, and sensemaking frameworks. As Machiavelli (1532) wrote in *The Prince*, "There is nothing more difficult to take in hand, more perilous to conduct, or more uncertain in its success, than to take the lead in the introduction of a new order of things." Offering convincing contemporary support for Machiavelli's caution are studies of the success rate of planning organizational change efforts, which indicate that as few as 30% of these initiatives are considered successful (Aiken & Keller, 2009; Kotter, 1996a; Smith, 2002). Technical and resource considerations are often the first to be blamed for a high failure rate, but as we shall discuss, failure to understand and address personal, cultural, and communication issues generally are the more fundamental sources of the problem. These factors are especially problematic in complex organizations such as colleges and universities.

Lemons to Lemonade: Resistance to Planned Change

Critical to these failure statistics is what the literature has termed *resistance*. Resistance to personal as well as organizational change results from any number of factors. A proposed change:

- May not be deemed necessary;
- Requires a substantial investment of time, when there is already too much to do;
- Comes as a surprise;
- Calls for new routines, knowledge, or skills;
- Assumes resources that may not be forthcoming;
- Undermines our sense of self and our identity;
- Threatens our present status, stature, or roles;
- May introduce mistrust and lack of confidence in leaders; and
- Implies a criticism of the present systems, processes, or structures.

The expression of resistance can take many forms—some quite obvious, others much less so. Depending on the organizational culture, organizational climate, and other factors, expressions of resistance may include avoidance, questioning, challenging, redirecting, delaying, withdrawal, or overt or covert sabotage

Because resistance is recognized as an impediment to planned change, we tend to think of it as a problem, and we regard avoiding or overcoming it as the solution, which certainly is the norm in higher education. But resistance can also have benefits, and the determination of its valence sometimes depends on its advocate's role or goal. People who are advocating change will tend to view resistance in negative terms, as an impediment to achieving the intended outcome, yet those who are the intended targets of change —or who will be the most affected by it—may view it differently.

Even when resistance thwarts a change agenda, its presence can be helpful. For instance, resistance can signal the potential inappropriateness of a change being advocated, insufficiencies in the way advocates have explained the need for change, or failures to create appropriate engagement, commitment, or action. In such cases, the resistance may indicate a need to revise the change agenda or the way in which it is being communicated. It may point to a need for further revision or consultation, and ultimately it may lead to a refined plan and broader acceptance by stakeholders as the change initiative moves forward. In his bestselling book about the Olympic champion rowing team from the University of Washington, Daniel James Brown (2014) shares a quote by George Pocock, a leading designer and builder of racing shells, about the mechanics of rowing that is particularly relevant to this discussion of resistance: "It is hard to make that boat go as fast as you want to. The enemy, of course, is resistance of the water, as you have to displace the amount of water equal to the weight of men and equipment, but that very water is what supports you and that very enemy is your friend. So is life: the very problems you must overcome also support you and make you stronger in overcoming them" (p. 53). Similarly, the ways that leaders respond to and navigate resistance to change may result in a more meaningful, constructive, mutually agreed upon, and enduring outcome.

Stages of Change Acceptance or Resistance

The process of accepting or resisting proposed changes—in whole or in part—is complex, and many authors have suggested that it occurs in a series of stages (e.g., Kotter, 1996b; Lewis, 2010; Ruben et al., 2008). The numbers of and labels for these stages vary across authors. Ruben and colleagues (2008) described five such stages, which they apply in their analysis of the dynamics of change associated with the Spellings Commission on Higher Education; that framework has proved useful more generally in understanding, planning, and leading higher education change efforts. As illustrated in Figure 15.1, the first stage in the model is *attention*, and relates to gaining an awareness of and perceiving a need for change. Clearly, if one sees no need for change and is unaware of proposals to address these needs, nothing happens. Once an individual becomes cognizant of the need, the second stage in the change process is *engagement*. To become engaged is to personally consider the potential need and issues involved, to discuss them with others, and generally to invest time and effort in the process. When this engagement occurs, the process of change moves forward. Conversely, without such engagement, it is unlikely that an individual will be motivated to further consider the need for change or prospects for new or innovative ideas, behaviors, or actions. Particularly in colleges and universities, where dialogue and analysis are so highly valued, engagement is critical to both the quality and likelihood of acceptance of new directions. It is also the case, however, that the penchant for extensive conversation and analysis in higher education can lead to loss of momentum and the potential for the change process to stall at this stage.

Figure 15.1. Stages in the change process.

Note. From Ruben, B.D., Lewis, L., Sandmeyer, L., and Immordino, K. (2008). *Assessing the impact of the Spellings Commission: The message, the messenger, and the dynamics of change.* Washington, DC: National Association of College and University Business Officers.

Commitment is the third stage and refers to the progression toward accepting—or in some cases rejecting—the need for change or the directions being advocated. As the process continues, commitment ideally translates into the fourth stage, *action*—to move forward toward embracing a new direction or behavior, or to disengagement. In the fifth stage, *integration*, either a change initiative is accepted and incorporated into the lifestyle of an individual or the culture of an organization, or it lingers and ultimately fades from practice.

Generally, successful change requires a progression through all five stages, but the process can stall at any point. Consider an example of how these dynamics play out in health practices. Suppose you visit a doctor, and you learn based on exam results that your blood pressure is up from your last visit, that it is "borderline, tending toward the high side." Your physician tells you that you need to significantly reduce your sodium intake and increase exercise in order to lower your blood pressure, and you should return for a recheck in six months. If you are not successful in these efforts, medication or other intervention strategies will be necessary. Does this news get your attention? Is it sufficient to motivate behavior change? If it is, you may have questions for the doctor or a nutritionist, and you will likely want to do some reading and research about elevated blood pressure, sources of sodium, approaches to lowering sodium intake, and exercise and other lifestyle strategies for lowering blood pressure. Will you commit to a low-sodium diet and increased exercise? If so, will you follow through with the actions necessary to implement that commitment? Finally, will you incorporate these actions into your behavior to the point where they become routine, leading to the change advocated by your physician—and ultimately resulting in lower blood pressure? And, if you achieve this goal, will you be able to sustain that success? At any of these stages, you may resist, reject, falter, or delay and fail to move to the next step in the advocated direction. Unless all stages are completed, the physician's planned change efforts for you—and yours for yourself—will likely not be successful.

Strategies for Stage 1: Capturing Attention

Managing organizational change is an area of increasing importance for academic as well as administrative leaders in higher education. The aim of change leadership is to guide others successfully through the stages in the change process. As implied in the model and foregoing discussion, the first consideration has to be gaining the attention of those who need to understand and support the change initiative. While this undertaking may seem simple and straightforward, capturing the attention of others in a world with so many messages and people competing for time and interest can be a significant challenge—particularly if the topic seems to have little immediate relevance or consequence. Additionally, the often siloed context of higher education adds to the complexity of leading and mobilizing attention to organizational change initiatives.

As noted, gaining attention relates to clarifying the need for the advocated change and the need it addresses. This attention-gaining process should generate a sense of importance or urgency. Ideally, the stage also creates a *burning platform*, defined as imparting the sense that change is necessary because continuing on the present course of action (or inaction) will not be tenable in the long run, and is likely to lead to undesirable outcomes. Gaining attention for one's agenda and issues is essential, but avoiding the *attention paradox* is also a consideration. This term describes the phenomenon in which dramatic, fear-inducing, or shocking message are used to gain attention. However, if overdone, these strategies may lead to denial, avoidance, or alienation of its intended supporters, thereby inadvertently heightening resistance to the message because of the anxieties they evoke.

Strategies for Stage 2: Creating Engagement

Strategies that heighten awareness and receptivity should be followed by efforts to engage individuals in discussions of the need, challenge, or problem(s), and potential solutions. A key prior consideration in this stage is identifying the list of individuals (and groups) who need to participate actively in the process. This list would include key stakeholders—individuals and groups with a stake in the outcome of the proposed change. Depending on the circumstances, these stakeholders might include board members, administrators, faculty, staff, alumni, students, parents, donors, the media, and perhaps the local community. This stage also involves determining whether particular individuals within those groups would be especially important to engage—because of their insight or influence, or the resources they control. For example, along with faculty and staff, members of advisory boards, high-level donors, or political representatives might wield extensive influence relative to a planned construction project through vocal support or resistance. As noted, the primary goal at this point in the process is facilitating dialogue with internal and external stakeholders in order to generate a shared understanding of the reasons for the proposed change, what the change will involve, and what it will mean for them.

Strategies for Stage 3: Developing Commitment

Developing resolve—a commitment to the advocated change—is the third aim. This stage includes identifying and focusing on areas of agreement, and also addressing and working through obstacles. Typically, these goals include ensuring the availability of needed resources, providing opportunities for input and influence, and ultimately building consensus and working coalitions.

Strategies for Stage 4: Motivating Action

Motivating action is the fourth task. Success at this stage involves clarifying intended change outcomes, promoting the desired behavior, and identifying the tasks or actions that need to be implemented. The ultimate aim is enlisting the desired actions, which often requires providing the necessary resources and training to support the desired behaviors, prompting activities that move the initiative in the desired direction, and continuing these efforts until the intended change outcomes are realized.

Strategies for Stage 5: Assuring Integration

Once the envisioned goals have been achieved, the final challenge—and by no means a minor one—is assuring integration and sustaining the change. Often the passage of time, waning attention, or a change in leadership result in a gradual backsliding.

In Stage 5, strategies should be implemented to mitigate these tendencies, showcasing and celebrating changes, publicly recognizing and rewarding innovators, developing reinforcing processes and structures, and implementing mechanisms for regular review and improvement.

Unless these and other reinforcing steps are initiated, whether applied to planned personal or organizational advances, it is likely that recent advances will gradually regress to the older patterns, traditions, or behaviors. So it is, for instance, with the case of weight loss, as discussed earlier, where evidence suggests that losing weight, while difficult, is far easier than maintaining the lower weight.

Five-by-Five Matrix of Planned Change

In the preceding discussion we provided an overview of the dynamics and stages of change, the potential liabilities and benefits of resistance, and considerations for negotiating through the five stages. Five additional factors are critical in guiding planned change efforts. Each of these is cross-cutting—that is, these five concepts play a vital role in the tasks associated with each of the five stages of change. They are planning, leadership, communication, culture, and assessment.

1. *Planning* is defined as developing the change plan.

2. *Leadership* is defined as specifying and designating appropriate individuals or teams to guide the change initiative through the five stages.
3. *Communication* is defined as designing and implementing a process of information sharing, listening, and collaboration with those involved with, knowledgeable about, or affected by the planned change.
4. *Culture* is defined as taking account of the organization's language, history, norms, rules, and traditions that may influence the dynamics of change.
5. *Assessment* is defined as developing and implementing a systematic approach to monitoring progress and outcomes as the change process progresses, and of outcomes overall.

Overlaying these five cross-cutting success factors (listed vertically) across the five stages of change (listed horizontally) produces a five-by-five matrix for planned change (MPC) shown in Table 15.1. The matrix displays the five stages of change as columns and the five cross-cutting success factors as rows. Each cell represents a point of intersection between the two sets of considerations, and each highlights an important area for attention by academic and administrative leaders as they undertake a change initiative.

We have found that the MPC provides an exceptionally useful framework for *thinking* about a planned change strategy and also serves as a helpful tool for developing and implementing that strategy. Although one person can develop and implement strategy, the benefits are generally greater—in terms of the quality of the finished product as well as the value of the process—if the team with responsibility for the change efforts develops it in a collaborative way.

TABLE 15.1
The 5 x 5 Matrix for Planned Change

STAGES: SUCCESS FACTORS	1. Attention	2. Engagement	3. Commitment	4. Action	5. Integration
1. Planning					
2. Leadership					
3. Communication					
4. Culture					
5. Assessment					

In the following sections, each cross-cutting factor will be discussed in more detail, along with activities that may be used to apply the framework to change planning and implementation. Readers may find it helpful to apply the framework to a hypothetical or actual case study as a way to become familiar with how the matrix works.[1]

Factor 1: Planning Basics

The following discussion focuses on the basics of change planning. This framework is an adaptation of the more general strategic planning framework presented in Chapter 14.

The phrase *planning basics* refers to high-level planning. This is not a detailed project management model or program, although such models are sometimes a helpful way to keep track of the details of a plan as it progresses.

When is systemic planning for change necessary? There are several answers to this question: (a) when one person alone cannot easily accomplish the proposed initiative; (b) when there is a potential for multiple understandings—or misunderstandings—of the purposes of a change initiative; (c) where the actions and decisions that will be undertaken are likely to have substantial or lasting consequences; (d) when multiple stakeholders are involved; or (e) where the success of the venture depends on commitment, action, or ownership by a number of individuals or stakeholder groups. Planning basics can significantly improve outcomes in any situation with these characteristics.

The primary aim of planning basics is to achieve some degree of shared understanding of the purpose and intended outcomes of the project, and to coordinate action in the implementation of a plan. If the planning is done in an inclusive way rather than by a single individual, the process can also contribute to the quality of decision-making and to the morale and enthusiasm of those involved with or affected by the change.

The first step, and an important one, is to clearly and succinctly explain the purpose(s) of the planned change initiative or project, and why it is needed. The second step is to list all the groups that are directly affected by, or will have an interest or stake in, the planned change initiative. This stakeholder list is important because it will be used later to develop leadership, communication, cultural, and assessment strategies.

Implementing an environmental scan is the third step. This involves two components, as discussed in Chapter 14. The first component is an analysis of unit and institutional strengths, weaknesses, opportunities, and threats that are relevant to the change initiative. The second involves *benchmarking*—defined as identifying peer and aspirant programs, departments, and institutions whose offerings can provide a useful point of comparison for the changes being considered. Depending on the nature of the change initiative, a leader can perform this step via structured brainstorming by individuals intimately acquainted with the project, the unit, and the institution. On the basis of the change's complexity, scope, and magnitude, the environmental scan may require substantial research by a specially formed task force or external consultants. More extensive efforts would be appropriate, for instance, with a merger or restructuring of multiple units or institutions. However the scan is conducted, the aim is to identify factors in the environment that represent strengths, limitations, opportunities, and threats, and through benchmarking to consider how peer and aspirant programs, departments, or institutions may be addressing comparable needs and challenges. Information gained through these activities adds to considerations for establishing change goals.

Formulating specific goals that will address the need and purpose, as well as fulfill the aspirations of the change initiative, is the fourth step. These goals become the reference point for the various activities to be undertaken. Each goal statement should succinctly describe—in a sentence—*what* needs to be done to fulfill the envisioned change. Also, keep the number of goals manageable; four or five is probably the upper limit. Beyond that, the big picture that the goals are meant to define can slip out of focus. Goal statements should also be sufficiently precise so that it is possible to monitor progress toward their achievement(see Chapter 16).

Determining the best *strategies* for each goal—*how* each goal is to be accomplished—is the fifth step. Finally, action plans are developed. Aptly named, these plans provide the details of who needs to do what, and when. Action planning serves a number of purposes. When it comes to planning, unquestionably the devil is in the details of follow-through. Often, without specifying this level of detail as a part of the plan development, the critical link between the idea and the implementation gets lost. So, although it is sometimes tempting to defer or short-circuit this stage in the basics of planning, that maneuver almost always turns out to be a mistake.

Once all of the elements discussed thus far have been completed, they can be pulled together to provide an integrated change summary guide. The document and the thinking it embodies provide the foundation for the development of leadership, communication, cultural, and assessment strategies, as the following sections discuss.

Factor 2: Leadership Considerations

Leadership is indispensable to the success of every stage in the process of planned change, as it is for planning in general. In considering leadership issues relative to change, a couple of perspectives should be taken into account: (a) personal leadership—the personal roles and responsibilities of the individual who wants to promote successful change; and (b) leadership architecture—the roles and responsibilities of the leadership structure or team—recognizing that no successful organizational change initiative is ever accomplished by a single individual, regardless of how competent that person may be.

In the review of literature completed for *What Leaders Need to Know and Do*, discussed at several points in previous chapters, Ruben (2006) identified five competency clusters as necessary for exceptional leadership. In addition to positional competencies—those described as vertical, subject matter, discipline, and sector-related areas of expertise—are personal, organizational, communication, and analytic competencies. These four competency clusters refer to knowledge and skill sets that transcend specific fields, jobs, or situations. As discussed in Chapter 11, a commitment to enhancing one's competencies in each of these areas is one of the most meaningful professional development decisions a leader can make. These knowledge and skill sets are useful in a broad range of leadership roles and circumstances, yet few situations test individual leadership capabilities more than developing and implementing planned change. The personal and organizational reflection associated with analytic competencies, and the positional competencies that relate to the organization and field, are particularly critical in preparing for change initiatives and forming an appropriate leadership team. Personal, communication, and organizational competencies become essential in shepherding the effort through each of the five stages of change.

Another critical task, which also draws on personal leadership competencies, is establishing an appropriate leadership team and the broader leadership structure or architecture necessary to facilitate the process. The leadership structure may consist of one or several teams and possibly subteams, and depending on the specific nature of the initiative it may make sense for the composition of the team or teams to vary as the initiative moves through the various stages. The appropriate size, composition, and responsibilities of the leadership structure will vary greatly from initiative to initiative, depending on the complexity of the organization, the scope of the project, the number of constituencies involved, the extent of resources committed, and the length of time available to complete the project.

The strengths and limitations of those who will be asked to play a role in the effort should be carefully considered when forming leadership teams. A good strategy is generally to select participants whose competencies, knowledge, and skills augment those of the senior leader. It is also important to identify and involve individuals who understand and can effectively represent the perspectives of the various groups that the proposed change will affect—either directly or indirectly, who will understand and help to champion the planned change, and who have the competencies necessary to facilitate success at a particular stage in the process.

Table 15.2 provides an example of a template for the identification of a leadership group and/or architecture to guide planned change through each of the five stages. The guide focuses attention on the analysis and decisions regarding *who* (person or leadership team) will need to complete what *task(s)*, during what *time frame*, for each stage in the planned change process.[2]

If the project was being administered by a team within a larger organization, perhaps the senior leader or project leader would form an executive team. In this case, different team members might serve as coordinators of different tasks in different stages, with the goal of matching leadership knowledge and skills to the objectives of each stage. In any case, the leadership architecture guide provides a useful tool for encouraging the disciplined thinking necessary for successful leadership throughout the various stages of a project.

TABLE 15.2
Leadership Architecture Guide

Stage	*Leader (Person/team)*	*What the leader/ team should do*	*Time frame*
1. Attention			
2. Engagement			
3. Commitment			
4. Action			
5. Integration			

Factor 3: Communication Strategy and Framing

Along with planning and leadership, communication is a key determinant of the successful execution of the five stages of change. Communication can seem like a simple and straightforward activity to those who have not studied or thought seriously about the process. A person has an idea for an organizational change that he or she thinks makes sense. The individual creates a message (oral, visual, or written) and conveys it to others in the organization or persons they would like to inform or persuade, and that's that. However, as we know from previous discussions on communication, because of differences in experience, needs, perspective, motives, knowledge, roles, and a number of other factors, one cannot assume that the messages sent and the meanings intended by leaders or others will be received and interpreted as desired. This caution is particularly important when applied to such topics as planned change in higher education, where the need for better communication is not only about sending messages more effectively but also listening, empathizing, building support, and observing carefully to increase the likelihood that communication will function as intended. This is especially critical in communication on topics and with stakeholders for whom misunderstanding or resistance is predictable.

As noted previously, it is easy to assume that everyone else is as knowledgeable and concerned about the issues that matter to a leader, but typically that is not the case. When it comes to comprehending the purpose and need for change, for instance, those who have been intimately involved in the thought and preparation processes have already recognized the significance of the effort. But many others whose understanding and support are needed are unlikely initially to share that knowledge or enthusiasm. To move them to the desired point of insight and interest requires a systematic, time-release communication process that allows the relevant individuals and groups to work through and digest the information in the way a leader did. Then, ideally with encouragement and engagement, these audiences will reach conclusions similar to those of the leader.

Personal experience and the research literature indicate that a single message is seldom likely to have much impact when it comes to creating change. Telling someone, "This change is needed and important," will not get the job done. It takes a great deal of repetitive communication to create attention, engagement, commitment, action, and integration. Viewed from a leader's perspective, repetition can be agonizing and may begin to seem wasteful; however, the goal is not for the leader to enjoy his or her communication effort. Rather, the goal is to reach all the important stakeholders, so that they can understand, endorse, and support the initiative. As noted earlier, leaders are likely to become quite bored with the specific messages long before they reach everyone who needs to be familiar with and committed to the effort.

Charts that depict the hierarchy of an organization are helpful for describing lines of responsibility and control. They are generally much less helpful for describing—or helping to predict—the actual lines of communication and information flow, particularly in higher education. According to organizational folklore, information flows quite naturally in organizations from senior leaders to mid-level leaders and then throughout the organization. The realities of organizational life offer contrary evidence. In practice, organizational communication is much more complex, disorderly, and random. Particularly in colleges and universities, communication lines may not correspond at all to formal organizational reporting lines, but rather may often operate through informal channels, based on relationships—and these are often very well developed. Communication within an organization, therefore, may be a combination of top-down, bottom-up, horizontal, circular, looping, disjointed, and random patterns (Ruben & Stewart, 2016). Recognizing these realities—and developing strategies accordingly—is very helpful in leveraging the communication patterns that are likely to occur relative to a planned change.

In any communication situation, some fraction of receivers are relatively easy to reach via well-crafted messages that explain the purpose and need for a change. Those individuals will be willing to listen to the proposed change, and they will develop a basic understanding of the rationale for it. Individuals in this segment of the audience can contribute in very helpful ways to efforts to reach other members of the target audience.

Keep in mind also that it will not be possible to be equally successful with everyone in the total population of individuals with whom a leader must communicate throughout the change process. Of course, sincere effort needs to be made with all relevant stakeholders, and leaders cannot write off anyone. But leaders also must not burn out on efforts with those who are wholly unwilling to even entertain ideas related to the need for change.

There is always a fraction of the audience that is not easy to engage. They may lack interest in the initiative or simply be unable to relate to the new perspectives, purposes, goals, or needs as described. Even with repeated efforts, the message received will not even loosely correspond to the message sent. Efforts certainly must be made to gain the attention, engagement, and commitment of this group, but leaders cannot focus too much energy on people who are extremely resistant. Successful communication with all individuals is not a realistic or necessary goal. At some point, it becomes reasonable to conclude that the investment of time and effort directed toward particular individuals is no longer useful. Instead of contributing to progress toward the intended outcome, the efforts are creating frustrations and draining energies that could be better invested elsewhere.

Perhaps the most important place to invest significant effort is with the segment of the target audience that could respond either negatively or positively to the message. That response will depend mostly on the quality of the communication effort—how carefully messages are crafted and delivered, whether there is sufficient repetition and follow-up, and how fully questions and concerns are listened to and considered. In any situation, essentially this is an independent voter group that can understand and support the effort if the communication process is handled well—in speaking and writing, as well as listening and observing. On the other hand, if communication activities are not well planned and executed, this group may not understand, may be indifferent, or may resist your message and the directions it advocates—sometimes as much because of inadequate communication as because of fundamental reactions to the substantive aspects of the proposed change. Without active support from a large segment of this audience, success in moving successfully through the five stages of change is doubtful. Related to points made earlier in this book, followers play an active role in the coconstruction of leadership, and the value and necessity of a shared sense of purpose and direction are nowhere more critical than in efforts to lead successful organizational change. As these individuals come to understand and support an initiative, they become part of the de facto leadership team and can be particularly influential agents of change with other stakeholders. Indeed, they often make up the group that is most effective in explaining why they reached their particular conclusion because they are regarded as relatively objective parties, having no personal stake in the outcome.

As discussed earlier in a different context, efforts relative to change are easier if the messages created to explain the purpose of a change tell the story simply and briefly—about the time it takes to ride several floors in an elevator. Imagine a situation where a colleague says, "Fill me in on that project you're working on." What do you say? In this case, having a simple, focused, and well-rehearsed story is most helpful for improving the likelihood that your colleague takes away the intended message. A very unpromising start would be, "Well, let me begin by giving you some background. In October 1987 . . ." This is not a good beginning for a succinct explanation, and one that likely will not get beyond the mid-1990s before the elevator door opens and your colleague (gratefully) departs—with little or no understanding of the key points of the project and probably very little interest in inquiring further.

People are drawn to, remember, and retell messages that are simple and to the point. Longer messages with many details and qualifications are more difficult to understand, harder to remember, and more likely to be misinterpreted and distorted in retelling. Elevator stories intentionally provide very few details. If the person you are talking to is interested after hearing more about the project—and if time permits—you can provide additional details. If colleagues are motivated to ask questions, the answers given should be concise and responsive to the specific issues in question, rather than provided as part of a monologue. The more attention and meaningful engagement in the exchange, the better the chances for the desired commitment and action.

Framing is another relevant concept in change communication. There are many ways to describe a particular situation, change initiative, or project. These framing choices can have considerable influence on whether a message is noticed, how it is interpreted, whether it is remembered, and how it is described to others. Thoughtful attention to word choice, thematic focus, topics of emphasis, and whether the words convey a positive or negative connotation can be significant to the outcomes in face-to-face, written, and electronic communication.

Communication Strategies for Stages of Planned Change
As discussed in Chapter 13, communication concepts are translated into action through the communication strategy that a leader develops to support the change process. When applied to change leadership, specific communication strategies are needed for each stage in the change process. Key questions to consider include the following:

- Who are your internal and external target audiences (affected parties)?
- What are your intended outcomes?
- What are the potential sources of resistance?
- What are the appropriate messages for each audience?
- What are the most effective channels for reaching each audience with your message?
- Who is the most appropriate messenger?
- What impact are you expecting from your messages?

Clear goals, thoughtfully tailored messages, and purposefully selected channels that are appropriate for a particular stage and a specific audience are vital components in change communication. Many potential communication goals may be adopted, as shown in Table 15.3. Messages should be created to achieve the selected goal or goals, paying attention to the messages' substance, language, length, framing, and tone of the message.

Channel selection can also be a significant variable in communication planning and implementation. There are many different means of communication, and depending on the goals, audiences, and situation, some are more effective than others. In certain instances, the potential for immediate,

TABLE 15.3
Possible Communication Goals

• Gain attention	• Increase awareness
• Listen and understand	• Provide information
• Clarify	• Encourage
• Reinforce a point of view	• Persuade
• Engage	• Motivate
• Create buy-in	• Prompt action
• Heighten commitment	• Promote sustainability

face-to-face interaction is desirable. In these situations, one-on-one sessions and focus groups are appropriate. In other situations, a large group setting such as a town hall meeting and production video may be most appropriate. There may be other stages or situations wherein the possibility of spontaneous and immediate reactions could interfere with particular goals or be difficult for leaders to handle on the fly. In these circumstances, mediated channels—e-mail exchanges, blogs, or websites—may be more appropriate, because they provide the opportunity for leaders to think through their responses before reacting. Another consideration in media selection is the issue of how public and permanent you want messages to be. Face-to-face conversation is fleeting, while e-mails, blogs, and other media-based documents are far more permanent and portable. The extent of permanence can be a virtue or a liability, depending on factors such as the stage of the project, level of support for the project, assessed need for communication flexibility and adaptability, the comfort and skill level of the communicator, and especially the goals. As illustrated in Table 15.4, leaders may utilize many communication channel options, and in each case, the assets and liabilities of particular channels—and the extent to which they are most appropriate given the stage, goals, and audiences—point to the need for careful analysis and decision-making relative to their selection. Quite likely, different messages and channels will be best suited for differing internal and external audiences—perhaps even within each of these broad categories. A plan to expand a campus in a way that requires purchasing and tearing down a number of local homes would be an extreme example of a situation where the community, media, homeowners, local government, faculty, staff, and students would each require their own communication approaches, messages, and channels, given the specialized needs, concerns, and preferred communication channels of each group.

TABLE 15.4
Available Communication Channels

• Face-to-face	• E-mail
• Website	• Video
• The grapevine	• Cascade briefings
• Focus groups	• Surveys
• Meetings	• Blogs
• Social media	• Poster/bulletin boards
• Discussion lists	• Newsletters, reports, memos

One additional and important consideration is the selection of message sources. Is the president, an area vice president, a dean or director, one or more faculty or staff members, or an alumnus of a student group the appropriate source for particular goals, messages, and stages in the change process? Depending on the change initiative and the culture of the organization, individuals in each role may bring particular strengths and liabilities, and selections of people to serve as message sources should be made purposefully.

Ideally, communication planning will take account of each stage in the change process, along with the goals, messages, and channels. Generally speaking, a distinct strategy is required for each stage.

Table 15.5 provides an illustration of a template for Communication Strategy, Stage 1 that can be used to develop and record these decisions.[3] Individuals and groups can complete each of these templates to develop a systematic, sequential, and comprehensive communication strategy for a specific change initiative or project.

TABLE 15.5
Communication Strategy Guide: Stage 1—Attention

Communication . . . in order to connect to what audiences, to achieve what goals/outcomes, to overcome what anticipated resistance (e.g., needs, questions, concerns), with what message, through which channels, coming from whom?					
Audience	*Goal*	*Resistance*	*Message*	*Communication Channel*	*Message Source*

Adapted from: Tromp, S. A., Ruben, B. D. *Strategic Planning in Higher Education,* Washington, DC: National Association of College and University Business Officers, 2010, p. 77.

Factor 4: The Role of Organizational Culture

As discussed in Chapter 5, each of the major divisions, disciplines, and departments within the institution is likely to have its own distinctive culture. Change initiatives often affect more than one culture; therefore, attention to each group is another important component of change planning and implementation.

As noted previously, cultures are stable and naturally resist change. The more a group is affected directly or indirectly by a proposed change, the more thoughtful attention, creativity, and persistence are required for successful outcomes. The two largest and most critical employee groups within higher education institutions are the staff/administrators and the faculty. As discussed extensively in Chapter 5, fundamental and quite predictable differences often exist between faculty/academics and administrators, and these differences typically become quite significant when thinking about how planning for change should work.

Suppose that a university with a tradition of decentralized and collegial decision-making decided to consider enacting new policies and systems related to its online course offerings. Imagine that the new approach would include establishing a new university policy, a new university office, and a new centralized system through which all online courses would be designed and disseminated. Imagine further that a joint committee of faculty and administrators/staff was formed to consider this idea and make recommendations about the advisability of moving in this direction. Thinking first about the administrative and staff perspective, members of this group would likely focus on issues related to operational outcomes, cost, procedures, legal issues, and system needs and capabilities, while academics likely would begin with focused attention on issues related to the impact of potential changes on faculty autonomy and academic freedom, and ensuring appropriate inclusivity in the process of considering new directions.

Thinking about the planning process more generally, the administrative culture promotes a formalization of the planning process, while academics are often comfortable with a much more informal agenda. When it comes to evaluating the merits of change, the academic culture typically places greatest attention on the impact that new systems or procedures will have on the faculty and academic life—and, where appropriate, the perspective of students.

Considerable differences often occur in the ways in which administrators and faculty talk about organizational issues. Indeed, academics might not often use a phrase like "organizational issues," preferring to talk in specifics about an issue in Department X or School Y. This and other language differences reflect the view that, for most faculty members, each department, school, or university is a unique and special entity. Administrators, on the other hand, may be far more likely to see universities and the units within them in more general terms, and to perceive more parallels and relevancies for the language and thinking in other organizations, institutions, or sectors. The preceding discussion is full of generalizations, and they do not hold for all individuals, cultures, or institutions. The key point to keep in mind is that effective change leadership requires what we characterized earlier as ethnographic competencies—skills in predicting and detecting cultural differences with sensitivity, and finding creative ways to utilize and leverage the strengths of each perspective.

Table 15.6 provides a template that can be used for systematically approaching the issues related to culture that might be important for a particular initiative during each stage in the planned change process. The first column calls for a listing of the various groups and issues that need to be considered. The second column presents the details of precisely what needs to be done in particular stages to address the issues noted. For example, if strategic planning was recently conducted in a way that created annoyance and resistance, this item can be noted as a "Group/Cultural Issue" in the Culture Guide Worksheet in Table 15.6, recognizing that this issue should perhaps be considered in all stages of the change initiative. Given this situation, leaders should consider addressing this cultural baggage by labeling and describing the new initiative in ways that are unlikely to bring up past negative associations—an item to be discussed and noted in the "What Needs to Be Done" column of the worksheet. On the other hand, if previous experiences with "strategic planning" have been positive and well received, that knowledge can be useful in approaching and implementing a new initiative.

The worksheet allows space for comments and plans for each stage. Depending on the initiative, the number of groups involved, and overall complexity, it might make sense to create separate sheets for each stage in the change planning process. Leaders can also perform a more granular analysis of the cultural groups involved and the issues that must be considered. For instance, in some cases the cultural resistance of senior faculty and those who are currently making extensive use of online course design and delivery could certainly be greater than the resistance of junior or part-time faculty, so at some stages, different strategies and approaches might be appropriate for each group. Similarly, it might make sense to break out and consider staff and administrative subgroups. The staff group that would have direct responsibility for a new system might be one to consider. Auditors might be another, deans and unit business managers another, and so on. The decision about whether and how to break out separate groups would be made based on whether particular groups have their own cultural issues that need to be addressed separately.

TABLE 15.6
Culture Guide Worksheet

Stage	Group/Cultural Issue	What Needs to Be Done
1. Attention		
2. Engagement		
3. Commitment		
4. Action		
5. Integration		

Factor 5: Assessment—Monitoring Progress and Outcomes

In regard to planned change, the overriding goals are to be proactive and to adopt an approach to assessment that helps to ensure the successful completion of the initiative in a manner that is as simple and straightforward as possible. These aims are especially important with planned change initiatives, as an institution must be sure that the substantial resources dedicated to an initiative are leading in the intended direction, and that they ultimately result in the desired benefits.

Assessment efforts that focus on change initiatives—like those devoted to assessing other processes within the institution—typically meet with some resistance and a variety of arguments. Nonetheless, if done well, evaluation can be quite useful. If leaders assume responsibility for guiding the assessment process, it allows those who understand the intricacies of the institution and situation to play the central role in defining, implementing, and using the assessment techniques to be employed.

The basics of assessment—regardless of what one is assessing—are very straightforward. The core concepts are captured by four questions:

- Why is the change needed?
- What is the initiative intended to accomplish?
- How will success be evaluated?
- How will this knowledge be used for improvement?

As we discuss in greater detail in Chapter 16, these four questions can be applied to assessment of any type of initiative, at any level. The core considerations are the same. Table 15.7 provides a template for the creation of a plan to guide assessment through each of the five stages of planned change.

To illustrate how this guide can be used, let's use the online course development policy and program example, considering how one would design an

TABLE 15.7
Assessment Guide Worksheet

Stage	To Accomplish What?	What Will Be Assessed?	How?	How Will Info Be Used?
1. Attention				
2. Engagement				
3. Commitment				
4. Action				
5. Integration				

approach to assessment for Stage 1: Attention. Take a few minutes to think about how you might complete this portion of the assessment guide.

In Stage 1—leaders would assess the sources of satisfaction and dissatisfaction with the current policy and system among faculty, administrators, and staff. This assessment could be done using techniques such as focus groups and surveys or documenting comments made in town hall and other meetings. The information obtained could be used to clarify attributes that will be important for any new system and shortcomings to be avoided and could also provide input for the development of appropriate communication strategies to pursue in this and subsequent stages. These strategies would include determining how to encourage sufficient engagement with the topic, the shortcomings of the present system to highlight, what inefficiencies and costs are associated with the present system or policies, what potential attributes of a new system will be and how to emphasize these benefits, and so on.

It might also be useful to assess whether members of the community are informed about a proposed change, the need for that change, or possible options to address those needs. Depending on specific goals, leaders would probably want the community awareness level to be very high, implementing attention-gaining communication strategies until this goal is achieved. Awareness level could be assessed through surveys designed to gauge community members' ability to speak to the topic or by tracking attendance at town hall meetings or other events at which the topic is discussed.

An Integrated Approach

The foregoing sections have described the major components of the five-by-five MPC—the five stages of change, and the five cross-cutting key success factors. There is no magic bullet or foolproof formula that assures success in all situations. However, a disciplined approach using the MPC model in planning and implementing change initiatives certainly can enhance the effectiveness of the processes by which innovation or change is introduced, facilitate acceptance and recognition, reduce risk and resistance, and decrease the time it takes to achieve each of these outcomes.

This approach is helpful because it addresses many of the reasons why change initiatives fail, which include the following:

- The importance of each stage in the change process is not understood.
- Factors that are essential to change at each stage—planning, leadership, communication, culture, and assessment—are overlooked.
- Key constituencies are not engaged in appropriate ways and at appropriate times.

- An effective leadership architecture is never designed.
- The need for buy-in is underestimated.
- The dynamics of learning and change for individuals and organizations are misunderstood.
- There is an insufficient level of senior-level support.

Principles of Planned Change

In thinking broadly about successful planned change, it is helpful for leaders to keep in mind some foundational principles of planned change:

- No change is so small or insignificant that you can ignore issues of planning, leadership, communication, culture, or assessment.
- Assume that you know and care much more about the change initiative—and reasons for it—than those at other levels or other parts of the organization.
- Create a cadre of people who understand, support, and champion the change—a leadership team.
- Seek the perspectives of those who have insights, experience, and outlooks that you do not have.
- Realize that all change has both temporary and longer-term effects on members of the organization and other stakeholder groups. Consider the longer- as well as shorter-term impact.
- When it comes to understanding the dynamics of change, try to see things from the point of view of the affected parties, and apply the Golden Rule.

Conclusion

Rapidly changing environments call for organizations that are flexible and adaptable, which is certainly the case for American colleges and universities. As Blumenstyk (2015) noted in an article in the *Chronicle of Higher Education,*

> Leadership in higher education today requires a delicate balance: a posture that prevents both knee-jerk reactions to the latest trend and flat-footed reluctance to go after real opportunities. . . . Whatever the model, it's clear that cruise-control leadership is no longer an option, even for colleges that don't face immediate financial threats.

Change is inevitable. Effective leadership during times of planned change can shape the legacy of an individual or team. The concepts, principles, and tools offered in this chapter are intended to help leaders effectively guide their institutions through times of turbulence and significant change.

For Further Consideration

1. Personal Change Reflection

As a personal thought experiment, recall examples in which efforts were made by a family member, friend, or colleague at work to encourage you to make a significant change in your life—for example, to spend more time with family, learn new skills at work, or undertake a lifestyle or behavioral change. Were those efforts successful? Why or why not? Did you resist the change? Were you able to overcome that resistance? If resistance did occur, at what stage or stages in the process did it intervene? Can you analyze and explain the outcome of the planned change effort based on the five stages in the change model?

2. Recruitment and Selection at Corwin College

Traditionally, each search committee at Corwin College developed its own search process for recruiting and selecting new directors and deans. Several administrators have discussed the idea of creating a single search process or procedure and supporting materials for all senior leader searches college-wide. At this point, the idea is very much in its infancy, and the president has asked you to chair a committee to develop a framework for planning and implementing the new campus-wide search process. Recognizing the complexity and array of issues involved, the recommendation is to use the matrix for planned change (Table 15.1) as your guide. You also have been asked to annotate the suggestions in your plan with the rationale guiding your recommendations. The president looks forward to meeting with your committee when the proposal is complete. What would your plan and proposal include?

Notes

1. Guides Worksheets that can be used for these purposes are also provided in the appendices.

2. Copies of this and other worksheets are provided in the appendices.

3. Additional templates are available at odl.rutgers.edu

16

USING METRICS TO TRACK
PROGRESS, MEASURE
OUTCOMES, AND ASSESS
EFFECTIVENESS

In This Chapter

- What are the origins of the widespread interest in measures, metrics, evaluations, and assessments in higher education?
- What are the potential advantages and disadvantages associated with the use of metrics?
- What are the central elements of a mission-to-metrics framework, and how can the model be helpful for higher education leaders?
- How can metrics help clarify the institutional, departmental, programmatic, or project mission, vision, and goals?
- How can academic and administrative leaders use metrics to create shared understanding and commitment to organizational aspirations?

There is no mistaking the growing national, state, and local pressures for increased attention to measurement. These efforts are apparent in all organizations in all sectors, but perhaps nowhere have they been the focus of greater attention, controversy, and change efforts than in higher education.

Historically, the most critical considerations in evaluating the quality of colleges and universities were factors such as the stature of faculty and staff, the quality of the programs offered, the level of distinction of students selecting and attending the institution, the extent of library holdings, and the adequacy of financial and physical assets. Within this tradition, there was a notable emphasis on the quality of resources and the richness of opportunities that the institution provided. Today, that traditional emphasis is matched, if not surpassed, by efforts to assess the benefits that stakeholders, especially students, derive from these institutions—most particularly, what they learn, how they progress through the institution, and how their education benefits them following completion. This shift in emphasis has led to increasing efforts to assess outcomes related to all elements of an institution's, department's, or program's mission, aspirations, plans, and goals; not only those related to education and student learning, but also those associated with teaching, research, scholarship, service, and outreach.

The Assessment Craze in Higher Education

Assessing outcomes, rather than inventorying inputs and institutional resources and attributes, reflects a major shift in thinking and one that seems to have quite thoroughly captured the attention of most, if not all, of higher education's external stakeholders—parents, employers, state and national educational organizations, accrediting and regulatory agencies, and the general public. The 2006 Report of the Commission on the Future of Higher Education is more widely known as the Spellings Commission. Named after Margaret Spellings, former Secretary of Education under the George W. Bush administration and current president of the University of North Carolina, this report may have been the single greatest factor in creating momentum for more rigorous and systematic measurement of the effectiveness of higher education.

Representing a broad range of constituencies and perspectives, the 19-member commission focused its report broadly on the challenges facing U.S. higher education, voicing concerns about what was believed to be a pressing need for enhanced accountability and significant reform in many areas (Miller, 2006; Ruben et al., 2008; Schray, 2006; Spellings Commission, 2006). The preamble of the report, titled "A Test of Leadership: Charting the Future of U.S. Higher Education," acknowledged the many accomplishments of colleges and universities, but was also unequivocal in expressing concerns about the risks of complacency:

> This Commission believes U.S. higher education needs to improve in dramatic ways. As we enter the 21st century, it is no slight to the successes of American colleges and universities thus far in our history to note the unfilled promise that remains. Our yearlong examination of the challenges facing higher education also brought us to the uneasy conclusion that the sector's past attainments have led our nation to unwarranted complacency about its future. It is time to be frank. Among the vast and varied institutions that make up U.S. higher education, we have much to applaud, but also much that requires urgent reform. (Spellings Commission, 2006, pp. ix–xiii)

Although the substance of most of the issues raised in the Spellings Report was not particularly new, the strident language and broad distribution of the commission's reports and communiqués, coupled with the official status of the group and concerns about increased external regulation, prompted vigorous reactions from many quarters (Berdahl, 2006; Lederman, 2006, 2007; McPherson, 2006; Spellings Commission, 2006; U.S. Department of Education, 2006; Ward, 2006). A fundamental issue in the report and subsequent reactions to it is what Kennedy (1997) describes as a "kind of dissonance between the purposes our society foresees for the university and the way the university sees itself" (p. 2), and what Ruben (2004) characterized as a tension between the traditional values of the academy and the values of the contemporary marketplace.

As noted, the report included six specific recommendations. Of greatest relevance to this chapter, the commission recommended the following:

> To meet the challenges of the 21st century, higher education must change from a system primarily based on reputation to one based on performance. We urge the creation of a robust culture of accountability and transparency throughout higher education. Every one of our goals, from improving access and affordability to enhancing quality and innovation, will be more easily achieved if higher education embraces and implements serious accountability measures. (Spellings Commission, 2006, p. 21)

Of the various specific recommendations outlined in the report, this one was most controversial (Ruben et al., 2008). Greater focus on accountability and transparency—taken to imply more attention, and perhaps mandates, to measure performance and effectiveness—triggered emotions ranging from unbridled enthusiasm (most generally among external stakeholders and critics of the status quo) to acute anxiety and strong resistance among many college and university faculty and administrators and higher education organizations. For higher education, the recommendation signaled an increased focus on outcomes measurement, particularly the measurement of student learning, institutional effectiveness and efficiency, and value-added elements of colleges and universities. Many within higher education believed that the recommendation threatened the avowed purpose(s) of American higher education, including the tenets of academic freedom. These issues and concerns about underlying motives, hidden agendas, and the potential increase in national regulation were barriers to useful and constructive discussions. In the midst of the fray, the terms *assessment,* along with *measurement, metrics,* and *accountability* carried rather toxic connotations (Ruben et al., 2008).

Ironically, when assessment is described in neutral and generic terms, it would be difficult to find anyone inside or outside higher education who would argue with its value. Who would disagree with the assertion that it is essential to determine, document, and ensure the quality of the work within colleges and universities? Indeed, this is a core value within the academy—one that is fundamental to the work of faculty and staff. Issues related to the review of the contributions of students, faculty, staff, programs, and institutions have always been a central concern within colleges and universities, and substantial time and energy are devoted to these activities within all institutions.

Not everyone within higher education reacted negatively to the increased pressure for assessment. A number of individuals had long seen the need for a more explicit focus on the scholarship of education and on the application of higher education's research and professional expertise to examine and improve its own practices. Moreover, then and now, there has been no shortage of reflective writings on the topic in popular, professional, and academic literature (see Burke, 1997; Burke & Minassians, 2001; Burke & Serban, 1997; Ewell, 1994; Frank, 2001; Jackson & Lund, 2000; Kuh, 2001; Light, 2001; Newman & Couturier, 2001; Pascarella, 2001; Ruben, 2004, 2006; Selingo, 1999; Seymour, 1989; Spangehl, 2004; Terenzini & Pascarella, 1994).

Higher education associations and individual institutions advanced a number of new initiatives during this period, all intended to enhance outcomes measurement. One of the most popular of these efforts was the Voluntary System of Accountability (VSA). The VSA initiative was championed by the American Association of State Colleges and Universities (AASCU) and the Association of Public and Land-grant Universities (APLU; College Portrait, 2015). VSA, introduced in 2007, provided a standardized College Portrait—a web-based template composed of a number of institutional and learning-outcomes measures that permitted institutional comparisons. Originally, 70 public universities led the effort, and that number has grown to nearly 300 (College Portrait, 2015). VSA was envisioned as "a demonstration of the effectiveness of collective, voluntary action in responding to policymakers' demands for increased accountability and transparency. It . . . provided a space for a large group of institutions to experiment with new metrics for progress, completion, and learning outcomes" (Keller, 2014, p. 29).

With encouragement from multiple stakeholders, combined with the availability of models such as that afforded by VSA, the assessment and measurement of outcomes have become increasingly common features of higher education discourse and practice. Indeed, one recent publication, providing an inventory of developments in this area, lists more than 125 assessment instruments—a variety of software tools, benchmarking platforms, and customized services—available for leaders in higher education as they cultivate a culture of assessment and measurement (Borden & Kernel, 2012).

Origins and Evolution of Measurement in Other Sectors

While the measurement of outcomes has been a relatively recent trend in higher education, what we might think of as *assessment* has long been an accepted practice in other sectors. Outcomes assessment had its beginnings in the business world, where the approach was used for the evaluation of accounting and financial performance, reporting, and the comparison of performance across multiple organizations or divisions. Particularly for complex organizations with multiple units geographically dispersed and remote from management, quantitative measurement methods became an attractive alternative to narratives and anecdotes, which had been the traditional tools used for documenting and reporting accomplishments. Measurement techniques also offered a tool for making comparisons in performance over time and across organizations.

In the current period, measurement systems—variously termed *performance metrics, key performance indicators* (KPIs), *scorecards*, and *dashboards*—have become increasingly popular. Figure 16.1 provides an example of the ways in which assessment data can be displayed using graphics of various kinds. Figure 16.2 illustrates a hypothetical dashboard of the sort that might be used to display financial performance results. The dashboard concept draws its name from the analogy to the dashboard of an automobile, which

Figure 16.1. Displaying assessment results.

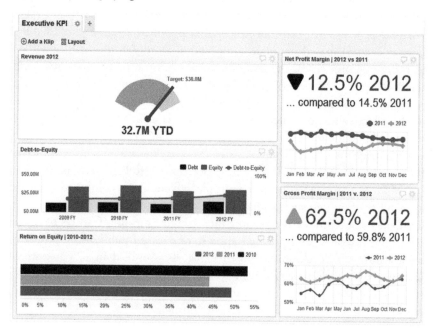

Figure 16.2. A sample financial performance dashboard.

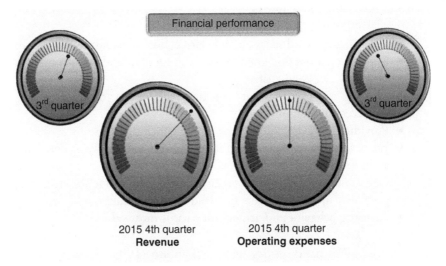

aggregates and displays a few critical measures that the driver can monitor without diverting attention from the fundamental task of driving—or, in the case of an organization, leading.

It was estimated in 2005 that a majority of business organizations had developed or were developing a performance measurement system (Eckerson, 2005). Performance measurement has also been widely adopted in healthcare, where measurement and reporting systems are used to track performance in areas such as treatment outcomes, hospital emergency room wait times, average length of patient stay, lab turnaround time, and patient satisfaction (Healthcare Dashboards, 2015). In public sector organizations, dashboards are used to document and communicate the levels of performance of civic and governmental agencies, such as city planning, parks and recreation, public health, and roads and highways (Government Dashboards, 2015). The application of performance measurement has been particularly extensive in community policing. The CompStat measurement system, originally developed for use in New York City, has since been widely adopted nationally and internationally (Bratton, 1998, 1999; Weisburd et al., 2004).

Benefits and Limitations

The continuing popularity of organizational measurement across sectors is not difficult to understand. In addition to their original uses for documenting and reporting performance and facilitating comparisons across organizations over time, measurement systems offer a number of additional benefits, including the following:

- Encouraging the discussion and clarification of aspirations and goals
- Motivating more fine-grained specification of intended outcomes and how they can be identified
- Helping to clarify what constitutes evidence of successful or unsuccessful outcomes
- Providing the basis for tracking performance over time
- Facilitating trend analysis and the possibility of identifying core issues and root causes of problems
- Contributing to the development of predictive models—identifying particular upstream factors that lead to downstream outcomes
- Focusing behavior and activity on what is most valued

On the other hand, critics such as Brancato (1995) point to various potential limitations. Because measures are historical, measurements may lack predictive power. They may fail to capture key changes until it is too late for the information to be useful strategically, and these measurements can be of limited value if they focus primarily on inputs and not outputs. Moreover, measures may have limited utility if they reflect localized functions rather than cross-functional processes or if they give inadequate consideration to difficult-to-quantify resources, such as intellectual capital and motivation. Finally, these measures can potentially discourage behaviors and activities that are desirable, but not easily measured.

Notwithstanding these concerns, measurement systems are widely used in organizations of various types and sectors. They are seen as beneficial not only for the data they provide but also the value of the process that is required to identify, establish, and develop consensus on selected metrics. In the process of creating organizational measures, it becomes necessary to focus attention on organizational purposes, aspirations, and goals as a prerequisite to selecting specific measures. Conversations associated with this process are often as valuable as the decision about specific metrics that result. Kaplan and Norton (1996, 2001, 2004, 2006), two authors who have written extensively about what is termed the *balanced scorecard*, note the following additional benefits related to the development and use of metrics:

- Guiding leadership strategy
- Clarifying and gaining consensus about vision and strategic direction
- Communicating and linking strategic objectives and measures throughout the organization

- Aligning individual and organizational goals and plans
- Establishing and aligning targets
- Conducting strategic reviews
- Obtaining feedback and responding proactively to accountability and performance measurement pressures
- Creating a culture of ongoing and integrated self-assessment, planning, and improvement
- Motivating constructive conversations about organizational purposes, aspirations, plans, and goals

Measurement in Higher Education

The assessment of the quality of the work within higher education has always been important in concept and practice; however, what is assessed, how it is assessed, and the terms used to describe the activity have evolved considerably over time. As noted previously, we have seen a noticeable shift in focus from the educational opportunities, resources, and facilities *provided* that characterized evaluation efforts in earlier years, to an emphasis on those outcomes or benefits *derived from* the institution, unit, or program in the current period.

So, while assessment is not necessarily a new topic for higher education, the growing challenge is to extend assessment models to include greater attention to outputs created as well as benefits derived. The primary push for outcomes assessment has been in teaching and learning, where, as noted previously, far greater attention is now being devoted to evaluating what is being learned rather than simply what is being taught. A secondary area where assessment is increasingly emphasized is the evaluation of institution, department, program, and service performance outcomes. The focus in this regard is shifting from what is provided and available in the way of resources and opportunities, to what the intended beneficiaries receive and use. The additional challenge is to usefully link these activities to planning and improvement, so that assessment does not occur in a vacuum and is part of an integrated program to increase the effectiveness of programs and services. For more information regarding the connections to strategic planning, see Chapter 14.

Measurement can be used to benefit any or all of the functions and services of higher education institutions. While one might think first of academic programs, assessment can be useful in any area of administration or student affairs, along with any of the other programs or offices that provide services to students, faculty, administrators, staff, parents, alumni, prospective students, employers, or other stakeholders.

The concept of assessment can also be applied at different levels. One can assess the effectiveness of the institution as a whole, or assessment might occur at a department or program level. These concepts can also be applied to evaluate a specific initiative. The appropriateness of particular measures of effectiveness will, of course, differ based on the level of assessment. In the case of institution- or campus-level organizational assessment, a question such as, "What are the university's primary goals?" initiates the conversation. At the general education level, we may ask, "What are the educational or learning goals of our core requirements, or what core knowledge and capability do we expect graduates of a particular institution to possess?" At the department level, the process may begin with the question, "What are our primary goals: organizational, educational, research, service?" And at the program or service level—which could be, for example, an academic or administrative program, or a service program or student life initiative—we are again asking, "What are the goals of our program or service?" One can also use the assessment framework to define and measure the effectiveness of strategic planning or other campus projects in fulfilling their intended purposes and goals.

Regardless of the terminology, setting, or level of analysis one chooses, the fundamental questions are the same (Ruben, 2014):

- What are we trying to accomplish?
- How do we evaluate our progress?
- How effective or successful are we in our efforts?
- How will we use this knowledge to improve what we do?
- How will it move us closer to our vision?

The Mission-to-Metrics Process

How does one go about creating a measurement system? The illustration in Figure 16.3 depicts the mission-to-metrics process, including the components and flow involved in moving from the selection of the *focus for assessment* to the *identification of a set of specific metrics* that are used in the formalization of a measurement system. In this process, the mission and vision of an institution, department, program, or project provide the essential focus and serve as the initial point of reference.

Step 1: Clarify the Focus of Assessment

The process begins by clarifying the focus of assessment. Will the reference point for the assessment be an institution, department, program, strategic plan, project, or some other activity? Next, determine if an existing statement describes the mission, vision, values, plans, or goals associated with the focus

Figure 16.3. Assessment: A broad "mission-to-metrics" framework.

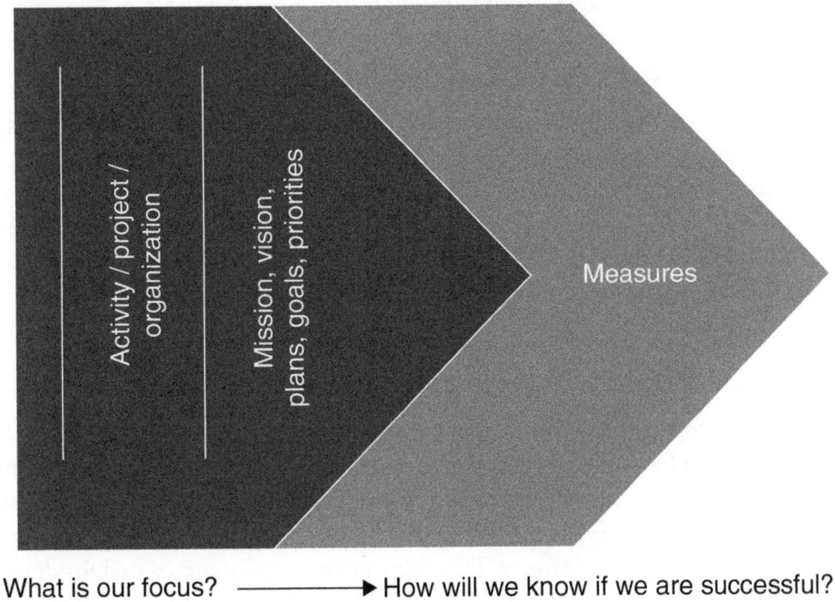

What is our focus?   ────────▶ How will we know if we are successful?

on assessment. Clear and shared statements of purpose and aspiration—in the form of mission and vision statements—are basic to the development of a measurement system, and identified priorities and goals are also helpful. If these have been established previously, they may simply be reviewed and reaffirmed as a way to begin assessment work. If these do not exist, then creating them is the important first step in establishing a measurement system. (A detailed discussion of mission, vision, and goals statements and their purpose and characteristics can be found in Chapter 14.) These statements provide the foundation for the selection of metrics. It is also important to identify or reaffirm primary stakeholders and the primary programs and services as a part of this discussion.

Step 2: Selecting Appropriate Metrics

The next step is to identify—and to reach agreement on—the most appropriate indicators or metrics to track in order to evaluate the organization's effectiveness relative to the focus of the assessment. For example, let's assume that the focus for assessment is a departmental strategic plan. Suppose that one of the goals of that plan is "to establish new and productive partnerships with other campus units." The question to be addressed next is, "What indicators will be the most appropriate measures of progress toward fulfillment of this goal?" One obvious metric would be the number of new partnerships established. As we discuss later, various other indicators in this case might be selected as useful as well—perhaps most obviously, one or more indicators designed to capture the meaning of *productive*.[1]

Step 3: Collecting and Organizing Information

Once metrics have been selected, a process for collecting and organizing data to support those measures is needed. In some cases, relevant information may already exist. In the strategic planning example, it is unlikely that the needed information is currently available; therefore, it will be necessary to develop a method for keeping track of the number of partnerships being established and perhaps a way to evaluate their contributions.

Step 4: Displaying, Disseminating, and Using Information

The final step involves the display, communication, and use of the information provided through the measurement system. Potential applications include documenting outcomes, communicating outcomes information internally and to relevant external stakeholders, and using the results for monitoring and improvement. This information can be aggregated for document outcomes during particular periods of time, aggregated to track trends, or used to establish improvement targets. Outcomes can also be compared to those of peers, aspirants, or leaders at one's own or another institution. The measures need to be reviewed from time to time to ensure that they continue to be appropriate for evaluating progress toward fulfillment of the mission, aspirations, priorities, and goals. In summary, the key steps in developing an assessment system are as follows:

- Clarify the focus for assessment, and review or develop clear statements of purpose, aspiration, and goals for the institution, program, service, strategic plan, or project on which assessment will focus. Assess outcomes and achievements relative to these purposes, aspirations, plans, and goals, as appropriate.
- Include comparisons of outcomes over time and with peers and other institutions and organizations.
- Monitor and use results to document outcomes and achievements, inform day-to-day decision-making and resource allocation, improve programs and service offerings, establish performance targets, and generally enhance quality, effectiveness, and efficiency relative to the focus of the assessment.

Note that the purpose of this assessment process is not usually to conduct the kind of rigorous research that is necessary for publication in academic journals, but rather to develop useful operational tools that are helpful guides for decision-making, evaluation, and planning efforts, and for monitoring and documenting outcomes.

Selecting Measures

To be useful, the measures you select need to be

- valid—accurate and objective, focusing on what you set out to measure;
- reliable—consistent and dependable; and
- useful—easily able to be understood and used.

The selected measures should also be

- *Strategic.* Measures should be chosen carefully to be helpful in monitoring the organization's success in pursuing the mission, aspirations, plans, goals, or projects that are the focus for assessment. The aim is to select a few metrics that are useful for documenting key outcomes and guiding strategy and improvement efforts.
- *Aligned with those of the larger organization.* Measures should take account of the mission, aspirations, plans, and goals of the larger units of which they may be a part, and those of the institution as a whole. Ideally, the selected measures will be useful in demonstrating how the focus for assessment fits with and contributes to the institutional directions and aspirations.
- *Appropriate.* To the extent possible, metrics chosen for use should reference factors over which the organization has control and that reflect its mission. Measures should also capture the priorities or concerns of constituents and beneficiaries—those in the position to evaluate your performance and whose judgments are important to your success and standing.
- *Sustainable.* Measures should be able to be supported over time. Consider at the time it is created what it will take to sustain a measurement system. Outcome information that is inexpensive and easy to gather is the ideal. Take care not to commit to elaborate systems of measurement and dissemination that may be costly and difficult to sustain. Adding additional metrics to a system over time based on need and capacity is preferable to overreaching in an initial system design.

Types of Measures

In choosing measures, selecting a variety of types of metrics is prudent. Following are metrics that can be used to assess an organization's performance:

- *Activity measures.* One approach is to count the number of activities (tasks, events, participants) associated with the organizational mission, aspirations, plans, or projects that are the focus of assessment. Returning to the illustration involving strategic planning goals mentioned previously, the *number of partnerships established* is an example of an activity measure.
- *Quality measures.* Evaluating the caliber of organizational activities against professional or disciplinary standards, compared to the standards employed by peer or aspirant organizations or based on third-party evaluations, can provide the basis for these measures. In the case of establishing productive partnerships, considering criteria used by other departments in defining productive interdepartmental partnerships—or metrics comparing the nature and character of partnerships established by your organization with similar partnerships at peer, aspiration, or leading departments or institutions—might be useful measures of professional quality.
- *Benefit and satisfaction measures.* The benefits and satisfaction levels of constituents or beneficiaries may also be desired metrics. The perceptions of those involved provide the basis for these measures. In the case of establishing productive partnerships with other departments, judgments by members of the departments involved regarding the effectiveness and value of newly established partnerships would provide a basis for this type of measure.
- *Impact measures.* These measures gauge the impact your programs or services have on their users in relation to overall organizational or project purposes, aspirations, plans, and goals. Although these measures are perhaps the most difficult to capture, they are often the most meaningful. Impact measures extend beyond activity, quality, and benefit or satisfaction measures and directly assess whether there was an impact—perhaps including a change or a key step in accomplishing ultimate purposes and goals. In the case of the goal of establishing productive interdepartmental partnerships, considerations of objective evidence that the newly established partnerships are productive would be appropriate measures. Examples might include metrics related to joint publication, collaborative grant applications, interdisciplinary events or programs, or joint course

offerings, depending specifically on the overarching goals envisioned for particular partnerships.

To illustrate with an example from an administrative area, consider an effort to develop measures for assessing the work of a campus parking office. Assume that the mission of the office is "To serve the university and the university community by issuing parking permits, overseeing parking operations, and enforcing parking policies and regulations." Some examples of organizational outcomes assessed by each of the measures are as follows:

- An *activity measure* could be the number or percentage of students purchasing parking permits.
- A *quality measure* could be the results from benchmarking reviews of local practices, policies, and procedures compared to those in similar offices at peer, aspirational, or leading institutions.
- A *benefit and satisfaction measure* might be the results or trends in user satisfaction evaluations for programs, services, policies, and procedures.
- An *impact measure* could be an evaluation of the effectiveness of the parking program and service in fulfilling its mission, or the effect parking has on the larger university goal of ease of parking as a measure of overall faculty, staff, and student satisfaction.

Each of these types of measures has value, and each is also limited in some ways. In most cases, activity, quality, benefit or satisfaction, and impact metrics complement one another, collectively providing the most useful portfolio of measures that offer a picture of the effectiveness of a project, program, department, or institution. Depending on the particular focus for assessment, *efficiency measures*—focusing on resource utilization of time, money, or human capital—might provide a useful fifth category of metrics to include.

During discussions regarding the selection of measures, questions sometimes arise about organizational purposes, aspirations, plans, and goals, and the way they are articulated. Such discussions often point to the need for greater clarity in the language of statements in order to make it possible to meaningfully evaluate progress and success in achieving the desired outcomes. To pick an extreme example, a mission or vision statement that identifies "becoming an excellent teaching and research department" is difficult to operationalize in terms of measurement. What would "excellent" mean? While identifying and agreeing upon definitions for *excellence* is possible, an alternative would be to craft a more precise, less ambiguous, and more easily assessed statement of aspiration—for instance, "to be internationally recognized as a center of excellence in bridging basic and clinical research and training."

To return to the strategic planning example, a discussion of what constitutes a productive partnership, and how "productive" would be assessed, could result in an extremely beneficial dialogue—helping to clarify exactly what the particular goal is intended to accomplish. Ultimately, the discussion may lead to identifying useful measures that correspond to the meaning that *productive* will have for the unit, or it might lead to the selection of a term or terms other than *productive* to include in the goal statement—terms that might clarify intentions and also make the appropriate choice of measures an easier and more precise task. Similarly, a discussion of the appropriate measures for assessing the effectiveness of a parking office in fulfilling its mission may ultimately lead to a conclusion that the mission statement should be revised to facilitate measurement. While these discussions can seem less-than-useful in the moment, conversations of this kind are often one of the genuine benefits of the development and implementation of measurement systems—ideally resulting in greater clarity in statements of direction and also more effective metrics.

Gathering Measurement Data

The idea of collecting the information needed for assessment may initially seem daunting, but as noted previously, most organizations already have much of the information. Thus, it makes sense to determine, first, what relevant information is currently available, and only then to think about how to gather the rest.

Other related questions about gathering measurement data need to be considered, including the following:

- Who has—or has access to—the information that is required?
- How can it be accessed?
- Can the information be used with confidence?
- Is it valid, reliable, and useful?

For instance, if participation, attendance, or submission data are available, and there is confidence as to their accuracy, these can be the basis for useful activity measures. An organization might make use of information that had been gathered for some other purpose, such as a report by an accreditation review group.

Instituting new methods to gather some of the information will likely be necessary. For instance, for some assessment purposes, it may be useful to conduct focus groups or surveys or enlist the services of mystery-shopper groups composed of students or alumni who could provide useful feedback based on their experiences with a program, department, or institution. New measures will also likely be needed, and purpose, creativity, and sustainability should guide in their selection.

A variety of sources are available for the information needed to establish and support the chosen measures, including the following options:

- *Archival*—information that already exists within the organization but may need to be located, reformatted, and analyzed
- *Unobtrusive*—information derived from observing behaviors
- *Solicited*—information collected through interview, focus groups, surveys, or other intentional information-gathering activities

Assessment may utilize measures that are direct, indirect, or inferential. The classic example of *direct* measurement in the case of learning outcomes is giving a test before and after taking a course as a direct measure of what a student learned. Another direct measurement would be the results from licensure exams after completion of a specialized program designed to prepare students to pass that exam. Direct measures are regarded as providing the most desirable form of evidence. *Indirect* measures are considered good, but less than ideal. *Inferential* metrics are sometimes helpful, but of less value. Each of these measures could shed light on the effectiveness of an institution, department, or program in fulfilling its mission; direct measures are most persuasive because they measure behaviors that are most clearly related to the desired outcomes. Direct measures of learning are considered more useful, for example, than those that would result from surveying students at the end of the course about how much they had learned, which would be an *indirect* measure. Recommending the course to friends as a valuable learning experience could represent an *inferential* measure of learning.

However, if the goal was to measure *satisfaction* as opposed to *learning*, asking students for their opinion as to how well they liked the course would be a direct measure. If the student recommends the course to friends, we might consider that an inferential measure of satisfaction. A pre- and post-test of learning would not be a particularly good measure here, since learning may not relate to a person's satisfaction. There are no perfect measures. Each has strengths and limitations, and the aim is to use the best and most appropriate measures available for each situation.

Measurement System: Planning, Displaying, Disseminating, and Sustaining Assessment

Measurement System Planning

Measures alone are not an assessment system. As discussed, a viable system requires a well-defined focus for assessment; clear statements of purpose, aspirations, plans, or goals; a list of appropriate indicators or measures; identified measurement methods; techniques for gathering and analyzing evidence; and a systematic approach to displaying, disseminating, and using the resulting information. A planning matrix such as that provided in Table 16.1 can be helpful in providing a framework for developing such a system.

Displaying Assessment Results

There are numerous ways to display assessment results, including standard report forms, tables, charts, dashboards, and other forms of graphic display. One illustration is provided by the tabular dashboard developed by James Madison University (JMU) to display performance measures associated with its strategic plan.[2] After an 18-month strategic planning process, JMU developed 11 of what it terms *core qualities*, or the key elements of the plan. Each core quality was supported by 4 to 7 university goals, which in turn were

TABLE 16.1
Measures Planning Matrix Sample

Focus of Measurement	Measure	Measure Type*	Data Collection Method	Process for Data Analysis/ Dissemination	Desired Outcome

* Activity, quality standards, benefit/satisfaction, impact, ineternal effectiveness

TABLE 16.2
A Sample of Strategic Planning Performance Dashboard Indicators for James Madison University.

5 Measures of Important Perspectives

Performance Measure		Target by 2020	2009–2010	2013–2014	2014–2015	2015–2016
32	Student satisfaction with JMU in general	Will be monitored	93%	98%	N/A	96%
33	Percentage of respondents who, on the JMU Continuing Student Survey (CSS), agree that JMU places "significant emphasis on the development of academic/scholarly/intellectual qualities."	Will be monitored	74%	74%	N/A	68%
36	Percentage of respondents who, on the JMU Continuing Student Survey, indicated "very satisfied" or "satisfied" with the condition of buildings and grounds.	Will be monitored	94%	98%	N/A	97%
37	Percentage of students who, on the JMU Continuing Student Survey, indicated "very satisfied or "satisfied" with personal security/safety at JMU.	Will be monitored	87%	98%	N/A	97%
39	Percentage of faculty, staff and students who indicated "very satisfied" or "satisfied" with JMU technology on the Technology Survey.	Will be monitored	Students: 89% Faculty & Staff: 94%	Students: 85% Faculty & Staff: 90%	Students: 88% Faculty & Staff: 94%	Students: 89% Faculty & Staff: 88%

Source. James Madison University Office of Institutional Research.

TABLE 16.3
Engagement at Purdue

Mission To design, guide and lead collaborations that drive innovation, prosperity and an improved quality of life throughout Indiana and beyond.	

Engagement Goals

- Connect and collaborate with businesses, communities, and regions to leverage talent, innovation, and resources to address current and emerging real-world issues and opportunities.
- Promote, facilitate and reward faculty and student engagement including the scholarship of engagement as a recognized channel for faculty advancement.
- Identify and deliver innovative programs and strategies to meet the informational, educational, and technical needs of the current and emerging workforce, businesses/industries, and communities/regions.

Source. "Engagement at Purdue University." Steve Abel, Associate Vice President for Engagement, Committee on Institutional Cooperation, November 7, 2015.

supported by a number of objectives (see www.jmu.edu/jmuplans/_docs/StrategicPlanMeasures.pdf).

In order to add critical levels of assessment, evaluation, and accountability to its plan, performance metrics were developed. These included a relatively short list of key measures to provide at-a-glance tracking of the plan in each of the following areas:

- Measures of academic quality
- Measures of engagement
- Measures of resources
- Measures of access, opportunity, and people development
- Measures of important perspectives

Table 16.2 provides a sampling of the way in which measures of important perspectives are presented on JMU's strategic plan webpage. The measures are tracked consistently, either affirming desired performance for elements of the plan or pointing to improvement needs in goals or objects (for the full set of measures, see www.jmu/edu/jmuplans/jmu-strategicplan/strategic_plan_perfomance_measures.shtml).

Other examples are given in Table 16.3, which includes three goals of the Purdue University Engagement (2015) initiative, and Figure 16.4, which provides an example of a way of displaying outcome results associated with those goals using graphics.

Figure 16.4. Engagement at Purdue University: Fast facts.

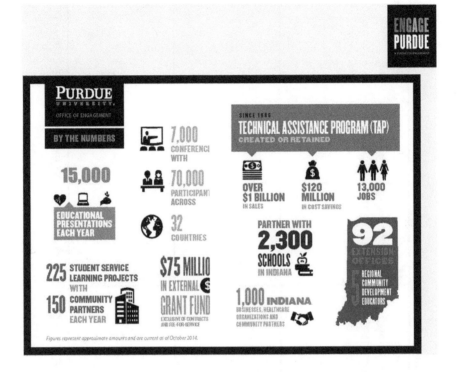

Dissemination

The ways in which data are displayed and communicated can be important to the attention and the use these results receive by internal and external constituents. They are also important for documenting outcomes, setting future targets, and telling internal and external groups one's story of accomplishments, progress, and future aspirations.

A closely related decision pertains to the list of who should receive assessment results. This list, of course, depends on the focus of assessment and the overall aims of the process. It is generally useful to create a list of internal and external groups with whom to share results as a part of the early planning process, being clear about the benefits this communication process could have for each. Under some circumstances, it may be useful to separate groups into segments and to customize the distribution based on interests, relevance, and other factors. Not all audiences will be equally interested in all outcomes data, and some results may be designated for internal use only. A planning guide to help think through these communication issues is illustrated in Table 16.4.

TABLE 16.4
Communication Planning Matrix

Communication Goal *What do we hope to accomplish? (desired Outcome)*	Target *For Whom?* *(key audiences)*	Audience Needs and Expectations *What matters to this group? What potential needs, questions, concerns exist?*	Content *What message is appropriate?*	Messenger *Who is the best person to deliver the message?*	Method used *What vehicle to deliver message?*	Pros and Cons of: *Chosen message, Messenger, vehicle*

Adapted from: Tromp, S. A., Ruben, B. D. Strategic Planning in Higher Education (SPHE) Washington, DC: National Association of College and University Business Officers, 2004, p. 69.

Outcomes information can be used to assess performance by comparing current outcomes with results from previous years and with peer, aspirant, or leading institutions. Measurement information can also be used to guide strategic planning; to review, refine, and update goals; to identify resource allocation priorities; and to inform day-to-day decision-making. Measurement results from a project, program, or department can be integrated with the university assessment results, used to document progress and effectiveness to external audiences, or used to identify opportunities for improvement. Particularly as it relates to the internal uses of outcome results, a well-documented system with attention to display and communication of outcomes information enables an organization to maximize the value of the system in support of improvement, planning, and decision-making.

Sustaining the Measurement System

Sustainability refers to the goal of maintaining the viability and usefulness of the measurement system over time. A good practice generally is to develop a measurement system slowly and resist the temptation of trying to measure too much at the outset. A better approach is to identify all relevant measures, but to collect data for only a few critical indicators initially, adding more over time.

Identifying and addressing key issues and barriers to the sustainability of the measurement system can be a challenge. To achieve this goal, it is critical to develop a plan for keeping measures relevant, which requires reviewing them on a regular basis to ensure that they continue to be the focus for assessment and reflective of current purposes, aspirations, plans, and goals. It is also important to periodically validate the relevance and usefulness of the measures for key internal and external constituencies. Finally, reviews of the assessment process should assure that results are displayed and communicated in a timely and easily accessible manner.

Conclusion

The assessment process is critical for evaluating the effectiveness of one's activities. Despite the limitations associated with the use of metrics, a culture that emphasizes evidence over anecdotes and narratives of personal experience is increasingly required by external stakeholders, and also increasingly useful to members of the organization. Monitoring outcomes is essential for ensuring accountability, guiding strategic planning, identifying the need for change and innovation, and promoting, advocating, and championing accomplishments of one's unit, program, or department. Through the use of metrics, academic and administrative leaders in higher education are also able to demonstrate a willingness to be transparent and accountable, establish priorities to advance the aims of the organization, and clarify how the work of faculty and staff throughout the institution contributes to these aspirations.

For Further Consideration

1. Developing Measures for Your Institution, Department, or Program

Develop a draft of measures for your institution, department, or program. Complete a first draft of a measurement system matrix using the worksheet provided in Table 16.6.

2. Aspen College

Figure 16.5 provides a statement of Aspen's aspirations—its vision statement—which is to be the focus for establishing a measurement system.

Figure 16.5. A commitment to leadership.

To realize our vision, Aspen will:

1. Sustain the highest standards in learning, discovery, and engagement with our constituents.
2. Serve our communities, our state, our nation, and the international community.
3. Advance scholarship and intellectual vitality in our academic disciplines.
4. Attract, welcome, develop, and retain outstanding students, faculty, and staff.
5. Encourage the open and civil exchange of ideas and perspectives.
6. Provide superior curricular and co-curricular opportunities for students at all levels.
7. Educate exceptional leaders and citizens for future generations.
8. Foster a supportive and collaborative social environment, and a community dedicated to valuing diversity.
9. Maintain a safe, clean, and attractive physical environment.
10. Maintain accessible, responsive, and cost-effective programs and services.
11. Dedicate our learning community to ongoing self-assessment and continuing improvement of all that we do.

TABLE 16.5
Potential Measures for Vision Element 4

4. Attract, welcome and retain outstanding students, faculty, and staff		
4.1 Students	*4.2 Faculty*	*4.3 Staff*
Preference	Preference	Preference
Selectivity	Selectivity	Selectivity
Diversity	Diversity	Diversity
Satisfaction	Satisfaction	Satisfaction
Recommendations	Recommendations	Recommendations
Others	Others	Others
Potential Measures		

Figure 16.6. Aspen dashboard for vision element 4.

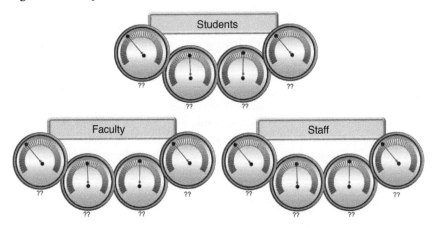

What measures would you select for each group?

TABLE 16.6
Aspen Measures Planning Matrix: Vision Element 4

Focus of Measurement	*Measure*	*Measure Type**	*Data Collection Method*	*Process for Data Analysis/ Dissmination*	*Desired Outcome*

*Activity, quality standards, benefit/satisfaction, impact

Table 16.5 identifies three subcomponents of vision element 4: students, faculty, and staff. A decision has been made that measures will be developed for each. The bullet listing under each identifies potential indicators that could be used in the dashboard illustrated in Figure 16.6.

The process would continue as described in the previous example until measures are developed for each vision element, and an overall system of measurement, interpretation, display, dissemination, and use is created.

- What questions do you have about this method for developing measures?
- What organizational challenges surfaced that need to be addressed as you develop measures within your organization?
- What could help make the selection of measures for your organization easier, more productive, or more useful?
- What challenges might you anticipate in closing the loop?
- How might you go about gaining buy-in and engagement in the assessment process?
- What are the probable challenges to sustaining the effort?

Notes

1. Metrics can also focus on finer-grained categories of organizational excellence, such as leadership, purposes and plans, relationships with beneficiaries and constituencies, programs and services, faculty and staff and climate, and others included in the Excellence in Higher Education (EHE) model (see Chapter 12).

2. Thanks to James Madison University's president Jon Alger and associate vice president Brian Charette for their assistance in providing this brief overview of the James Madison University planning and dashboard development process.

17

CRISIS LEADERSHIP

Upholding Institutional Values

Ralph A. Gigliotti and John A. Fortunato

In This Chapter

- What is crisis leadership, and how does it differ from crisis management?
- What differentiates a crisis from an emergency or incident?
- What types of crises are most likely to impact a college or university?
- Which communication strategies associated with crisis leadership are most relevant for academic and administrative leaders?

Many of the leadership principles and strategies offered in this text are useful for academic and administrative leaders during periods of normalcy for the organization. For example, most leaders are better able to think about developing strategic plans, formulating mission and vision statements, initiating change, and assessing performance metrics during times of stability. In ever-increasing and wide-ranging situations, however, leaders in higher education are forced to respond to explosive or potentially explosive circumstances on a regular basis—moments that some would characterize as organizational crises—leading a growing number of colleges and universities to craft "all hazards" emergency operations plans (McIntire, 2015). When crises occur, they can create havoc for the department or institution and for its faculty, staff, students, and other stakeholders. The extent to which such events are disruptive depends not only on the nature of the crises that transpire but also on the history, stability, and culture of the institution; the preparation and competencies of its leaders to make appropriate and timely decisions; and the tangible actions taken moving forward. Some recent examples of crises that directly influenced the higher education sector include, but are not limited to, on-campus shootings, child abuse scandals, cybercrimes, allegations of racism and demonstrations of racist behavior, athletic hazing scandals, academic integrity violations, natural disasters, faculty-board disagreements, sexual assaults, and violations of federal anti-discrimination laws. Unfortunately, this list only skims the surface of recent crises to impact American colleges and universities. Despite the critical role leaders at all levels must play in addressing crisis situations, little preparation is typically provided for these difficult situations. This lack of preparation is unfortunate, and also unnecessary.

In response to an extensive—and growing—set of crises facing college and university leaders, the American Council on Education (ACE) convened a roundtable with college and university presidents, media experts, and attorneys on the topic, "Leading in Times of Crises." This meeting led to the development of an article (Bataille, Billings, & Nellum, 2012) and a subsequent book (Bataille & Cordova, 2014) on the subject. Crisis preparation remains a top priority for college and university leaders for obvious reasons. As Genshaft (2014) suggests, "Higher education is particularly primed for poor handling of crises," (p. 10) in part because of the lack of preparation and an ongoing preoccupation with excellence. This claim is consistent with the survey findings of Mitroff, Diamond, and Alpaslan (2006), reporting much remains to be done in the area of crisis preparation in higher education. A number of long-term and short-term approaches to crisis leadership are relevant and important for the preparation of academic and administrative leaders. Much of the literature on this topic is applicable to an array of organizations, but in this chapter we focus particularly on principles and practices that are most relevant for leaders in higher education.

We begin with an overview of relevant background information on the topic of crisis and continue with a breakdown of the types of crises that may directly influence leaders in higher education. This introductory content provides a context for thinking through crisis leadership within units, departments, and institutions. In the remainder of the chapter we consider characteristics of crisis leadership—an important and broader framework for understanding the many elements associated with leading during these challenging moments.

Crisis Management Versus Crisis Leadership

The most common way of approaching this subject within the literature has been in terms of crisis management. Writings on crisis management generally focus on specific strategies and tactics to deal with events that threaten, disrupt, or endanger an organization, those it serves, or its employees and considers the threats to an organization's reputation that crises embody. The study of crisis management has its roots in the corporate sector, and only recently has there been an increase in writing on the topic within the context of higher education.

Managing a crisis, however, is only one part of a leader's responsibility. The concept of crisis leadership, as we discuss later, moves beyond a mechanistic or tactical view of the leader's role in crisis—often referred to as *crisis management*—to one that is systematic, anticipatory, proactive, and expansive—a perspective that is more appropriately labeled *crisis leadership*. In addition to coping with and preparing for crises, the notion of crisis leadership often involves the very decision to declare some social construction or event to be a crisis. Leaders may use the invocation of crisis as a strategic opportunity to cut through red tape, skip particular processes, and move quickly (L. Lewis, personal communication, December 18, 2015)—all of which are appealing within the slow-moving, committee-driven, and bureaucratic context of higher education. A crisis leadership framework is useful for academic and administrative leaders in thinking through both the unplanned, uncontrolled, and imposed emergence of crises as well as the purposeful or strategic declaration of a crisis label by leaders; such a framework is also useful for navigating those crises that are most germane to institutions of higher education.

The History, Definitions, and Stages of Crisis

Crisis History

The term *crisis* has its roots in the Greek language, where it represents a "turning point," similar to the medical usage of the term in Latin to imply the turning point of an illness. The origin of the word maintains a positive connotation, referring to the turning point in sickness, tragedy, or peril (Ulmer, Sellnow, & Seeger, 2015). These turning points, often reflecting human choice and human decision, could fundamentally shape the future of an individual or organization (Shrivastava, 1993). Beginning in the eighteenth century, *crisis* evolved to mean a difficult situation or dilemma, presumably a more negative conceptualization of a turning point. Sellnow and Seeger (2013) present another interesting interpretation of the concept from the Chinese *wei chi,* which translates to "dangerous opportunity" (p. 22). This interpretation of the term captures the ambivalence associated with the concept of crisis, as the fear and danger associated with crisis intersect with the opportunity and turning point of what might lie ahead.

Crisis Definitions

Crises—and the ways in which they are handled—are a particularly significant concern in colleges or universities because of the lofty standards to which higher education institutions aspire and by which they are judged by society. Crises are unpredictable, yet not unexpected, moments (Coombs, 2015) that in many instances can have damaging, injurious, or hurtful consequences for the victims most impacted by the crisis, along with reputational implications for the organization and its leaders. Crises often have an interdependent impact on human lives, institutional structures, and leadership or organizational reputation. Additionally, crises impact various individuals and groups inside and outside the institution, and they often challenge the core values and principles that the organization esteems. These multifaceted consequences make it especially challenging for organizational leaders as they predict, respond to, navigate, and learn from these situations. Distinct from more localized emergencies or incidents, crises have the potential to "disrupt the entire organization" (Pauchant & Mitroff, 1992, p. 3).

Like leadership and communication, myriad definitions exist for *crisis*. Labeling something as a "crisis" involves an element of subjectivity. The identification of a particular incident or moment as a crisis involves a level of judgment, leading it to become a widely used—and potentially overused—word. For example, an issue may become a crisis on one campus, but the same issue may fail to rise to the level of crisis on another campus. Adding to this complexity, a failure to act or communicate in an appropriate and timely way may result in emergent and difficult situations transforming into crises. This idea is explored in subsequent sections of this chapter.

Mitroff (2004) cautions against predicting crisis with any degree of certainty. He defines a *crisis* as "an event that affects or has the potential to affect the whole organization" (p. 6). Reviewing the many definitions of *crisis*, several themes stand out as being most important for leaders in higher education. First, crises present a disruption from normal activity that threatens the well-being of organizational stakeholders (Irvine & Millar, 1998; Weick, 1988). In the case of colleges and universities, these crisis situations often impact students, faculty, staff, alumni, and the local community in a range of dramatic ways. Additionally, crises threaten the reputation of the organization and its leaders. Although crises present a substantial threat that must be addressed, they also present a significant opportunity for leaders to articulate, demonstrate, model, and reaffirm the core values and principles of the college or university. The ability to be guided by institutional values is not limited to the initial response to the situation, but rather precedes the crisis and is embedded in its aftermath. Crises test these core values—and also provide a venue to display and communicate them. Finally, perception matters in moments of crisis (Benoit, 1995, 1997; Coombs, 2015; Mitroff, 2004). Institutions of higher education have an important role to play in establishing and maintaining high standards and core values in a way that instills confidence in the institution and also demonstrates care for members of the institution. The challenge for leaders is negotiating the complexities of the crisis itself, while also responding in a way that cultivates hope, trust, and safety for those whom one leads, as well as maintains a favorable reputation for the institution and its leaders. Ideally, the reputational concerns, while important, are addressed as a natural consequence of competent leadership.

One final note about the definition of *crisis* deserves mention. Many of the existing definitions treat crisis as an objective phenomenon—something that lives in the world to be discovered and named. As Lewis suggests, however, crises are only a "thing" when someone with influence names them and people jointly construct them as a "thing" through talk (L. Lewis, personal communication, December 18, 2015). In this sense, the tendency to objectify crises and present them as something existing and in need of discovery by leaders can be problematic. The objectification of crisis may overlook the subjective nature of identifying, framing, and making sense of the incident in the first place. If we think about the social construction of crises, communication is more than a strategy for dealing with or responding to crisis. Communication becomes a broader mechanism through which crises are strategically bracketed, defined, and labeled as such. Leaders and other stakeholders play a creative—and subjective—role in identifying and treating some event, incident, or state of affairs as a crisis.

Crisis Stages

The life cycle of a crisis is another important issue raised in the crisis literature that often reflects the progression of crises in higher education. Within the disruption and confusion associated with crises often lies an underlying order and pattern (Li & Yorke, 1975; Lorenz, 1963; Wheatley, 2006). One model divides crisis management into five phases: (a) signal detection, (b) probing and prevention, (c) damage containment, (d) recovery, and (e) learning (Mitroff, 1994). Coombs (2015) identifies a model for crisis development that includes three general stages of precrisis, crisis event, and postcrisis. These phases are helpful in that they provide an order to the crisis, yet crises by their very nature are unpredictable and call for leaders to be both flexible and prepared. In some ways, these models cast the crisis as a linear process and put forward a set of prescriptive strategies for best managing the isolated incident (Gigliotti, 2016). The notion of crisis leadership that is central to this chapter can help us to better understand the broader system and explore and explain crisis in a more nuanced way for leaders in higher education. For example, in the child sex abuse scandal at Penn State, the public announcement of the many allegations against the former assistant football coach might be viewed as the commencement of the crisis. However, as outlined in the Freeh Report commissioned by the Penn State Board of Trustees, critical facts relating to Coach Jerry Sandusky's child abuse were concealed from and by leaders across the university—a troubling finding that points to the many historical factors leading to the public components of crisis (Freeh Report, 2012). This case is one of many that capture the subjectivity involved in defining something as a *crisis*, let alone identifying its beginning and end.

Crisis Taxonomies

As illustrated in Table 17.1, there are a number of crisis taxonomies in the existing literature. As you read the distinct types of crises listed here, notice that a number of incidents are more relevant to the higher education sector. In particular, natural disasters, technical breakdowns, and incidents of violence are increasingly common types of crises to which leaders must attend. Like other institutions, these crises in higher education may range in severity and level of impact.

As the lists in Table 17.1 seem to suggest, there are numerous ways to categorize crises, one obvious way being based on whether they are the results of human actions or natural disasters (Lindell, Prater, & Perry, 2007). Cole, Orsuwan, and Ah Sam (2007) present the following list of disasters that are the product of human behavior and most applicable to colleges and universities: sexual assault, stalking, campus dating violence, hate crimes, hazing, celebratory violence (riots), attempted suicides, suicides, murder/suicides, manslaughter, aggravated assault, arson, and attacks on faculty and staff. This list is inherently limited and fails to capture the full range of areas where colleges and universities are most susceptible, such as cybercrimes, student protests, and violations of academic. Disasters that are the result of nature require different responses than those that are a consequence of human action. For example, a college or university may be a "victim" to the forces of Mother Nature, yet culpable for neglecting to prepare for—or deal effectively with—the potential disaster. Leaders must be prepared to look within and beyond the institution as they consider the types of crises that may impact the college or university.

A Test of Organizational Core Values

In very fundamental ways, crises test the core values of an organization—and by understanding the various dimensions, phases, and types of crises as outlined in the literature, academic and administrative leaders may better prepare for these potentially troubling, yet not entirely unexpected, situations.

TABLE 17.1
Crisis Taxonomies

Lerbinger (1997)		
Natural	Technological	Skewed management values
Confrontation	Malevolence	Deception
Management misconduct	Business and economic	

Meyers and Holusha (1986)		
Public perception	Sudden market shifts	Product failure
Top management succession	Cash crises	Industrial relations crises
Hostile takeover	Adverse international events	Regulation/deregulation

Coombs and colleagues (1995)		
Natural disasters	Malevolence	Workplace violence
Technical breakdowns	Human breakdowns	Rumors
Challenges	Organizational misdeeds	

Mitroff and Anagnos (2001)		
Economic	Informational	Natural disasters
Human resource	Reputation	Psychopathic acts
Physical loss of key plants and other facilities		

Coombs (2007)		
Victim crises: Minimal crises responsibility	Accident crises: Low crises responsibility	Preventable crises: Strong crises responsibility
Natural disasters	Challenges	Human-error accidents
Rumors	Technical-error accidents	Human-error product harm
Workplace violence	Technical-error product harm	Organizational misdeeds
Product tampering/ malevolence		

Two cases are widely discussed in the literature on crisis leadership/ management and provide valuable lessons for leaders across sectors. The response by Johnson & Johnson to the 1982 poisonings of Tylenol capsules is the first such classic case. The oil leakage associated with the Exxon *Valdez* is the second. In fact, various writers have indicated that the positive response by Johnson & Johnson juxtaposed against the notoriously poor response to the Exxon *Valdez* oil spill in Prince William Sound in 1989 led to the emergence of the field of crisis management (Heath & O'Hair, 2009; Mitroff, 2004). Many of the leadership characteristics distilled from these classic cases remain relevant to today's higher education environment. In particular, there remains great value in approaching crisis leadership through a values-centered lens—an orientation that positions clarity, consistency, and congruency between the way that one leads during crisis and those core values that are most critical to an institution. In the instance of Johnson & Johnson, the company had to deal with a situation that was devastating in its impact on the victims of the poisoning. Beyond the immediate effect on health and safety, organizational leaders were forced to take decisive action to prevent future injuries—and to also act in a way that would restore trust in the good name of the company. The bold decision to act quickly and recall Tylenol from every provider had a costly impact on the share price of the company, but the long-term financial and reputational benefit for Johnson & Johnson was notable. This case demonstrates how dealing with crisis in an appropriate and timely way is a function of the nature of the organization and its core values—a function that goes beyond those tactical strategies for managing reputation. Crises test the core values of an organization. The decision to pull the Tylenol product from all shelves is a natural response that embodies the values and priorities of the Johnson & Johnson (2016) credo, which gives priority to the health of patients.

This case is often juxtaposed with examples of organizations that failed to respond to crisis in a way that is consistent with their core values. Some examples include the failed response by Exxon and BP, respectively, to oil spills in Prince William Sound, Alaska, and the Gulf of Mexico; the Catholic Church's lack of leadership during an ongoing child abuse scandal; and the lack of preparation for and ineffective management of the response to Hurricane Katrina by federal and local government leaders. A common thread runs through the core values of Exxon, BP, the Roman Catholic Church, and FEMA—a commitment to the welfare of others. This core value was tested by the aforementioned crises; but, unlike Johnson & Johnson's response, the leadership behaviors demonstrated in the face of these crises were absent, ineffective, or disingenuous. Crisis leadership involves the alignment of decisions with the organization's core values. As these values are tested, the very mission of the unit, department, or organization provides a compass for decision-making when the stakes are quite high.

Understanding Crisis in Higher Education

One does not have to look far to identify the scope of crisis examples in higher education or to see the relevance of the classic cases discussed in the previous sections. Higher education news outlets and general news outlets often report on the array of crises that is affecting colleges and universities. It is often difficult to pinpoint the complex and multifaceted causes for these crises, yet a useful first step for academic and administrative leaders is to consider which types of crises are most likely to impact their institution, and how the institution's values and purposes can serve as a useful guide in directing the actions of leaders at all levels. Whether the crisis is a flood, an act of violence, or an athletics scandal, the mission, vision, and values of the institution provide a useful foundation for thinking about the appropriate ways to approach this situation—before, during, and after the crisis.

Crisis leadership in higher education shares much in common with the Johnson & Johnson case offered in the previous section. In November 1999 Texas A&M University continued with its autumn tradition of building and burning a bonfire as part of its rivalry with the University of Texas at Austin. During the construction of this particular bonfire, the bonfire logs—which weighed the equivalent of two 747 jumbo jets—collapsed, killing 12 students and injuring 27 more. In her reflection on the crisis, the executive director of university relations at Texas A&M at the time of the bonfire collapse, Cynthia Lawson (2014), commented on the power of leadership during this dark period in the university's history. Consistent with the mission and values of the university, the priorities during the crisis involved the rescue and recovery of the victims at the site of the bonfire and the immediate support of students, parents, and other key university stakeholders. The crisis response is often recognized as one of the "best managed in higher education," due to the prompt response, the development and implementation of a process to investigate the cause of the accident, the emotional support from leaders across the institution throughout and following the crisis, and the creation of a task force charged with identifying the university's vulnerabilities and risks (Lawson, 2014). When President Ray Bowen was asked about his expectations for media relations in the aftermath of the crisis, Lawson described his response: "'That's what I hired you for,' he said. And then, looking me directly in the eyes, he added, 'Just do the right thing, Cindy'" (Lawson, 2014, p. 40).

This desire to "do the right thing" is consistent with other examples of effective crisis leadership in higher education, including Tulane University's response to Hurricane Katrina, the University of Oklahoma's response to racist chants by members of a fraternity, and Duquesne University's response to an on-campus shooting incident. When core values drive the crisis leadership response, the reputation of the unit, department, or institution is not the primary area of focus. Rather, the reputation is upheld by the commitment to these articulated values such as protecting the safety and well-being of students, staff, and faculty; taking responsibility for mistakes and oversights; and seeing that they are corrected. Like the Tylenol case, "doing the right thing" based on aligning behaviors with one's core mission and values during crisis is paramount.

Effective crisis leadership requires, first and foremost, an understanding of the importance of maintaining the core values of the institution, along with the context for crisis prevention, reputation management, and crisis management. The complexity of higher education crises makes colleges and universities especially vulnerable, leading to the necessity of both crisis management and crisis prevention and an understanding of the importance of communication during these moments of organizational disruption. It is essential for both academic and administrative leaders to understand the nuances of crisis management and crisis prevention, recognizing the importance of ethics, integrity, and core values in guiding leadership behavior throughout all phases of the crisis.

Crisis Leadership: Beyond Public Relations

Much of the writing on crises in organizations focuses primarily on the public relations implications—how to protect the reputation of the institution, maintain a favorable impression in the eyes of many stakeholders, and view and use communication as a tactic to shape public opinion. And while these perspectives may be sufficient for crisis leadership in organizations in some sectors, they provide a limited perspective when thinking about higher education and the leader's role and responsibility. Leaders at all levels, as we have discussed throughout this book, have the responsibility of establishing and sustaining a culture and climate where core values are maintained and practiced. Crisis situations present major challenges that test the organization and leaders in their ability to deal with multiple challenges simultaneously—analyzing the situation; mobilizing appropriate resources to attend to injury, the loss of life, or damage to the physical structure of the institution; and planning and executing appropriate internal communication with faculty and staff, as well as communication with students, safety and emergency personnel, media, the public, and other affected parties.

As discussed in Chapter 8, many leadership and social influence outcomes are often unplanned, unintentional, unpredicted, and unpredictable. The message sent by a leader, particularly during times of crisis, is not guaranteed to be received by those most affected by the crisis; in fact, the gap between message sent and message received is particularly likely to occur in times of crisis. Single messages seldom have much impact on broader impressions. Furthermore, the historical context is significant in shaping the design, interpretation, and evolution of messages related to an organizational crisis. For example, when a crisis strikes, it is important to consider the organization's history with crises of this type, the leader's past experiences in dealing with crises, and the susceptibilities and expectations of those stakeholders most impacted by the crisis. For these reasons, crisis management and crisis prevention are only part of the story. The notion of crisis leadership, particularly crisis leadership in higher education, extends beyond reputation management, the prevention of a crisis, and the public relations–oriented management of a unit, department, or institutional crisis. Rather, crisis leadership presents a broader framework for understanding what's most at stake during these periods of disruption.

Within the various phases of a unit, department, or organizational crisis, a number of communication implications are at stake for academic and administrative leaders. A summary of writings on organizational crises indicates that differing leadership competencies are important at specific stages of the crisis (Booker, 2014). These competencies include the detection of early warning signs in the environment; the strategic use of communication in preventing, preparing, and containing the crisis; and the promotion of learning throughout the process and at the conclusion of the crisis. This emphasis on learning and improvement in operating procedures and communication practices is especially relevant in colleges and universities that place learning at a premium. The focus on risk assessment, postcrisis learning, and crisis leadership more broadly reflects a more proactive and holistic approach to dealing with crises in colleges and universities (Mitroff, 2004).

DuBrin (2013) extends this summary of crisis leadership behaviors to include the following:

- Stay calm during a crisis.
- Plan before and during a crisis.
- Make good use of your team.
- Avoid stonewalling the problem.
- Reestablish the work routine.

- Exercise transformational leadership.
- Give recognition for accomplishments.
- Do not waste the crisis. (p. 15)

These strategies are most useful in thinking through how one might deal with some of the challenges in the aftermath of a crisis, but we would first make note of the centrality of the core institutional values in leading during crisis. If these core values become lived values, leaders are often able to maintain trust in order to proceed through the behaviors offered here. If these values are violated prior to or during the crisis, however, no communication strategies can be expected to offset the loss of trust in a leader.

In a time when more, rather than fewer, campus crises seem probable, leadership competencies for crisis leaders become ever more indispensable. For example, the ability to adapt is understood to be a critical competency for leaders (Muffet-Willett & Kruse, 2008). The continuum depicted in Figure 17.1 highlights the unique demands on leaders during times of crisis.

Figure 17.1. Crisis leadership continuum.

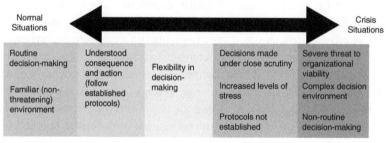

Source. Muffet-Willett and Kruse, 2008. Reprinted with permission.

These demands call for leaders who can make appropriate and timely decisions and lead effectively in a complex environment.

Tactical (or persuasive) communication, clarity of vision and values, and caring relationships are critical components of crisis leadership (Klann, 2003). This emphasis on communication and relationships is also central to Muffet-Willett's (2010) summary of crisis leadership actions that are most relevant to colleges and universities, as illustrated in Figure 17.2. Communication and feedback mechanisms are situated at multiple junctures in the process. Administrative decision-making is critical, but so too are those mechanisms for soliciting feedback from key stakeholders

Figure 17.2. Higher education crisis leadership practical process model.

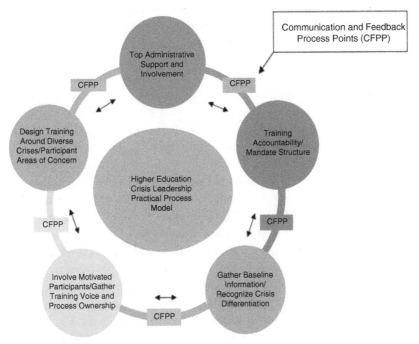

Source. Muffet-Willet, 2010. Reprinted with permission.

across the institution. Not surprisingly, this emphasis on creating dialogue is a value shared across the higher education sector. The model also indirectly speaks to the inherent limitations of a focus on crisis management or crisis prevention. Crisis leadership encompasses the communication that occurs at senior-level decision-making, in organization-wide training initiatives, and in the messages that occur before, during, and following the crisis.

Key Communication Considerations for Crisis Leadership Practice

Crisis leadership involves more than simply saying the right things to the right audiences to uphold the reputation of an institution in the face of crisis, what Mitroff (2004) may describe as an "integrated design" (p. 9) of crisis leadership. Rather, crisis leadership calls for a more expansive understanding of the types of risks that a unit, department, or institution faces—and a continual emphasis on personal and institutional learning at all phases of the crisis process.

Focusing only on the delivery of appropriate responses is a simplistic view of communication that violates much of what we currently understand about human communication. Rather, communication theory would point to the importance of understanding the organization's history with crises, appreciating the diverse needs of stakeholders, and leading with integrity throughout the entire crisis process (i.e., before, during, and after). Crisis leadership involves prevention and management, consistency and clarity, trust and transparency—with communication playing a critical role during each phase. By building and maintaining a reservoir of goodwill at the individual and collective levels, a foundation is set for authentic, values-centered dialogue when crises do occur. Specifically, it seems likely that the reputation and history that serve an individual leader and collective organization well during times of normalcy are essential for effective leadership and performance during times of crisis. This reputation provides a solid and sturdy foundation upon which to stand when crises strike.

Recognition of the organization's history and an acknowledgment of future vulnerabilities are critical for crisis leadership. This broader paradigm for understanding crisis does not diminish the importance of communication during the crisis itself. To the contrary, there is generally a need to use communication strategy to inform, educate, and inspire those most impacted by the crisis—and to do so in a way that builds confidence in the institution and its leaders. A number of strategies that are useful in these ways are widely acknowledged in the public relations literature. Strategies and tactics such as those associated with reputation management, crisis prevention, and internal and external communication may be very useful for academic and administrative leaders as they address the multiple challenges associated with crisis leadership.

Reputation Management Strategies

As discussed in Chapter 4, higher education institutions may contain more interested stakeholders than any other sector. These stakeholders, or constituency groups (Fortunato, 2005), include current and prospective students, faculty, staff, parents, alumni, and donors along with a wide range of external audiences (e.g., governmental agencies, employers, high schools, and the media). Reputation management is an important communication-oriented principle for effective crisis leadership. The recognition of stakeholders is critical in understanding which constituency groups the crisis might impact, which relationships might be threatened, and with whom one needs to communicate. Reputation management begins with an identification of these stakeholders and the prioritization of these various audiences. A number of principles capture the essence of reputation management, including the following:

- No organization exists by itself.
- The function is to constantly evaluate the relationship between the organization and its constituency groups, questioning how to strengthen the relationship.
- Communication is the key to improving these relationships.
- People involved in communication interactions between the organization and its constituency groups must have the requisite competencies and resources to improve the relationship.
- Communication between the organization and different constituency groups can be tailored to address their specific concerns.
- Reputation management ideally results in mutually beneficial relationship outcomes.

It is easier to manage reputations when things are going well. Crises test these relationships, and various stakeholders will closely evaluate the response of the organization during a crisis. To add to the complexity, one group of stakeholders might also be evaluating the response of other stakeholders during a crisis (e.g., alumni and parents may monitor how corporate sponsors react to an on-campus scandal, which is then reported by the media).

Within a broader crisis leadership framework, reputation follows naturally from a firm and predictable adherence to an institution's values. If managing reputation is the explicit goal of crisis communication, then communication is understood to be a strategy for positively influencing how others view the organization. If upholding the core mission and values is the goal, however, the communication strategies and ultimate perception from stakeholders should fall naturally into place during times of crisis. In the seminal Tylenol case mentioned earlier, the Johnson & Johnson credo served as a guide in shaping the organization's actions following the crisis. The case is heralded as a classic, not because of the adoption of clever communication strategies for managing the company's reputation, but because of the company's responding to crisis in a way that very much aligns with the mission, vision, and values of the organization. The decision to pull the drugs from the shelves in the aftermath of the crisis was more than a public relations strategy—it embodied the core values of the company. Integrity and ethics are not secondary to reputation management and crisis leadership; rather, they are paramount to the success of leading before, during, and following these critical moments.

Crisis Prevention Strategies

Crisis prevention is a recommended philosophy; however, it is naïve to think that all crises will or even can be prevented. Although many crises are unpredictable, an understanding of the nature of crisis and a sophisticated awareness of organizations, leadership communication, and culture allows for a richer and broader understanding of ways to prevent specific college and university crises. If one considers first the array of crises that might impact institutions, along with those areas of vulnerability across units and departments, we can begin to take an important first step in preventing future crises from occurring.

If we consider the parallels between colleges and universities and local cities, the characteristics are fairly similar. Colleges provide services to a diverse group of residents and commuters. They have a responsibility to care for these individuals—to provide food, shelter, security, and opportunities for fulfillment. Just like cities, colleges and universities are also vulnerable to a host of crises that could threaten this mission of protection, security, and fulfillment. Tabletop simulations, crisis preparation training sessions, and the development of a sophisticated crisis prevention plan are all examples of ways that leaders can proactively think through the nuances of particular crises. These tools allow leaders and members to evaluate the vulnerability of the unit, department, or organization. The crisis prevention plan should assess the unit, department, or organization on two dimensions—first, how likely or probable it is that a specific crisis would impact the group, and second, how devastating could this crisis be (Fearn-Banks, 2011)? Based on the responses to these two questions, leaders can then determine specific actions that can and should be taken in an effort to prevent certain crises from occurring. In many instances an investment in crisis prevention can be less than the resources that would be needed to manage the crisis, engage in litigation and have the organization regain its credibility following the crisis.

The development of protocols following crises is another useful strategy for preventing similar scenarios in the future. For example, learning about the strengths and weaknesses of past crisis responses to natural disasters, active campus crime situations, or hate crimes can strengthen the collective capacity of the institution to better prepare for future episodes of similar magnitude. In thinking through the design of these protocols, there is a need for academic and administrative leaders to consider the following questions as a way of minimizing the severity of the crisis:

- In what types of situations is your unit, department, or institution most vulnerable?

- Depending upon these vulnerabilities, which internal and external stakeholders are most at risk?
- Who needs to be engaged throughout the crisis response process?
- What communication is needed, to whom, and through which delivery method?

The goal of the protocols is to prevent these serious events from rising to the level of a crisis during and after the active situation has occurred. Other issues are more complex, such as student uprisings, misconduct by high-profile leaders, or unanticipated market crashes. For these crises, along with others, it becomes especially important to privilege and emphasize learning across the institution as a way of creating a collective awareness about those issues that might lie on the horizon.

Internal and External Communication Strategies

As noted, communication is a critical component to crisis leadership. According to Gores (2014),

> When tragedy strikes, the campus community, stakeholders, and the local community look to leadership for direction and guidance. How leaders respond in the first several hours and in the days that follow offers tremendous opportunity to bring a campus together or put the campus at risk. It is not possible to predict or control a crisis, but it is possible to control the response and the way in which the institution reacts to it. (p. 147)

Leaders in higher education must grapple with the in-the-moment complexities of crisis in order to audit where things stand and to detect vulnerabilities for future crises. Adding to this complexity is the notion that there may be moments where the leader can be proactive and frame the situation for others, whereas other crises may already have been identified and labeled a crisis by other stakeholder groups and in need of immediate attention by the leader. In both instances, the following three critical questions need to be answered when a situation develops that is perceived by all key parties to be a crisis:

1. What happened?
2. Will it happen again?
3. What tangible actions has the organization undertaken to prevent the crisis from reoccurring?

These questions allow institutional leaders to consider the short- and long-term impact of the crisis while also informing how leaders might communicate about the crisis and the subsequent changes made after it.

Communication in a crisis is especially important for its ability to either improve the situation or make it worse. One of the goals is for leaders to avoid escalating or compounding the crisis through communication, recognizing Benson's (1988) point that crisis communication can significantly diminish or magnify the harm. Three fundamental concepts should guide communication during times of crisis (Coombs, 2006). First, *be quick*. A prewritten press release, for example, can demonstrate that the organization is aware of the crisis, already dealing with it, and working toward responding to the key question of what happened. This statement could express empathy toward the situation, if applicable. Social media has facilitated the speed with which an initial communication can be provided. Second, *be consistent*. The presentation of conflicting responses can be especially problematic for the institution. Again, one of the goals is to avoid creating a secondary crisis due to poor communication surrounding the primary crisis. Finally, *be open*. Crises inevitably lead to information vacuums. It is necessary for the college or university to fill that vacuum with truthful information that reflects well on the organization. If higher education leaders are not filling that vacuum, others might be—and they may be providing information that is detrimental to the organization.

Depending on the crisis, a number of core communication principles should be considered at the unit, department, and institutional levels (Nelson, 2014):

- Activate timely and early alert messages.
- Provide frequent updates.
- Incorporate a variety of tools and media.
- Leverage the university's, department's, or unit's homepage.
- Educate and involve stakeholders such as parents, leadership councils, and alumni.

The design of crisis response messages requires careful consideration of the needs of those most affected by the situation, while also recognizing that as a leader you are simultaneously communicating with internal and external stakeholders.

Crisis communication and the leader's response must align with the severity of the crisis. In other words, not every crisis requires the same response. Furthermore, expectations will vary based on the institution. Leaders in higher education must be aware of the different types of responses available; the particular vulnerabilities of one's unit, department, or institution; and the potential sensitivities associated with the unique culture of a given college or university. This is especially the case as leaders consider those crises that are self-imposed. For example, the decision to arm public safety officers or expand the number of surveillance cameras across campus may trigger different sets of reactions at various institutions—incidents that may be characterized as internal crises or may create the conditions for a perceived crisis. In this sense, crisis leadership involves the ability to forecast the anticipated reactions from campus stakeholders prior to major announcements and decisions.

Interactions With Media

Because of the significant role of a university as part of the geographic community in which it is located and the standing it has in society, a crisis at a university often becomes a local or national media story. For these crisis situations, academic and administrative leaders are expected to interact with the media, taking on the roles of information providers and advocates, and representing the organization at large. Through these roles, leaders may provide relevant information on behalf of the institution, both highlighting and emphasizing certain aspects of the issue at stake. Recognizing the critical role of the stakeholder, crisis communication is informed by the various audiences that will receive the message—with the media taking on the role of a conduit for the message itself. Doug Lederman, editor of *Inside Higher Education*, provides the following advice for speaking with the media: "I can say that in a crisis, one should be honest and forthright. Don't ever try to hide the truth, because if the media believe you are covering up the truth, or if it is found that there were truths being covered up, there is a good chance that will be worse than the actual crisis itself" (as cited in Parrot, 2014, p. 171).

The media, an important stakeholder for any college or university, have the responsibility to make decisions about what becomes part of their coverage. Colleges and universities are often the target for a great deal of media attention when crises strike. In some instances, crises challenge or call into question the noble mission of higher education—leading many to criticize these institutions for failing to live up to their articulated values. As discussed in Chapter 8, agenda-setting theory is important for understanding the communicative role of leaders. It is also a foundational theory for the study of the mass media's role during times of crisis. The theory suggests that the selection of stories—along with the selection of certain facts—increases audience salience of the issues as well as the facts themselves (McCombs & Shaw, 1972; McCombs, Shaw, & Weaver, 2014). There is competition for media coverage and to have certain facts presented within the coverage, so it is imperative for higher education leaders to have a plan in place for interacting with the media during periods of crisis. There are a number of mechanisms through which to communicate with the media during crises, including prewritten press releases, spokesperson/spokespeople, press conferences, website updates, and the use of social media. All of these approaches call for an established chain of command, carefully calibrated plans, and sophisticated media training. Parrot (2014) offers additional advice for higher education leaders who are communicating with the media:

> Trepidation for working with the media is understandable, but fear should never delay the issuance of a response or participation in an interview. [Leaders] must model the highest levels of leadership possible by pro-actively sharing their institution's story—a story that must be rooted in truth and framed with engaging language—and providing a plan for future direction. (p. 179)

When interacting with the media, two crisis communication models are especially useful for higher education leaders. The first of the most often referenced approaches to crisis management focuses on the idea of image restoration (Benoit, 1995). As summarized in Benoit and Pang (2008), there are five tactics that may be used to restore the image of an organization during a crisis, some of which may be used simultaneously with one another:

1. Denial—the organization claims there is no crisis and offers a simple denial that it did not perform the act in question.
2. Evasion of responsibility—the organization attempts to reduce responsibility for the crisis by claiming it was either forced into the crisis by another culprit, it did not have the ability to prevent the crisis, it made a mistake, or there were good intentions in its act.
3. Reduction of the offensiveness of the act—the organization attempts to reinforce the good traits of the organization, thus creating a more complete context with which the organization should be evaluated.
4. Corrective action—the organization implements steps to solve the problem and prevent a repeat of the crisis.
5. Mortification—the organization accepts responsibility for the act and apologizes. (pp. 247–251)

In decisions relative to the use of these approaches, we would emphasize choosing the strategies that honestly reflect the stance of the unit, department, or organization. For example, an apology can show remorse for the crisis and reinforce the good traits of the college and university. This serves to shift the context to evaluate the organization. Corrective action, responding to the speculation as to whether the crisis will occur again, has the potential to enhance the organization's image following the crisis and offers the potential for the institution to emerge as a leader in directly confronting the issue. Once corrective action measures have been implemented, the organization has something positive to talk about. It should be noted that these general strategies are mitigated by two important factors: (a) the nature of the transgression—some acts are so egregious, it is difficult and perhaps impossible to overcome regardless of the strategies implemented; and (b) stakeholders' loyalty toward the leader or institution—some may be willing to overlook the transgression because of their unwavering support for and commitment to their college or university. For these reasons, higher education leaders would respond differently to an on-campus shooting than they would to a crisis of lesser magnitude. Furthermore, the effectiveness of these communication strategies rely on the integrity of the claims, the authenticity of the postcrisis actions, and the leadership and organizational behaviors that preceded the crisis.

The second crisis communication model outlines seven response strategies organized by their perceived level of acceptance on behalf of the stakeholders (Coombs, 2015). These seven strategies are summarized as follows:

1. Full apology—very high acceptance
2. Corrective action—high acceptance
3. Denial—no acceptance
4. Attack the accuser—no acceptance
5. Ingratiation (organization reminds stakeholders of past good acts)—mild acceptance
6. Justification (organization claims the damage from the crisis was minimal)—mild acceptance
7. Excuse (organization denies intent)—mild acceptance

The role of the leader is to understand the magnitude of the situation as well as the importance of the situation in the eyes of various stakeholders. Essentially, if the stakeholders view the issue as a crisis, the organization must respond accordingly. Leaders at the University of Missouri, for example, were forced to resign for not recognizing the severity of a racial crisis and for failing to respond in a timely and appropriate fashion to the concerns of multiple constituency groups. Some have also criticized the university leadership for reacting to racial incidents without fully addressing the deeper systemic issues plaguing the campus community (Parker, 2015). Recognizing that the issue in many instances cannot be dismissed as irrelevant, higher education leaders must ensure not only that the appropriate messages are being sent, but also that the right person is delivering the message, depending on the type and severity of the crisis. This protocol will likely appear in a formalized crisis management plan—one designed by a collaborative crisis management team that outlines key individuals and policies for best responding to immediate crises. Leaders must be willing to participate in media training, if needed, and during the crisis itself the leader must be visible to internal as well as external audiences. Finally, the college or university must be willing to invest resources in the crisis management process and any subsequent corrective action procedures in order to restore trust from the many stakeholders who have an interest in the institution. Referring back to the University of Missouri example, it was important for the appropriate university official(s) to respond to the racial incidents impacting the community; but as these cases have also demonstrated, effective crisis leadership involves more than reacting to a problematic incident on the college campus. Effective crisis leadership relies on having a deep understanding of the needs, expectations, goals, and attitudes of these stakeholders as university officials create communities of inclusivity, respect, and mutual understanding—with communication occupying a critical role.

Conclusion

The strategies and tactics raised in this chapter are useful for crisis leadership in practice, yet they are only part of a much more extensive story—one in which ongoing adherence to core institutional values is central. If a college or university has a history with a certain type of crisis, or if there is a pattern of leaders not considering the needs of certain stakeholders, no right mix of tactical strategies can guarantee a satisfactory crisis response. To think otherwise is indicative of a rudimentary understanding of communication theory. It is worth repeating that a message being by a leader, particularly during times of crisis, provides no guarantee that the message will be received by those most affected by the situation. Single messages seldom have much impact on broader impressions as with the ongoing crash of waves shaping the ocean shoreline, these tactical communication strategies during a crisis may help to manage expectations, ensure transparency, and provide a framework for collective sensemaking to occur. Crisis leadership in higher education involves recognition of the critical role of communication, including the tactics used during crises and the broader communication infrastructure that shapes both what is accepted and what is expected by one's stakeholders. Finally, and it is worth repeating, reputation management and the communication strategies offered in the latter half of this chapter are of secondary importance. The reputation of a leader and an organization is reflective of those values-centered leadership strategies that precede and emerge during the crisis.

In his recent analysis of his time as president of Tulane University during Hurricane Katrina, Scott Cowan (2014) offered 10 leadership principles that reflect the nuances of crisis leadership presented in this chapter:

1. Do the right thing.
2. Seek common ground.
3. Marshal facts.
4. Understand reality.
5. Aim high.
6. Stand up for your beliefs.
7. Make contact.
8. Innovate.
9. Embrace emotion.
10. Be true to core values.

In many instances, individual crises are isolated occurrences that can attract a great deal of attention. The principles that Cowan offers speak to the importance of embodying an approach to leadership that prepares a leader for these isolated moments, while also serving the leader and his or her unit, department, or institution well during periods of normalcy. *Crisis leadership* in higher education—a broader term that embodies and goes beyond both crisis management and crisis prevention—involves recognition of the needs, expectations, and values of the many stakeholders who have an interest in colleges and universities. Crisis leadership positions communication as a critical competency for navigating tumultuous terrain. Finally, crisis leadership extends the unit of analysis from the crisis itself to the culture, relationships, history, and leadership decisions that underlie the unit, department, or institution.

Crisis leadership remains a timely and important area of focus for all current and aspiring academic and administrative leaders in preventing, managing, responding to, and recovering from the crises that may tear at the institution and that may dramatically impact the lives of those who live, learn, and work in American colleges and universities. The emphasis on crisis leadership presented in this chapter highlights the critical role of communication and feedback throughout the process—and suggests a more holistic approach to leading during times of crisis.

For Further Consideration

1. Recent Case Analysis

Select a recent case involving a college or university crisis. Review the messages delivered by university leader(s) in response to the crisis.

1. Using Benoit's (1995) approach to image restoration, which of the following strategies did the university leader(s) utilize: denial, evasion of responsibility, reducing the offensiveness of the act, corrective action, or mortification?
2. Were these strategies effective or ineffective? Why?
3. In what ways did the strategies align or fail to align with the severity of the crisis?
4. Is there anything you would have done differently in responding to this particular crisis?

2. Crisis Prevention Inventory

Conduct a crisis prevention inventory by determining the types of crises that are most likely to affect your unit, department, or institution.

1. Have you encountered any crises that were sudden and took the organization by surprise—or were slowly creeping and growing increasingly problematic over time (Seymour & Moore, 2000)?
2. Are there any specific areas where you find your unit, department, or institution to be most vulnerable?
3. In which of the phases of the crisis do you feel most prepared or least prepared as a leader?

As you think through this inventory, consider the recommendations put forward by the Society for College and University Planning for leading during these increasingly common—and increasingly troubling—moments (see www.scup.org/page/knowledge/crisis-planning/diamond; Mitroff, Diamond, & Alpaslan, 2006).

3. Crisis Leadership Training and Development

What areas of training are most important for the leader of your specific area (e.g., media training, understanding of organizational processes and protocols, tabletop simulations of potential crises)? In what ways might these areas of training help that leader better respond to a crisis?

4. Core Values in Responding to Crisis

Describe the core values of your unit, department, or institution.

1. Can you think of examples where the core values of your specific unit, department, or school would help to prevent crises from occurring?
2. What role can these core values play in providing guidance for leaders during times of crisis?
3. Core values can also provide guidance in suggesting what *not* to do when crises strike. In what ways might your core values inform how you will *not* respond to a particular crisis?

18

ORGANIZATIONAL CONTINUITY AND CHANGE

Leadership Succession Planning

In This Chapter

- What is leadership succession planning, and how does it contribute to organizational excellence efforts?
- What is the current state of leadership succession planning in higher education?
- What are the critical elements of leadership succession planning?
- In what ways can some or all of the leadership succession planning elements be useful to colleges and universities?
- What are the steps in a leadership development and succession program?

College and university leaders typically engage with faculty, staff, and other stakeholders, including governing boards, in systematic planning activities such as strategic planning (Chapter 14), master planning, and contingency/emergency planning. Despite familiarity with and reliance on planning processes, most colleges and universities do not engage in leadership succession planning (Calareso, 2013). This chapter describes leadership succession planning and explores its potential value for higher education. This chapter also identifies factors that are fundamental to successful practices in this area and explores options for approaches to leadership succession that governing boards, college presidents, chancellors, and other senior leaders might find useful.

What Is Leadership Succession Planning?

The U.S. Office of Personnel Management (2005) provides a succinct description of the purpose and process of succession planning:

Succession planning is a systematic approach to:

- Building a leadership pipeline/talent pool to ensure leadership continuity
- Developing potential successors in ways that best fit their strengths
- Identifying the best candidates for categories of positions
- Concentrating resources on the talent development process yielding a greater return of investment (p. 1)

At its core, *leadership succession planning* is "the preparation to replace one leader with another" (Mamprin, 2002). Underpinning these practices is the view that some jobs are the lifeblood of the organization and too critical to be left vacant or filled by any but the best, most knowledgeable, and most qualified persons. In this way of thinking, "Succession planning is critical to mission success and creates an effective process for recognizing, developing, and retaining top leadership talent" (U.S. Office of Personnel Management, 2005, p. 1).

In corporate sector organizations, where succession planning is most widely practiced, an essential goal is identifying and developing new leaders from within the organization to succeed current leaders (Cascio, 2011). Typically, this preparation occurs long before the incumbent leader departs. Developing a detailed profile and description of a position can be part of the leader's portfolio of responsibilities, and in some instances, incumbent leaders can play a meaningful role in the review and selection of their successors. For example, as a part of the transition process, leaders might be asked to articulate a set of goals, describe general competencies required for the position, highlight current pressing challenges and aspirations, and identify key markers that he or she would regard as critical for the next generation of leadership, given his or her evaluation of the organization's current and future needs.

Succession Planning in Higher Education

Most institutions of higher education do not have comprehensive succession programs in place. In one of the few systematic studies on the topic, Richards (2009) identified three possible approaches to leadership succession planning in higher education.[1] The first and least sophisticated approach is labeled "back of the envelope." In this approach, an institution does not really plan for leadership succession but instead addresses immediate needs as they arise. The second approach is known as "replacement planning." Here, a college or university might have backup charts specified for a few positions with one-to-one or single replacements specified. For example, in case of death or prolonged disability, the campus provost assumes the presidency on an interim basis. Within the replacement planning model, other succession plans are oriented toward the next one to two years only. The third and most complex approach to campus-based leadership succession planning is "talent management" and has four components: (a) considers long-term and future planning, (b) focuses on key leadership positions, (c) builds management bench strength, and (d) adopts a competency-based approach (Richards, 2009).

Based on the limited research and writing on the topic, it is clear that very few colleges and universities have implemented a talent management approach to succession planning, especially for academic roles. More typical is the ad hoc, back-of-the-envelope approach or consideration of leadership successions on a case-by-case or replacement-as-needed basis (Calareso, 2013; Richards, 2009).

Approaches to succession planning on the staff-administrative side of higher education are increasingly likely to use approaches that are more closely associated with components of the talent management model. For example, the College and University Professional Association for Human Resources offers resources on its website for leadership development and leadership succession planning.[2] The information provided relies heavily on best practices for leadership succession planning from the business-corporate sector.

A number of factors—some historical, some philosophical, and others operational—help to explain the current state of affairs in higher education. Perhaps the most fundamental explanation can be traced to the lack of systematic processes for institutional assessment and evaluation of current leaders. Such assessment systems provide the foundation for rational and effective succession planning. Without a larger process of institutional assessment and current leader evaluation, colleges and universities are not well positioned to have a strong and successful leadership succession planning process in place. Leadership development programs, as discussed in Chapter 19, represent an additional element that is important for leadership succession planning. Even when robust leadership development programs are in place, however, institutions need to make a commitment to promote those who have successfully completed these programs when open positions become available, rather than routinely favoring external hires.

Why Engage in Leadership Succession Planning?

A corporate mind-set. Many leading organizations in the corporate sector believe that the best approach to leadership succession is to be proactive, develop an internal talent pool, and plan and carefully manage transitions. For organizations that embrace leadership succession planning, the underlying belief is that the costs of leadership training for employees who exemplify and contribute positively to the corporate culture often yield greater benefits than hiring candidates from outside the organization. No matter how thorough a search process may be, hiring organizations are likely to be less certain of the capabilities and competencies of external candidates than of employees already in residence. Moreover, even if strong external candidates are selected, under the best of conditions these individuals still require a good deal of time to understand the new organization and its culture. Well-prepared internal candidates are predictably more knowledgeable about the organization's strengths, weaknesses, and unique challenges and opportunities. For these and other reasons, succession planning that includes thoughtful identification and training of the next-in-line for key leadership posts within the organization has many benefits.

With succession planning and leadership preparation as its default, the corporate sector can, when deemed appropriate, pivot to filling positions with people outside the organization. This might occur if a judgment is made that a cultural shift is necessary, or the knowledge and competencies required are not present within the organization. Thus, an investment in leadership succession planning gives such organizations two options for leadership succession: building strength from within and shopping the marketplace as necessary.

A higher education mind-set. Identification and training of internal candidates for next-in-line succession is atypical in higher education. The default approach for filling many leadership posts is an external search that relies on the marketplace—often with the assistance of search firms—to identify new leaders. This is especially true for academic posts above the level of department chair, including positions such as dean, provost, vice presidents, and presidents. Of course, internal candidates are often permitted to apply when external searches are conducted, but as Mrig and Fusch (2014) report, a recent survey found that only 30% of responding institutions filled more than half of their VP-level positions with internal candidates. While next-in-line succession appointments are generally not looked upon with favor in higher education, exceptions exist; for some academic positions, such as department chair, selection of internal candidates is commonplace. The next department chair is typically found from within the current members of the faculty, often following a turn-taking or "sorry, you drew the short straw" approach. Clearly, this approach does not parallel the ideal talent management approaches to succession planning. Indeed, without prior training, a new leader, selected in this manner—with little planning or preparation—is not necessarily in a good position to lead, even if he or she is an internal candidate who has knowledge of the departmental, college, and institutional culture.

A similar circumstance exists on the staff-administrative side. For entry-level positions of leadership, current staff employees who meet and exceed expectations may be promoted. Like a new department chair, such a staff member is now responsible for managing persons who had previously been peer colleagues. Although position descriptions from the human resources department make it clear that the new leader has the responsibility and authority to manage others or set strategic priorities, there is often little prior assessment of the person's suitability to lead. For many, the learning curve is very steep, especially if institutional leadership development programs are absent or ineffective.

The guiding philosophy, particularly as it relates to senior academic hiring, is built on the assumption that a change in perspective is important to organizational vitality. Regarding academic leadership, the thinking holds that so-called organization inbreeding can undermine growth and advancement. While this may be the case in some instances, continuity can often be a very important value. In either circumstance, the goal should be to select a candidate whose competencies best match the needs and aspirations of the department, college, or institution. In an ideal circumstance, where a talent management approach is integrated with leadership assessment and preparation, potential internal candidates and the needs of the organization would have been assessed over months or even years. In addition to being more sensitive to individual and organizational needs and capabilities, this approach has the advantage of providing more time and opportunity for greater in-depth analyses of internal candidates than are processes typically used to evaluate external and internal candidates. The importance of institutional continuity and leadership succession planning is nicely illustrated in the reflections offered by David Ward in Box 18.1.

Unexpected leadership vacancies in higher education. The need for talent management approaches to leadership succession planning in higher education is perhaps most obvious in cases where current leaders—including directors, deans, and department chairs—vacate their positions unexpectedly and with little advance notice. Unexpected vacancies can be disruptive for the institution as well as for the faculty and staff employees (Calareso, 2013). In some cases, no suitable internal candidate is available to assume a leadership position, and a suitable external candidate may not be readily found, recruited, and hired. This can create a serious and disruptive leadership gap for a semester, a year, or even longer (Bennett, 2015). It is unclear how representative Bennett's description may be, especially given a paucity of scholarly research on leadership succession planning in higher education. However, anyone who has worked in higher education for 20 years or more can cite examples like Bennett's, in which the question, "Who can we appoint to fill

BOX 18.1
Succession Planning

Leadership transitions in any kind of enterprise present so many opportunities and challenges that the process lies outside normal concepts of planning. Nevertheless, transitions are critical, and the search process is usually designed to consolidate continuity of mission and vision or to ignite some transformational process. Often this choice is linked to preferences for an inside or outside candidate. In the academic world, it is fair to conclude that there is very little succession management but there are always high hopes of transformational change. Yet the tempo and duration of change require consistency of direction that outlasts the tenure of individual leaders.

For about 20 years the University of Wisconsin–Madison did experience a consistency of direction under the leadership of three different chancellors—Donna Shalala, myself, and John Wiley. We were, I believe, quite different in our leadership styles, and while Donna was clearly an outside appointment invested with a mandate for change, John and I were long-standing faculty members who had previously served as provost. There was certainly no explicit succession plan, and each of us aroused different kinds of loyalty and commitments from different segments of the university community and its constituencies.

I believe that the continuity was rooted in the success of the self-study of the regional accreditation process in the late 1980s. The success of that study must be attributed to Donna's predecessors and in particular their choice of key faculty and staff who emphasized deeply the problems that needed to be addressed. This document was refreshed 10 years later by a similar self-study process, and the challenge of leadership was not the legitimacy of the issues before us but their willingness to address them.

All three leaders chose from these issues and addressed them—there were both common, high-priority issues and other issues more specifically identified with each of these leaders. The entire process of continuity was amplified by the high level of trust that each leader placed in the senior financial officer, John Torphy, who was both a critical and creative partner in the implementation processes. This mutual trust was not confined to the senior leaders but was also the basis of broad and flexible levels of implementation by the cabinet, deans, directors and other functional and cross-functional unit leaders.

If leadership is embedded in a broadly supported set of goals rooted in the traditions and expectations of the university and its constituencies, leadership style is less critical, and the merits of inside or outside appointments matter less. An agenda rooted in a representative process greatly

(Continues)

BOX 18.1 *(Continued)*

> diminished the inevitable conflicts based on prior loyalties and unfamiliar personal styles of successive leaders.
>
> Succession planning certainly helps develop leadership skills within an institution, but without some kind of campus commitment to issues and goals, no amount of succession planning or assumptions about the transformational capacities will work.
>
> David Ward, University of Wisconsin–Madison
> Former President of the American Council on Education
> Former Chancellor of the University of Wisconsin—Madison

this vacancy, at least on an acting basis?" hits very close to home. Note that emergency appointments of internal candidates (including those specified in policy documents) can have a domino effect, such that as higher positional vacancies are filled with existing faculty or staff members, vacancies are created at lower levels. For example, if a dean is appointed interim provost, who becomes dean? If a department chair becomes interim dean, who becomes department chair? Also, individuals promoted to acting positions with no real prospect of being selected permanently for the role run the risk of displacing a leader who may be well matched to the needs of their present role, and may also create a lasting morale problem for the individual.

Other Problems Resulting From an Absence of Succession and Transition Planning

The manner in which colleges and universities fill vacancies has been critiqued even aside from failures to engage in leadership succession planning. Focusing on presidential transitions, Greenberg (2014) maintains that using a search committee is unnecessary, since the pool of available (external) candidates is rather small due to the stratification of institutions. For example, a sitting president at a liberal arts institution is unlikely to make the short list of candidates at a research-intensive university. Greenberg also maintains that the typical list of desired characteristics in presidential job positions in the *Chronicle of Higher Education* is so generic as to be unhelpful. Such qualifications include the following:

- Ability to articulate a vision
- A collaborative working style
- A capacity to lead and inspire diverse groups
- A commitment to excellence

- Superb communication skills
- Distinguished scholarly and professional achievement
- Well-developed interpersonal skills
- An ability to work effectively with a wide range of constituents
- A commitment to diversity (Greenberg, 2014, p. 144)

As Greenberg notes, such a list of desired competencies, taken alone, is not all that helpful. The competencies need to be contextualized in terms of specific organizational strategic goals. Identification of competencies is helpful in selecting a leader when it flows from a larger process of institutional assessment. Campus-based leadership development programs for aspirational leaders should be tailored not only to organizational needs but also to specific individual leadership profiles. With effective programs in place, a college or university positions itself to avoid an external search altogether and hire from within.

Greenberg asserts that it is a myth to believe that search firms can do a better job than duly constituted search committees working unaided to recruit a president, largely because of the small size of the available external talent pool at peer or aspirant institutions. While it may not have been his intention, when Greenberg (2014) refers to the limited pools of strong external candidates, he also makes a good case for institutions to use the talent management approach to leadership succession planning, whereby a cadre of strong, internal candidates would be available for consideration. This analysis may be valid not only for top posts at colleges and universities but also for many other faculty and staff leadership positions.

Another potential problem with the replacement model of leadership succession planning that relies on external searches to screen and recruit candidates is the likely introduction of unnecessary organizational discontinuities. If a department or institution is doing well, the need to introduce change and the turbulence that is inevitably associated with recruitment of an outside candidate who is unfamiliar with the organization may be unnecessary or wasteful, and, in some instances, potentially harmful. When perceived organizational weaknesses or needs exist, the recruitment of external candidates is a potentially effective strategy, but attention to developing internal candidates can be another viable alternative.

Succession Planning in Higher Education: Key Considerations

A General Model

A general model of leadership succession planning in higher education appears in Figures 18.1 to 18.4. There are several considerations for effective leadership succession planning in a higher education context. First and most important, planning for leadership transitions can and should be nested within a larger, more comprehensive process of institutional assessment that, in turn, should include a systematic process for the evaluation of current leaders, utilizing a framework such as that discussed in Chapter 12. Taken together, these activities can inform whether a change in leadership is needed, while also identifying the leadership competencies desired as regular terms expire and new leaders are recruited. As depicted in Figure 18.1, a key outcome of this first step is an organizational decision as to whether the future should be more heavily weighted in terms of organizational continuity or discontinuity.

Figure 18.1. Starting point for leadership succession planning in higher education.

As illustrated in Figure 18.2, developing a strong bench of potential leaders is the second major component needed for leadership succession planning. In parallel with systematic efforts to identify desired or needed leadership competencies, an institution can intentionally develop the leadership skills of those who work at the college or university by affording opportunities to participate in in-house leadership programs or by relying on programs external to the organization. Developing a strong bench of internal leaders should be the responsibility of current leaders.

Leadership development programs need to be carefully monitored and assessed, as they are the fundamental component to succession. We favor programs that occur over weeks, months, or even longer; that have a specific focus on developing both knowledge and skills (i.e., competencies); and that go beyond a classroom setting and require completion of a real-world project or activity. These components are depicted in Figure 18.3. The time it takes to train internal employees so that they are ready to assume leadership positions within the organization may be more cost-effective than the

Figure 18.2. Developing a strong bench for leadership succession.

Figure 18.3. Critical components of leadership development programs.

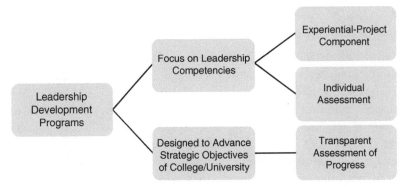

time it takes for untrained leaders to get up to speed or the time it takes for externally selected candidates to conduct listening tours as they seek to learn about the culture and climate of their new institutions. If an institution lacks the resources for leadership program development or for placement of employees in programs offered by outside agencies, then transition plans for specific faculty and staff positions should be developed. Transition plans can also complement participation in and completion of leadership development programs by current or future employees who become leaders on campus.

Assuming that current employees have completed well-designed leadership development programs, the final component of succession planning is an institutional commitment or willingness to go to the bench when leadership openings occur (see Figure 18.4). This step may be the most difficult to implement for a variety of reasons, as described in the next section. However, taken together, the steps depicted in Figures 18.1 to 18.4 represent a general model of leadership succession planning for use in higher education.

Figure 18.4. The "final" step in leadership succession planning: To search or not to search?

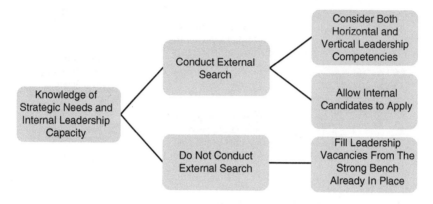

Implementation Considerations

Given the diversity of institutions, a one-size-fits-all approach to succession planning is not realistic. While we encourage all institutions to adopt at least some of these steps (especially those depicted in Figure 18.1), we recognize that some campuses may not or will not adopt all of the steps. In fact, there are several reasons why colleges and universities have limited succession plans that fall short of the talent management approaches used in the corporate sector. Historically, higher education has systematically underinvested in leadership development, instead relying on external searches to fill top leadership posts. Reliance on external searches is part of the cultural fabric (Mrig & Fusch, 2014). Apart from cultural norms and traditions, many institutions are simply too small in size to have the capacity to develop a talent pool for internal leadership succession. Succession planning requires an investment of human and financial resources. Colleges and universities may not have the resources on hand to conduct leadership identification and leadership training. Identification of future leaders and placement into leadership development programs can create internal friction and jealousy between those selected and those not selected. This situation can be problematic for everyday operations, especially if departments are small in size. Finally, the academic culture and policies and procedures governing faculty promotions also render aspects of leadership succession planning for faculty members problematic. Faculty members might not want to invest their time and energy in leadership development, especially if advancement to a leadership position is not guaranteed. Such an investment during one's mid-career period, for example, might interfere with advancement to higher faculty

ranks, especially if participation in and completion of training is not considered in promotion evaluation systems. Many institutions offer academic
leadership training programs for new chairs and even for new deans. In contrast, very few institutions offer leadership training programs for prospective
chairs and prospective deans. Multicampus leadership development programs such as the Big Ten Academic Alliance and other examples discussed
in Chapter 19 are notable exceptions. Some institutions have begun to initiate such programs in recent years, several of which appear in Appendix D.
While there are many reasons for the pervasive lack of leadership succession
planning in higher education, it is useful to consider the consequences of
this general state of affairs and consider what, if anything, might be done to
improve transitions to leadership in higher education.

Transition Planning: An Important Bridge to Succession Planning

Although it appears that the vast majority of colleges and universities do
not engage in talent management approaches to succession planning, some
institutions are intentional about managing the transition when leadership
vacancies are anticipated (e.g., due to term limits), and an employee already
in place will assume a new role either on an interim or permanent basis. For
both entry-level and more advanced faculty and staff leadership positions—
such as academic department chair or staff manager, in which internal candidates are routinely selected—having a detailed plan for the leadership
transition is recommended (Mandelbaum, 2007). Such transition planning
can stand alone or may be a component of a larger process of succession
planning.

As Mandelbaum (2007) discussed, an academic department chair
vacating the position can document useful information (about operations, budget, and personnel issues, for example), create a detailed timeline
with to-do activities (e.g., for submission of course schedule and budget
requests), and make arrangements for the incoming leader to shadow the
outgoing leader. The examples that Mandelbaum gives can be generalized
to higher levels of academic leadership, such as dean. For example, a department chair who agrees to serve as interim dean, or who has been appointed
as the next dean, can be invited to attend dean council or cabinet meetings with the existing dean. With this approach, the new dean can get an
understanding of how the provost or vice president conducts meetings and
can learn about fellow dean participants. Similarly, the dean designate can
accompany the existing dean to meetings with key donors and other important external stakeholders. In general, such transition plans can flatten the
learning curve relative to both managing up and leading outside the institution—two key arenas that are not visible to those who are moving into

an interim role at a higher level than their present role. Staff managers and directors can engage in these same activities to ease the transitions for their successors.

Elements of transition planning can also be used when external candidates are appointed and for academic and staff positions above the level of dean or director. For example, Jon Alger, president of James Madison University, reported that in the first several months after he assumed the presidency, the former president accompanied him to meetings with key external stakeholders in order to make introductions and ease the transition (J. Alger, personal communication, November 2, 2015).

Importantly, planning for a leadership transition needs to go beyond the workload and salary adjustments that are used to entice an individual to assume a leadership position. Such adjustments are important for the individual but are not educative nor preparatory for the new leadership responsibilities. Mechanisms such as shadowing, attendance at meetings with one's superiors and external stakeholders, and discussions of these meetings can flatten the learning curve. Detailed "when-to" documents developed by the departing leader, manager, or director also put a fine point on general policy and procedure documents that may or may not provide helpful advice to an incumbent leader. Although documentation is difficult to obtain, many institutions engage in deliberate and thoughtful approaches to managing leadership transitions, as discussed herein. Colleges and universities can build on these approaches to develop even more intentional approaches to leadership succession.

Reprise: What Works in Business-Corporate and Government Sectors

The need for greater attention to leadership succession planning in higher education seems apparent. Best-practice approaches in the corporate sector can prove helpful as a guide to get started. In the corporate sector, succession planning has the best chance of being successful when the following are met:

- Senior leaders are involved and hold themselves accountable for developing new leaders,
- Succession is linked to strategic planning and organizational assessment,
- Needed leadership competencies are identified,
- A pool of talent is identified and developed with an eye toward future needs of the organization, and
- Factors such as diversity, recruitment, and retention of leaders are considered. (U.S. Office of Personnel Management, 2005)

There is every reason to expect that these same elements hold for leadership succession planning in higher education.

Adaptations for Higher Education

Working from a higher education perspective, Richards (2009) presents five strategies for comprehensive leadership succession planning. The first strategy is *culture*; leadership succession must be aligned with the institution's culture, mission, vision, and values. The second strategy is *champions*; implementation of succession planning needs the active support of the college or university president, governing board, and human resources department. The third strategy for succession planning discussed by Richards (2009) is *communication*: "Any succession planning should be carefully communicated within the collegial culture, and academic institutions must balance perceptions of entitlement for a few with leadership development for many" (p. 109). The fourth strategy is *competency based*, identifying individuals based on specific competencies that match the school's goals and needs. The fifth strategy that Richards identifies is *continuous* implementation; evaluations of an individual's needs should continue even after one's formal training. Monitoring of individuals and the succession plan itself is an ongoing process.

A Step-by-Step Approach to Leadership Succession Planning in Higher Education

Despite the diversity in types of institutions of higher education—especially in overall size and resource availability—we close this chapter by highlighting one step that all institutions should take to move in the direction of leadership succession planning. We then present additional steps that, if adopted in full, would constitute talent management approaches to succession planning in higher education.

Leadership transitions need to be placed in the larger context of overall institutional assessment and accountability. Careful monitoring of progress toward institutional goals is part and parcel of the evaluation of current leaders. Such monitoring and ongoing assessment by supervisors of current leaders (including presidents and chancellors) should provide the foundation to determine the types of competencies that future leaders need. Assessment of institutional progress is a critical and necessary component of leadership evaluation and of leadership succession. For example, if an institution judges that it is making good progress toward stated goals and is satisfied with its current trajectory, then a leadership transition might seek to maximize continuity and avoid disruption. On the other hand, if an institution judges that progress is severely lacking, then a leadership transition might seek to introduce discontinuity and disrupt the current trajectory.

Whether leadership transitions are expected or unexpected, and whether external candidates or internal candidates are appointed, organizations have a greater chance of having successful outcomes when an ongoing process of institutional assessment is in place. The EHE framework described in Chapter 12 provides a model assessment practice. Assessment can and should inform decisions about the need for radical changes or discontinuities in leadership versus relative stability or continuity in leadership. Either desired outcome—discontinuity or continuity—might result in an external or internal candidate assuming leadership of the unit, department, or institution. The key is to connect institutional needs with leadership competencies. As described in Chapter 9, leadership competencies have a vertical and a horizontal dimension. The vertical dimension—education and accomplishment in one's field—might be heavily weighted in the search and leadership transition process. If a school has as its top goal increasing donations from individuals and foundations, then prior success in development should be heavily weighted in screening candidates. Similarly, if a school wants to increase success with faculty applications for external research funding, then it makes sense to look for an accomplished researcher with a large grant portfolio. Note, however, that having determined an institutional need for certain vertical competencies in the next leader, identification or training of existing faculty and staff might occur to fulfill this need in anticipation of a vacancy.

To summarize, institutions need to

- systematically assess institutional needs and current leaders' performance, and
- identify future organizational directions and leadership competencies needed to move forward.

All institutions of higher education are encouraged to take these two steps, which are necessary but not sufficient for leadership succession planning. The following additional steps, listed in order of importance, are necessary for leadership succession planning:

- Add leadership succession planning to the portfolio of requirements for top leaders in the institution. A culture in which current leaders take responsibility for leadership succession, even their own replacements, ensures consideration of and conversations about leaders' roles in attainment of strategic organizational goals.

- Encourage and enable faculty and staff employees to enroll in leadership development programs to create a pool of internal candidates for future leadership positions. Building a strong bench is critical for leadership successions at an institution.
- Develop transition plans for key leadership positions, extending beyond presidencies, that address expected as well as unexpected vacancies. This step can include mandatory participation in either in-house or external leadership development programs for those who are newly appointed to leadership positions.
- Garner support and assistance from the institutional human resources department to help manage the process in which existing employees are identified as next in line for promotion.
- Establish a process to assess the outcomes derived from leadership succession planning.
- Modify plans within a continuous improvement framework.

Conclusion

Leadership succession planning entails a simultaneous and coordinated focus on developing human capital and organizational excellence, and as such, this form of planning can be a key tool for institutions striving for improvement and excellence. This result is more likely to occur when leadership succession planning is paired with other key tools, such as vision setting and strategic planning. Although leadership succession planning can be resource intensive, the benefits to the organization should outweigh the costs of time and financial resources needed for a successful program.

Adoption of the elements depicted in Figures 18.1 to 18.4 would move an institution of higher education beyond minimal and ad hoc approaches to leadership succession in the direction of comprehensive, systematic, and intentional leadership succession planning. By adopting all of these leadership succession planning components, an institution is not obligated to promote a current employee who has completed some type of training. The option to do so would be available, however, as would the option of searching externally. By taking an incremental approach, institutions of higher education can slowly move toward a full-scale, talent management approach to leadership succession planning—an approach that may yield dividends beyond those accrued from ad hoc, nonstrategic approaches to leadership transitions.

For Further Consideration

1. Approaches to Leadership Transitions

Describe your unit or department's approach to leadership transitions.

1. Is the approach best described as ad hoc, one-to-one replacement, or talent management as discussed in this chapter?
2. Is your home unit's approach typical of the entire college or university?
3. Check to see if your college's or university's policy documents designate a successor for the president or chancellor in cases of sudden death or disability. Do any other leadership positions have a successor designated by policy?

2. Leadership Development Programs

Consider the larger organization in which you operate.

1. Does your institution offer leadership development programs, and if so, for whom? Prospective leaders, newly appointed leaders, or both?
2. Are these professional development programs linked to organizational needs, and do they focus on specific leadership competencies?

Construct a two-by-two grid in which organizational needs and goals are columns and specific leadership competencies are rows. How many cells are filled, and how many are empty?

3. Leadership Succession Plan

Based on For Further Consideration #2, outline a leadership succession plan for your home institution, assuming one is not already in place. If a plan is in place, propose ways that it might be improved. Make sure your plan is realistic and takes account of your institution's culture.

Notes

1. Richards adapted this framework from the Leadership Advantage Forum published by Personnel Decisions International.
2. See www.cupahr.org/search.aspx?x=0&y=0&terms=leadership+succession+planning

PART FOUR

LEADERSHIP DEVELOPMENT MODELS

19

LEADERSHIP DEVELOPMENT IN HIGHER EDUCATION

A Snapshot of Approaches, Characteristics, and Programs

In This Chapter

- How do organizational dynamics influence the role of leadership development in programs, departments, and institutions?
- What approaches are available for developing leadership capacity within colleges and universities?
- What are the characteristics of the following types of leadership development models: early intervention model, institutional model, multi-institutional model, and association-based model?
- What factors are important for successful leadership development within colleges and universities?

The need for leadership development initiatives has long been recognized in the military and business worlds. For instance, American corporations spend nearly $160 billion annually on training and development programs (Association for Talent Development, 2015). Leadership programs have also become increasingly popular in healthcare and government. Somewhat ironically, higher education institutions have been considerably more ambitious in promoting and offering leadership and management development programs to other sectors than in embracing these programs for their own use. In general, these efforts have been slower to reach the education industry, particularly colleges and universities, often because of the presumption that subject-matter expertise and experience were the primary ingredients necessary to provide effective leadership within colleges and universities. The suggestion that a faculty or professional staff member would need training has sometimes been regarded as insulting. Why would thought leaders in colleges and universities need training? Are they not already outstanding leaders by definition?

With the growing recognition that subject-matter expertise, in and of itself, is not sufficient to assure outstanding leadership, these traditions are changing. An increasing number of institutions have begun to see the need to focus greater attention on leadership development. As Gmelch and Buller (2015) point out:

> Through academic leadership programs, institutions benefit from making the most effective use of this resource, building connections across campus, promoting purposeful leadership diversity, tapping hidden talent, retaining campus talent, expanding people's potential, and ensuring institutional renewal, effectiveness, and dedication. (p. 198)

Creating successful leadership development initiatives is a complex undertaking, particularly if programs are designed to address insufficiencies in current practice. As discussed in Chapter 5, organizational cultures and climates exert a powerful and pervasive influence, for better or worse—and their influence on present and future leaders is no exception. Organizational cultures clearly provide a natural and inevitable informal training process, one that takes place each day in the workplace as future leaders observe and are socialized to the leadership behaviors and practices that are characteristic of the institution. The education offered by organizational culture is informal, yet extremely potent. Cultures provide training on an array of fundamental leadership practices, such as how future leaders will relate to and interact with their colleagues, how conflict is handled, what colleague behaviors are valued and rewarded, how decisions are made and implemented, if and how leadership performance is reviewed, and how superior performances and failures are handled. The culture also creates powerful lessons on issues such as the tone and frequency of in-person and e-mail communication, the ways that meetings are conducted, and many other facets of organizational life. These informal leadership education moments operate on every campus, in every department, and in every meeting. In ideal circumstances, these natural institution-wide lessons are the ones we wish to impart to future leaders. When this is the case, the role of formal leadership programs is to reinforce and supplement current leadership practices. Often, however, dissatisfaction with some elements of current leadership practice and the perceived need for change provides the motivation for initiating leadership development programs. When this is the case, core themes and behaviors being promoted in the program must compete for attention and adoption with pervasive and sometimes contradictory elements of current practice. The greater the contrast between the state of current and ideal organizational and leadership practices, the more formidable the challenges that must be addressed in leadership development programming.

In any case, the process should begin with an assessment of the current organizational and leadership culture and practices, a clear formulation of program goals, and consideration of the various dynamics of personal and organizational change that must be addressed in order for the program to succeed. The next step is a review and selection from among alternative leadership development programming approaches and teaching/learning methodologies considered in light of the influences of everyday forces at play that may support, compete with, or potentially undermine the goals of the effort. McCauley, van Velsor, and Ruderman (2010) underscore the importance of organizational climate in this regard:

> The climate for development is established and reinforced through six organizational processes: priorities of top management, recognition and rewards, communication, efforts to track and measure, resource allocation, and skilled employees. These processes are a powerful part of a development system because they are the drivers and motivators of development within the system and therefore provide support for leader development above and beyond that provided by the methods of development. (p. 50)

Clearly, organizational climate directly influences the design and perceptions of formal leadership programs, while also shaping their potential outcomes.

Approaches to Formal Leadership Education and Development

Any number of themes can be components in leadership development programs; many of potential value have been examined in this volume, including the higher education landscape, theories of leadership, the unique nature of higher education leadership, the distinction between formal and informal leadership, communication and influence strategies, leader self-assessment, leadership styles, and the variety of tools that are most germane for academic and administrative leaders in higher education—planning, change, and the use of rubrics and metrics, for example. Additionally, in their research on the topic, Gmelch, Hopkins, and Damico (2011) found three ingredients of an effective leadership development program that represent the needs and expectations for college and university administrators: (a) habits of mind (an understanding of concepts), (b) habits of practice (a demonstration of skills), and (c) habits of heart (a commitment to reflective practice). Many of the effective leadership programs for college and university leaders attempt to integrate these three critical themes.

In addition to the number of worthy program themes, numerous leadership development philosophies, theories, and models are available. Each of these models highlights particular concepts and considerations that are important to successful leadership development programming. Prior to examining several specific approaches to education and development in higher education in some detail, we begin by highlighting two general models. One leadership development model that provides a template for designing and implementing programs of this type is the J-Curve Leadership Model (Bolea & Atwater, 2015), which is shown in Figure 19.1. The model consists of the following nine essential elements of leadership mastery:

1. Set direction.
2. Build a team of people.
3. Create key processes.
4. Steward structure.
5. Nurture behaviors.
6. Promote conversations.
7. Provide support.
8. Set boundaries.
9. Ensure space to deliver.

Through these identified elements, leaders develop their own capacities while also enhancing the leadership capacities of people around them.

Figure 19.1. J-Curve Leadership Model.

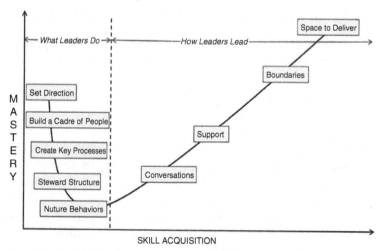

Source. From Bolea and Atwater, 2015. Reprinted with permission.

Another model for developing leaders was developed and is in use within the Center for Creative Leadership (McCauley, van Velsor, and Ruderman, 2010). This two-part model consists, first, of those elements that make for powerful, richer, and more developmental experiences: assessment, challenge, and support. The second part of the model describes the relationship among several aspects of the developmental process, including a variety of developmental experiences, individual leadership development, and the ability to learn. This model also considers the significant role of the context for leader development, which, as discussed at the outset of this chapter, is a very important influence in leadership development.

Leadership development at a collective, organizational level includes—but also extends beyond—individual leader development. As McCauley, van Velsor, and Ruderman (2010) note,

> Leadership development is an ongoing process. It is grounded in personal development, which is never complete. It is embedded in experience: leaders learn as they expand their experiences over time. It is facilitated by interventions that are woven into those experiences in meaningful ways. And it includes, but goes well beyond, individual leader development. It encompasses the development of the connections among individuals, the development of the capacities of collectives, the development of the connections among collectives in an organization, and the development of the culture and systems in which individuals and collectives are embedded. (p. 26)

As discussed in Chapter 11, personal leader development is an intentional process that individuals engage in to enhance their own leadership capabilities. With an eye toward organizational change, improvement, and learning, organizational leadership development is a process designed to enhance the leadership capacity of the organization's members. Personal leader development is, of course, embedded in the very processes, strategies, and structures of the organization's culture and in the approach taken for collective leadership education and development.

The leader and leadership development needs of individuals in leadership roles vary as a function of the stage and level of one's position within an organization, and leadership development initiatives may be designed for differing circumstances, including (a) the level of leadership, (b) the leader's life-cycle stage, and (c) the leader's role-cycle stage (Guillen & Ibarra, 2009). For example, the level of leadership for which the initiative could focus may be at a project, unit, department, or institutional level. The life-cycle stage could consider the specific leadership needs and competencies for entry-level coordinators, mid-career professionals, or senior vice presidents. Finally, the role-cycle stage distinguishes the needs of those entering a specific leadership role in the institution as compared to those who are nearing the end of their leadership tenure. Both models highlight those elements that are most critical to the process of leadership development, focusing on specific tasks to enhance one's individual leadership effectiveness and also on the broader context that allows for leadership growth and development.

Snapshots of Leadership Education and Development Models in Higher Education

Formal leadership development programs embodying these philosophies and concepts may be designed and offered by colleges and universities, external consulting firms, and professional associations. The remainder of this chapter offers snapshots of various approaches to leadership development in higher education, focusing particularly on examples of programs that represent four approaches: programs that offer leadership preparation as a component of graduate education across disciplines (early intervention model); institutional, or campus-based programs; a multi-institutional model illustrated by the Committee on Institutional Cooperation (which changed its name to Big Ten Academic Alliance [BTAA] in 2016); and cross-institutional programs offered by professional associations. The aim will be to highlight various approaches to leadership development and to identify common goals, features, and areas of distinction.

Early Intervention Model

Many if not most leadership positions in higher education are eventually filled by individuals who have received graduate education. Thinking more specifically of academic leadership positions, current doctoral students across the range of academic disciplines will eventually occupy many if not most of these roles, yet leadership is not a topic that most disciplines explore, nor is it a primary goal in doctoral education in programs other than in select fields. The PreDoctoral Leadership Development Institute (PLDI) at Rutgers was developed to address this gap. PLDI is an early-intervention approach to leadership education and development that cuts across academic disciplines and is specifically geared for doctoral students who are recognized as both scholars-in-training and leaders-in-training (Gigliotti et al., 2016). The aim of PLDI is to better prepare doctoral students for future leadership roles through a two-year fellowship program. Initiated in 2009, the PLDI is offered through the Graduate School–New Brunswick, with sponsorship and support from the Center for Organizational Development and Leadership (ODL); Office of the Chancellor, Rutgers–New Brunswick; Office of the Senior Vice President for Academic Affairs; the School of Communication and Information; and the Graduate School of Education (Rutgers PreDoctoral Leadership Institute, 2014).[1]

Upon being nominated, approximately 15 students are competitively selected across a number of academic disciplines at Rutgers for acceptance into the program each year. There is no additional cost to their normal registration and course fees. Students who complete the two-year program receive a modest stipend and recognition of their participation in the program on their transcripts. Students are required to enroll in a four-course sequence over a two-year period. These noncredit courses are taught by an interdisciplinary team of faculty and administrators from across the institution.

Semesters one and two: The context of higher education leadership
Recognizing that PLDI students enter the program with varying academic experiences, the program begins with an introduction to the broader context of higher education. The first two courses, Leadership Issues in Higher Education I and II, provide (a) an introduction to the general context of higher education and (b) an introduction to organizational and leadership theory and competencies. Key readings, including scholarly articles as well as relevant news articles, present a broad overview of the state of American higher education.

One of the primary objectives of these two courses is to familiarize students with the "important dimensions of higher education and administration in colleges and universities, including mission, organizational structure, governance, finance, legal and regulatory issues, diversity, and ethics" (Rutgers PreDoctoral Leadership Institute, 2014). Topics in the first semester include an overview of the history of American higher education, an introduction to higher education organization and administration, and key issues related to the legal and financial functions within colleges and universities. Students are also introduced to an understanding of the various cultures and broad range of stakeholders associated with colleges and universities. This introductory content accomplishes two important goals.

First, the content provides students with the foundational knowledge related to the study of higher education. Also, by becoming familiar with the broader context of higher education, PLDI participants begin to think more substantively about the various leadership expectations and challenges in the academy, most of which cut across disciplines and institutional types. The second major goal of the first year is to introduce core concepts related to organizational leadership, culture, assessment, communication, and change, and to promote the development of enhanced personal competencies related to organizational analysis, leadership development, and leadership style and strategy, among others.

During these seminars, students have an opportunity not only to discuss these issues but also to interact with current university leaders who deliver firsthand information about their particular approach to leadership in addressing challenges in their organizations. The use of case studies, role playing, simulations, and other interactive experiential learning techniques are also incorporated into the classes.

Semester three: Mentoring

During this semester, fellows are independently matched with distinguished university leaders so that they can discuss and observe leadership behavior as it unfolds in real time. This experience allows for direct, one-on-one interactions with administrators representing the academic and administrative sides of the institution. Over the years, these mentors have included the chancellor; chief financial officer; executive vice presidents; the university librarian; and multiple deans, directors, and chairs. Through the mentor program, students have the opportunity to study the application of leadership competencies in real time, while also taking note of the consequences of one's approach to leadership. Subsequently, by discussing and observing the leadership behaviors of others, fellows have an opportunity to identify their own strengths and areas for improvement as aspiring leaders. The mentoring relationship blends the theory and concepts presented in the first year with the practice of leadership in a unique experiential learning environment.

Semester four: Capstone project

In the final semester of the program, PLDI fellows use the knowledge from the PLDI experience as they collaborate to design and develop a capstone presentation on an important issue in higher education that will be presented in a university-wide forum at the end of the semester. Through this collaborative experience, students are able to explore a leadership issue through the lenses of multiple stakeholders, learn about the challenges and opportunities of interdisciplinary collaboration, and process the various roles that individuals demonstrate in the group setting. Once again, the emphasis on experiential learning and continual reflection is critical to the success of this capstone project. Recent capstone presentations addressed the academic freedom in higher education, the Penn State child abuse scandal and its implications for higher education, advancements and challenges related to online education, and the challenges and opportunities presented by diverging perspectives on the role of higher education.[2]

Preliminary assessment data point to the initial success of the program.[3] The PLDI program has been featured in the *Chronicle of Education* (June,

2010) and at invited presentations to the BTAA, the Council of Independent Colleges, the Council of Graduate Studies, and the Council of Academic Deans at Research Education Institutions.

Programs with a comparable framework have been implemented or are being planned at the University of South Florida, the University of Missouri, the University of Tennessee, Northwestern University, and Fordham University.[4] These programs point to the importance of an early intervention approach to leadership development in higher education—programs that introduce and begin to prepare doctoral students for the realities of higher education leadership.

Institutional or Campus-Based Model

Another approach to leadership education is to create campus-based programs for individuals who are current or aspiring leaders. An increasing number of institutions are creating programs of this type. In research on institutional or campus-based approaches to leadership development in higher education, Gigliotti (forthcoming) identified the following types of initiatives offered by the Association of American Universities member institutions (Association of American Universities, 2015):

- Roundtable conversations with peers, senior leaders, and outside leaders, which facilitate conversations on topics of interest with campus and community leaders
- Coaching sessions—one-on-one confidential executive coaching sessions for on-campus leaders
- Leadership/management assessments—self-assessment tools used to identify strengths and areas of growth, including, but not limited to, the Leadership Practices Inventory, the Campbell Leadership Descriptor, the Management Effectiveness Profile, the Leadership Effectiveness Assessment, Myers-Briggs, DiSC, and Life Styles Inventory
- Leadership profile/individual career plans/Career Development Passport—electronic portals, typically organized by human resources offices, to track and monitor leadership accomplishments in current positions and identify the skills necessary to advance in a professional context
- Leadership certificate programs—customized workshop series on various topics of interest for aspiring faculty and staff leaders
- Leadership development courses—leadership courses

- Executive leadership academies/fellowship programs—ongoing leadership workshops for a cohort of aspiring leaders, which often include a mentor component and capstone presentation at their conclusion
- Onboarding opportunities—organizational socialization initiatives used to introduce new leaders to the knowledge, skills, and competencies required to succeed in the organization
- Speaker series—keynote speakers from on campus and the community who offer various perspectives on leadership in higher education
- Performance management programs—appraisal programs that assess individual performance in the institution
- Leadership webinars/self-directed online leadership resources—virtual seminars and resources on topics of interest for emerging leaders in higher education
- Mentor programs—formal pairing of emerging leaders with senior leaders from the campus offered to help individuals learn more about each other and to strengthen their organizational and professional knowledge
- Consultation opportunities—on-campus professionals with leadership and organizational development expertise are available to assess and offer recommendations on individual and group performance.
- Leadership libraries—collections of texts and resources related to leadership in higher education
- Succession planning resources—resources for identifying and developing future leaders in higher education
- Coffee conversations/leadership lunches—casual conversations facilitated by presenters from across campus
- Group leadership forums—introduction to the complexities and nuances of leading project teams and work groups in higher education, with an emphasis on managing group and organizational dynamics.
- 360-degree leader assessments—method for collecting opinions from a wide range of coworkers and stakeholders related to one's leadership performance
- Talent accelerators—incubators and other physical spaces used to encourage creativity and address areas of growth from leadership assessments
- Supervisory development labs/new executive officer training sessions—workshops and training programs offered for new and current supervisors within the institution
- Women's leadership initiatives—tailored experiential leadership programs for women in higher education, which often include female mentors from the campus community

- Leadership newsletters—bulletins issued routinely throughout the year to share information related to leadership in higher education and to formally recognize the accomplishments of campus leaders
- Alumni leadership networks—formal and informal networking opportunities for graduates of on-campus leadership initiatives and new participants from these respective programs

These instructional methods are consistent with the broader set of instructional methods that Gmelch and Buller (2015) provide. Some of their recommended methods include case studies, simulations, expert facilitation, retreats, and self-appraisals.

Gigliotti and Ruben (2015) also collected a comprehensive list of campus-based leadership programs offered by the Big Ten Academic Alliance universities (2015a). These education and development initiatives are designed to advance leadership capabilities and address relevant leadership needs within their own institutions. The Association of American Universities and Big Ten member institution snapshots describe differentiated activities and services for academic leadership development that vary in size, duration, sponsoring departments, program themes, and targeted audiences—each delivered through a variety of approaches and methodologies. Michigan State University, for instance, organizes its leadership opportunities into the following categories: orientations, administrator briefings, workshops and seminars, cohort programs, and services (Michigan State University, 2015).

In general the publicized leadership development programs reflect the unique character of the university, with a particular emphasis on outcomes that are most germane to the institution. These direct linkages connect current and future academic leaders to the institution's mission, vision, and values. For example, the University Leadership Education and Development (U-LEAD) program at the University of North Carolina provides emerging leaders with the space to think through "real [UNC] issues," in order to then produce practical and actionable outcomes that are most relevant to the institution (University of North Carolina, 2015). Finally, cultivating small communities of practice is another common theme among a number of these programs. For instance, according to the Rutgers Center for Organizational Development and Leadership website, the Academic Leadership Program creates "a collaborative network of administrators and faculty members charged with providing academic leadership for the institution" (Rutgers University, 2015). In many instances, participants are paired with mentors from within the organization for both guidance and support in their leadership development. In summary, the programs variously include classroom instruction, workshops, experiential activities, self-assessment inventories, conversations with campus leaders, project team assignments, leadership coaching, and activities aimed at cultivating smaller communities of practice, in some cases including structured feedback and one-on-one mentoring experiences. Appendix D provides a snapshot of one notable program for each member institution.[5]

Multi-Institutional: The Big Ten Model

The BTAA, formerly known as the Committee on Institutional Cooperation (BTAA, 2015a) is a collaborative organization that provides a unique and expansive approach to leadership education and development among its member institutions. The consortium was established by the presidents of the Big Ten Athletic Conference members in 1958 as the athletic league's academic counterpart. This consortium of 15 influential research universities has historically included the members of the Big Ten Conference, along with the University of Chicago. The impact of this collaboration is reflected in the $110 million in library book volumes and the $10.8 billion in combined research across the institutions. These large research institutions have a substantial impact on a national and international scale, and one of the goals of the consortium is to provide an infrastructure for enhanced collaboration in a way that enables them to leverage and coordinate their expertise. The BTAA provides the infrastructure for these institutions to save money, share assets, and create new opportunities that might not otherwise occur.

Peer-to-Peer Learning. Within the context of leadership training and development, the BTAA provides a broad range of formal and informal peer-to-peer and institution-to-institution programs, each of which promotes leadership networking and the sharing of practices among individuals who occupy comparable leadership roles in particular academic and administrative specialty areas. The BTAA provides the infrastructure for groups to assemble and collaborate. Many BTAA groups convene on a regular basis and typically fall into one of three categories: executive leadership, program management, and peer groups. The executive leadership groups include senior leaders at BTAA member universities who govern, make investments, or both in BTAA activities. The program management groups are typically convened by an executive leadership group to accomplish a particular analysis or coordinate a BTAA project or program. These two types of groups have support from BTAA staff. Peer groups are typically self-organizing peers from member universities who convene virtually or face-to-face, or both, to share ideas and best practices. Peer groups often are self-guided. Among all groups, knowledge sharing is a key benefit to their involvement.

Department Executive Officers Seminar and Academic Leadership Program. Two of the BTAA program groups focus explicitly on faculty leadership development: Department Executive Officers (DEO) liaisons (BTAA, 2015b) and the Academic Leadership Program (ALP) liaisons (BTAA, 2015c). The groups are responsible for the development and implementation of the DEO Seminar and ALP program. Both are unique in that these consortium-wide professional development opportunities allow campuses to draw upon talented speakers and facilitators who would not be financially feasible to bring to one individual campus each year. Additionally, the programs develop a talent pool of future leaders for the institution as well as all BTAA universities.

Launched in 1997, the DEO Seminar is a leadership development program for newly appointed department heads and chairs at BTAA universities. Each BTAA institution invites five fellows to participate in the annual three-day seminar. Individuals are selected by their respective campuses. The seminar focuses on topics involving departmental leadership skills, including but not limited to conflict resolution, time management, leadership style, and performance review of faculty. The objectives of the seminar are threefold:

1. To hone the skills of the participants in these (and other) key areas,
2. To develop a cadre of highly trained and motivated individuals who could be more effective in inculcating their skills and experience on their own campuses, and
3. To develop an infrastructure of department heads and chairs who can communicate regarding key topics at BTAA institutions.

The seminar serves as a venue to generate resource materials, network with colleagues across the BTAA, and take part in group problem-solving. It provides a venue for sharing of best practices with best practitioners.

The ALP Seminar is a yearlong, more extensive BTAA leadership development opportunity established eight years before DEO. ALP is one of the longest-serving professional development programs that the BTAA offers. Although campus participation in ALP is voluntary, all BTAA member institutions actively participate in the program. It is an intensive program that develops the faculty's leadership and managerial skills and provides a better understanding of university-level academic leadership and its challenges and rewards. The primary goal of the program is to help a select group of talented and diverse faculty further develop their ability to be effective academic leaders at all levels of research universities. Each BTAA institution establishes its own recruitment and selection process for identifying five fellows to participate in the program each year. Fellows are faculty or select executive-level professional staff who are recognized as emerging academic leaders. Since its inception, more than 1,400 participants have completed the program. Many of them have gone on to serve with distinction as college presidents, provosts, and deans.

The program comprises three campus-based seminars, each three days in length. Host campus responsibilities rotate among the BTAA universities. The seminars follow a format designed to maximize interaction among all the fellows. Over the three days, guest speakers address the group on identified thematic topics through case studies, workshops, and other group exercises, and the participants engage in small group discussions and networking opportunities. Each seminar focuses on a central theme: (a) contemporary issues in higher education; (b) internal and external relationships; and (c) money, management, and strategies. Table 19.2 provides a general framework for the three seminars.

Each campus chief academic officer appoints one or more institutional liaisons to serve as the central coordinator for the ALP, and the liaison also serves as the campus contact with the BTAA office. Liaisons usually hold positions in the Provost's Office, with responsibilities in areas such as academic leadership, faculty and staff development, and human resources, but also in a range of other academic administrative roles. They are responsible for supervising all aspects of the Fellows' activities at their home institutions. Liaisons play an important role in recruiting and selecting fellows and are essential in

TABLE 19.2
BTAA Academic Leadership Program Framework

Seminar I: Contemporary Issues in Higher Education	Seminar II: Internal and External Relationships	Seminar III: Money, Management, and Strategies
President and provost	President and provost	President and provost
Campus tour	Campus tour	Campus tour
Globalization	Faculty	Strategic planning
Diversity and inclusion	Staff	Financial planning/ budget models
Public engagement	Students	Philanthropy and advancement
Contemporary issues in higher education	External constituents/ stakeholders	Space/infrastructure
Teaching and learning	Research	Prioritization and time management
Academic leadership	Leadership values, styles, skills	Leading into your future

the program planning and implementation of the seminars, as well as the on-campus enrichment programs that support the ALP experience.

To support the ALP fellows, each BTAA institution conducts its own series of on-campus enrichment programs. These supplemental programs often include scheduled discussion sessions between the fellows and a variety of campus senior leaders and, on occasion, external stakeholders. Examples of those leaders included are the president/chancellor, provost, regents/trustees, vice presidents (e.g., student affairs, development, general counsel, finance, and operations), athletic director, deans, and so on. The range is quite varied. Minimally, to ensure that the three campus seminars are as effective as possible, each campus is asked to coordinate a meeting between its fellows and campus officials whose portfolio includes topics to be discussed at the upcoming seminar. For example, before the seminar session that focuses on strategic planning and budgeting, ALP liaisons are asked to schedule a meeting with their campus budget officer.

ALP liaisons and BTAA staff design seminars and on-campus experiences to meet the specific program objectives with a balance of informational and interactive sessions and opportunities to network and socialize. By participating in the program, fellows may learn more about the organization, operations, finances, and structure of their own university and research universities in general. Additionally, fellows are able to think more deeply about the challenges and rewards of academic leadership, while building relationships with other aspiring leaders from across the participating BTAA universities.

Program evaluations. Topics and speakers for both programs are evaluated regularly. DEO participants are encouraged to complete a seminar evaluation, and ALP participants are encouraged to complete a preseminar questionnaire, an evaluation for each seminar, and a postseminar evaluation. The survey responses provide critical feedback regarding the sessions, speakers, and logistics. Based on this feedback and the liaisons' recommendations, speakers and topics are adjusted and adapted to ensure that the seminar remains a progressive and innovative professional development opportunity. Additionally, the BTAA completes program evaluations for key programs on a rotating schedule. The program review is a process of refinement and an opportunity to reflect on what works well and what improvements could be made based on feedback from the provosts, fellows, and liaisons. The most recent surveys for the programs indicate that both have a profound impact on the fellows' leadership development.

Association-Based Model

A number of external organizations offer training and development for higher education audiences, although their expertise and area of focus often extend beyond leadership programming. The types of organizations that might fall under this category include external consulting entities (e.g., McKinsey & Co., the Boston Consulting Group, IDEA Education), multi-institutional consortia (e.g., American Council on Education; Association of American Universities; Higher Education Resource Services; National Consortium for Change and Continuous Improvement in Higher Education; National Association of Women Deans, Administrators, and Counselors; Harvard Institutes for Higher Education), and professional associations, research centers, and private training firms (e.g., Center for Creative Leadership; Higher Education Research Institute; International Leadership Association; ATLAS: Academic Training, Leadership, and Assessment Services; the Center for the Study of Academic Leadership, along with a myriad of sector-specific professional associations). These organizations provide a wide array of services and resources for faculty and staff leaders in higher education, including program-specific support (e.g., crisis leadership consulting, assistance with strategic planning), a variety of online and in-person resources for navigating one's role as a leader, and extensive networking opportunities with other leaders in higher education. Additionally, many of these organizations provide specific programs and services for underrepresented groups. Some examples include the Women's Leadership Forum and the Spectrum Executive Leadership Program sponsored by the American Council on Education, the Association of American Colleges and Universities Teaching to Increase Diversity and Equity in STEM (TIDES) initiative, and the numerous institutes sponsored by the Higher Education Resource Services (HERS).

There are certainly a number of advantages in pursuing the leadership services offered by these and similar organizations. Unencumbered by the culture of one's own institution, these association-based training and development opportunities may provide participants with anonymity as they develop as a leader outside of their specific institution. Furthermore, these associations can allow for learning from peers who are often dealing with a host of similar challenges. The disadvantage, of course, is that the programs and services are often not tailored to the specific needs, values, and goals of one's home institution. Additionally, upon returning from an impactful conference or leadership training program, the desire to initiate new practices at one's home institution is predictably met with the reality of the routine pressures facing college and university leaders.

Implications for Evaluating Leadership Development Efforts

The success of leadership development depends to a great degree on the culture of one's home institution. The influence of role modeling, outlook, knowledge, skills, and support on behalf of current leaders cannot be underestimated. The current leaders in higher education are those who can cultivate a climate where effective leadership practice is prized and encouraged, and where meaningful leadership development is nurtured and supported. Often this approach involves welcoming change and supporting a reexamination of new approaches to leadership practices and styles. Borrowing from Maxwell (1995), if leadership efforts are to be valued, "Creating an environment that will attract leaders is vital. . . . Doing that is the job of leaders. They must be active; they must generate activity that is productive; and they must encourage, create, and command changes in the organization. They must create a climate in which potential leaders will thrive" (p. 17). The onus is most certainly on current leaders to create this supportive environment for leadership development—an environment on which the future of their institutions depends.

To be successful, leadership educational programs and interventions must leverage the learning that occurs within the ongoing, everyday environment. The programs must also compete successfully for attention with the natural and uncontrolled socializing influences of the college or university culture.

Here are a number of options available to evaluate leadership development programs. Indicators might include the number of participants who complete specific modules or the entire program, or completion of assignments or projects that are included in the curriculum of a leadership development program. Alternatively—or additionally—those involved with program design may look at the data from self-evaluations where leaders assess the knowledge or skills they believe they have gained from a program, or one might analyze evaluative feedback from multirater assessments of the leader completed by peers and colleagues. These quantitative and qualitative evaluation methods may explore both the immediate and the long-term impact of the program on one's leadership behavior. The triangulation of various data sources is likely the best approach to assessing the ultimate impact of a leadership development initiative. In the end, the evaluative process must be embedded within the larger context in which the mission, aspirations, and goals of the program are articulated. The success of any program should be evaluated in terms of these purposes.

In thinking about the many options for leadership development, a number of central topics can be seen as critical components, including the following:

- Myriad obstacles and opportunities facing higher education as a sector
- General and specific difficulties confronting aspiring leaders in higher education

- Obstacles to personal and professional change and development
- Array of potentially relevant tools available for leaders

All of these central topics combine to provide the context and potential components that could be considered as core elements of leadership development programming, and strategies for evaluation would vary substantially from one to another. The programs and approaches highlighted in this chapter and in Appendix D vary in scope, duration, intended audience, and outcomes, and it becomes critical to think through precisely what one hopes to achieve in initiating or attending such programming. These leadership programs might emphasize issues that are specific to the higher education landscape, or they may focus on leadership or organizational theory, research, or skills. They might feature self-assessment approaches or tools and strategies for organizational assessment. Such leadership programs might include participation in team-building exercises or hands-on leadership projects as a component, along with a host of other methods for instruction and engagement. For higher education, as for leadership development programming in other sectors and contexts, no single approach is correct.

One further comment about expectations: Questions are often posed about the preparation time and effort required for leadership development. What does one have to learn to become an effective leader, and how long does that take? Can it occur in a workshop or by reading particular books or attending a two-day program? No doubt any of these may be helpful in some way, but realistic expectations are important. No workshop, multiday program, or book alone can be expected to have a transformative effect on a person's leadership capability. As Gmelch and Buller (2015) suggest, "If we assume that it takes ten to twenty years for a highly intelligent person to become an expert in an academic discipline, why do we assume that we can train academic leaders in a three-day workshop?" (p. 8). An individual may learn new terms and concepts; may hear about and practice newly acquired skills; and, it is hoped, come away with renewed motivation to make a difference as a leader, but even that may be a lot to expect from short-term workshops that are typical of so many leadership enhancement efforts. Remember that we are taught to be leaders through daily lessons in our organizations and in other interactions within our social and civic activities—for example, by observing the news, watching leaders around us, listening to political debates, and so on. The waves of messages that have brought us to our current understanding of leadership—as with communication—have been substantial and continuous. So the issues of what kind of programming we need, and how long the duration of the program or educational efforts needs to be, depend very much on where one is starting and where one wants to end up—specifically, how appropriate have the role models and organizations been in which we have participated to date, and how much can we—as organizations and individual leaders—become committed to pursuing new concepts, new capabilities, and new behaviors. Thus, in setting expectations, one should probably not look to reading a couple of self-help books, participating in a daylong workshop, or joining a training session by a noted consultant to dramatically reshape the leadership shoreline of our colleges and universities. We can hope for a tsunami or recognize the reality that systematic improvement of leadership is a critically important yet long-term process. Expecting otherwise invites disappointment.

Conclusion

Formalized leadership development programs occupy an increasingly visible, popular, and important role in higher education—nationally and on a growing number of campuses. The goals of these programs are easy to embrace as we face a growing array of challenges at all levels within higher education. A variety of programs exist to address these needs, ranging from self-study programs or occasional campus roundtables that focus on specific issues and associated leadership strategies, to intensive longer-term programs designed to substantially enhance participants' knowledge and behavioral competencies. Some programs are aimed at those in existing formal roles; others are designed to prepare participants for future positions. Still others have more general aims, seeking to enhance participants' informal leadership capabilities.

Gmelch and Buller (2015) provide a comprehensive overview of strategies for academic leadership in their text. They categorize the strategies based on three levels of intervention: personal, institutional, and professional. Additionally, as noted earlier, one can distinguish leadership development strategies according to the three areas of emphasis: habits of mind (conceptual understanding), habits of practice (skill development), and habits of heart (reflective practice).

Drawing on various lessons learned from their academic leadership programs at Iowa State University, Gmelch and Buller (2015) go on to outline the following qualities that are characteristic of effective academic leadership programs:

1. Cohort groups can play a key role in most leadership development programs.
2. Leadership development programs should not serve merely as training programs; they should also act as support groups.

3. Leadership development must be an ongoing process.
4. Leaders can create and deliver their own learning opportunities.
5. Successful leadership development programs require a supportive culture.
6. Leadership programs tend to be most successful when they capitalize on small wins as they proceed.
7. Leadership development is most effective when it occurs within a specific context.
8. Setting aside time and space for the administrators' reflection is indispensable.
9. Regardless of institutional mission or personal beliefs, effective leadership development must have moral, ethical, and (in many cases) spiritual dimensions.
10. Leaders must leave campus occasionally to gain a broader perspective and vision.
11. Much of the value of leadership development is lost if institutions do not provide incentives for administrators to stay long enough to make a difference and sustain the change.
12. Leadership development programs work best when they are built around a single, well-delineated model of leadership development (pp. 27–33).

In conceptualizing, designing, implementing, or adopting any program, it is important to begin with an assessment of organizational needs, as well as the knowledge and competencies required for effective leadership. Also important is a realistic assessment of the current organizational and leadership culture to determine the extent to which current practices are in line with organizational and leadership aspirations. When alignment is present, formal leadership programming is a far easier task than when more fundamental gaps exist. In either case, the design or selection of a program should reflect the sense of what's needed, and these same assessments should inform one's expectations of the outcomes.

When selecting an approach to preparing future leaders, we are reminded of the point made in Chapter 11 that the development of leaders and leadership competencies is an ongoing and continuous process. Pointing to the inadequacy of one-time, short-term, and isolated workshops, Connaughton, Lawrence, and Ruben (2003) note,

> It is unrealistic to expect that enhanced leadership capabilities can be developed in a two-hour or even a week long leadership workshop. Rather, leadership competencies are best developed over time through a program that fosters personalized integration of theory and practice and that conceives of leadership development as a recursive and reflective process. (p. 46)

A highly focused, intentional, and multidisciplinary approach to leadership development seems to be the most desirable option, particularly for those programs that align teaching methods with desired outcomes, encourage direct application and reflection, and offer various opportunities for learning about leadership (Connaughton et al., 2003; Prince, 2001).

To conclude, it is interesting to compare leadership development through participation in a one-time initiative (e.g., a program, workshop, or leadership book) with leadership development through one's long-term socialization in an organization (e.g., through culture, process, a set of experiences over time, and ongoing role modeling). It parallels the difference between learning how to parent from attending a workshop or reading a couple of how-to books and the learning that takes place through the influence of the multitude of experiences, observations, and insights developed over years of learning from one's own parents and other parents. In both instances, communication is central to learning. The former case, however, typically involves a few messages in a concentrated period of time, whereas long-term socialization involves an ongoing immersion in an environment filled with myriad verbal and nonverbal messages, some provided intentionally and others unintentionally, that both shape and reinforce what is learned—as implied by the waves against the shoreline analogy introduced earlier. One's expectations for significant change in knowledge and skills should be modest in the case of the former, recognizing that these few messages compete for influence with the vast array of accumulated insights and observations on the topic that have been gleaned through the natural communication processes within the culture of the organizations of which one has been a part.

For Further Consideration

1. Leadership Development Climate Reflection

Reflect upon your own unit, department, or organization:

- In what ways are leadership education and development encouraged or discouraged by your organizational climate?
- How might you describe this climate to a new aspiring leader?
- How does your organization incentivize, recognize, reward, or celebrate leadership development?
- What can one learn about leadership as a result of observing the behaviors of leaders in your unit, department, or institution?

2. The Design, Justification, and Evaluation of a Campus-Wide Leadership Development Program

As someone who is committed to leadership education and development, you would like to propose a new program for mid-career faculty and staff at your college or university. In talking to colleagues from other departments, you begin to recognize several troubling themes. There is a growing malaise across the institution, and many individuals lack the motivation for taking on formal leadership roles as department chairs or directors in major department or institutional committees. When you discuss the issue informally with colleagues, they report questioning their ability to function effectively in these roles and the value attached to this work by the institution.

- How might you further assess the organization and leadership development needs within your institution in order to further clarify the dimensions of the problems, strategies for addressing the issues you discover, and the role a formalized leadership development program might play?
- Given this context, what type of approach to leadership development (e.g., components, structure, duration, target audience) might be most effective or appropriate?
- What themes or competencies would you emphasize in the curriculum of this newly developed program?
- How would you evaluate the success of a leadership development program? What measures and methods might be most appropriate?

Notes

1. PLDI is one component of the Center for Organizational Development (ODL) leadership development programs, which have been supported by contributions from Johnson & Johnson, AT&T, the Mellon Foundation, Anne Thomas, Francis and Mary Kay Lawrence, and other Rutgers faculty and staff.

2. For a summary of these topics and capstone presentations, visit odl.rutgers .edu/pldi

3. A summary of the preliminary evaluation is provided at odl.rutgers.edu/wp-content/uploads/2015/03/pldi-presentation.pdf

4. See www.fordham.edu/info/21273/graduate_community/7058/fellowship_in_higher_education_leadership

5. A more comprehensive collection of academic and senior leadership education programs offered by these institutions can be found at odl.rutgers.edu/wp-content/uploads/2015/03/btaa-leadership-programs.pdf

While recognizing that each unit, department, and institution in higher education has special and unique features, our intent in writing this book has been to emphasize core concepts, competencies, and tools that cut across institutional types and structures, positions, roles, disciplines, and experiences in higher education.

The voluminous literature on leadership theory and practice and the popularity of leadership development programs—individual and organizational—are evident within higher education, as in other sectors. But, as more attention is devoted to these leadership initiatives, it has become increasingly clear that the challenges of preparing better and more effective leaders and improving organizational leadership practices are formidable. As mentioned in the concluding chapter of this volume, no leadership program, book, or resource can be expected to dramatically reshape the behavior of a leader or the culture of a college or university. That said, translating the lessons from these programs into everyday practice can have an incremental and cumulative impact on leaders and organizations. To the extent that current leaders are positive role models for future leaders, the process becomes significantly more effective. But none of us—even with a solid grasp of leadership concepts, a commitment to reflection practice, and the best of intentions—is able to consistently and effectively enact leadership behaviors to meet the complex and changing situations we face.

More than any other single factor, the future of higher education will be determined by its leadership. In order to continue to occupy a special place in society, higher education institutions need leaders who can do the following:

- Espouse and maintain the highest standards of personal integrity.
- Embrace innovation and change, while being mindful of the importance of higher education's traditions, history, and enduring values.
- Respect and acknowledge predecessors and their contributions.
- Demonstrate confidence in the new perspectives and possibilities they bring to their positions, but maintain humility about the value and merits of any one person's ideas.
- Pursue academic excellence and excellence in organizational practices.

A great deal of responsibility comes with higher education leadership. As a process of social influence that can be planned and unplanned, formal and informal, used for purposes that may be good or evil, much of leadership is about communication. Ultimately, leadership involves both what one says and what one does. As custodians of one of the most important sectors of society, we are ambassadors for the values printed in our mission statements and promoted on our college and university websites. If our behaviors fail to align with these articulated values, then none of the concepts, competencies, or tools presented in this volume can be expected to have much impact on the larger institution.

Finally, in the context of discussing role modeling, we think it is important to comment on values and ethics in leadership practice. Here, too, through the examples we set as leaders at the organizational level (e.g., the vision set forth in a strategic plan, the recovery plan initiated from a large-scale campus crisis, the broader systems developed for employee recruitment, selection, retention, and engagement) and the personal level (e.g., acknowledging the good work of others in public, treating our colleagues with mutual respect and care, actively listening and participating during meetings) are extremely important in shaping the cultural fabric of our institutions. As leaders in higher education, we cannot *not* communicate. Indeed, the ways we enact our roles as leaders become part of the "leadership curriculum" for future leaders of our colleges and universities.

Our hope is that the ideas and the ideals offered in this book will strengthen leadership performance, encourage active self-reflection, and empower future leaders of our colleges and universities to recognize leadership as a phenomenon that is coconstructed with our followers through acts that are conscious and accidental, part of our formal roles and our informal behaviors, through actions small and large.

Intercultural Communication Behavior Scales

Behavioral Observation Guide A: Respect

Date: _____

Participant: _____

Observer: _____

Individuals vary in the extent to which they express respect and regard for others' thoughts, opinions, or feelings. Their actions may take many forms ranging from verbal and nonverbal expressions of minimal regard to statements, gestures, and tones that are extremely respectful and indicative of very positive regard. Please indicate on a 1 to 5 continuum the pattern of expression that was most characteristic during the period of observation.

Description

1. The verbal and nonverbal expressions of the individual suggest a *clear lack of respect and negative regard* for others around him or her. By his or her actions, the individual indicates that the feelings and experiences of others are not worthy of attention or consideration. Examples include a condescending tone, lack of eye contact, and general lack of attention or interest.

2. The individual responds to others in a way that communicates *little respect* for others' feelings, experiences, or potential. The individual may respond mechanically or passively or may appear to ignore many of the thoughts and feelings of others.

Adapted in 2015 from "Assessing Communication Competency for Intercultural Adaptation" by B. D. Ruben, 1976, *Group and Organization Management, 1*(3), 34–354; and "Behavioral Assessment of Communication Competency and the Prediction of Cross-Cultural Adaptation" by B. D. Ruben and D. J. Kealey, 1979, *International Journal of Intercultural Relations, 3*(1), 15–47.

3. The individual indicates some respect for others' situations and *some concern* for their feelings, experiences, and potential. He or she may indicate some attentiveness to others' efforts to express themselves.
4. The individual indicates (through eye contact, general attentiveness, and tone) a *concern* for the thoughts, opinions, or feelings of others. The individual's verbal and nonverbal behavior encourages others to feel worthy of interaction and provides a sense that others' thoughts, opinions, and feelings are of interest and valued.
5. The individual indicates a *deep respect* for the worth of others' thoughts, opinions, and feelings. The individual indicates (through eye contact, general attentiveness, and tone) a clear respect and valuing of the thoughts and feelings of others and encourages continuing interaction.

Rating

Circle the number that best describes the individual's behavior.

1	*2*	*3*	*4*	*5*
Low Respect				High Respect

Behavioral Observation Guide B:
Interaction Posture

Date: _____

Participant: _____

Observer: _____

Instructions: Responses to another person or persons in an interpersonal or group situation range from *descriptive, nonvaluing* to *highly evaluative.* Indicate on a 1 to 4 continuum which interaction pattern was most characteristic during observation.

Description

1. *Highly evaluative.* The individual reacts immediately to others' verbal and nonverbal contributions in a highly judgmental and evaluative manner. The individual appears to measure the contributions of others in terms of a highly structured, predetermined, and rigid framework of thoughts, beliefs, attitudes, and values. Responses, therefore, communicate clearly and quickly whether the individual believes others to be "right" or "wrong." Reactions are made in declarative, often dogmatic fashion and will closely follow the comments of others, indicating little or no effort to digest what has been said before judging it.

2. *Evaluative.* The individual responds to others verbally and nonverbally in an evaluative and judgmental manner and measures the comments of others using a predetermined framework of thoughts, beliefs, attitudes, and values. The framework is not totally rigid but does provide a clear basis for determining whether others' contributions are "right" or "wrong,"

Adapted in 2015 from "Assessing Communication Competency for Intercultural Adaptation" by B. D. Ruben, 1976, *Group and Organization Management, 1*(3), 34–354; and "Behavioral Assessment of Communication Competency and the Prediction of Cross-Cultural Adaptation" by B. D. Ruben and D. J. Kealey, 1979, *International Journal of Intercultural Relations, 3*(1), 15–47.

and he or she is visibly impatient and interrupts others. Responses tend to follow fairly closely on the heels of termination of discussion by others, but there is some break, indicating a minimal attempt to digest and consider others' ideas before responding positively or negatively.

3. *Evaluative-descriptive.* The individual appears to measure the responses of others in terms of a framework based partly on information, thoughts, attitudes, and feelings gathered from the particular interaction and the individuals involved. He or she offers evaluative responses, but they appear to be less-than-rigidly held and subject to negotiation and modification. The time lapse between others' comments and the individuals' response suggests an effort to digest and consider input before reacting either positively or negatively.

4. *Descriptive.* The individual responds to others in a manner that draws out information, thoughts, and feelings, but only after gathering sufficient input so that the evaluative framework and responses relate to the individual(s) with whom he or she is interacting. The individual asks questions, restates others' ideas, and appears to gather information prior to responding with his or her opinions.

Rating

Circle the number that best describes the individual's behavior.

1	2	3	4	5
Highly Evaluative				Descriptive

Behavioral Observation Guide C:
Orientation to Knowledge

Date: _____

Participant: _____

Observer: _____

Instructions: People explain themselves and the world around them in varying ways. Some personalize their explanations, knowledge, and understandings, prefacing their statement with phrases such as, "*I* feel," or, "*I* think," and might say, "I don't like Mexican food." Others tend to generalize their explanations, understandings, and feelings, using statements such as, "It's a fact that . . . ," "It's human nature to . . . ," and so on. This pattern could lead an individual to say, "Mexican food *is* too spicy," indicating that the food is perceived to be the basis of the problem rather than the person's own tastes. Indicate on a 1 to 4 continuum which expression was most characteristic during the period of observation.

Description

1. *Physical orientation.* The individual treats perceptions, knowledge, feelings, and insights as inherent in the people and objects being perceived and assumes other people will always share the individual's perceptions, attitudes, and feelings if they are mature, knowledgeable, or insightful. Thus, differences with others' perceptions imply that the other persons are "wrong" or lack maturity or knowledge. Such an orientation might lead to a statement such as, "Mexican food is too hot." An individual with this orientation might use phrases such as, "We're all familiar with

Adapted in 2015 from "Assessing Communication Competency for Intercultural Adaptation" by B. D. Ruben, 1976, *Group and Organization Management, 1*(3), 34–354; and "Behavioral Assessment of Communication Competency and the Prediction of Cross-Cultural Adaptation" by B. D. Ruben and D. J. Kealey, 1979, *International Journal of Intercultural Relations, 3*(1), 15–47.

the way Xs act in such a situation," "It's inevitable that . . . ," "What else would you expect from . . . ," and so on.

2. *Cultural orientation.* The individual treats perceptions, knowledge, feelings, and insights as highly generalizable from one individual to another within a culture and assumes that other persons of similar cultural heritage will tend to share common views and perceptions. A representative statement might be, "North Americans find Mexican food far too hot for their tastes." He or she may use phrases such as, "In my country . . . ," "Canadians are typically . . . ," "In American cities, people are . . . ," or "In this culture . . ."

3. *Interpersonal orientation.* The individual treats perceptions, knowledge, and feelings as personal, but also potentially generalizable to others to some extent and tends to assume that others in an immediate group share the individual's perceptions, feelings, or thoughts (as with friends, colleagues, family, other members of a group). An individual whose orientation to knowledge is of this sort might say, "No one in my family would like these tacos," or may use phrases such as, "We feel . . . ," "My husband and I believe . . . ," "Most of you in the group know that . . . ," "Many people in my department . . . ," and so on.

4. *Intrapersonal Orientation.* The individual treats perceptions, knowledge, feelings, and insights as personally based, as shown by a statement such as, "I don't like Mexican food," which makes clear that the mismatch between the food and the taster is a consequence of the taster's particular tastes, perceptions, likes, and so on, and may have nothing necessarily to do with Mexican food. He or she does not regard differences in perception as inherently right or wrong. Examples of phrases that may be characteristic of this orientation are "I feel that . . . ," "It is my view that . . . ," "I believe . . . ," and so on.

Rating

Circle the number that best describes the individual's behavior.

1	2	3	4
Physical Orientation		Intrapersonal Orientation	

Behavioral Observation Guide D: Empathy

Date: _____
Participant: _____
Observer: _____

Instructions: Individuals vary in their ability to convey the sense that they understand things from another person's point of view. Some individuals seem to communicate a fairly complete awareness of another person's thoughts, feelings, and experiences; others seem unable to display any awareness of another's thoughts, feelings, or state of affairs. Indicate on a 1 to 5 continuum which pattern of behavior was most characteristic during your observations.

Description

1. *Low-level empathy.* The individual indicates little or no awareness of even the most obvious, surface feelings and thoughts of others. The individual appears to be bored or disinterested or simply operating from a preconceived frame of reference that totally excludes others' experience around at a particular point in time.

2. *Medium-low empathy.* The individual may display some awareness of obvious feelings and thoughts of others. He or she may attempt to respond based on this awareness; often the responses seem only superficially matched to the thoughts and feelings of others involved in the interaction.

Adapted in 2015 from "Assessing Communication Competency for Intercultural Adaptation" by B. D. Ruben, 1976, *Group and Organization Management*, *1*(3), 34–354; and "Behavioral Assessment of Communication Competency and the Prediction of Cross-Cultural Adaptation" by B. D. Ruben and D. J. Kealey, 1979, *International Journal of Intercultural Relations*, *3*(1), 15–47.

3. *Medium empathy.* The individual responds to others with reasonably accurate understandings of the surface feelings of others around but may not respond to, or may misinterpret, less obvious feelings and thoughts.
4. *Medium-high empathy.* The individual displays an understanding of responses of others at a deeper-than-surface level and thus enables others involved in the interaction to express thoughts or feelings they may have been unwilling or unable to discuss around less empathic persons.
5. *High empathy.* The individual appears to respond with great accuracy to apparent and less apparent expressions of feeling and thought by others. He or she projects interest and provides verbal and nonverbal cues that he or she understands the state of affairs of others.

Rating

Circle the number that best describes the individual's behavior.

1	*2*	*3*	*4*
Low Empathy			High Empathy

Behavioral Observation Guide E: Role Behavior

Date: _____

Participant: _____

Observer: _____

Instructions: Indicate how often participants exhibited each pattern of role behavior during the time periods observed.

Description

Task Roles. Individuals differ in the extent to which they engage in behavior that contributes to group problem-solving activities. Activities associated with the completion of tasks include initiating ideas, requesting further information or facts, seeking clarification of group tasks, clarifying task-related issues, evaluating suggestions of others, or focusing a group on task. Circle the number on the continuum that best describes the frequency of this behavior.

1	2	3	4	5
Never	Seldom	Occasionally	Frequently	Continually

Relational Roles. Individuals differ in the extent to which they devote effort to building or maintaining relationships within a group. *Group-development activities,* as they are sometimes termed, may consist of verbal and nonverbal displays that provide a supportive climate for the group members and help to solidify the group's feelings of participation. Behaviors that lead to these outcomes include efforts to harmonize or mediate arguments or conflicts between group members, comments offered relative to the group's dynamics, indications of a willingness to compromise one's own position for the sake of group consensus, displays of interest (nods of agreement, eye contact, general

Adapted in 2015 from "Assessing Communication Competency for Intercultural Adaptation" by B. D. Ruben, 1976, *Group and Organization Management, 1*(3), 34–354; and "Behavioral Assessment of Communication Competency and the Prediction of Cross-Cultural Adaptation" by B. D. Ruben and D. J. Kealey, 1979, *International Journal of Intercultural Relations, 3*(1), 15–47.

attending behaviors), and others. Circle the number on the continuum that best describes the frequency of this behavior.

1	*2*	*3*	*4*	*5*
Never	Seldom	Occasionally	Frequently	Continually

Individualistic Roles. Some individuals operate in groups in a highly individualistic manner and, as a consequence, may serve to block the group's efforts at both problem-solving and relationship building. Behaviors of this sort include displays by individuals who are highly resistant to ideas of others, or who return to issues and points of view previously discussed and acted upon or dismissed by the group. Other behaviors include attempting to call attention to him- or herself; projecting a highly positive image by noting achievements, qualifications, vocational and professional experience, or other factors that are designed to increase the individual's credibility; manipulating the group by asserting authority through flattery, sarcasm, and interrupting; actively avoiding and resisting participation; remaining insulated from the group when the individual feels he or she is not getting his or her way, and so on. Circle the number on the continuum that best describes the frequency of this behavior.

1	*2*	*3*	*4*	*5*
Never	Seldom	Occasionally	Frequently	Continually

Behavioral Observation Guide F:
Interaction Management

Date: _____

Participant: _____

Observer: _____

Instructions: People vary in their skill at managing interactions in which they take part. Particularly in regard to taking turns in discussion and initiating and terminating interaction based on the needs of others, some individuals display great skill, while others do not. For each participant, indicate on the 1 to 5 continuum which pattern was most characteristic during the period of observation.

Description

1. *Low management.* The individual is unconcerned with taking turns in discussion. The individual may dominate or refuse to interact at all, may be unresponsive to or unaware of other's needs for involvement and time sharing, may initiate and terminate discussion without regard for the wishes of other individuals, may continue to talk long after obvious displays of disinterest and boredom by others, or may terminate discussion—or generally withhold information—when there is clear interest expressed by others for further exchange.
2. *Moderately low management.* The individual is minimally concerned with taking turns in discussion. The individual often either dominates or is reluctant to interact, is unresponsive to other's needs for involvement and time sharing, and initiates or terminates conversations with minimal regard for other individuals.

Adapted in 2015 from "Assessing Communication Competency for Intercultural Adaptation" by B. D. Ruben, 1976, *Group and Organization Management, 1*(3), 34–354; and "Behavioral Assessment of Communication Competency and the Prediction of Cross-Cultural Adaptation" by B. D. Ruben and D. J. Kealey, 1979, *International Journal of Intercultural Relations, 3*(1), 15–47.

3. *Moderate management.* The individual is somewhat concerned with taking turns in discussion. The individual seldom either dominates or is reluctant to interact with most persons at most times and generally shows a concern for time sharing and initiating and terminating interaction in a manner that is responsive to the needs of other participants.

4. *Moderately high management.* The individual is quite concerned with taking turns in discussion. He or she seldom either dominates or withdraws from interaction and at most times shows a concern for time sharing and initiating and terminating interaction in a manner that is responsive to the needs of other participants.

5. *High management.* The individual is extremely concerned with providing equal opportunity for all participants to share in contributions to discussion. In the initiation and termination of discussion, he or she always indicates concern for the interests, tolerances, and orientation of others who are involved in discussions.

Rating

Circle the number that best describes the individual's behavior.

1	2	3	4	5
Low Management				High Management

Behavioral Observation Guide G: Ambiguity Tolerance

Date: _____

Participant: _____

Observer: _____

Instructions: Some individuals react to new situations with greater comfort than others. Some are excessively nervous, highly frustrated, or hostile toward the new situation or those who may be present (who may be identified as sources of their problems). Others encounter new situations as a challenge; they appear to function best wherever the unexpected or unpredictable occurs and quickly adapt to the demands of changing environments. On a 1 to 5 continuum, indicate the manner in which the individual observed seemed to respond to new or ambiguous situations.

Description

1. *Low tolerance.* The individual seems quite troubled by new or ambiguous situations and exhibits excessive nervousness and frustration. He or she seems slow to adapt to the situation and may express hostility toward those in authority or leadership roles. Negative feelings may also lead to verbal hostility directed toward other individuals present in the environment and especially toward those perceived to be in control of the immediate environment.
2. *Moderately low tolerance.* The individual seems somewhat troubled by new or ambiguous situations, exhibits nervousness and frustration, is somewhat slow to adapt to the situation, and may express some hostility toward those perceived as in control.

Adapted in 2015 from "Assessing Communication Competency for Intercultural Adaptation" by B. D. Ruben, 1976, *Group and Organization Management, 1*(3), 34–354; and "Behavioral Assessment of Communication Competency and the Prediction of Cross-Cultural Adaptation" by B. D. Ruben and D. J. Kealey, 1979, *International Journal of Intercultural Relations, 3*(1), 15–47.

3. *Moderate tolerance.* The individual reacts with moderate nervousness and frustration to new or ambiguous situations but adapts to these environments with reasonable speed and resilience. There are no apparent personal, interpersonal, or group consequences as a result of the individual's uneasiness. Those perceived as being in leadership or authority positions may be the target of minor verbal barbs—sarcasm, joking, and mild rebukes—but there are no significant signs of hostility.

4. *Moderately high tolerance.* The individual reacts with some nervousness and frustration to new or ambiguous situations. He or she adapts to the situation quite rapidly with no personal, interpersonal, or group-directed expressions of hostility. Those in leadership and authority positions are not a target for verbal barbs or sarcasm, nor are other individuals in the environment.

5. *High tolerance.* The individual reacts with little or no nervousness or frustration to new or ambiguous situations. He or she adapts to the demands of the situation quickly with no noticeable personal, interpersonal, or group consequences and seems to adapt very rapidly and comfortably to new or changing environments.

Rating

Circle the number that best describes the individual's behavior.

1	*2*	*3*	*4*	*5*
Low Tolerance				High Tolerance

Leadership Competencies Scorecard 2.0

> **Leadership Competencies Scorecard 2.0**
> **(LCS 2.0)**
>
> **Developed by**
>
> **Brent D. Ruben, PhD**

The Leadership Competencies Scorecard 2.0 is the 2012 version of the Leadership Competency Scorecard (LCS), first published in *What Leaders Need to Know and Do: A Leadership Competencies Scorecard* (Ruben, 2006/2012). The scorecard provides a competency-based framework that identifies and integrates a diverse array of characteristics described in scholarly and professional writings as being important for effective leadership.

The LCS identifies and defines five major competency themes, each of which includes a number of specific competencies. *Analytic competencies* are associated with thoughtful reflection on one's own and others' behaviors and careful consideration of the consequences of alternative leadership options and strategies. *Personal competencies* refer to one's standards, character, and expression of values. *Communication competencies* relate to the knowledge and skills necessary for effective interaction in interpersonal, group, organizational, and public settings. *Organizational competencies* include administrative capabilities that are important for leading in organizations of varying purpose, function, and size. *Positional competencies* include knowledge and skills related to the particular context, setting, field, or sector in which a leader is serving.

The scorecard can be used to inventory and develop a profile of one's own or another person's leadership competencies, using ratings from 1 to 5 for each of the 35 competencies. LCS ratings allow individuals to rate "understanding of the concept," and "effectiveness in practice." *Understanding* refers to theoretical knowledge that provides a foundation for anticipating and adapting to leadership needs of varying situations, organizations, cultures, or sectors. *Effectiveness* relates to skill in translating knowledge and applying it to practice. Both dimensions can be important to assessing and enhancing leadership capability. When using the scorecard for self-assessment, rate both *understanding* and *effectiveness*. When using the LCS to assess others, the ratings should generally be limited to effectiveness. Effectiveness assessment is based on behavioral observation, and an individual's level of understanding or knowledge of particular competencies may not be apparent from his or her behavior.

Reference

Ruben, B. D. (2006/2012). *What leaders need to know and do: A leadership competencies scorecard.* Washington, DC: National Association of College and University Business Officers.

Figure A.B.1. Analytical competencies.

1 (low) ⟷ 5 (high)

Analytic Competencies		Understanding of the Concept					Effectiveness in Practice				
1. SELF-ASSESSMENT	Analyzing one's own thoughts, emotions, and reactions	1	2	3	4	5	1	2	3	4	5
2. PROBLEM-DEFINITION	Identifying underlying issues, concerns, problems, and tasks that need to be addressed in a given situation	1	2	3	4	5	1	2	3	4	5
3. STAKEHOLDER ANALYSIS	Assessing perspectives of those likely to be affected by the decisions, policies, or practices of a leader or organization	1	2	3	4	5	1	2	3	4	5
4. SYSTEM, ORGANIZATIONAL, SITUATIONAL ANALYSIS	Focusing on "the big picture," including short- and long-term concerns and outcomes, for all those affected by leadership decisions, policies, or practices	1	2	3	4	5	1	2	3	4	5
5. ANALYSIS OF TECHNOLOGY TO SUPPORT LEADERSHIP	Assessing available technologies, and their potential strengths and weaknesses for supporting leadership efforts	1	2	3	4	5	1	2	3	4	5
6. PROBLEM-SOLVING	Analyzing a situation, identifying possible/appropriate leadership styles and courses of action; ensuring follow through	1	2	3	4	5	1	2	3	4	5
7. REVIEW AND ANALYSIS OF RESULTS	Debriefing and analyzing outcomes to derive "lessons learned" that can be applied in a future situation	1	2	3	4	5	1	2	3	4	5

Subtotals - Analytic Competencies

Figure A.B.2. Personal competencies.

Personal Competencies		Understanding of the Concept					Effectiveness in Practice				
8. CHARACTER, PERSONAL VALUES, AND ETHICS	Maintaining personal and professional standards	1	2	3	4	5	1	2	3	4	5
9. COGNITIVE ABILITY AND CREATIVITY	Demonstrating insight and imagination	1	2	3	4	5	1	2	3	4	5
10. ENTHUSIASM	Maintaining a positive attitude	1	2	3	4	5	1	2	3	4	5
11. HIGH STANDARDS	Expecting excellent performance from oneself and others	1	2	3	4	5	1	2	3	4	5
12. PERSONAL CONVICTION AND PERSISTENCE	Being dedicated and persevering	1	2	3	4	5	1	2	3	4	5
13. SELF-DISCIPLINE AND SELF-CONFIDENCE	Having self-control, focus, and confidence in one's capabilities	1	2	3	4	5	1	2	3	4	5
14. ROLE MODELING	Enacting the values and behaviors that one advocates for others	1	2	3	4	5	1	2	3	4	5

Subtotals - Personal Competencies

Figure A.B.3. Communication competencies.

1 (low) ⇔ 5 (high)

Communication Competencies		Understanding of the Concept					Effectiveness of Practice				
		1	2	3	4	5	1	2	3	4	5
15. CREDIBILITY AND TRUST	Being admired, seen as magnetic, authoritative, honest, competent and trustworthy	1	2	3	4	5	1	2	3	4	5
16. INFLUENCE AND PERSUASION	Convincing others to adopt advocated ideas, points-of-view, or behaviors	1	2	3	4	5	1	2	3	4	5
17. INTERPERSONAL RELATIONS AND TEAM-BUILDING	Creating effective interpersonal relationships, groups, and teams	1	2	3	4	5	1	2	3	4	5
18. LISTENING, ATTENTION, QUESTION-ASKING AND LEARNING	Attending verbally and visually to the thoughts, behaviors and actions of others	1	2	3	4	5	1	2	3	4	5
19. WRITING AND PUBLIC SPEAKING	Conveying information, ideas, and opinions clearly through writing and oral presentations	1	2	3	4	5	1	2	3	4	5
20. DIVERSITY AND INTERCULTURAL RELATIONS	Valuing and working effectively with both men and women, and individuals of varying cultural, racial, ethnic, political or lifestyle orientations	1	2	3	4	5	1	2	3	4	5
21. FACILITATION, NEGOTIATION, AND CONFLICT RESOLUTION	Encouraging discussion and the expression of varying points of view, encouraging compromise, and effectively addressing tensions and conflicts	1	2	3	4	5	1	2	3	4	5

Subtotals - Communication Competencies

Figure A.B.4. Organizational competencies.

Organizational Competencies		Understanding of the Concept					Effectiveness of Practice				
22. VISION-SETTING, STRATEGY DEVELOPMENT, AND GOAL ATTAINMENT	Motivating and providing a sense of purpose and direction, development approaches and goals, and ensuring follow through	1	2	3	4	5	1	2	3	4	5
23. MANAGEMENT AND SUPERVISION	Overseeing financial, physical, and human resources	1	2	3	4	5	1	2	3	4	5
24. INFO/KNOWLEDGE MANAGEMENT AND BOUNDARY SPANNING	Facilitating the flow and sharing of information within a group or organization, and across organizational boundaries	1	2	3	4	5	1	2	3	4	5
25. TECHNOLOGICAL CAPABILITY	Using appropriate communication technology and media to support leadership initiatives	1	2	3	4	5	1	2	3	4	5
26. COLLABORATIVE DECISION-MAKING AND EMPOWERMENT	Effectively engaging others in decision-making and other activities	1	2	3	4	5	1	2	3	4	5
27. TEACHING AND COACHING	Encouraging the development of leaders and leadership capacity	1	2	3	4	5	1	2	3	4	5
28. CHANGE, RISK, AND CRISIS MANAGEMENT	Promoting and effectively guiding change and innovation, anticipating and managing risks, and coping effectively with unexpected and crisis situations	1	2	3	4	5	1	2	3	4	5

Subtotals – Organizational Competencies

Figure A.B.5. Positional competencies.

1 (low) ⟷ 5 (high)

Positional Competencies		Understanding of the Concept					Effectiveness in Practice				
29. EDUCATION	Having relevant formal education and/or training in sector-related competencies	1	2	3	4	5	1	2	3	4	5
30. EXPERIENCE	Having prior relevant experience in the sector (e.g., business, healthcare, government, or education)	1	2	3	4	5	1	2	3	4	5
31. EXPERTISE	Having appropriate and/or required job competencies	1	2	3	4	5	1	2	3	4	5
32. KNOWLEDGE OF FIELD	Understanding of the field, its issues, challenges and opportunities (e.g., business, healthcare, government, or education)	1	2	3	4	5	1	2	3	4	5
33. KNOWLEDGE OF ORGANIZATION	Understanding the particular organization, its issues, challenges, and opportunities	1	2	3	4	5	1	2	3	4	5
34. FAMILIARITY WITH WORK	Knowing about and being comfortable with tasks or work activities that are specific to the sector and organization	1	2	3	4	5	1	2	3	4	5
35. PROFESSIONAL INVOLVEMENT	Pursuing opportunities for personal and professional learning, growth, and advancement	1	2	3	4	5	1	2	3	4	5

Subtotals - Positional Competencies

Figure A.B.6. Scoring instructions to chart each competency category.

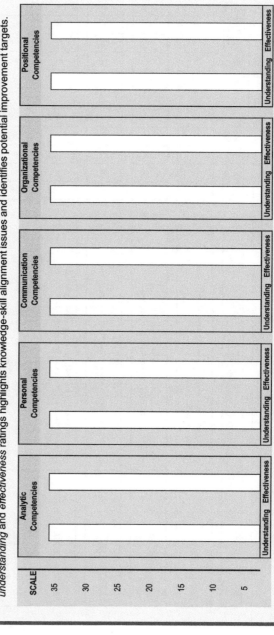

Scoring Instructions

- Total the ratings for each competency category. If you used the LCS 2.0 for self-assessment and completed both *understanding of the concept* and *effectiveness in practice*, total your ratings for both dimensions. If you used the LSC 2.0 for assessing others, you may only have completed the *effectiveness in practice* ratings and would only total the effectiveness columns.

- Transfer the subtotal scores to the blank bar graph below by drawing a horizontal line at the level which corresponds to your particular score. Then, color in the area below each scoreline to create bar charts for each competency area.

- Note: Comparing totals across competencies highlights strengths and areas where improvement may be beneficial. Comparing *understanding* and *effectiveness* ratings highlights knowledge-skill alignment issues and identifies potential improvement targets.

Change Planning Worksheets

Steps in the Change Planning Process

1. Develop a clear statement of the mission, need, purpose, and vision for the proposed change.

2. Identify stakeholder groups that are potential collaborators, beneficiaries, and other groups affected by the proposed change.

3. Identify potential strengths, weaknesses, opportunities, and threats of the proposed change. Who are your peers and aspirants?

4. Identify key themes and goals to be pursued. What needs to be done?

5. Develop strategies and action plans for each goal. How does it need to be done, by whom, when, and so on?

6. Draft a plan summarizing 1 to 6, to be updated over time with outcomes and achievements.

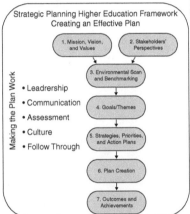

Strategic Planning Higher Education Framework
Creating an Effective Plan

1. Mission, Vision, and Values

2. Stakeholders' Perspectives

Making the Plan Work

- Leadrership
- Communication
- Assessment
- Culture
- Follow Through

3. Environmental Scan and Benchmarking

4. Goals/Themes

5. Strategies, Priorities, and Action Plans

6. Plan Creation

7. Outcomes and Achievements

Adapted from: Tromp, S. A., Ruben, B. D. *Strategic Planning in Higher Education* (SPHE) Washington, DC: National Association of College and University Business Officers, 2010, p. 9.

Define the Purpose
Draft Statement

What is the *purpose* of the planned change?

Clarify the Need

Why is the change needed?

Identify Affected Parties and Key Stakeholders

What groups will be directly affected?

What groups will be indirectly affected?

SWOT Analysis–Items That Could Affect Accomplishing Your Strategic Goals

Organizational strengths that could affect the accomplishment of your strategic goals **S**	Organizational weaknesses that could affect the accomplishment of your strategic goals **W**
O Opportunities that could affect the accomplishment of your strategic goals	**T** Threats to the organization that could affect the accomplishment of your strategic goals

From: Tromp, S. A., Ruben, B. D. *Strategic Planning in Higher Education* Washington, DC: National Association of College and University Business Officers, 2010, p. 62.

Environmental Factors

What are the pluses/strengths/assets that should be considered?

Environmental Factors

What are the negatives/weaknesses/liabilities that should be considered?

Environmental Factors

What are the opportunities that should be considered?

Environmental Factors

What are the threats/risks that should be considered?

Environmental Factors—Benchmarking Peers and Aspirants

- How have peer or aspirant organizations addressed a similar change need?

- What peer or aspirant organizations have adopted the changes you're considering?

- What key lessons can be derived from their experience?

Define Goals—*Draft Statement*

List goals and desired outcomes that need to be achieved in order for the planned change to be successful in fulfilling the intended purposes.

What needs to be done?

1.

2.

3.

Goal 1 Strategies

How can Goal 1 be achieved?

   1.1 ...

   1.2 ...

   1.3 ...

Goal 2 Strategies

How can Goal 2 be achieved?

   1.1 ...

   1.2 ...

   1.3 ...

Goal 3 Strategies

How can Goal 3 be achieved?

    1.1 ...

    1.2 ...

    1.3 ...

Develop Action Plans

Priority/Goal #_____   _____Short-term (6 months or less)
Strategy Description   _____Longer-term (7 months to 1 year)

Key steps/activities:	Potential members:
	Convener:

Funding considerations:

Deliverables:

Communication and engagement issues:

Timeframe (start-up, milestones, target completion date):

Effectiveness measures(s):

How to move the project to action (multiple choice):

❏ Delegate to existing group (if so, which one?)
❏ Delegate to individual (if so, which one?)
❏ Delegate to leadership
❏ Form task force

From: Tromp, S. A., Ruben, B. D. *Strategic Planning in Higher Education* (SPHE) Washington, DC: National Association of College and University Business Officers, 2010.

Action Planning

Priority/Goal #_____

_____Short-term (6 months or less)
_____Longer-term (7 months to 1 year)

Strategy Description: In one or two sentences, how can you clearly define the scope of the project?

Key steps/activities: What kinds of broad activities need to be part of the project plan?	Potential members: Which individuals/positions need to be represented in the group to bring the best input, ideas, and expertise to the project? Who should lead the group? Convener:

Funding considerations: What resources are required to make the project a reality? To sustain it? What sources currently exist? What issues exist?

Deliverables: At the end of the project, what items will the group produce (e.g., a report, a new/revised process, a survey, a website, publications)?

Communication and engagement issues: How will you keep others abreast of your progress? How will you promote two-way communication about the project? How will you let others know about recommendations/changes?

Timeframe (start-up, milestones, target completion date): What is a reasonable amount of time for the project? (Keep in mind operational calendar, lead time for notification of changes, etc.)

Effectiveness measures(s): What information will tell you whether the planning has been successful in reaching the desired outcomes?

How to move the project to action (multiple choice): What needs to be done to ensure the project moves forward?

☐ Delegate to existing group (if so, which one?)

☐ Delegate to individual (if so, which one?)

☐ Delegate to leadership

☐ Form task force

From: Tromp, S. A., Ruben, B. D. *Strategic Planning in Higher Education* (SPHE) Washington, DC: National Association of College and University Business Officers, 2010.

Leadership Architecture Guide

	Stage	Leader (Person/Team)	What the Leader/Team Should Do	Timeframe
Attention	1.			
Engagement	2.			
Commitment	3.			
Action	4.			
Integration	5.			

Communication Guide: Stage 1—Attention

Communication . . . in order to connect to what <u>audiences</u>, to achieve what <u>goals/outcomes</u>, to identify/overcome what <u>resistance</u> (e.g., needs, questions, concerns) with what <u>message</u>, through which <u>channels</u>, coming from <u>whom</u>?

Audience	Goal	Resistance	Message	Communication Channel	Message Source

Adapted from: Tromp, S. A., Ruben, B. D. *Strategic Planning in Higher Education* Washington,

Communication Guide: Stage 2—Engagement

Communication . . . in order to connect to what <u>audiences</u>, to achieve what <u>goals/outcomes</u>, to identify/overcome what <u>resistance</u> (e.g., needs, questions, concerns) with what <u>message</u>, through which <u>channels</u>, coming from <u>whom</u>?

Audience	Goal	Resistance	Message	Communication Channel	Message Source

Adapted from: Tromp, S. A., Ruben, B. D. *Strategic Planning in Higher Education* Washington,

Communication Guide: Stage 3—Commitment

Communication . . . in order to connect to what <u>audiences</u>, to achieve what <u>goals/outcomes</u>, to identify/overcome what <u>resistance</u> (e.g., needs, questions, concerns) with what <u>message</u>, through which <u>channels</u>, coming from <u>whom</u>?

Audience	Goal	Resistance	Message	Communication Channel	Message Source

Adapted from: Tromp, S. A., Ruben, B. D. *Strategic Planning in Higher Education* Washington,

Communication Guide: Stage 4—Action

Communication . . . in order to connect to what <u>audiences</u>, to achieve what <u>goals/outcomes</u>, to identify/overcome what <u>resistance</u> (e.g., needs, questions, concerns) with what <u>message</u>, through which <u>channels</u>, coming from <u>whom</u>?

Audience	Goal	Resistance	Message	Communication Channel	Message Source

Adapted from: Tromp, S. A., Ruben, B. D. *Strategic Planning in Higher Education* Washington,

Communication Guide: Stage 5—Integration

Communication . . . in order to connect to what <u>audiences</u>, to achieve what <u>goals/outcomes</u>, to identify/overcome what <u>resistance</u> (e.g., needs, questions, concerns) with what <u>message</u>, through which <u>channels</u>, coming from <u>whom</u>?

Audience	Goal	Resistance	Message	Communication Channel	Message Source

Adapted from: Tromp, S. A., Ruben, B. D. *Strategic Planning in Higher Education* Washington,

Cultural Guide

	Stage	Group/Cultural Issue	What Needs to Be Done?
Attention	1.		
Engagement	2.		
Commitment	3.		
Action	4.		
Integration	5.		

Assessment Guide

	Stage	What Will Be Assessed?	How?	How Will Info Be Used?
Attention	1.			
Engagement	2.			
Commitment	3.			
Action	4.			
Integration	5.			

Snapshot of Signature Leadership Programs at Big Ten Academic Alliance Member Institutions

University of Chicago

Program: Executive Program for Emerging Leaders (EPEL)

Coordinating Office: The University of Chicago Booth School of Business

Website: www.iedp.com/University_of_Chicago/Executive_Program_for_Emerging_Leaders

Program Description: The Executive Program for Emerging Leaders (EPEL) is designed for University of Chicago administrators with high potential. It will deliver new approaches to leadership development, build and develop high-performance teams, manage cross-functional and cross-organizational relationships, and craft strategy. This program will benefit administrators responsible for improving the performance of their organizational unit, as well as contribut to the University of Chicago's broader strategic goals.

The content is based on the general management and leadership programs at the University of Chicago Booth School of Business. EPEL features highlights from our best programs taught by our faculty. This program also offers specific content sessions led by officers, vice presidents, and deans focusing on critical challenges and opportunities at the University of Chicago.

University of Illinois

Program: Academic Leadership Seminar Series

Coordinating Office: Office of the Provost

Website: provost.illinois.edu/als/index.html

Program Description: The Academic Leadership Seminar Series is a year-long program for academic unit leaders including department heads and chairs, program and center directors, and assistant and associate deans. It consists of two separate series of seminars, one for new executive officers and one for all executive officers.

New Executive Officer Leadership Seminars

The New Executive Officer Leadership Seminar Series is designed to help acquaint newly appointed executive officers with university policies and procedures. It also provides a forum in which executive officers can meet with colleagues, share experiences, and gain knowledge of pertinent on-campus resources. Programs focus on helping the executive officer better understand the overall strategy and mission of the campus and the university.

Executive Officer Roundtables

The Executive Officer Roundtable Series is designed for new and experienced executive officers who wish to engage in dialogue and discuss best practices pertaining to current issues affecting academic leaders. In-depth discussion of topics such as leadership challenges, financial and strategic planning, and faculty development is featured.

Indiana University

Program: Management Training Series (MTS)

Coordinating Office: Human Resources and Organizational Development

Website: www.indiana.edu/~uhrs/training/man-training.html

Program Description: The MTS is a university-wide leadership development series that offers Indiana University leaders a unique opportunity to participate in a professional development program with colleagues from around the state. Since its inception in 1991, MTS has "graduated" a cadre of leaders who, to this day, are key players in the successes of Indiana University.

MTS is designed to empower a select group of leaders, from throughout Indiana University, to master the organizational and leadership challenges they face now and in the future. Drawing upon resources from both inside and outside the university, MTS presents leading-edge sessions designed to assist participants in improving performance in their current positions, as well as prepare them for possible additional responsibilities. Participants meet one day a month, for seven months, beginning in October and cover topics such as planning, managing change transitions, accountability, expectations, coaching, leadership, and more. In addition to the monthly sessions, participants are expected to participate in project teams that will afford them the opportunity to apply what they are learning to a real-life situation in real time. They are also be expected to establish their own professional leadership development goals with action plans and outcomes.

Indiana University continues to demonstrate its support and investment in employees through support of this program. MTS is supported by each vice president, provost, and chancellor and is funded by the University Human Resource Services office. Each participant is selected by his or her vice president, provost, and/or chancellor and must have leadership responsibilities at the director/assistant director level or above.

University of Iowa

Program: UI LEAD (Leadership Education, Assessment, and Development)

Coordinating Office: University Human Resources

Website: hr.uiowa.edu/lead

Program Description: UI LEAD is a comprehensive leadership program for University of Iowa faculty and staff. With one-to-one coaching at its core, UI LEAD focuses on individualized feedback, goal-setting, and skill development over a six-month to two-year period.

UI LEAD is a competency-based leadership program. It is focused on increasing participants' awareness of and effectiveness with specific leadership behaviors that create and sustain organizational success. Our approach is based upon the creation of a powerful partnership centering on the participant, the participant's supervisor/administrator, and his or her UI LEAD coach.

Through this partnership, the candidate is able to identify the following:

- Current leadership strengths and limitations
- Specific leadership competencies desired
- Individualized leadership goals
- Tailored action plan to achieve goals
- Progress and measure success

University of Maryland

Program: University of Maryland (UMD) Academic Leadership Forums

Coordinating Office(s): Associate Provost for Faculty Affairs

Website: N/A

Program Description: The Academic Leadership Forums are designed to build a stronger sense of community of academic administrators across the campus, particularly heads of departments, schools, and colleges, and to provide programs that facilitate discussion of important campus issues. Titles of talks have included the following:

- A Conversation with Senior Vice President and Provost Mary Ann Rankin: Initiatives and Future Directions
- Parental Leave, Family and Medical Leave, Tenure Clock Delay, and Related Issues: How to Counsel Your Faculty
- Budget Issues for Academic Administrators
- Strategic Plan Update
- Diversity Charges for Appointments, Promotion, and Tenure (APT) Committees
- University Budget
- Professional-Track Faculty
- Issues Surrounding Retirement, Post-Tenure Review, and Emeritus Status
- Changes in APT Policy and Guidelines

University of Michigan

Program: ADVANCE Program

Coordinating Office: University of Michigan ADVANCE Program

Website: advance.umich.edu

Program Description: The ADVANCE program promotes faculty diversity in all fields. The ADVANCE program aims to support university faculty in the following general areas:

- Recruitment—focuses on development and use of equitable recruiting practices
- Retention—focuses on preemptive strategies to prevent the loss of valued faculty, in part by encouraging their promotion and advancement
- Climate—focuses on creation and maintenance of departmental work environments that support faculty satisfaction, promotion, and retention
- Leadership—focuses on support for development of leadership skills and opportunities for all faculty as well as on support for development of skills among all appointed academic leaders to encourage positive work environments

Michigan State University

Program: New Administrator Orientation (NAO)

Coordinating Office: Office of Faculty and Organizational Development (F&OD)

Website: fod.msu.edu/orientation-new-administrators

Program Description: NAO is a three-day experience required for new academic deans, department chairs and school directors, and other new administrators upon request, including new associate deans. In addition to requiring attendance at NAO, Michigan State University's Academic Human Resources now requires new administrators to attend the following leadership development programs (all LEadership and ADministrator [LEAD] seminars)[1] during the first two years of their appointments: "Budget," "Hiring," and "Faculty Performance Review." These programs offered over a two-year period provide materials and skill development beyond what can be offered in the NAO event itself, and are deemed of high importance for administrators and the success of their units, faculty, and staff. One important elaboration of NAO has been the addition of "Informal Conversations with the Associate Provost and Associate Vice President for Academic Human Resources" that is comprised of five meetings throughout the year with new academic administrators on topics of high interest that they identify. Although attendance at the Informal Conversation sessions is not required, it has a significant following because of its high value in answering questions about important dimensions of their work. As a complement to NAO and its related activities, there are several leadership development offerings throughout the year including Conversations with the President and Provost, additional LEAD Seminars, and the Executive Leadership Academy Seminar Series focused on the development of individual leadership competencies and style.

Note

1. The LEAD Seminar Series is designed to promote ongoing communication among academic administrators, provide leadership development opportunities, and support campus leaders (deans, chairs, directors, and executive managers) in their efforts to foster organizational change in their units.

University of Minnesota

Program: Provost's Department Heads and Chairs Leadership Program

Coordinating Offices: Provost's Office, Office of Human Resources

Website: www1.umn.edu/ohr/leadership

Program Description: The provost's department Heads and Chairs Leadership Program supports department chairs' leadership and provides critical information and resources to chairs and heads. This yearlong academic leadership program for new chairs and heads is a collaborative effort between the provost's office and human resources. The vice provost for faculty and academic affairs hosts these meetings throughout the year. The program includes two half-day retreats and six dinner meetings. While aimed at new chairs and heads, new associate deans for faculty are also invited to participate in the program.

University of Nebraska–Lincoln

Program: Organization Development Services

Coordinating Office: Human Resources

Website: hr.unl.edu/orgdev#whatis

Program Description: Organization development is a practice to help organizations build the capacity to change and achieve greater effectiveness.

Organization Development Services (ODS) helps enhance congruence among organizational structure, process, strategy, people, and culture by developing new and creative organizational solutions.

Two services of interest to this leadership development snapshot document include the following:

- Management and leadership development—assisting managers to develop best practices for their work at the University of Nebraska-Lincoln (UNL).
- Administrators consultation program—confidential, individualized coaching to help new administrators adjust to their role at UNL by offering assistance in their roles as managers of people and finances.

Northwestern University

Program: Heading an Academic Unit at Northwestern: Leadership Among Peers

Coordinating Offices: Office of Human Resources, Learning and Organization Development and Office of the Provost

Website: No website

Program Description: The program is designed to give department chairs, research center directors, and academic program directors an opportunity to

- Develop a greater understanding of the roles and responsibilities common to heads of Northwestern University academic units
- Increase familiarity with internal and external resources
- Build a multidisciplinary community of supportive colleagues

Ohio State University

Program: New Department Chair Orientation

Coordinating Office: Office of Academic Affairs

Website: No website

Program Description: The office of academic affairs at The Ohio State University offers a nine-month program for individuals entering into their first year as a chair. The program helps new chairs explore best practices in leading departments and supports their transition in year one. The program emphasizes how to do the following:

- Collaborate and build effective relationships
- Optimally deploy people, space and money
- Develop and retain faculty and staff
- Interact effectively with administration and communicate with key stakeholders

Additionally, the program facilitates ongoing collegial exchanges with other chairs and leaders so as to build a network of contacts and resources. Participants will engage in discussions, exercises, and simulations on key issues facing chairs at Ohio State today. Specific program elements include skill development workshops led by academic leaders from across the university, a cohort experience to build community, individualized mentoring support to help navigate specific challenges and needs, as well as contact with key college resources to gain administrative support.

Skill Development

Workshops are designed to provide information, tools and contacts related to managing the department and the people in it, as well as navigating relevant university processes. The preliminary topic titles include the following:

- The Life of a Chair
- Budget and Compensation
- Promotion and Tenure
- Strategic Planning
- Decision-Making
- Legal Issues
- Evaluation

Cohort Experience

Sessions are intended to support new chairs in developing leader relationships throughout the university as well as provide a supportive network of colleagues to benefit each chair in being an effective leader. The preliminary titles include the following:

- Luncheon With the Provost
- Communicating for Understanding

- Building Trust
- Influencing Others
- Conflict and Difficult Dialogue
- Luncheon and Celebration With the President

Mentoring Support

Mentoring support aims to strengthen a chair's transition into the new role by providing an experienced colleague who can draw from her or his experience to guide the new chair. A mentor will be matched with each new department chair and is available to meet one-on-one for counsel that illuminates the role of chair and supports the effectiveness and engagement of the new chair.

College Resources

Each college provides support to help new chairs get up to speed on administrative resources (fiscal, human resources, legal/compliance, grant support, etc.), advancement resources (fund-raising and development, special events, communication, alumni relations), enrollment management, curriculum management, and scheduling. New chairs can expect support and guidance from associate deans, fiscal and human resources professionals, college advancement and communications staff, and college facilities staff, in addition to other staff and faculty. Each dean provides strategic guidance and performance expectations as well as counsel on navigating the university and accessing college resources.

Pennsylvania State University

Program: Academic Leadership Forum (ALF)

Coordinating Office: Office of the Vice Provost for Academic Affairs

Website: www.psu.edu/dept/vprov/academicleader.htm

Program Description: The Office of the Vice Provost for Academic Affairs conducts four or five half-day ALF sessions each year for our deans, associate deans, department heads, and other academic administrators. An ALF planning committee helps to identify topics and speakers for the sessions. The topics vary each year depending upon what contemporary issues are occurring in higher education and more specifically at Penn State. Some recent titles include the following:

- Educating and Communicating With Our Increasingly Diverse Student Body
- Monsters in the Forest: Legal Issues for Academic Administrators
- Performance Counseling of Senior Faculty
- Managing Your Time, Stress, and Conflict (Taking Care of Yourself and Your Employees)
- Resiliency: Rebounding From Personal and Institutional Circumstances
- Academic Bullying 101: Enhancing Department Climate
- Leading Academic Change With Today's Uncertainties

Also, each year we ask the president and provost to participate in one session to share their thoughts about topics of interest to them and to engage in a question-and-answer session with the administrators. To bring an outside perspective to at least one of the sessions, we invite speakers from another university, a government agency, a corporation or business, or an educational group. The other speakers are from within the university. From a structural perspective, we use multiple formats, such as panels, small group discussion, case studies, and role plays. Given the diversity of the university with its 24 campuses, we begin each session with a continental breakfast so the participants can get to know each other and develop informal relationships.

Purdue University

Program: Council for Manager Development (CMD)

Coordinating Offices: Office of the Treasurer and Chief Financial Officer and Office of the Vice President for Human Resources

Website: www.psu.edu/dept/vprov/academicleader.htm

Program Description: Purdue University has a rich tradition of professional development for high-potential future leaders. Since 1956, CMD has worked with senior staff leaders from across the West Lafayette campus to develop future leaders in the following areas:

- Professional networks
- Project management skills
- Leadership and teaming skills
- Management certifications

- Understanding of the university's strategic initiatives
- One-on-one mentoring from key university leaders
- Individualized career preparation and coaching

Over 700 leaders have graduated from the CMD program. Eight high-potential future leaders were admitted to the CMD program in September 2015. As candidates for the CMD program, each individual demonstrated a strong potential for career advancement within two years of admittance into the CMD program.

Rutgers University

Program: Rutgers Leadership Academy (RLA)

Coordinating Office: Center for Organizational Development & Leadership

Website: odl.rutgers.edu/leadership-programs

Program Description: RLA is a two-year program for midcareer faculty and staff from across the institution who aspire to broadened leadership roles within their units, the University, and/or higher education more generally. RLA focuses on the development of cross-cutting leadership concepts, competencies, and tools to enhance professional capabilities for those in academic, professional, and administrative leadership roles.

Target Audience

The program focuses on midcareer faculty and staff in Rutgers–New Brunswick and Rutgers Biomedical and Health Sciences with an interest in and potential for expanded leadership roles. The program is open to those with or without prior leadership experiences in higher education.

Fellows Nomination Process

Nominations for participation in the Academy are submitted by VPs, deans, directors, chairs, or other senior administrative leaders who see a need for an expanded pool of future leaders within their unit and want to recognize and encourage the development of particular colleagues to assume increasing leadership responsibility. Nominators will agree to serve a facilitating and mentoring role throughout the program and will identify projects through which RLA participants can exercise a leadership role.

Program Structure

The program consists of 18 3-hour sessions over the course of four semesters. This is a cohort program in which participants will develop leadership skills and competencies by exploring case studies, simulations, presentations, and readings and leading field-based projects under the mentorship of senior campus leaders.

RLA Topics

Topics include institutional structure and missions, organizational dynamics, leadership theories and concepts, formal and informal leadership roles and responsibilities, disciplinary and institutional cultures, decision-making, internal and external communication, the influence of multiple publics, and the leader's role in organizational planning and change.

Rutgers University

Program: Academic Leadership Program (ALP)

Website: http://odl.rutgers.edu/academic-leadership-program/

Program Description: The Rutgers ALP provides a forum for disseminating information on policies and practices, addressing theoretical and practical problems of academic leadership, sharing effective practices across disciplines, and creating a collaborative network of administrators and faculty members charged with providing academic leadership for the institution. Components of the program include an orientation for new deans and chairs, a breakfast discussion series, and an academic leadership website. ALP is sponsored by the Center for Organizational Development and Leadership; the Office of the Chancellor, Rutgers–New Brunswick; the Office of Senior Vice President for Academic Affairs; the Graduate School–New Brunswick, University Human Resources; and the School of Communication and Information

Rutgers University

Program: PreDoctoral Leadership Development Institute (PLDI)

Website: http://odl.rutgers.edu/pldi

Each year, PLDI welcomes a select group of Rutgers doctoral students from a broad array of disciplines to its two-year program. Traditional discipline-based doctoral education is devoted to preparing students for careers in scholarship and teaching, but often these future faculty members complete their degree with little preparation for academic and administrative leadership roles in their institutions. A critical need exists for individuals who also understand the structure and dynamics of colleges and universities, know the challenges these institutions face, and possess the interpersonal and organizational knowledge, competencies and aspirations to provide effective and ethical leadership in addressing the critical issues confronting higher education.

While it may be years before new doctoral graduates move into formal leadership roles, leadership expertise is needed immediately for working in teams and workgroups, pursuing research funding and support, participating in mentoring and advising relationships with students and colleagues, and for assuming the many informal leadership roles at their institutions. Through participation in the Institute, students can become more effective members of the academic community, more capable leaders and collaborators within their disciplines and their future places of employment, and for these reasons, more marketable and well-prepared for influential careers.

Senior leaders from both Rutgers and other institutions serve as guest speakers throughout the program, and key readings from higher education news outlets and higher education leadership texts provide a foundation for the weekly class seminars. Building upon the seminars from the first year, PLDI Fellows are paired with an on-campus mentor for the third semester of the program. Fellows shadow their mentors—consisting of deans, directors, vice presidents, and chancellors—and analyze the leadership competencies utilized in their specific roles. In the final semester, Fellows participate in a capstone presentation to leadership-minded faculty and peers on a complex and multifaceted topic of interest for leaders in higher education.

PLDI is sponsored by the Center for Organizational Development and Leadership, the Office of the Chancellor, Rutgers–New Brunswick, the Graduate School–New Brunswick, Office of the Senior Vice President for Academic Affairs, the Graduate School of Education, and the School of Communication and Information.

University of Wisconsin–Madison

Program: Chairs Chats and Chairs Chats Plus

Website: No website

Program Description: The Chairs Chats program at the University of Wisconsin–Madison is a highly popular and extremely successful program that brings department chairs, center directors, and department managers together to discuss issues of common concern, to problem solve, and to forge best practices. This 14-year-old program is sponsored by the office of the vice provost for faculty and staff and supported by the Office of Quality Improvement.

The format of the Chairs Chats has varied little over the years. After attendees have checked in and have had a chance to eat and socialize, the vice provost begins the session by announcing the topic, asking attendees to introduce themselves, and reviewing the format: peer discussion (there is no designated leader, though from time to time two or three of the attendees are "tapped" beforehand to be prepared to discuss their own perspective on the issue should the conversation lag) with a focus on individuals' experiences and with an emphasis on *solving* the problem rather than on the problem itself. The vice provost makes clear that the sessions operate on so-called Vegas rules: specific cases and names can be used with the confidence that what is said in the room stays in the room. The vice provost then lays out a set of questions or issues that may be discussed, and the conversation generally takes on a momentum of its own; the vice provost serves as moderator, steering the conversation in the event it meanders or gets stuck on problems more than solutions.

The Chairs Chats Plus format is a variation of Chairs Chats. Because it is designed for new chairs and directors, the topics tend to be of an introductory nature; during the past year titles included the following:

- University Finances 101
- What Do Chairs Need to Know About the Tenure/Promotion Process?
- Building a Team in the Chair's Office
- "Who's Who": A Primer on Key People and Offices on Campus

Typically, the vice provost calls on chairs or former chairs who have some experience to serve as lead discussants (an informal panel), though they are urged to keep their presentations brief so that the panel discussion itself takes no longer than 15 or 20 minutes, in order to leave substantial time for questions/answers and discussion. Vegas rules apply to these sessions as well, and the goal of the vice provost, as moderator, is to keep the focus on best practices. Chats are generally held during the lunch hour, though some breakfast sessions have been held in order to allow those who teach during the day to attend. Lunch or breakfast is provided free by the sponsoring offices. Tables are arranged in a circle to foster discussion; generally between 15 and 35 department chairs, center directors, and department managers attend. Typically there are six Chairs Chat sessions, and four Chairs Chat Plus sessions, each academic year, generally held about three weeks apart during the fall and spring semesters.

Topics of the sessions vary; topics have included the following:

- Achieving work-life balance as chair
- Working closely with department managers and staff
- Mentoring colleagues
- Strategic planning
- Advancement, development, communicating with alumni and friends, and fund-raising
- Managing budgets
- Helping assistant professors achieve tenure
- Recruiting and retaining faculty
- Addressing climate and morale issues

Generally topics are selected and set at the beginning of the academic year by surveying department chairs and center directors at the leadership summit held each August prior to the beginning of classes. Adjustments are made in the schedule as needed and as new issues emerge.

REFERENCES

Aiken, C., & Keller, S. (2009, April). The irrational side of change management. *The McKinsey Quarterly, 2.* http://www.mckinsey.com/insights/organization/the_irrational_side_of_change_management

Alger, J. R. (2015, November 2). *Public or private good? The role of public higher education in modern society.* Presented at Rutgers University, New Brunswick, NJ.

Allen, I. A., & Seaman, J. (2008). *Staying the course: Online education in the United States, 2008.* Retrieved from http://www.sloan-c.org/publications/survey/pdf/staying_the_course.pdf

Allison, M., & Kaye, J. (2005). *Strategic planning for nonprofit organizations* (2nd ed.). Hoboken, NJ: Wiley.

Altbach, P. G., Gumport, P. J., & Berdahl, R. U. (2011). *American higher education in the twenty-first century. Social, political, and economic challenges* (3rd ed.). Baltimore, MD: Johns Hopkins University Press.

Anderson, T., & Elloumi, F. (Eds.). (2005). *Theory and practice of online learning.* Canada: Athabasca University.

Arum, R., & Roska, J. (2010). *Academically adrift: Limited learning on college campuses.* Chicago, IL: University of Chicago Press.

Associated Press. (2015, February 4). Walker backs off removing "Wisconsin Idea" from UW mission. *The New York Times.* Retrieved from www.nytimes.com/aponline/2015/02/04/us/ap-us-xgr-wisconsin-budget-uw.html

Association for Talent Development. (2015). *2015 State of the industry.* Retrieved from www.td.org/Publications/Research-Reports/2015/2015-State-of-the-Industry

Association of American Colleges and Universities. (2004). *Taking responsibility for the quality of the baccalaureate degree.* Washington, DC: Association of American Colleges and Universities.

Association of American Universities. (2015). *Home.* Retrieved from www.aau.edu

Axley, S. (1984). Managerial and organizational communication in terms of the conduit metaphor. *Academy of Management Review, 9,* 428–437.

Ayyad, C., & Andersen, T. (2000). Long-term efficacy of dietary treatment of obesity: A systematic review of studies published between 1931 and 1999. *Obesity Reviews, 1*(2), 113–119.

Baldrige National Quality Program. (2015a). *Baldridge homepage.* Retrieved from www.nist/gov/baldridge

Baldrige National Quality Program. (2015b). *The 2015 criteria for performance excellence in education.* Washington, DC: National Institute of Standards and Technology. Retrieved from http://www.nist.gov/baldrige/enter/education.cfm

Baldrige National Quality Program. (2015c, February 11). *More evidence that Baldrige criteria help organizations perform better.* Retrieved from www.nist.gov/baldrige/2015_evidence_criteria.cfm.

Baldrige National Quality Program. (2015d). *Why Baldrige? Any organization can improve and excel using this management framework.* Retrieved from www.nist.gov/baldrige/enter/index.cfm

Barge, J. K. (2007). The practice of systemic leadership. *OD Practitioner, 39*(1), 10–14.

Barge, J. K., & Fairhurst, G. (2008). Living leadership: A systemic constructionist approach. *Leadership Quarterly, 4*(3), 227–251.

Barnshaw, J., & Dunietz, S. (2015). Busting the myths: The annual report on the economic status of the profession. *Academe, 101*(1), 4–19.

Bass, B., & Avolio, B. J. (1994). *Improving organizational effectiveness through transformational leadership.* Thousand Oaks, CA: Sage.

Bataille, G.M., Billings, M.S., & Nellum, C. J. (2012). *Leadership in times of crisis: "Cool head, warm heart."* Washington, DC: American Council on Education.

Bataille, G. M., & Cordova, D. I. (Eds.). (2014). *Managing the unthinkable: Crisis preparation and response for campus leaders.* Sterling, VA: Stylus.

Baum, S., Karuse, C., & Ma, J. (2013). *How college shapes lives: Understanding the issues.* Retrieved from www.trends.collegeboard.org

Baum, S., & Ma, J. (2014). *Trends in college pricing 2014.* Retrieved from www.trends.collegeboard.org

Baum, S., Ma, J., & Payea, K. (2013). *Education pays 2013. The benefits of higher education for individuals and society.* Retrieved from www.trends.collegeboard.org

Becker, C., Bianchetto, M., & Goldstein, L. (2012). *Budget models and process: Challenges facing institutions today.* Presentation at the annual meeting of the National Association of College and University Business Officers, Washington, DC.

Bender, B. (2002). Benchmarking as an administrative tool for institutional leaders. In B. Bender & J. Schuh (Eds.), *Using benchmarking to inform practice in higher education* (pp. 113–120). San Francisco, CA: Jossey-Bass.

Benne, K. D., & Sheats, P. (1948). Functional roles of group members. *Journal of Social Issues, 4*(2), 41–49.

Bennett, N. (2015, July 22). Our leader left. Who is left to lead? *The Chronicle of Higher Education.* Retrieved from m.chronicle.com/article/Our-Leader-Left-Who-s-Left/231159/?cid=at&utm_source=at&utm_medium=en

Bennis, W. (1997). *Managing people is like herding cats.* Provo, UT: Executive Excellence Publishing.

Bennis, W. (2007). The challenges of leadership in the modern world. *American Psychologist, 62*(1), 2–5.

Bennis, W., & Nanus, B. (1985). *Leaders: The strategies for taking charge.* New York, NY: Harper & Row.

Benoit, W. L. (1995). *Accounts, excuses, and apologies: A theory of image restoration.* Albany, NY: State University of New York Press.

Benoit, W. L. (1997). Image repair discourse and crisis communication. *Public Relations Review, 23*(2), 177–186.

Benoit, W. L., & Pang, A. (2008). Crisis communication and image repair discourse. In Tricia L. Hansen-Horn & Bonita Dostal Neff (Eds.), *Public relations: From theory to practice* (pp. 244–261). Boston, MA: Pearson.

Benson, J. A. (1988). Crisis revisited: An analysis of strategies used by Tylenol in the second tampering episode. *Central States Speech Journal, 39*(1), 49–66.

Berdahl, R. (2006). *Comments on the second draft of the Report of the Commission on the Future of Higher Education.* Retrieved from www.aau.edu/education/AAU_Response_to_Higher_Education_Commission_Second_Draft_Report-2006–07-31.pdf

Berger, P. L., & Luckmann, T. (1966). *The social construction of reality.* New York, NY: Doubleday Anchor.

Berrett, D., & Hoover, E. (2015, November 13). When pursuing diversity, victory is hard to define. *The Chronicle of Higher Education.* Retrieved from http://chronicle.com/article/When-Pursuing-Diversity/234190

Bertalanffy, L. V. (1968). *General system theory: Foundations, development, applications.* New York, NY: George Braziller.

Big Ten Academic Alliance. (2015a). *Home.* Retrieved from https://www.btaa.org/home

Big Ten Academic Alliance. (2015b). *Department executive officers (DEO) seminar.* Retrieved from https://www.btaa.org/projects/leadership/deo/introduction

Big Ten Academic Alliance. (2015c). *Academic leadership program (ALP).* Retrieved from https://www.btaa.org/projects/leadership/alp/introduction

Birnbaum, R. (1988). *How colleges work: The cybernetics of academic organization and leadership.* San Francisco, CA: Jossey-Bass.

Blake, R. R., & McCanse, A. A. (1991). *Leadership dilemmas: Grid solutions.* Houston, TX: Gulf Publishing.

Blumenstyk, G. (2015, March 9). Culture of change. *The Chronicle of Higher Education.* Retrieved from chronicle.com/article/Culture-of-change-Successful/228169/?key=QD91dgVjYXNKZX41NT1AbztcPSFsMB8mZX4cOihxblFREA==

Boehner, J. (2015). Highlights of Speaker Boehner's resignation speech. *The Washington Post.* Retrieved from https://www.washingtonpost.com/video/national/highlights-of-speaker-boehners-resignation-speech/2015/09/25/64e1ba94-63c0-11e5-8475-781cc9851652_video.html

Bok, D. (2013). *Higher education in America.* Princeton, NJ: Princeton University Press.

Bolden, R. (2011). Distributed leadership in organizations: A review of theory and research. *International Journal of Management Reviews, 13*(3), 251–269.

Bolden, R., Petrov, G., & Gosling, J. (2009). Distributed leadership in higher education: Rhetoric and reality. *Educational Management Administration & Leadership, 37*(2), 257–277.

Bolea, A., & Atwater, L. (2015). *Applied leadership development: Nine elements of leadership mastery.* New York, NY: Routledge.

Bolman, L. G., & Gallos, J. V. (2011). *Reframing academic leadership.* San Francisco, CA: Jossey-Bass.

Booker, L., Jr. (2014). Crisis management: Changing times for colleges. *Journal of College Admission, 222,* 16–23.

Borden, M. H., & Kernel, B. (2012). *Measuring quality in higher education: An inventory of instruments, tools, and resources.* Retrieved from apps.airweb.org/surveys/

Brancato, C. K. (1995). *New corporate performance measures.* New York, NY: Conference Board.

Bratton, W. J. (1998). *Turnaround: How America's top cop reversed the crime epidemic.* New York, NY: Random House.

Bratton, W. J. (1999). Great expectations: How higher expectations for police departments can lead to a decrease in crime. In Robert H. Langworthy (Ed.), *Measuring what matters: Proceedings from the Policing Research Institute meetings* (pp. 11–26). Washington, DC: National Institute of Justice.

Brown, D. (2011, February 28). Inside the busy, stressful world of air traffic control. *The Atlantic.* Retrieved from www.theatlantic.com/technology/archive/2011/02/inside-the-busy-stressful-world-of-air-traffic-control/71776/

Brown, D. J. (2014). *The boys in the boat: Nine Americans and their epic quest for gold at the 1936 Berlin Olympics.* New York, NY: Penguin Books.

Brown, S. (2015, November 20). At Yale, painful rifts emerge over diversity and free speech. *The Chronicle of Higher Education.* Retrieved from chronicle.com/article/At-Yale-Painful-Rifts-Emerge/234112

Brown, S. (2016, January 27). A university softens a plan to cut tenured faculty, but professors remain wary. *Chronicle of Higher Education.* Retrieved from http://www.chronicle.com/article/A-University-Softens-a-Plan-to/235061

Bruni, F. (2013, April 20). Questioning the mission of college. *The New York Times,* p. SR3.

Bruni, F. (2015, August 8). A prudent college path. *The New York Times.* Retrieved from www.nytimes.com/2015/08/09/opinion/sunday/frank-bruni-a-prudent-college-path.html?rref=collection%2Fcolumn%2Ffrank-bruni&action=click&contentCollection=Opinion&module=Collection&region=Marginalia&src=me&pgtype=article

Bryson, J. M. (2011). *Strategic planning for public and nonprofit organizations* (4th ed.). San Francisco, CA: Jossey-Bass.

Buller, J. L. (2012). *The essential department chair. A comprehensive desk reference* (2nd ed.). San Francisco, CA: Jossey-Bass.

Buller, J. L. (2014). *Change leadership in higher education: A practical guide to academic transformation.* San Francisco, CA: Jossey-Bass.

Burke, J. C. (1997). *Performance-funding indicators: Concerns, values, and models for two- and four-year colleges and universities.* Albany, NY: Nelson A. Rockefeller Institute of Government.

Burke, J. C., & Minassians, H. (2001). *Linking state resources to campus results: From fad to trend—the fifth annual report.* Retrieved from www.rockinst.org/publications/higher_ed/5thSurvey.pdf

Burke, J. C., & Serban, A. M. (1997). *Performance funding and budgeting for public higher education: Current status and future prospects.* Albany, NY: Nelson A. Rockefeller Institute of Government.

Burkhart, P. J., & Reuss, S. (1993). *Successful strategic planning: A guide for nonprofit agencies and organizations.* Thousand Oaks, CA: Sage.

Calareso, J. P. (2013). Succession planning: The key to ensuring leadership. *Planning for Higher Education Journal, 41*(3), 27–33.

Carey, K. (2014, September 5). On the immense good fortune of higher education. *The Chronicle of Higher Education.* Retrieved from chronicle.com/article/On-the-Immense-Good-Fortune-/148541/

Carey, K. (2015). *The end of college: Creating the future of learning and the university of everywhere.* New York, NY: Riverhead Books.

Carpenter-Hubin, J., & Snover, L. (2013). Key leadership positions and performance expectation. In P. J. Schloss & K. M. Cragg (Eds.), *Organization and administration in higher education* (pp. 27–49). New York, NY: Routledge.

Cascio, W. F. (2011). Leadership succession: How to avoid a crisis. *Ivey Business Journal, 75*(3), 6–8.

Centers for Disease Control and Prevention. *Current cigarette smoking among adults—United States, 2005–2013.* Retrieved from www.cdc.gov/mmwr/preview/mmwrhtml/mm6347a4.htm?s_cid=mm6347a4_w

Chatterjee, A., & Hambrick, D. C. (2007). It's all about me: Narcissistic chief executive officers and their effects on company strategy and performance. *Administrative Science Quarterly, 52*(3), 351–386.

Cherniss, C. (2010). Emotional intelligence: Toward clarification of a concept. *Industrial and Organizational Psychology, 3*(3), 110–126.

Chronicle of Higher Education. (2015). *The view from the top: What presidents think about financial sustainability, student outcomes, and the future of higher education.* Retrieved from http://www.maguireassoc.com/wp-content/uploads/2015/08/2015-PresidentsReport_Chron-Maguire-2.pdf

Cole, D., Orsuwan, M., & Ah Sam, A. (2007). Violence and hate crimes on campus against international students and students of color: Uncovering the mystique. In M. C. Terrell & J. Jackson (Eds.), *Creating and maintaining safe college campuses: A sourcebook for enhancing and evaluating safety programs* (pp. 34–57). Sterling, VA: Stylus.

College Board. (2014). *Trends in college pricing 2014.* Retrieved from https://trends.collegeboard.org/sites/default/files/2014-trends-college-pricing-final-web.pdf

College Portrait. (2015). *Voluntary system of accountability.* Retrieved from www.collegeportraits.org/about

Collins, J. (2001). *Good to great. Why some companies make the leap . . . and others don't.* New York, NY: Harper Business.

Connaughton, S. L., Lawrence, F. L., & Ruben, B. D. (2003). Leadership development as a systematic and multidisciplinary enterprise. *Journal of Education for Business,* 46–51.

Coombs, W. T. (2006). *Code red in the boardroom: Crisis management as organizational DNA.* Westport, CT: Praeger.

Coombs, W. T. (2007). Protecting organization reputations during a crisis: The development and application of situational crisis communication theory. *Corporate Reputation Review, 10*(3), 163–176.

Coombs, W. T. (2015). *Ongoing crisis communication: Planning, managing, and responding* (4th ed.). Thousand Oaks, CA: Sage.

Coombs, W. T., Hazelton, V., Holladay, S. J., & Chandler, R. C. (1995). The crisis grid: Theory and application in crisis management. In L. Barton (Ed.), *Proceedings for the new avenues in risk and crisis management conference* (vol. 4; pp. 30–39). Las Vegas, NV: University of Las Vegas Publications.

Costa, G. (1993). Evaluation of workload in air traffic controllers. *Ergonomics, 36*(9), 1111–1120.

Covey, S. R. (1989). *The 7 habits of highly effective people: Powerful lessons in personal change.* New York, NY: Simon & Schuster.

Cowan, S. (2014). *The inevitable city: The resurgence of New Orleans and the future of urban America.* New York, NY: Palgrave Macmillan.

Curry, J. R., Laws, A. L., & Strauss, J. C. (2013). *Responsibility center management: A guide to balancing academic entrepreneurship with fiscal responsibility.* Washington, DC: National Association of College and University Business Officers.

Dargis, M. (2013). A college where the exams are terrifying: "Monsters University" unfolds before "Monsters Inc." *The New York Times,* p. C12.

Day, D. V. (2001). Leadership development: A review in context. *Leadership Quarterly, 11*(4), 581–613.

Day, D. V., Zaccaro, S. J., & Halpin, S. M. (Eds.). (2004). *Leader development for transforming organizations: Growing leaders for tomorrow.* Mahwah, NJ: Erlbaum.

DePree, M. (1999). My mentors' leadership lessons. In F. Hasselbein & P. M. Cohen (Eds.), *Leader to leader* (pp. 15–24). San Francisco, CA: Jossey-Bass.

Department of Education. (2008). *Comments by Margaret Spellings.* Invitational Summit on Higher Education. Washington, DC.

Dewey, J. (1933). *How we think.* Boston, MA: D. C. Heath & Co.

DeZure, D., Shaw, S., & Rojewski, J. (2014). Cultivating the next generation of academic leaders: Implications for administrators and faculty. *Change: The Magazine of Higher Learning, 46*(1), 6–12.

Dodd, A. H. (2004). Accreditation as a catalyst for institutional effectiveness. In M. J. Dooris, J. M. Kelley, & J. F. Trainer (Eds.), *Successful strategic planning: New directions for institutional planning* (pp. 13–25). San Francisco, CA: Jossey-Bass.

Donathen, E. A., & Hines, C. A. (1998). Growing our own future leaders: A case study in Texas leadership training. *A Leadership Journal: Women in Leadership—Sharing the Vision, 2*(2), 93–106.

Dooris, M. J., Kelley, J. M., & Trainer, J. F. (2004). Strategic planning in higher education. In M. J. Dooris, J. M. Kelley, & J. F. Trainer (Eds.), *Successful strategic planning: New directions for institutional planning* (pp. 5–11). San Francisco, CA: Jossey-Bass.

Downey, M., Parslow, S., & Smart, M. (2011). The hidden treasure in nursing leadership: Informal leaders. *Journal of Nursing Management, 19*(4), 517–521.

DuBrin, A. J. (2013). Conclusions about crisis leadership in organizations. In A. J. DuBrin (Ed.), *Handbook of research on crisis leadership in organizations* (pp. 333–340). Northampton, MA: Edward Elgar.

DuBrin, A. W. (2004). *Leadership*. New York, NY: Houghton Mifflin.

Duneiere, M. (2000). *Sidewalk*. New York, NY: Farrar, Straus and Giroux.

Ebersole, J. (2014, January 13). Top issues facing higher education. *Forbes*. Retrieved from www.forbes.com/sites/johnebersole/2014/01/13/top-issues-facing-higher-education-in-2014/

Eckerson, W. W. (2005). *Performance dashboards: Measuring, monitoring, and managing your business*. New York, NY: Wiley.

Edmunds, E. F., & Boyer, R. K. (2015, July 19). How great colleges distinguish themselves. *The Chronicle of Higher Education*. Retrieved from chronicle.com/article/How-Great-Colleges-Distinguish/231623/?cid=at&utm_source=at&utm_medium=en

Eisenberg, E. M. (1984). Ambiguity as strategy in organizational communication. *Communication Monographs, 51*(3), 227–242.

Ellerby, J. M. (2009, July 21). Views from both sides now. *Inside Higher Education*. Retrieved from www.insidehighered.com/views/2009/07/21/ellerby

Entman, R. M. (1993). Framing: Toward clarification of a paradigm. *Journal of Communication, 43*(4), 51–58.

Ewell, P. (1994). Developing statewide performance indicators for higher education. In S. S. Ruppert (Ed.), *Charting higher education accountability: A sourcebook on state level* (pp. 147–166). Denver, CO: Education Commission of the States.

Fain, P. (2015, November 17). College completion rates decline more rapidly. *Inside Higher Ed*. Retrieved from https://www.insidehighered.com/quicktakes/2015/11/17/college-completion-rates-decline-more-rapidly

Fairhurst, G. T. (2005). Reframing the art of framing: Problems and prospects for leadership. *Leadership, 1*(2), 165–185.

Fairhurst, G. T. (2007). *Discursive leadership: In conversation with leadership psychology*. Thousand Oaks, CA: Sage.

Fairhurst, G. T. (2009). Considering context in discursive leadership research. *Human Relations, 62*(11), 1607–1633.

Fairhurst, G. T., & Connaughton, S. L. (2014a). Leadership: A communicative perspective. *Leadership, 10*(7), 7–35.

Fairhurst, G. T., & Connaughton, S. L. (2014b). Leadership communication. In L. L. Putnam & D. K. Mumby (Eds.), *The SAGE handbook of organizational communication: Advances in theory, research, and method* (pp. 401–423). Thousand Oaks, CA: Sage.

Fairhurst, G. T., & Putnam, L. (2004). Organizations as discursive constructions. *Communication Theory, 14*(1), 5–26.

Fairhurst, G. T., & Sarr, R. (1996). *The art of framing: Managing the language of leadership*. San Francisco, CA: Jossey-Bass.

Fearn-Banks, K. (2011). *Crisis communications* (4th ed.). New York, NY: Routledge.

Feiner, M. (2004). *The Feiner points of leadership. The 50 basic laws that will make people want to perform better for you*. New York, NY: Warner Business Books.

Fiedler, F. E. (1967). *A theory of leadership effectiveness*. New York, NY: McGraw-Hill.

Flaherty, C. (2016, January 26). Divided over diversity. *Inside Higher Ed*. Retrieved from https://www.insidehighered.com/news/2016/01/26/did-baylor-us-new-provost-step-down-over-controversy-surrounding-diversity-program

Fleirscher, B. (2015, August 19). Stop universities from hoarding money. *The New York Times*. Retrieved from www.nytimes.com/2015/08/19/opinion/stop-universities-from-hoarding-money.html?ref=opinion

Flynn, W. J., & Vredevoogd, J. (2010). The future of learning: 12 views on emerging trends in higher education. *Planning for Higher Education, 38*(2), 5–10.

Fortunato, J. A. (2005). *Making media content: The influence of constituency groups on mass media*. Mahwah, NJ: Erlbaum.

Frank, R. H. (2001). Higher education: The ultimate winner-take-all market? In M. E. Devlin & J. W. Meyerson (Eds.), *Forum futures: Exploring the future of higher education—2000 papers* (pp. 3–12). San Francisco, CA: Jossey-Bass.

Freeh Report of the actions of Penn State University. (2012). Retrieved from www.scribd.com/doc/99901850/Freeh-Report-of-the-Actions-of-Penn-State-University

Freeman, R. E. (1984). *Strategic management: A stakeholder approach*. Boston, MA: Pitman. [Reprinted 2010, Cambridge University Press.]

Friedman, T. L. (2013). Revolution hits the universities. *The New York Times*. Retrieved from http://www.nytimes.com/2013/01/27/opinion/sunday/friedman-revolution-hits-the-universities.html

Gallup. (2014). *Gallup-Lumina Foundation Study 2014 Report*. Retrieved from www.gallup.com/poll/182462/postsecondary-education-aspirations-barriers.aspx

Gallup. (2015). *Gallup-Purdue Index 2015 Report*. Retrieved from products.gallup.com/168857/gallup-purdue-index-inaugural-national-report.aspx

Geertz, C. (1973). *The interpretation of cultures*. New York, NY: Basic Books.

Genshaft, J. (2014). It's not the crime, it's the cover-up (and the follow-up). In G. M. Bataille & D. I. Cordova (Eds.), *Managing the unthinkable: Crisis preparation and response for campus leaders* (pp. 7–17). Sterling, VA: Stylus.

George, B. (2003). *Authentic leadership: Rediscovering the secrets to creating lasting value*. San Francisco, CA: Jossey-Bass.

Georgetown University. (n. d.). *School of medicine mission statement*. Retrieved from https://som.georgetown.edu/

Gigliotti, R. A. (2016). Leader as performer; Leader as human: A post-crisis discursive construction of leadership. *Atlantic Journal of Communication, 24*(3).

Gigliotti, R. A. (forthcoming). Academic leadership education within the Association of American Universities. *Journal of Applied Research in Higher Education*. Manuscript submitted for publication.

Gigliotti, R. A., Agnew, B., Goldthwaite, C., Sahay, S., Dwyer, M., & Ruben, B. D. (2016). Scholar in training; leader in training: The Rutgers University PreDoctoral Leadership Development Institute. In P. Blessinger & D. Stockley (Eds.),

Emerging directions in doctoral education (pp. 39 -59). Bingley, UK: Emerald Group Publishing.

Gigliotti, R. A., & Ruben, B. D. (2015). *Academic leadership development matrix.* Prepared for the Center for Organizational Development & Leadership, Rutgers University.

Gignac, G. (2010). On a nomenclature for emotional intelligence research. *Industrial and Organizational Psychology, 3*, 131–135.

Gill, R. (2012). *Theory and practice of leadership* (2nd ed.). Thousand Oaks, CA: Sage.

Gilley, J., Fulmer, K., & Reithlingshoefer, S. (1986). *Searching for academic excellence: Twenty colleges and universities on the move and their leaders.* New York, NY: Macmillan.

Gittleman, S. (2015, November 20). Higher education has always been a mess. That's what makes it great. *The Chronicle of Higher Education Review.* Retrieved from chronicle.com/article/Higher-Ed-Has-Always-Been-a/234162

Gmelch, W. H., & Buller, J. L. (2015). *Building academic leadership capacity: A guide to best practices.* San Francisco, CA: Jossey-Bass.

Gmelch, W. H., Hopkins, D., & Damico, S. (2011). *Seasons of a dean's life: Understanding the role and building leadership capacity.* Sterling, VA: Stylus.

Goffman, A. (2014). *On the run: Fugitive life in an American city.* Chicago, IL: University of Chicago Press.

Goleman, D. (1998). *Working with emotional intelligence.* New York, NY: Bantam Books.

Goleman, D. (2004, January). What makes a leader. *Harvard Business Review.* Retrieved from hbr.org/2004/01/what-makes-a-leader/ar/1

Gores, C. J. (2014). Courage, compassion, communication. In G. M. Bataille & D. I. Cordova (Eds.), *Managing the unthinkable: Crisis preparation and response for campus leaders* (pp. 147–156). Sterling, VA: Stylus.

Graen, G. B., & Uhl-Bien, M. (1995). The relationship-based approach to leadership: Development of LMX theory of leadership over 25 years: Applying a multilevel, multi-domain perspective. *Leadership Quarterly, 6*(2), 219–247.

Grant, A. (2013). *Give and take: Why helping others drives our success.* New York, NY: Penguin Books.

Greenberg, M. (2014, September 5). You don't need a search firm to hire a president. *The Chronicle of Higher Education, 61*, 144.

Greenleaf, R. (1977). *Servant leadership.* Mahwah, NJ: Paulist Press.

Grint, K. (2000). *The arts of leadership.* Oxford, UK: Oxford University Press.

Guillen, L., & Ibarra, H. (2009). Seasons of a leader's development: Beyond a one-size-fits-all approach to leadership development. *Academy of Management Best Paper Proceedings.*

Haberaecker, H. J. (2004). Strategic planning and budgeting to achieve core missions. In M. J. Dooris, J. M. Kelley, & J. F. Trainer (Eds.), *Successful strategic planning: New directions for institutional planning* (pp. 71–87). San Francisco, CA: Jossey-Bass.

Hackman, M. Z., & Johnson, C. E. (2013). *Leadership: A communication perspective* (6th ed.). Long Grove, IL: Waveland Press.

Harden, N. H. (2012). The end of the university as we know it. *The American Interest, 8*(3). Retrieved from http://www.the-american-interest.com/2012/12/11/the-end-of-the-university-as-we-know-it

Heaphy, M. S., & Gruska, G. F. (1995). *The Malcolm Baldrige National Quality Award: A yardstick for quality growth.* Reading, MA: Addison-Wesley Publishing.

Heath, R. L., & O'Hair, H. D. (Eds.). (2009). *Handbook of risk and crisis communication.* London, UK: Routledge.

Hernandez, M., Eberly, M. B., Avolio, B. J., & Johnson, M. D. (2011). The loci and mechanisms of leadership: Exploring a more comprehensive view of leadership theory. *Leadership Quarterly, 22,* 1165–1185.

Hersey, P. (1984). *The situational leader.* Escondido, CA: Center for Leadership Studies.

Hersey, P., & Blanchard, K. H. (1969). Life-cycle theory of leadership. *Training and Development Journal, 23,* 26–34.

Higher Learning Commission. (n.d.). *The criteria for accreditation: Guiding values.* Retrieved from www.ncahlc.org/Criteria-Eligibility-and-Candidacy/guiding-values-new-criteria-for-accreditation.html

Hirsch, W. Z., & Weber, L. E. (Eds.). (1999). *Challenges facing higher education at the millennium.* Washington, DC: American Council on Education and Oryx Press.

Hoover, E. (2013, July 2). Monsters U.'s site just might give you "website envy." *The Chronicle of Higher Education.* Retrieved from chronicle.com/blogs/headcount/monsters-u-s-site-just-might-give-you-web-site-envy/35333

Hunger, J. D., & Wheelen, T. L. (2010). *Essentials of strategic management* (5th ed.). Upper Saddle River, NJ: Prentice Hall.

Ibarra, H. (2015a). *Act like a leader, think like a leader.* Boston, MA: Harvard Business Review Press.

Ibarra, H. (2015b, January–February). The authenticity paradox. *Harvard Business Review,* 52–59.

iDashboards. (2015). *Government dashboards.* Retrieved from www.idashboards.com/Solutions/For-YourIndustry/Government.aspx

iDashboards. (2015). *Healthcare dashboards.* Retrieved from www.idashboards.com/Solutions/For-YourIndustry/Healthcare.aspx

Immordino, K. M., Gigliotti, R. A., Ruben, B. D., & Tromp, S. (2016). Evaluating the impact of strategic planning in higher education. *Educational Planning, 23*(1), 35–47.

Inside Higher Ed. (2011). *The 2011 Inside Higher Ed survey of college and university business officers.* Retrieved from https://www.insidehighered.com/sites/default/server_files/files/insidehigheredcfosurveyfinal7-5-11.pdf

International Civil Aviation Organization. (2005). *Annex 2 to the Convention on International Civil Aviation* (10th ed.). Retrieved from www.icao.int/Meetings/anconf12/Document%20Archive/an02_cons%5B1%5D.pdf

Irvine, R. B., & Millar, D. P. (1998). *Crisis communication and management: How to gain and maintain control.* San Francisco, CA: International Association of Business Communicators.

Jackson, N., & Lund, H. (2000). *Benchmarking for higher education.* London, UK: Society for Research into Higher Education and Open University Press.

Jacob, R. A., Madu, C. N., & Tang, C. (2012). Financial performance of Baldrige Award winners: A review and synthesis. *International Journal of Quality & Reliability Management, 29*(2), 233–240.

Jacobs, J. (1961). *The death and life of great American cities.* New York, NY: Random House.

Jaschik, S. (2015). *2015 survey of chief academic officers.* Retrieved from https://www.insidehighered.com/news/survey/2015-survey-chief-academic-offcers

Jasinski, J. (2004). Strategic planning via Baldrige: Lessons learned. *New Directions for Institutional Research, 123,* 27–31.

Johnson & Johnson. (2016). *Our credo values.* Retrieved from www.jnj.com/about-jnj/jnj-credo

June, A. W. (2010, December 10). Rutgers program helps Ph.D. students learn the ropes of academic leadership. *The Chronicle of Higher Education.* Retrieved from chronicle.com/article/Rutgers-Program-Helps-PhD/125679/

Juntrasook, A. (2014). "You do not have to be the boss to be a leader": Contested meanings of leadership in higher education. *Higher Education Research & Development, 33*(1), 19–31. Retrieved from dx.doi.org/10.1080/07294360.2013.864610

Kalamazoo College. (n.d.). *Introduction and mission.* Retrieved from www.kzoo.edu/college

Kanter, R. M. (1983). *The change masters: Innovation & entrepreneurship in the American corporation.* New York, NY: Simon & Schuster.

Kaplan, R. S., & Norton, D. P. (1996). *The balanced scorecard.* Boston, MA: Harvard Business School Press.

Kaplan, R. S., & Norton, D. P. (2001). *The strategy-focused organization.* Boston, MA: Harvard Business School Press.

Kaplan, R. S., & Norton, D. P. (2004). *Strategy maps: Converting intangible assets into tangible outcomes.* Boston, MA: Harvard Business School Press.

Kaplan, R. S., & Norton, D. P. (2006). *Alignment: Using the balanced scorecard to create corporate synergies.* Boston, MA: Harvard Business School Press.

Katz, E. (1957). The two-step flow of communication: An up-to-date report on a hypothesis. *Public Opinion Quarterly, 21*(1), 61–78.

Katz, E., & Lazarsfeld, P. (1955). *Personal influence: The part played by people in the flow of mass communications.* New York, NY: The Free Press.

Katz, R. L. (1974). Skills of an effective administrator. *Harvard Business Review, 52*(5), 90–102.

Kegan, R. (1982). *The evolving self: Problem and process in human development.* Cambridge, MA: Harvard University Press.

Keller, C. M. (2014). Lessons from the Voluntary System of Accountability (VSA). The intersection of collective action and public policy. *Change, 46*(5), 23–29.

Keller, G. (1983). *Academic strategy: The management revolution in American higher education*. Baltimore, MD: Johns Hopkins University Press.

Kennedy, D. (1997). *Academic duty*. Cambridge, MA: Harvard University Press.

Keyton, J. (2011). *Communication and organizational culture: A key to understanding work experiences* (2nd ed.). Thousand Oaks, CA: Sage.

Kiley, K. (2013, June 21). College is scary. *Inside Higher Education*. Retrieved from www.insidehighered.com/news/2013/06/21/monsters-university-explores-value-diversity-college-settings

Kingdon, J. W. (1984). *Agendas, alternatives, and public policies*. Boston, MA: Little, Brown.

Klann, G. (2003). *Crisis leadership: Using military lessons, organizational experiences, and the power of influence to lessen the impact of chaos on the people you lead*. Greensboro, NC: CCL Press.

Kolowich, S. (2015, March 28). How Sweet Briar's board decided to close the college. *The Chronicle of Higher Education*. Retrieved from https://chronicle.com/article/How-Sweet--Board/228927

Kotter, J. P. (1996a). Kotter's 8-step change model. Retrieved from www.kotterinternational.com/the-8-step-process-for-leading-change/

Kotter, J. P. (1996b). *Leading change*. Boston, MA: Harvard Business Press.

Kotter, J. P. (2012). Accelerate! *Harvard Business Review, 90*(11), 45–58.

Krahenbuhl, G. S. (2004). *Building the academic deanship. Strategies for success*. Westport, CT: American Council on Education.

Kuh, G. D. (2001). Assessing what really matters to student learning. *Change, 33*(3), 10–17, 66.

Labaree, D. F. (1997). Public goods, private goods: The American struggle over educational goals. *American Educational Research Journal, 34*(1), 39–81.

Lawson, C. (2014). The power of leadership at a time of tragedy. In G. M. Bataille & D. I. Cordova (Eds.), *Managing the unthinkable: Crisis preparation and response for campus leaders* (pp. 37–46). Sterling, VA: Stylus.

Lederman, D. (2006, June 15). A stinging first draft. *Inside Higher Ed*. Retrieved from insidehighered.com/news/2006/06/27/commission

Lederman, D. (2007, March 21). Assessing the Spellings Commission. *Inside Higher Ed*. Retrieved from www.insidehighered.com/news/2007/03/21/commission

Lederman, D. (2015a, April 3). *An insider's perspective on American higher education*. Presented at Rutgers University, New Brunswick, NJ.

Lederman, D. (2015b, April 3). *Higher education 2015: A SWOT analysis*. Presented at Rutgers University, New Brunswick, NJ.

Lerbinger, O. (1997). *The crisis manager: Facing risk and responsibility*. Mahwah, NJ: Erlbaum.

Lewin, K. (1952). Group decision and social change. In G. W. Swanson, T. M. Newcomb, & E. L. Hartley (Eds.), *Readings in social psychology* (pp. 459–473). New York, NY: Henry Heath & Co.

Lewin, K., Lippitt, R., & White, R. K. (1939). Patterns of aggressive behavior in experimentally created "social climates." *Journal of Social Psychology, 10*, 271–299.

Lewis, L. K. (2010). *Implementing change in organizations: A stakeholder communication perspective*. Malden, MA: Blackwell.

Li, T., & Yorke, J. A. (1975). Period three implies chaos. *American Mathematical Monthly 82*(10): 985–992.

Liden, R. C., Wayne, S. J., Zhao, H., & Henderson, D. (2008). Servant leadership: Development of a multidimensional measure and multi-level assessment. *Leadership Quarterly, 19*(2), 161–177.

Light, R. J. (2001). *Making the most of college: Students speak their minds*. Cambridge, MA: Harvard University Press.

Lindell, M. K., Prater, C., & Perry, R. W. (2007). *Introduction to emergency management*. Hoboken, NJ: Wiley.

Lorenz, E. N. (1963). Deterministic nonperiodic flow. *Journal of Atmospheric Sciences, 20*, 130–148.

Loyola University. (n. d.). *Division of finance and administration mission statement*. Retrieved from http://finance.loyno.edu/about-finance-administration

Luke, J. S. (1998). *Catalytic leadership*. San Francisco, CA: Jossey-Bass.

Luria, G., & Berson, Y. (2013). How do leadership motives affect informal and formal leadership emergence? *Journal of Organizational Behavior, 34*, 995–1015.

Luthans, F., & Avolio, B. J. (2003). Authentic leadership: A positive developmental approach. In K. S. Cameron, J. E. Dutton, & R. E. Quinn (Eds.), *Positive organizational scholarship* (pp. 241–261). San Francisco, CA: Barrett-Koehler.

Macfarlane, B. (2011). Professors as intellectual leaders: Formation, identity and role. *Studies in Higher Education, 36*(1), 57–73.

Machiavelli, N. (1532). *The prince*. Chapter VI, Concerning new principalities which are acquired by one's own arms and ability. Retrieved from www.constitution.org/mac/prince06.htm

Mamprin, A. (2002). *Five steps for successful succession planning*. Washington, DC: The Center for Association Leadership.

Mandelbaum, J. (2007). Managing the transition between chairs. *Effective Practices for Academic Leaders, 2*(8), 1–15.

March, J. G., & Weil, T. (2005). *On leadership*. Malden, MA: Blackwell.

Marelli, A., Tondora, J., & Hoge, M. (2005). Strategies for developing competency models. *Administration and Policy in Mental Health, 32*(5/6), 533–561.

Martin, J. (1992). *Cultures in organizations: Three perspectives*. Oxford, UK: Oxford University Press.

Maxwell, J. C. (1993). *Developing the leader within you*. Nashville, TN: Thomas Nelson.

Maxwell, J. C. (1995). *Developing the leaders around you*. Nashville, TN: Thomas Nelson.

Maxwell, J. C. (1999). *The 21 indispensible qualities of a leader*. Nashville, TN: Thomas Nelson.

Mayer, J. D., Salovey, P., & Caruso, D. R. (2000). Models of emotional intelligence. In R. J. Sternberg (Ed.), *Handbook of intelligence* (pp. 396–420). Cambridge, UK: Cambridge University Press.

McCauley, C. D., Kanaga, K., & Lafferty, K. (2010). Leader development systems. In E. Van Velsor, C. D. McCauley, & M. N. Ruderman (Eds.), *Center for Creative Leadership handbook of leadership development* (pp. 29–61). San Francisco, CA: Jossey-Bass.

McCauley, C. D., Van Velsor, E., & Ruderman, M. N. (2010). Introduction: Our view of leadership development. In E. Van Velsor, C. D. McCauley, & M. N. Ruderman (Eds.), *Center for Creative Leadership handbook of leadership development* (pp. 1–26). San Francisco, CA: Jossey-Bass.

McCombs, M. E., & Shaw, D. L. (1972). The agenda-setting function of mass media. *Public Opinion Quarterly, 36*(2), 176–187.

McCombs, M. E., & Shaw, D. L. (1993). The evolution of agenda-setting research: Twenty-five years in the marketplace of ideas. *Journal of Communication, 43*(2), 58–67.

McCombs, M. E., Shaw, D. L., & Weaver, D. H. (2014). New directions in agenda-setting theory and research. *Mass Communication & Society, 17*(6), 781–802.

McGee, J. (2016). *Breakpoint: The changing marketplace for higher education.* Baltimore, MD: Johns Hopkins University Press.

McGrath, J. E. (1962). *Leadership behavior: Some requirements for leadership training.* Washington, DC: US Civil Service Commission, Office of Career Development.

McDaniel, E. A. (2002). Senior leadership in higher education: An outcomes approach. *Journal of Leadership and Organizational Studies, 9*(2), 80–88.

McIntire, M. E. (2015, October 20). Many colleges' new emergency plan: Try to account for every possibility. *Chronicle.* Retrieved from chronicle.com/article/Many-Colleges-New-Emergency/233841/?key=UvQFoZhHCM9_6bonWiw3nxXlSiml_OgEstaSzwVmLiJSWmltSkI1cEN5NHBhUV80bFJoTy1DRDJDN-llzZ-k5yZXh1R2NpRzIyOS0w

McPherson, P. (2006). NASULGC President Peter McPherson responds to the Commission on the Future of Higher Education Report. *National Association of State Universities and Land-Grant Colleges.* Retrieved from www.nasulgc.org/CAA/NASULGC_Commission_Response8–10.pdf

Meindl, J. R., & Ehrlich, S. B. (1987). The romance of leadership and the evaluation of organizational performance. *Academy of Management Journal, 30*(1), 91–109.

Meyers, G. C., & Holusha, J. (1986). *When it hits the fan: Managing the nine crises of business.* Boston, MA: Houghton Mifflin.

Michigan State University. (2015). *The Academic Advancement Network (AAN) at Michigan State University.* Office of Faculty & Organizational Development. Retrieved from fod.msu.edu/

Middle States Commission on Higher Education. (2014). *Standards for accreditation and requirements of affiliation* (13th ed.). Philadelphia, PA: Middle States Commission on Higher Education.

Miller, C. (2006). Issue paper 2: Accountability/consumer information. *Secretary of Education's Commission on the Future of Higher Education.* Retrieved from www.ed.gov/about/bdscomm/list/hiedfuture/reports/miller.pdf

Miller, J. G. (1965). Living systems: Basic concepts. *Behavioral Science, 10*(3), 193–237.

Mitroff, I. I. (1994). Crisis management and environmentalism: A natural fit. *California Management Review, 36*(2), 101–113.

Mitroff, I. I. (2004). *Crisis leadership: Planning for the unthinkable.* Hoboken, NJ: Wiley.

Mitroff, I. I., & Anagnos, G. (2001). *Managing crises before they happen: What every executive and manager needs to know about crisis management.* New York, NY: AMACOM.

Mitroff, I. I., Diamond, M. A., & Alpaslan, C. M. (2006). *How prepared are America's colleges and universities for major crises? Assessing the state of crisis management.* Ann Arbor, MI: Society for College and University Planning. Retrieved from www.scup.org/page/knowledge/crisis-planning/diamong

Moneta, L., & Kuh, G. (2005). When expectations and realities collide. In T. Miller, B. Bender, & S. Schuh (Eds.), *Promoting reasonable expectations: Aligning student and institutional views of the college experience* (pp. 65–83). San Francisco, CA: Jossey-Bass.

Montez, J. M., Wolverton, M., & Gmelch, W. H. (2002). The roles and challenges of deans. *The Review of Higher Education, 26*(2), 241–266.

Morphew, C. C., & Taylor, B. J. (2009, August 19). College rankings and dueling mission statements. *The Chronicle of Higher Education.* Retrieved from chronicle.com/article/College-RankingsDueling/48070/

Mrig, A., & Fusch, D. (2014, February). Innovative practices in higher-ed leadership development. *Academic Impressions.* Retrieved from www.academicimpressions.com/news/innovative-practices-higher-ed-leadership-development

Muffet-Willett, S. L. (2010). *Waiting for a crisis: Case studies of crisis leaders in higher education.* (Unpublished doctoral dissertation.) Akron, OH: University of Akron.

Muffet-Willett, S. L., & Kruse, S. D. (2008). Crisis leadership: Past research and future directions. *Journal of Business Continuity & Emergency Planning, 3*(3), 248–258.

National Center for Education Statistics (2012). *Fast facts.* Retrieved from nces.ed.gov/fastfacts/display.asp?id=98

National Center for Education Statistics. (2013). *Table 301.20: Historical summary of faculty, enrollment, degrees, and finances in degree-granting postsecondary institutions: Selected years, 1969–70 through 2011–12.* Retrieved from nces.ed.gov/programs/digest/d13/tables/dt13_301.20.asp

National Center for Education Statistics. (2014, July). *Digest of education statistics.* US Department of Education and the Institute of Education Sciences. Retrieved from nces.ed.gov/programs/digest/d13/tables/dt13_317.50.asp

National Center for Education Statistics. (2015, May). *Digest of education statistics.* US Department of Education and the Institute of Education Sciences. Retrieved from nces.ed.gov/programs/digest/d14/tables/dt14_317.40.asp

Nelson, M. D. (2014). Preparation, response, and recovery: The everydayness of crisis leadership. In G. M. Bataille & D. I. Cordova (Eds.), *Managing the unthinkable: Crisis preparation and response for campus leaders* (pp. 74–81). Sterling, VA: Stylus.

Neubert, M. J., & Taggar, S. (2004). Pathways to informal leadership: The moderating role of gender on the relationship of individual differences and team member network centrality to informal leadership emergence. *Leadership Quarterly, 15*, 175–194.

Neustadt, R. (1960). *Presidential power and the modern presidents.* New York, NY: John Wiley and Sons.

Neustadt, R. E. (1976). *Presidential power: The politics of leadership with reflections on Johnson and Nixon.* New York, NY: Wiley.

New England Association of Schools and Colleges Commission on Institutions of Higher Education. (2011). *Standards for accreditation.* Retrieved from cihe .neasc.org/standard-policies/standards-accreditation/standards-effective-july-1-2011#standard_one

New, J. (2016, February 11). Get ready for more protests. *Inside Higher Ed.* Retrieved from https://www.insidehighered.com/news/2016/02/11/survey-finds-nearly-1-10-freshmen-plan-participating-campus-protests

Newman, F., & Couturier, L. K. (2001). The new competitive arena: Market forces invade the academy. *Change, 33*(5), 10–17.

New York Times index. (2015). *Articles, "university" or "college."* Retrieved from www.nytimes.com/ref/membercenter/nytarchive.html

North Central Association of Colleges and Universities, Higher Learning Commission. (2015). *The Criteria for Accreditation and Core Components.* Retrieved from www.ncahlc.org/Criteria-Eligibility-and-Candidacy/criteria-and-core-components.html

Northern Arizona University. (n. d.). *Social work mission statement.* Retrieved from http://nau.edu/SBS/SSW/Degrees-Programs/Mission-statement/

Northouse, P. G. (2015). *Leadership: Theory and practice* (7th ed.). Thousand Oaks, CA: Sage.

Obama, B. H. (2013, August 22). *Remarks by the president on college affordability— Buffalo, NY. State University of New York Buffalo.* Retrieved from www.whitehouse.gov/the-press-office/2013/08/22/remarks-president-college-affordability-buffalo-ny

Organisation for Economic Co-operation and Development (OECD). (2015). *Population with tertiary education.* Retrieved from https://data.oecd.org/eduatt/population-with-tertiary-education.htm

Oxford Dictionaries. (2015). *Welcome.* Retrieved from www.oxforddictionaries.com/

Paris, K. A. (2004). Moving the strategic plan off the shelf and into action at the University of Wisconsin-Madison. *New Directions for Institutional Research, 123*, 121–127.

Parker, E. T. (2015, December 3). Hire a chief diversity officer, check! *Diverse Education.* Retrieved from diverseeducation.com/article/79300/

Parker, P. S. (2005). *Race, gender, and leadership.* Mahwah, NJ: Lawrence Erlbaum.

Parks, S. D. (2005). *Leadership can be taught: A bold approach for a complex world.* Boston, MA: Harvard Business Review.

Parrot, T. V. (2014). Working effectively with the media: Advice from the front line. In G. M. Bataille & D. I. Cordova (Eds.), *Managing the unthinkable: Crisis preparation and response for campus leaders* (pp. 170–180). Sterling, VA: Stylus.

Pascarella, E. T. (2001). Identifying excellence in undergraduate education: Are we even close? *Change, 33*(3), 19–23.

Pauchant, T. C., & Mitroff, I. I. (1992). *Transforming the crisis-prone organization: Preventing individual, organizational, and environmental tragedies.* San Francisco, CA: Jossey-Bass.

Perez, L. (2015, November 5–7). *Address to committee for institutional cooperation Academic Leadership Program.* Presented at University of Wisconsin–Madison, Madison, WI.

Peters, L., & O'Connor, E. (2001). Informal leadership support: An often overlooked competitive advantage. *Physician Executive, 27*(3), 35–39.

Pfeiffer, J. W., Goodstein, L. D., & Nolan, T. M. (1986). *Applied strategic planning: A how to do it guide.* San Diego, CA: University Associates.

Pfeffer, J., & Sutton, R. I. (2000). *The knowledge-doing gap: How smart companies turn knowledge into action.* Boston, MA: Harvard Business School Press.

Pielstick, C. D. (2000). Formal vs. informal leading: A comparative analysis. *Journal of Leadership & Organizational Studies, 7*(3), 99–114.

Pierce, S. R. (2011). *On being presidential. A guide for college and university leaders.* San Francisco, CA: Jossey-Bass.

Pondy, L. R. (1978). Leadership is a language game. In M. W. McCall & M. M. Lombardo (Eds.), *Leadership: Where else can we go?* (pp. 87–99). Durham, NC: Duke University Press.

Porath, C. (2015, June 19). No time to be nice at work. *The New York Times.* Retrieved from www.nytimes.com/2015/06/21/opinion/sunday/is-your-boss-mean.html?_r=0

Prince, H. (2001). Teaching leadership: A journey into the unknown. *Concepts and Connections: A Newsletter for Leadership Educators, 9*(3), 1–5.

Przasnyski, Z., & Tai, L. S. (2002). Stock performance of Malcolm Baldrige National Quality Award winning companies. *Total Quality Management, 13*(4), 475–488.

Rae, K. (Producer), & Scanlon, D. (2013). *Monsters University* [Motion picture]. Emeryville, California: Pixar Animation Studios.

Richards, C. L. (2009). A new paradigm: Strategies for succession planning in higher education. (Unpublished doctoral dissertation). Capella University, Minneapolis, MN.

Roberts, S., & Rowley, J. (2004). *Managing information services.* London, UK: Facet Publishing.

Rost, J. C. (1993). *Leadership for the twenty-first century.* Westport, CT: Praeger.

Rothman, S., Kelly-Woessner, A., & Woessner, M. (2010). *The still divided academy: How competing visions of power, politics, and diversity complicate the mission of higher education.* Lanham, MD: Rowman & Littlefield.

Rowley, D. J., & Sherman, H. (2001). Implementing the strategic plan. *Planning for Higher Education, 30*(4), 1–14.

Ruben, B. D. (1975). General systems theory: An approach to human communication. In R. W. Budd & B. D. Ruben (Eds.), *Approaches to human communication* (pp. 120–144). Rochelle Park, NJ: Hayden.

Ruben, B. D. (1976). Assessing communication competence for intercultural communication adaptation. *Group and Organization Studies, 1*(3), 334–354.

Ruben, B. D. (1977). Guidelines for cross-cultural communication effectiveness. *Group and Organization Studies, 2*(4), 470–479.

Ruben, B. D. (1988). Human communication and cross-cultural effectiveness. In L. A. Samovar & R. E. Porter (Eds.), *Intercultural communication: A reader* (5th ed.; pp. 338–346). Belmont, CA: Wadsworth.

Ruben, B. D. (1989). Cross-cultural communication competence: Traditions and issues for the future. *International Journal of Intercultural Relations, 13*(3), 229–240.

Ruben, B. D. (1994). *Tradition of excellence: Higher education quality self-assessment guide.* Dubuque, IA: Kendall-Hunt.

Ruben, B. D. (2003). General system theory: An approach to human communication. In R. W. Budd & B. D. Ruben, *Approaches to human communication* (2nd ed.; pp. 95–118). New Brunswick, NJ: Transaction Publishers.

Ruben, B. D. (2004). *Pursuing excellence in higher education: Eight fundamental challenges.* San Francisco, CA: Jossey-Bass.

Ruben, B. D. (2005). Linking communication scholarship and professional practice in colleges and universities. *Journal of Applied Communication Research, 33*(4), 294–304.

Ruben, B. D. (2006). *What leaders need to know and do: A leadership competencies scorecard.* Washington, DC: National Association of College and University Business Officers.

Ruben, B. D. (2011). *Understanding, planning and leading organizational change.* Washington, DC: National Association of College and University Business Officers.

Ruben, B. D. (2012). *What leaders need to know and do: A leadership competencies scorecard* (2nd ed.). Washington, DC: National Association of College and University Business Officers.

Ruben, B. D. (2015a). Communication theory and health communication practice: The more things change, the more they stay the same. *Health Communication,* 1–11.

Ruben, B. D. (2015b). Intercultural communication competence in retrospect: Who would have guessed? *International Journal of Intercultural Relations.* Retrieved from www.sciencedirect.com/science/article/pii/S0147176715000334

Ruben, B. D. (2015c). *Excellence in higher education guide: An integrated approach to assessment, planning, and improvement in colleges and universities.* Wuhan, China: Wuhan University Press.

Ruben, B. D. (2016a). *Excellence in higher education: A framework for the design, assessment, and continued improvement of institutions, departments, and programs* (8th ed.). Sterling, VA: Stylus.

Ruben, B. D. (2016b). *Intercultural communication behavior scales.* Retrieved from odl.rutgers.edu/research-development/intercultural-communication-behavioral-guides/

Ruben, B. D. (2016c). *Excellence in higher education workbook and scoring instructions*. (8th ed.). Sterling, VA: Stylus.

Ruben, B. D. (2016d). *Excellence in higher education facilitator's guide*. (8th ed.). Sterling, VA: Stylus.

Ruben, B. D., Connaughton, S. L., Immordino, K., & Lopez, J. M. (2004). *What impact does the Baldrige/excellence in higher education self-assessment process have on institutional effectiveness?* Paper presented at the annual conference of the National Consortium for Continuous Improvement in Higher Education, Baltimore, MD.

Ruben, B. D., & Fernandez, V. (2013). Growing your own: A proactive approach to leadership development. *The Higher Education Workplace*, pp. 37-40. Retrieved from odl.rutgers.edu/wp-content/uploads/2015/03/growing-your-own.pdf

Ruben, B. D., & Gigliotti, R. A. (in press). Leadership as social influence: An expanded view of leadership communication theory and practice. *Journal of Leadership and Organizational Studies*.

Ruben, B. D., & Gigliotti, R. A. (under review). Are higher education institutions and their leadership needs unique? Vertical and horizontal perspectives.

Ruben, B. D., & Jurow, S. (2012). *Leading in tough times: Case studies for higher education leaders*. Washington, DC: NACUBO.

Ruben, B. D., & Kealey, D. J. (1979). Behavioral assessment of communication competency and the prediction of cross-cultural adaptation. *International Journal of Intercultural Relations, 3*(1), 15–47.

Ruben, B. D., & Kim, J. Y. (1975). *General systems theory and human communication*. Rochelle Park, NJ: Hayden.

Ruben, B. D., Lewis, L., Sandmeyer, L., Russ, T., Smulowitz, S., & Immordino, K. (2008). *Assessing the impact of the Spellings Commission: The message, the messenger, and the dynamics of change in higher education*. Washington, D.C.: National Association of College and University Business Officers.

Ruben, B. D., Russ, T., Smulowitz, S. M., & Connaughton, S. L. (2007). Evaluating the impact of organizational self-assessment in higher education: The Malcolm Baldrige/*excellence in higher education* framework. *Leadership and Organizational Development Journal, 28*(3), 230–250.

Ruben, B. D., & Stewart, L. P. (2016). *Communication and human behavior* (6th ed.). Dubuque, IA: Kendall Hunt.

Ruiz, R. R. (2011, October 13). Florida governor wants funds to go to practical degrees. *The New York Times*. Retrieved from thechoice.blogs.nytimes.com/2011/10/13/rick-scott/

Rutgers Center for Organizational Development and Leadership. (2014). *PLDI*. Retrieved from www.odl.rutgers.edu/pldi/

Rutgers University. (2015). *Academic leadership program*. Retrieved from odl.rutgers.edu/academic-leadership-program.html

Ruud, G. (2000). The symphony: Organizational discourse and the symbolic tensions between artistic and business ideologies. *Journal of Applied Communication Research, 28*(2), 117–143.

Salovey, P., & Mayer, J. D. (1990). Emotional intelligence. *Imagination, Cognition, and Personality, 9*, 185–211.

Sandmeyer, L. E., Dooris, M. J., & Barlock, R. W. (2004). Integrated planning for enrollment, facilities, budget, and staffing: Penn State University. In M. J. Dooris, J. M. Kelley, & J. F. Trainer (Eds.), *Successful strategic planning: New directions for institutional planning* (pp. 89–96). San Francisco, CA: Jossey-Bass.

Scarborough, S. (2009). The case for decentralized financial management. *Business Officer Magazine.* Retrieved from http://www.nacubo.org/Business_Officer_Magazine/Magazine_Archives/April_2009/The_Case_for_Decentralized_Financial_Management.html

Schaefer, C. (2015, August 20). A Baldrige award-winning restaurant chain that makes education its business. *Blogrige: The official Baldrige blog.* Retrieved from nistbaldrige.blogs.govdelivery.com/2015/08/20/a-baldrige-award-winning-restaurant-chain-that-makes-education-its-business/

Schein, E. H. (1999). *The corporate culture survival guide.* San Francisco, CA: Jossey-Bass.

Schein, E. H. (2015). The concept of organizational culture: Why bother? In G. R. Hickman (Ed.), *Leading organizations: Perspectives for a new era* (3rd ed.; pp. 280–291). Thousand Oaks, CA: Sage.

Schneider, B. (Ed.). (1990). Organizational climate and culture. San Francisco, CA: Jossey-Bass.

Schön, D. A. (1984). *The reflective practitioner: How professionals think in action.* New York, NY: Basic Books.

Schray, V. (2006). *Issue paper 14: Assuring quality in higher education.* Secretary of Education's Commission on the Future of Higher Education. Retrieved from www.ed.gov/about/bdscomm/list/hiedfuture/reports/schray2.pdf

Selingo, J. (1999, July 14). Businesses say they turn to for-profit schools because of public colleges' inertia. *Chronicle of Higher Education.* Retrieved from chronicle.com/daily/99/07/99071401n.htm

Selingo, J. J. (2013). *College (un)bound: The future of higher education and what it means for students.* Las Vegas, NV: Amazon Publishing.

Sellnow, T. L., & Seeger, M. W. (2013). *Theorizing crisis communication.* Hoboken, NJ: Wiley Blackwell.

Sendjaya, S., & Sarros, J. C. (2002). Servant leadership: Its origin, development, and application in organizations. *Journal of Leadership and Organization Studies, 9*, 47–64.

Sevier, R. A. (2000). *Strategic planning in higher education: Theory and practice.* Washington, DC: Council for Advancement and Support of Higher Education.

Seymour, D. T. (1989). *On Q: Causing quality in higher education.* New York, NY: American Council on Education and Macmillan.

Seymour, M., & Moore, S. (2000). *Effective crisis management: Worldwide principles and practice.* London, UK: Cassel.

Shrivastava, P. (1993). Crisis theory/practice: Towards a sustainable future. *Industrial & Environmental Crisis Quarterly, 7*, 23–42.

Silver, H. (2008). Does a university have a culture? *Studies in Higher Education, 28*(2), 157–169.

Smircich, L. (1983). Concepts of culture and organizational analysis. *Administrative Science Quarterly, 28,* 339–358.

Smircich, L., & Morgan, G. (1982). Leadership: The management of meaning. *Journal of Applied Behavioral Science, 18*(3): 257–273.

Smith, A. A. (2015, July 15). Reshaping the for-profit. *Inside Higher Education.* Retrieved from www.insidehighered.com/news/2015/07/15/profit-industry-struggling-has-not-reached-end-road

Smith, Z. (2007). *Creating and testing the higher education leadership competencies (HELC) model: A study of athletics directors, senior student affairs officers, and chief academic officers.* Unpublished doctoral dissertation, University of Nevada, Reno.

Smith, Z. A., & Wolverton, M. (2010). Higher education competencies: Quantitatively refining a qualitative model. *Journal of Leadership and Organizational Studies, 17*(1), 61–70.

Snow, C. P. (2012). *The two cultures.* New York, NY: Cambridge University Press.

Society for College and University Planning. (2016). *SCUP: Integrated planning for higher education.* Retrieved from http://www.scup.org/page/about

Southern Association of Colleges and Schools Commission on Colleges. (2012). *The principles of accreditation: Foundations for quality enhancement* (5th ed.). Retrieved from www.sacscoc.org/pdf/2012PrinciplesOfAcreditation.pdf

Spangehl, S. D. (2004). The North Central Association of Colleges and Schools, Academic Quality Improvement Project. In B. D. Ruben (Ed.), *Pursuing excellence in higher education: Eight fundamental challenges* (pp. 179–189). San Francisco, CA: Jossey-Bass.

Spellings Commission. (2006). A test of leadership: Charting the future of U.S. higher Education: A report of the commission appointed by Secretary of Education Margaret Spellings. *Commission on the Future of Higher Education.* Retrieved from www.ed.gov/about/bdscomm/list/hiedfuture/index.html

Spradley, J. P. (1979). *The ethnographic interview.* Belmont, CA: Wadsworth.

Spunt, R. P., & Adophs, R. (2015). Folk explanations of behavior: A specialized use of a domain-general mechanism. *Psychological Science, 26,* 724–736.

Stincelli, E., & Baghurst, T. (2014). A grounded theory exploration of informal leadership qualities as perceived by employees and managers in small organizations. *International Journal of Business Management & Economic Research, 5*(1), 1–8.

Stolberg, S. G. (2015, June 20). Sweet Briar reaches deal to stay open. *The New York Times.* Retrieved from www.nytimes.com/2015/06/21/us/sweet-briar-reaches-deal-to-stay-open.html

Stone, B. (2015, June). Twitter's cofounder on creating opportunities. *Harvard Business Review,* 39–42.

Society for College and University Planning. (2016). *SCUP: Integrated planning for higher education.* Retrieved from http://www.scup.org/page/about

Strauss, J. C., & Curry, J. R. (2002). *Responsibility-centered management: Lessons from 25 years of decentralized management.* Washington, DC: National Association of College and University Business Officers.

Tagg, J. (2012). Why does the faculty resist change? *Change: The Magazine of Higher Learning, 44*(1), 6–15.

Tagiuri, R., & Litwin, G. L. (Eds.). (1968). *Organizational climate: Explorations of a concept.* Cambridge, MA: Harvard University Press.

Terenzini, P. T., & Pascarella, E. T. (1994). Living with myths: Undergraduate education in America. *Change, 26*(1), 28–32.

Thayer, L. (1968). *Communication and communication systems.* Homewood, IL: Richard D. Irwin.

Thayer, L. (2003). Communication: *Sine qua non* of the behavioral sciences. In R. W. Budd & B. D. Ruben (Eds.), *Approaches to human communication* (2nd ed.; pp. 7–31). New York, NY: Spartan-Hayden.

Thelin, J. R. (2011). *A history of American higher education* (2nd ed.). Baltimore, MD: Johns Hopkins University Press.

Tierney, W. G. (1988). Organizational culture in higher education. *The Journal of Higher Education, 59*(1), 2–29.

Tromp, S. A., & Ruben, B. D. (2010). *Strategic planning in higher education: A guide for leaders* (2nd ed.). Washington, DC: NACUBO.

Tuckman, B. W. (1965). Developmental sequence in small groups. *Psychological Bulletin, 63*(6), 384–399.

Tuckman, B. W., & Jensen, M. A. C. (1977). Stages of small-group development revisited. *Group and Organization Management, 2*(4), 419–427.

Ulmer, R. R., Sellnow, T. L., & Seeger, M. W. (2015). *Effective crisis communication: Moving from crisis to opportunity* (3rd ed.). Thousand Oaks, CA: Sage.

University of Michigan. (n.d.). *Mission and integrity.* Retrieved from www.accreditation.umich.edu/mission

University of North Carolina. (2015). *University leadership education and development (ULEAD).* Retrieved from hr.unc.edu/training-talent-development/specialized-programs-and-resources/ulead/

U.S. Department of Education. (2006, April 6–7). *Commission on the future of higher education.* Retrieved from www.connectlive.com/events/highered0406/

Useem, M. (1998). *The leadership moment.* New York, NY: Random House.

U.S. Office of Personnel Management (2005). *Succession planning process.* Retrieved from www.opm.gov/policy-data-oversight/human-capital-management/reference-materials/leadership-knowledge-management/successionplanning.pdf

Velsor, E. V., McCauley, C. D., & Ruderman, M. N. (2010). *The Center for Creative Leadership handbook of leadership development.* San Francisco, CA: Jossey-Bass.

Ward, D., & American Council on Education. (2006). *President to President, 7*(30). Retrieved from www.acenet.edu/Content/NavigationMenu/GovernmentRelationsPublicPolicy/PresidenttoPresident/Default877.htm

Waterman, R. H. (1990). *Adhocracy: The power to change.* Memphis, TN: Whittle Direct Books.

Watzlawick, P., Beavin, J. & Jackson, D. (1967). *Pragmatics of human communication: A study of interactional patterns, pathologies, and paradoxes.* New York, NY: Norton.

Weick, K. E. (1979). *The social psychology of organizing.* Reading, MA: Addison-Wesley.

Weick, K. E. (1976). Educational organizations as loosely coupled systems. *Administrative Science Quarterly,* 21(1), 1–19.

Weick, K. E. (1988). Enacted sense-making in crisis situations. *Journal of Management Studies, 25,* 305–317.

Weisburd, D., Mastrofski, S. D., Greenspan, R., & Willis, J. J. (2004). *The growth of Comstat in American policing.* Police Foundation Reports. Retrieved from assets.lapdonline.org/assets/pdf/growthofcompstat.pdf

Westchester Community College. (n.d.). *Mission and goals of the college.* Retrieved from www.sunywcc.edu/about/about-the-college/mission-and-goals-of-the-college

Western Association of Schools and Colleges, Accrediting Commission for Senior Colleges and Universities. (2013). *Handbook of accreditation.* Retrieved from hilo.hawaii.edu/uhh/congress/documents/12WASCDraft2013HandbookofAccreditation.pdf

Wexler, E. (2016, January 27). Endowments fall to Earth. *Inside Higher Ed.* Retrieved from https://www.insidehighered.com/news/2016/01/27/endowment-returns-24-percent-fiscal-year-2015

Wheatley, M. (2006). *Leadership and the new science: Discovering order in a chaotic world* (3rd ed.). San Francisco, CA: Berrett-Koehler Publishers.

Wisniewski, M. A. (1999). Leadership competencies in continuing higher education: Implications for leadership education. *Continuing Higher Education, 47*(1), 14–23.

Witherspoon, P. D. (1997). *Communicating leadership: An organizational perspective.* Boston, MA: Allyn & Bacon.

Witt/Kieffer. (2013). *Leadership traits and success in higher education.* Retrieved from www.wittkieffer.com/file/thought-leadership/practice/Leadership%20Traits%20and%20Success%20in%20Higher%20Education_a%20Witt%20Kieffer%20Study_final.pdf

Woodhouse, K. (2015, April 28). Money talk. *Inside Higher Education.* Retrieved from www.insidehighered.com/news/2015/04/28/communication-issue-college-administrators-and-faculty-during-era-financial-change

Yukl, G. (2012). *Leadership in organizations* (8th ed.). Upper Saddle River, NJ: Prentice Hall.

Zaleznik, A. (1992, March/April). Managers and leaders: Are they different? *Harvard Business Review,* 126–135.

Zeier, H. (1994). Workload and psychophysiological stress reactions in air traffic controllers. *Ergonomics, 37*(3), 525–539.

Zhang, Z., Waldman, D. A., & Wang, Z. (2012). A multilevel investigation of leader-member exchange, informal leader emergence, and individual and team performance. *Personnel Psychology, 65*(1), 49–78.

ABOUT THE AUTHORS AND CONTRIBUTORS

Authors

Brent D. Ruben, PhD, is a distinguished professor and executive director of the Center for Organizational Development and Leadership at Rutgers University. He is also a member of the faculties of the Rutgers PhD program in higher education and the Robert Wood Johnson School of Medicine. Ruben's academic interests include human communication, organizational leadership, planning, assessment, and change. He has authored numerous publications including *Excellence in Higher Education Guide* (Stylus, 2016), *What Leaders Need to Know and Do* (National Association of College and University Business Officers, 2006), and *Communication and Human Behavior* (Kendall Hunt, 2014; 5th edition with L. Stewart). Ruben was a founder of the Rutgers School of Communication and Information, and he served as a department chair and graduate program director. He is Rutgers liaison to the Big Ten Academic Alliance leadership programs and serves as an adviser to colleges and universities nationally and internationally.

Richard De Lisi, PhD, is a university professor of educational psychology at the Graduate School of Education at Rutgers University. De Lisi joined the faculty in 1976 and has more than 20 years of experience as a formal leader at Rutgers as department chair, graduate program director, and dean of the Graduate School of Education from 2003 to 2014. He is a developmental psychologist who has investigated cognitive development and sex-related differences in academic achievement. De Lisi's most recent scholarly interests pertain to leadership, excellence, and accountability for student learning and development in higher education.

Ralph A. Gigliotti, MA, MPA is assistant director for the Center for Organizational Development and Leadership at Rutgers University, where he is also a doctoral candidate and part-time lecturer in communication. His research interests explore the intersection of organizational communication, leadership, and crisis communication, particularly in the context of higher education. Gigliotti's research appears in numerous books and journals, including the *Journal of Leadership and Organizational Studies, Journal of Leadership Education,* and *Atlantic Journal of Communication.*

Contributors

Barbara E. Bender, EdD, is associate dean of the Graduate School–New Brunswick at Rutgers University and founding director of the Teaching Assistant Project and the Rutgers Academy for the Scholarship of Teaching and Learning. She has held such roles as associate provost and dean of students, and has taught a wide variety of classes in higher education, including college teaching and building leadership skills for PhD students. Active in accreditation, she is the author of numerous articles, book chapters, and edited works, as well as a frequent presenter at national conferences. She served as editor of the *NASPA Journal.*

John A. Fortunato, PhD, is a professor at Fordham University in the School of Business, and chair of the area of communication and media management. He is the author of four books, including *Commissioner: The Legacy of Pete Rozelle*; *Making Media Content* (Taylor Trade Publishing, 2006); and *Sports Sponsorship: Principles and Practices* (McFarland, 2013). He has published articles in *Public Relations Review*, the *Journal of Sports Media*, the *Journal of Brand Strategy*, and multiple law reviews. Fortunato previously taught at the University of Texas at Austin in the Department of Advertising and Public Relations, and he received his PhD from Rutgers University in the School of Communication.

Susan E. Lawrence, PhD, is the vice dean for undergraduate education in the School of Arts and Sciences, Rutgers University–New Brunswick. She is responsible for the development, implementation, and ongoing assessment of the New Brunswick Core Curriculum; broad educational programs, including the SAS Signature Course Initiative and career readiness initiatives; and oversight of student support services, programs, and academic departments. A tenured member of the Department of Political Science, her current work focuses on the future of liberal arts undergraduate education at the research university and mission-centered instructional and institutional effectiveness assessment as a response to the political demands facing higher education today.

Sherrie Tromp is associate director for the Center for Organizational Development and Leadership at Rutgers University. Sherrie is primary author (with Brent Ruben) of *Strategic Planning in Higher Education: A Guide for Leaders* (NACUBO, 2004, 2010), and coauthor of several articles and book chapters on strategic planning and leadership in higher education, including "Evaluating the Impact of Strategic Planning in Higher Education" (with K. M. Immordino, R. A. Gigliotti, and B. D. Ruben), published in *Educational Planning* in 2016. She has served as a consultant to higher education organizations and the Rutgers Advisory Board for the Kellogg Leadership for Institutional Change Initiative.

Excellence in Higher Education
Workbook and Scoring Instructions

8th Edition

Brent D. Ruben

This workbook is generously illustrated with PowerPoint presentations for use in facilitating workshops and includes additional background on the each of the EHE categories and structured exercises that can be used by individuals or in a group context to support the assessment and planning process within a particular program, department, or institution. The scoring guidelines will help you interpret results and gauge your institution's performance.

Excellence in Higher Education
Facilitator's Materials

8th Edition

Brent D. Ruben

These materials—available only in e-book format—provide everything a facilitator needs to lead an EHE program and enable the customization and adaptation of the exercises to the needs of particular organizations.

Sty/us

22883 Quicksilver Drive
Sterling, VA 20166-2102

Subscribe to our e-mail alerts: www.Styluspub.com

Also available from Stylus

Excellence in Higher Education Guide
A Framework for the Design, Assessment, and Continuing Improvement of Institutions, Departments, and Programs

8th Edition

Brent D. Ruben

The new edition of the *Excellence in Higher Education Guide* updates and extends the classic Excellence in Higher Education (EHE) series. This edition includes a broad and integrated approach to design, assessment, planning, and improvement of colleges and universities of all types, as well as individual academic, student affairs, administrative and services units. The framework included in the *Guide* is adaptable to institutions and units with any mission and is consistent with the current directions within regional and programmatic accreditation.

Based on the Malcolm Baldridge National Quality Award framework, this bestseller is the definitive tool for college and university administrators. The flexibility of the EHE model makes it appropriate for use with administrative or academic departments, with administrative or faculty councils or senate, and with programs, centers, or institutes. Moreover, the framework can be used by an entire college or university or with a particular department, division, or campus.

The EHE program includes everything you need to conduct a self-assessment workshop. The *Guide* provides facilitators with a solid understanding of the EHE model, offering detailed guidance in each of the following seven areas:

- Leadership
- Purposes and Plans
- Beneficiary and Constituency Relationships
- Programs and Services
- Faculty/Staff and Workplace
- Metrics, Assessment, and Analysis
- Outcomes and Achievements

(Continues on previous page)